Protestant Metaphysics after Karl Barth and
Martin Heidegger

Protestant Metaphysics after Karl Barth and Martin Heidegger

Timothy Stanley

CASCADE *Books* • Eugene, Oregon

PROTESTANT METAPHYICS AFTER KARL BARTH
AND MARTIN HEIDEGGER

Copyright © 2010 Timothy Stanley. All rights reserved. Except for brief quotations in critical publications or reviews, no part of this book may be reproduced in any manner without prior written permission from the publisher. Write: Permissions, Wipf and Stock Publishers, 199 W. 8th Ave., Suite 3, Eugene, OR 97401.

First published in Great Britain in the Veritas series, by SCM Press, 13–17 Long Lane, London EC1A 9PN, England.

First U.S. edition published by Cascade Books under license from SCM Press.

Cascade Books
An imprint of Wipf and Stock Publishers
199 W. 8th Ave., Suite 3
Eugene, OR 97401
www.wipfandstock.com

ISBN 13: 978-1-60899-691-9

Cataloging-in-Publication data:

Stanley, Timothy

    Protestant metaphysics after Karl Barth and Martin Heidegger / Timothy Stanley

    xxii + 276 p. ; 23cm. —Includes bibliographical references and index.

    ISBN 13: 978-1-60899-691-9

    1. Metaphysics. 2. Philosophical theology. 3. Barth, Karl, 1886–1968. 4. Heidegger, Martin, 1889–1976. I. Title.

BT40. S69 2010

Manufactured in the U.S.A.
Typeset by Regent Typesetting, London, UK.

If, however, you feel and are inclined to think you have made it, flattering yourself with your own little books, teaching, or writing, because you have done it beautifully and preached excellently; if you are highly pleased when someone praises you in the presence of others; if you perhaps look for praise, and would sulk or quit what you are doing if you did not get it – if you are of that stripe, dear friend, then take yourself by the ears, and if you do this in the right way you will find a beautiful pair of big, long, shaggy asses ears. Then do not spare any expense! Decorate them with golden bells, so that people will be able to hear you wherever you go, point their fingers at you, and say, 'See, See! There goes that clever beast, who can write such exquisite books and preach so remarkably well'. That very moment you will be blessed and blessed beyond measure in the kingdom of heaven. Yes, in that heaven where hellfire is ready for the devil and his angels. To sum up: Let us be proud and seek honor in the places where we can. But in this book the honor is God's alone, as it is said, 'God opposes the proud, but gives grace to the humble' [1 Pet. 5.5]; to whom be glory, world without end, Amen.

Martin Luther, *Luther's Works*, ed. Jaroslav Jan Pelikan, Hilton C. Oswald and Helmut T. Lehmann, American ed., 55 vols, vol. 34 (Philadelphia, PA: Fortress Press, 1999), p. 287.

Contents

Acknowledgements	xv
Preface	xvii
Introduction	1

Part One Martin Heidegger's Onto-Theology	31
1 Heidegger's Cross	33
2 Protestant Theology after Heidegger	62

Part Two Karl Barth's Theological Ontology	93
3 Barth's 'God is God'	95
4 Returning Barth to Anselm	126
5 The Being of the *Church Dogmatics*	160
6 The Humanity of God	214

Conclusion	236
Bibliography	249
Index	269

Acknowledgements

No book is written alone. I have my wife Barbara first and foremost to thank for her love and willingness to support a calling which began in our pastoral ministry together in Seattle. Truly, 'let her works praise her in the city gates' (Proverbs 31.31). At its heart, this book is the result of an academic adventure, and no one has been more responsible for my progress in that regard than Professor Graham Ward. Thinking is a practice which requires good guidance. Graham is one such guide. I must thank Universities UK for the Overseas Research Scholarship and the School of Arts, Histories and Cultures at the University of Manchester for their financial support during my doctoral research. So too, the Religions and Theology Subject Area provided vital financial assistance which allowed me to present papers at a number of important conferences relevant to my work. Thanks are due as well to the Centre for Religion and Political Culture at the University of Manchester where my current postdoctoral fellowship is held, and which has provided the support necessary to craft this book into its present shape. Lastly, to Professor William Dyrness, Professor George Brooke, Dr Todd Klutz, Dr David Law, Dr Daniel Langton and last but not least Dr Michael Hoelzl, thank you for all the pints, corridor conversations and encouragement you have given over my time in Manchester.

Chapter 2 was based upon an article entitled 'Heidegger on Luther on Paul', which was published in *Dialog: A Journal of Theology*, vol. 46, no. 1, Spring 2007. As well, an earlier version of Chapter 4 appeared in *Modern Theology*, vol. 24, no. 3, July 2008. I would like to thank the editors and Wiley-Blackwell for allowing my work to be republished here in its present form.

Preface

What is the relationship between Karl Barth's understanding of onto-theology and Martin Heidegger's? The simplicity of this question shouldn't mislead us from the controversial nature of its potential implications. As in any juxtaposition the comparison narrows our enquiry into their shared interests and themes. In this case, both Barth and Heidegger understood that attributing existence to God was just as much of a problem for theology as it was for philosophy. As such, the category of being would be treated with great care in their work. So too, they both developed very particular understandings of theology's relationship to their various understandings of ontology. In the case of Heidegger, as we shall see, his critique of onto-theology was deeply imbued with his interpretation of Luther's early critiques of late scholasticism. This insight into the Protestant nature of Heidegger's thought brings greater clarity concerning his relation to Barth's theology. Barth, the overtly Protestant theologian, drew upon Luther's work as well, but in a way that differs significantly from Heidegger's. This is not to say, however, that Barth's theology was ontologically naïve. Rather, through and after his explication of Anselm's *Proslogion*, Barth himself developed a sophisticated ontology. Our aim in what follows, therefore, is to go beyond those accounts of Barth's theology which portray him as a forerunner to Heidegger or attempt to interpret Barth's theology in the onto theological terms of Heidegger.[1]

In so far as our primary focus is upon the understanding of ontology and theology in Barth and Heidegger's work, there is no way to fully extricate our task from its contemporary relevance to post-

---

1 Merold Westphal, *Transcendence and Self-Transcendence: On God and the Soul* (Bloomington: Indiana University Press, 2004), p. 145; Graham Ward, *Barth, Derrida, and the Language of Theology* (New York: Cambridge University Press, 1995), p. 102.

ontological philosophy and theology today. It is this context which justifies our return to this well rehearsed comparison between Barth and Heidegger.[2] Martin Heidegger is often cited as a crucial progenitor in a plethora of recent essays examining the future of theology without or after metaphysics.[3] Our goal is not to explicate this literature in detail, but rather step back to ask post-Heideggerian theologians a key question. Just what forms of theology are being inherited when we begin to articulate a *God without Being*?[4] This is particularly important when interpreting the work of Roman Catholic scholars taking up positions in a post-Heideggerian space, but so too, for Protestant theologians as well. As Hans Jonas puts it, 'the theologian must ask, before he reimports his original product: what have you done with my little ones? ... Can I take them back from you? and what, *if* I take them, will I take *with* them?'[5] By paying close attention to these questions we can begin to discern the different and unique theological dispositions Heidegger draws

---

2 For a good summary of the early debates which began around the work of Heinrich Ott's *Denken und Sein*, see James McConkey Robinson and John B. Cobb, *The Later Heidegger and Theology* (New York: Harper & Row, 1963). We will explain how this project goes beyond these debates in more detail below, but suffice to say for now that the academic understanding of both Heidegger and Barth's work has moved on since this time and opens up new possibilities of comparison.

3 Although we will mention a few of the post-ontological theologians in this essay and those that follow, I will list here a selection of influential contemporary essays and compilations: Mark A. Wrathall, *Religion after Metaphysics* (Cambridge: Cambridge University Press, 2003); Kevin J. Vanhoozer, *The Cambridge Companion to Postmodern Theology* (Cambridge: Cambridge University Press, 2003); Francis Schüssler Fiorenza, 'Being, Subjectivity, Otherness: The Idols of God', in *Questioning God*, ed. John D. Caputo, Mark Dooley, and Michael J. Scanlon (Bloomington: Indiana University Press, 2001), pp. 341–70; John D. Caputo, *Radical Hermeneutics: Repetition, Deconstruction, and the Hermeneutic Project* (Bloomington: Indiana University Press, 1987), pp. 153ff; Regina M. Schwartz, *Transcendence: Philosophy, Literature, and Theology Approach the Beyond* (New York: Routledge, 2004); John D. Caputo, 'Introduction: Who Comes after the God of Metaphysics?', in *The Religious*, ed. John D. Caputo (Malden, MA: Blackwell, 2002), pp. 1–22; Merold Westphal, *Postmodern Philosophy and Christian Thought* (Bloomington: Indiana University Press, 1999); Merold Westphal, *Transcendence and Self-Transcendence: On God and the Soul*, Merold Westphal, *Overcoming Onto-theology: Toward a Postmodern Christian Faith* (New York: Fordham University Press, 2001).

4 Jean-Luc Marion, *God without Being: Hors-texte* (Chicago: University of Chicago Press, 1991).

5 Hans Jonas, *The Phenomenon of Life: Toward a Philosophical Biology* (Chicago: University of Chicago Press, 1982), p. 243.

Preface

upon as he develops his account of the problem of onto-theology. In so doing, we can discern alternative accounts of the problem he raises.

The first section on Heidegger, therefore, helps us see how the question of post-ontological, postmodern theology is ultimately and centrally a question of Protestant metaphysics. In this regard we justify the dominant role Barth will play in the second section of this book. In an introduction to the issues surrounding Barth's relationship to postmodern thought, John Webster, rightly retains 'the term "postmodern" for those theologies which analyse the cultural situation of Christianity through the turns from substance-oriented accounts of being, time and selfhood characteristic of postmodern philosophy'.[6] What we will demonstrate below is that Barth's understanding of Protestant theology can be located at the heart of the contemporary debate concerning the virtues and inadequacies of post-ontological theology. In this regard it is all the more striking just how different Barth's own thinking is from Heidegger's. Furthermore, it is our contention that Barth's theology can best be brought to bear upon contemporary post-ontological theology in so far as he is allowed to speak as a concomitant and *alternative* voice at the Heideggerian origins of postmodern philosophy and theology. Although the dialogue between Heidegger and Barth appears particularly relevant today, it ultimately finds its roots in their shared context in the early part of the twentieth century. This is not only because their respective accounts of the relationship between theology and ontology both mature throughout the 1920s and 1930s, but because of the genuine similarity between their recognition of the problem the attribution of existence to God poses. Crucially, however, we must aim to delineate just what that difference is between them rather than glossing over it or interpreting Barth's theology through the onto-theological lens of Heidegger. It is as we take account of Barth's pathway through the problem that we can begin to see why Barth and Heidegger differed so dramatically.

Given our specific interest in Heidegger and Barth the application of Protestant to the title of this book deserves some comment. Especially given 'the sheer immensity of [Protestantism's] history

---

6 John Webster, 'Barth, Modernity and Postmodernity', in *Karl Barth – A Future for Postmodern Theology?*, ed. Christiaan Mostert and Geoff Thompson (Adelaide: Australian Theological Forum, 2000), p. 5.

across the entire globe and its unique manifestations and impact therein'.[7] Although in many ways we could narrow Barth's and Heidegger's use of the term Protestantism to their reference to the magisterial Reformation 'linked with the Lutheran and Reformed churches',[8] in fact, the understanding of Protestantism which can be found in their work is much more specifically defined in terms of its critical appraisal of metaphysical reflection. It is this insight which produces our focal concern in the introductory chapter below – one which speaks to the 'post-modern charge that Protestantism is nothing more than religious modernity'.[9] As we shall see, far from it, for both Heidegger and Barth, Protestantism is woven into the uniquely postmodern character of their thought. By comparing Barth and Heidegger we enquire into the nature of the relationship between Protestant theology and metaphysics – a relationship which goes back to the earliest progenitors of the Protestant tradition. [10]

Lastly, a few notes should be kept in mind concerning the translations in the texts we will be engaging below. Barth and Heidegger both developed highly technical modes of communication in

---

7 Alister E. McGrath and Darren C. Marks, *The Blackwell Companion to Protestantism* (Oxford: Blackwell, 2004), p. xv.

8 Alister E. McGrath, *Reformation Thought: An Introduction*, 3rd ed. (Oxford: Blackwell Publishers, 1999), p. 5.

9 McGrath and Marks, *The Blackwell Companion to Protestantism*, p. xv.

10 We will note in more detail Barth's way of appropriating Reformation thinking below, and I do not take this as an extraordinary idea given Barth is unashamedly a Protestant theologian. What is in question is whether or not, or maybe more accurately, how Barth's thought can be considered as metaphysical. In regards to Heidegger however, to cite his roots in Protestant thought may seem a bit odd, so I will make a brief comment. As we will note below, but has been documented by others such as John Van Buren in his essay 'Martin Heidegger, Martin Luther', in *Reading Heidegger from the Start: Essays in His Earliest Thought*, ed. Theodore J. Kisiel and John Van Buren (Albany, NY: State University of New York Press, 1994), Heidegger is interested in the deconstructive approach Luther often takes to scholastic metaphysics. An example of where this arises in Luther's works is as follows: 'But alas, how deeply and painfully we are ensnared in categories and questions of what a thing is; in how many foolish metaphysical questions we involve ourselves' Martin Luther, *Luther's Works*, ed. Jaroslav Jan Pelikan, Hilton C. Oswald and Helmut T. Lehmann, American ed., 55 vols, vol. 25 (Philadelphia, PA: Fortress Press, 1999), p. 153. Here we find an example of the reasons why Heidegger's interpretation of Luther is so compelling for postmodern thought today. Essentially Heidegger sees passages like these and takes them one step further to note that Luther's critique of Aristotle and scholastic metaphysics is in fact a critique of all metaphysics and the unfinished beginnings of an a-metaphysical theology.

Preface

German. Although I will often be citing published English translations, wherever possible I have consulted the original German texts in order to include the German terminology in the citations, and in some cases adjusting the translations accordingly. Where it was not possible to offer a satisfactory translation the German was left as it is. Most often I was able to engage Heidegger's *Gesamtausgabe,* and although I did not have access to Barth's *Gesamtausgabe,* I was able to consult the German versions of his major works, all of which are cited alongside the English. Given the importance of the ontological language in both Barth and Heidegger's accounts of the relation between ontology and theology, a further note should be kept in mind. First, because different translators of their work have sometimes capitalized Being as a translation for Heidegger's notion of *Sein,* I have left these translations as such. However, in my own use of the term I will refer to *Sein* as being and *Seiendes* as beings. This helps bring some consistency when we turn to Barth's understanding of *Existenz, Dasein* and *Sein* as he develops these terms. Second, it should be noted that I will be making a distinction between ontotheology, as the Heideggerian account of the relationship between theology and ontology, and Barth's understanding of this same problem which, because of its difference from Heidegger will be referred to as Barth's theological ontology. As such, onto-theology will be used throughout this dissertation to refer to Heidegger's thought, and theological ontology to refer to Barth's. Finally, both Barth and Heidegger sometimes cite Greek sources which I have not transliterated but left in their original language.

Introduction

The Future of Protestant Theology

In a purposely provocative essay, 'The Future of Protestantism: Postmodernity',[1] Graham Ward begins with the following thesis: 'Protestantism is one of the key developments in modernity and, to the extent that postmodernity offers itself as a critique of modernity, then the ethos it fosters is antithetical to Protestantism.'[2] The logic here is simple,[3] but depends heavily upon the meaning of the key terms involved, Protestantism, modernity and postmodernity. Ward will therefore set out to demonstrate how key themes such as 'the autonomy of the reasoning subject',[4] 'nominalism and ... the univocity of being',[5] share both a Protestant and modern pattern of

---

1 Graham Ward, 'The Future of Protestantism: Postmodernity', in *The Blackwell Companion to Protestantism*, ed. Alister E. McGrath and Darren C. Marks (Malden, MA: Blackwell, 2004), pp. 453–67.
2 Ward, 'The Future of Protestantism', p. 453.
3 If p is postmodernity, x is Protestantism and m is modernity, then Ward's thesis is that if m ≈ x and p ≠ m, then p ≠ x. The question is whether m's approximation to x is adequate to account for x's relation to p.
4 Ward, 'The Future of Protestantism', p. 453.
5 Ward, 'The Future of Protestantism', p. 456. In this regard, Ward cites those narrations that trace modernity's roots to medieval scholastic metaphysics (and in particular to the univocal ontology of John Duns Scotus) in the work of *nouvelle théologie* Roman Catholics such as Michel de Certeau and Henri de Lubac. Importantly, these narrations are continued in Radical Orthodox theologians such as John Milbank, Catherine Pickstock and Conor Cunningham. Ward, 'The Future of Protestantism', p. 464, n. 3. For specific examples of their interpretation of Scotist univocity for instance, see John Milbank, *Theology and Social Theory: Beyond Secular Reason*, 2nd ed. (Malden, MA: Blackwell Publishers, 2006), p. 305; Catherine Pickstock, *After Writing: On the Liturgical Consummation of Philosophy* (Oxford: Blackwell Publishers, 1998), p. 122; Conor Cunningham, *A Genealogy of Nihilism: Philosophies of Nothing and the Difference of Theology* (London and New York: Routledge, 2002), pp. 19ff, 26ff. For a critical debate regarding these Radically Orthodox interpretations see October 2005's *Modern Theology*, volume 21, issue

development. Following prominent interpreters of the postmodern such as Stephen Toulmin and Jean-François Lyotard, Ward presents postmodernity as the other side of modernity – that which, 'in the modern, puts forward the unpresentable in the presentation itself'.[6] For Toulmin, it is possible to notice proto-postmodern notions within modern history,[7] and in this sense, postmodernism was always a possibility of modernity.[8] This helps us understand postmodern critique as a radicalization of those masters of suspicion, Karl Marx, Friedrich Nietzsche and Sigmund Freud.[9] However, this narration of the relation between modernity and postmodernity is complicated in so far as Ward recognizes these themes to be reified 'ideologies of modernity',[10] which are largely constructed from the hindsight of the postmodern disposition itself. Here, the postmodern provides the vehicle and conditions for these reifications. It is in this light that we must interpret 'the extent that postmodernity offers itself as a critique of modernity'[11] in Ward's thesis. For whatever is to be understood by the 'post' in a postmodern emphasis or sensibility, it cannot be reduced to a simple negation. Rather, the critical nature of postmodernity is complicated by the fact that it

---

number 4, which was dedicated to this topic. In particular, for an example of someone who challenges the perceived implications of univocal ontology in the modern or postmodern period, see Thomas Williams, 'The Doctrine of Univocity is True and Salutary', *Modern Theology* 21, no. 4 (2005), pp. 575–85. Cf. Pickstock's response as well, Catherine Pickstock, 'Duns Scotus: His Historical and Contemporary Significance', *Modern Theology* 21, no. 4 (2005), pp. 543–74.

6 Jean François Lyotard, *The Postmodern Condition*, trans. Geoff Bennington and Brian Massumi (Minneapolis, MN: The University of Minnesota Press, 1984), p. 81.

7 Toulmin's argument turns on the relationship between the beliefs (cosmos) and the political outworkings of those beliefs (polis). He argues that the modern cosmopolis began around the time of Baroque culture in the seventeenth century and began to dissipate around the time of the Second World War. However, it did not fully shift to postmodernity until well after 1945. Stephen Edelston Toulmin, *Cosmopolis: The Hidden Agenda of Modernity* (Chicago: The University of Chicago Press, 1992), pp. 160–1.

8 Graham Ward, *The Blackwell Companion to Postmodern Theology* (Oxford: Blackwell Publishers, 2001), p. xiv.

9 Ward, 'The Future of Protestantism', p. 460. Interestingly, Ward does not mention Luther, but it is, as we shall demonstrate below, wholly consistent with his thesis to suggest that Luther was a progenitor of the modern age of suspicion.

10 The reified and constructed nature of his depiction of both modernity and Protestantism is a point Ward is acutely aware of. Ward, 'The Future of Protestantism', p. 464, n. 9.

11 Ward, 'The Future of Protestantism', p. 453.

Introduction

is first and foremost a work of smuggling and rebranding. This is a point Ward explicitly makes in his depiction of postmodernity as the implosion of modernity,[12] and the liquidation of epistemological and metaphysical principles of the modern period.[13] On the one hand, therefore, Ward presents a picture of postmodernity which is interwoven and bound up with modern problematics. On the other, however, Ward maintains that the postmodern is an example of how 'new emphases and sensibilities are making themselves felt and older ways of looking at and explaining the significance of the world are becoming otiose or no longer credible'.[14] Crucially however, the future of Protestantism is predicted according to the negative attribution of the 'post' which critiques and supersedes the modern.

The strength of Ward's analysis is the manner in which he enquires into Protestantism's relationship to postmodernity in a fundamental, and as such, metaphysical way. Much of what we have to contend with in Ward's account will not depart from the metaphysical nature of this enquiry. Ward should rightly be commended for attempting to face the question of Protestantism's future in light of a philosophical and theological account of the cultural shifts at work in our world today. However, in so far as Ward posits Protestantism's end under the conditions of the postmodern negation of modernity, he fails to account for the full range of possibilities his analysis implies. If the shift from modernity to postmodernity is to be understood as an act of smuggling as much as innovation, then the question of Protestantism's future must reflect this ambiguity and complexity. *The possibility which opens itself out before us is that Protestantism plays a much more pervasive role in the philosophical narration of the metaphysics of*

---

12 Ward, *The Blackwell Companion to Postmodern Theology*, p. xix.

13 Ward addresses this in his second heading 'Advancing Nominalism and the Liquidation of the Protestant Faith'. Ward, 'The Future of Protestantism', p. 457.

14 Ward, *The Blackwell Companion to Postmodern Theology*, p. xiv. It is important to note that Ward draws a distinction between postmodernism and postmodernity. The former represents a critical set of ideas capable of critiquing a cultural expression. Thus, Ward can claim to formulate a postmodern theology which is critical of postmodernity. We will not be holding to this distinction in this text. Our reasons will become clear as we reflect upon Heidegger's depiction of technology, but in brief, there is simply too much interrelationship between the postmodern critique and the cultural expressions referred to as postmodernity.

postmodernity than Ward's analysis allows. As we shall see, no two intellectual figures of the last century have contributed more pervasively to our understanding of these possibilities than Karl Barth and Martin Heidegger. This is not to say that Barth and Heidegger are agreed on this future, but rather that both recognized the value and importance of the ontological intrigue at the heart of the theology of Protestant progenitors such as Martin Luther. Although the chief aim of the following chapters is to explore the relationship between Protestantism and postmodernity in the work of Barth and Heidegger, as Ward's essay demonstrates, we must first orient ourselves to the difficulty of asking what Protestantism is. Our aim here is not to offer a definitive account of Protestantism at the outset, but rather to set the stage for Barth and Heidegger's own unique and sometimes idiosyncratic understandings of this matter.

Two Histories of Protestantism

What is Protestantism? Because of its origins in the sixteenth century, we might assume that the historian is best suited to answer this question. For instance, the term Protestant came into practical use in 1529 at the second Diet of Speyer,[15] around the controversies instigated by the call for ecclesial reform by figures such as Martin Luther. Answering the question historically, however, raises a series of deeper questions about the nature of the question itself. What is meant by the 'is' in the question 'What is Protestantism?' and to what degree is a historical investigation implied by Ward's identification of Protestantism with modern metaphysics? What we must come to understand is how the historical approach to this question demands an account of Protestant metaphysics more directly. Nowhere is the metaphysical inheritance of the historian's approach more apparent than in the difference between Adolf von Harnack's

---

15 'The Term derives from the Latin, *protestatio*. Even as late as 1547 during the coronation of King Edward VI, the term Protestant was reserved for the German diplomatic representatives staying in London at the time.' Diarmaid MacCulloch, *The Reformation* (New York: Viking, 2004), p. xx.

Introduction

'The Essence [*Wesen*] of Christianity'[16] and Ernst Troeltsch's critical response 'What Does "Essence of Christianity" Mean?'[17] As was pointed out early on by Roman Catholic critics such as Alfred Loisy,[18] Harnack's enquiry into Christian essences smuggled a deeply Protestant critique of Greek metaphysics into the question of Christian identity. Loisy recognized that to determine the unchangeable nature of the essence of Christianity was to 'transform it into a metaphysical entity, into a logical quintessence, into something resembling the scholastic notion of species'.[19] How else could an account of Christ's teaching and work be understood cohesively alongside the diverse manifestation of historical Christian practices and traditions? Loisy therefore highlighted Harnack's anti-metaphysical understanding of the 'essence of Christianity in a sentiment – filial confidence in God, the merciful Father',[20] precisely in order to expose it as a Protestant infatuation with disregarding the historical husk of Christianity for an un-realistic idea.[21] In

---

16 Adolf von Harnack, *Das Wesen des Christentums*, 1. Aufl. ed. (Gütersloh: Gütersloher Verlagshaus Mohn, 1977). We will be citing this as WC below, preceded by the English translation, Adolf von Harnack, *What is Christianity?* (Philadelphia: Fortress Press, 1986).

17 Ernst Troeltsch, 'Was heißt "Wesen des Christentums"?', in *Gesammelte Schriften: Zur religiösen Lage, Religionsphilosophie und Ethik* (Aalen: Scientia Verlag, 1962), pp. 386–451. We will be citing the second volume of the *Gesammelte Schriften* as GS below, preceded by the English translation, Ernst Troeltsch, 'What Does "Essence of Christianity" Mean?', in *Writings on Theology and Religion*, ed. Robert Morgan and Michael Pye (London: Duckworth, 1977), pp. 124–79.

18 This was a point confirmed by Ernst Troeltsch as well, and, although contested by Stephen Sykes as he seeks to shift the question of essence to one of identity, one which he nonetheless acknowledged as follows: 'In a sense, then, the essence of Christianity discussion is an episode in the history of Christian theology. Moreover as an episode, it is in truth primarily a Protestant discussion, with Roman Catholic contributions of an apparently disdainful kind', Stephen Sykes, *The Identity of Christianity: Theologians and the Essence of Christianity from Schleiermacher to Barth* (Philadelphia, PA: Fortress Press, 1984), p. 5. It should be noted that Sykes does his best to justify the broader interest in Christian identity, as a broadly ecumenical enquiry. However, this does not in any way take away from our interest in the particularly Protestant nature of the 'is' which resides at the heart of our question here. See also Alfred Firmin Loisy, *The Gospel and the Church* (Buffalo, NY: Prometheus Books, 1988), pp. 16ff, and, Troeltsch, 'What Does "Essence of Christianity" Mean?'

19 Loisy, *The Gospel and the Church*, p. 14.

20 Loisy, *The Gospel and the Church*, pp. 14–15.

21 To be fair, Harnack forthrightly admonished his readers for assuming that his quest for an essence of Christianity was like that of a child looking for the core of a

Loisy's words, 'Why not find the essence of Christianity in the fullness and totality of its life, which ... has grown in accordance with a law which affirms at every step the initial force that may be called its physical essence revealed in all its manifestations'?[22] What Loisy demonstrates, is that there is a problem in Harnack's question of a Christian essence itself, and it is one which is displayed all the more openly in the English translation, as 'What is Christianity?'

The irony in Harnack's 'is' arises in so far as his history of Christianity is understood in the terms of a particularly transhistorical and a-metaphysical essence. In other words, Harnack was interested in an essence which transcended the ontic manifestations of Christianity in history. Here, we must remember that Harnack is a pupil of Albrecht Ritschl, and the liberal, or as it may better be described, positivist theology which followed from his work.[23] Although it is not fair to reduce Harnack to Ritschl, they nonetheless share an attitude towards metaphysical reflection, which they believed wholly consistent with the Reformation critique of medieval scholasticism.[24] It is in this light that we must read Harnack's

---

bulb only to find that it is all leaves. Harnack, *What is Christianity?*, pp. 14–15/WC, p. 9.

22 Loisy, *The Gospel and the Church*, p. 16, in Sykes, *The Identity of Christianity*, p. 138. Sykes makes the point that Harnack and Loisy are in fact not as far off as Loisy makes out. As he concludes, 'Both Harnack and Loisy struggle with the question of "original Christianity" in a way which makes them instructive to ourselves', Sykes, *The Identity of Christianity*, p. 146. Having said that, this is not to say that Loisy is not correct to find in Harnack a particularly Protestant question.

23 This is the term John Macquarrie gives what is often called liberal theology. He rightly focuses on the desire by liberal Protestants to sidestep the strictures of Kant's critique of traditional metaphysical speculation and, more positively, assess the truth of Jesus in his ethical, historical and social context. 'A positivist philosophy excludes from consideration metaphysical or speculative questions, on the ground that they are in principle unanswerable, and perhaps also useless for practical purposes. So the positivist in Christology would be an investigator who eschewed all metaphysical questions about Jesus Christ – questions such as whether he had two natures, two wills, whether he was "one in being" with the Father, whether the one person of Christ is a human person or a divine person, and so on.' John Macquarrie, *Jesus Christ in Modern Thought* (London: SCM Press, 2003), p. 251.

24 Ritschl will explicitly cite Philip Melanchthon's 1521 *Loci theologici* in order to challenge any who would confuse the efficacious benefits to Christians with a metaphysics of the incarnation. Albrecht Ritschl, 'Theology and Metaphysics', in *Three Essays* (Philadelphia, PA: Fortress Press, 1972), p. 204. Ritschl's anti-metaphysical posturing is critically noted in Karl Barth, *Protestant Theology in the Nineteenth Century: Its Background & History*, trans. G. W. Bromiley, new ed. (London: SCM

Introduction

distillation of the essence of Christianity as 'Firstly, the Kingdom of God and its coming. Secondly, God the Father and the infinite value of the human soul. [And] Thirdly, the higher righteousness and the commandment of love'.[25] This is the core message which Harnack sets out to excavate from its historical circumstances,[26] and, as he will repeatedly emphasize, more adequately apprehends the 'metaphysical significance [*metaphysische Bedeutung*]'[27] of the Logos in early Christian theology.[28] Such metaphysical notions only served to draw 'into the domain of cosmology and religious philosophy a person who had appeared in time and space'.[29] Although Harnack does not disparage the Hellenization of the Christian tradition in so far as it occurred in a particular time and place,[30] he nonetheless will interpret the Reformation in utter contrast to Roman Catholicism, and chiefly in so far as it recovered this essential core of 'the Word of God and to faith' from its previously confused condition.[31] In sum, Harnack's, 'What is Christianity?' inherits a rarefied 'is' from Luther, and represents one possible way of interpreting the Reformer's ontology. In this sense, the essence of Christianity was seen to be fully compatible with the essence of the Reformation, and it was not only Catholics who saw the Protestant tone which rang through Harnack's history of Christianity, but, as well, Harnack's fellow Protestant historians also raised critical questions about the nature of the essence Harnack evinced, few more eloquently than Ernst Troeltsch.

Troeltsch responded to Harnack's interpretation of the history of Christianity through a methodological investigation into the meaning of 'essence' as such. Troeltsch's aversion is not to the notion of an essence, but rather the manner in which one might arrive

---

Press, 2001), p. 641. Cf. Alister E. McGrath, *The Making of Modern German Christology, 1750–1990*, 2nd ed. (Grand Rapids: Zondervan, 1994), pp. 91–2.

25 Harnack, *What is Christianity?*, p. 51/WC, p. 33.
26 Harnack, *What is Christianity?*, p. 15/WC, pp. 9–10.
27 Harnack, *What is Christianity?*, p. 204/WC, p. 128.
28 'The identification of the Logos with Christ was the determining factor in the fusion of Greek philosophy with the apostolic inheritance and led the more thoughtful Greeks to adopt the latter.' Harnack, *What is Christianity?*, p. 204/WC, p. 128.
29 Harnack, *What is Christianity?*, p. 204/WC, p. 128.
30 'But a man must be blind not to see that for that age the appropriate formula for uniting the Christian religion with Greek thought was the Logos.' Harnack, *What is Christianity?*, p. 205/WC, p. 128.
31 Harnack, *What is Christianity?*, p. 269/WC, p. 168.

at such an essence, and in this sense Troeltsch raises the possibility of an alternative Reformation inheritance. This helps explain his ambivalence towards Loisy's critique of Harnack. For instance, Troeltsch will agree that the notion of an essence is itself a product of Protestant theology.[32] Although Troeltsch is fully aware of the manner in which the history of Protestant theology was presented by Ritschl and Hermann as 'anti-philosophical theology [*antiphilosophische Theologie*]' and 'free of metaphysics [*metaphysik-freien*] in the way Luther thought',[33] he himself attributes this Protestant essentialism to German Idealism.[34] Furthermore, Troeltsch and Loisy are agreed that Harnack's essence is far 'too one-sidedly abstracted [*einseitige Abstraktion*] from the preaching of Jesus',[35] and therefore disjointed from the complexity of historical Christian phenomena. The question Troeltsch raised, therefore, concerned the distance between Harnack's essence and the ontic manifestation of historical Christianity.[36] However, although Troeltsch and Loisy agreed upon the form of the problem with Harnack's essentialism, Troeltsch parted with Loisy in so far as his history of Christianity was too quick to replace the 'concept of the essence [*Wesensbegriff*] by that of church'.[37] Rather, Troeltsch accepted that Harnack's essentialism was rooted in the historical consciousness that arose

---

32 Troeltsch, 'What Does "Essence of Christianity" Mean?', pp. 126–7, 134/GS, pp. 389–90, 398.

33 Ernst Troeltsch, 'Half a Century of Theology: A Review', in *Writings on Theology and Religion*, ed. Robert Morgan and Michael Pye (London: Duckworth, 1977), p. 62, Ernst Troeltsch, 'Rückblick auf ein halbes Jahrhundert der theologischen Wissenschaft', in *Gesammelte Schriften: Zur religiösen Lage, Religionsphilosophie und Ethik* (Aalen: Scientia Verlag, 1962), p. 204.

34 Troeltsch, 'What Does "Essence of Christianity" Mean?', pp. 129–30/GS, pp. 392–3.

35 Troeltsch, 'What Does "Essence of Christianity" Mean?', p. 134/GS, p. 398.

36 Troeltsch, 'What Does "Essence of Christianity" Mean?', p. 134/GS, p. 398. This is a point made even more forcefully by Albert Schweitzer as follows: 'Harnack, in his "What is Christianity?" almost entirely ignores the contemporary limitations of Jesus' teaching, and starts out with a Gospel which carries him down without difficulty to the year 1899.', Albert Schweitzer, *The Quest of the Historical Jesus: A Critical Study of Its Progress from Reimarus to Wrede*, trans. W. Montgomery (New York: Dover Publications, 2005), p. 252.

37 Troeltsch, 'What Does "Essence of Christianity" Mean?', p. 134/GS, p. 398. This is yet another way in which we might understand Loisy and Harnack to be working under a 'broadly similar purpose', Sykes, *The Identity of Christianity*, p. 142.

Introduction

out of the Enlightenment era, and as such demanded that this essentialism be taken to more radical metaphysical conclusions. Unlike Loisy, Troeltsch's solution was to raze the dogmatic presuppositions at work in Harnack's thought in order to allow the historical phenomena to speak all the more forcefully. In Troeltsch's words, 'the "essence" can only be found in *a broad view over the totality of all the manifestations [Erscheinungen] which are related to this idea*, and its discovery demands the exercise of historical abstraction'.[38] Troeltsch is therefore not averse to an idealist reification, but rather, the methodological rigour one employs in order to arrive at such an essence. It is in this light that Troeltsch's ultimate response to Harnack comes to the fore.

Troeltsch's method demanded that the essence of Christianity be understood on the terms of a singular historical phenomenon,[39] and the primary task in this endeavour was to locate religion within this phenomenon.[40] To this end, 'neither the semi-materialistic metaphysics of positivism nor an idealist metaphysic'[41] will be allowed to predetermine this religious data. Rather, he would follow the work of Friedrich Schleiermacher as well as William James's *Varieties of Religious Experience*,[42] by beginning with feeling [*Gefühl*]. Whether

---

38 Troeltsch, 'What Does "Essence of Christianity" Mean?', p. 130/GS, p. 393.

39 Troeltsch will reject the dogmatic historical method's means of resolving this issue in the terms of the 'duality in the divine nature [*Doppelheit im göttlichen Wesen*]', Ernst Troeltsch, 'Historical and Dogmatic Method in Theology (1898)', in *Religion in History* (Minneapolis: Fortress Press, 1991), p. 23; Ernst Troeltsch, 'Historische und dogmatische Methode in der Theologie', in *Gesammelte Schriften: Zur religiösen Lage, Religionsphilosophie und Ethik* (Aalen: Scientia Verlag, 1962), p. 743.

40 Ernst Troeltsch, 'Religion and the Science of Religion', in *Writings on Theology and Religion*, ed. Robert Morgan and Michael Pye (London: Duckworth, 1977), p. 86/GS, p. 459.

41 Troeltsch, 'Religion and the Science of Religion', p. 87/GS, p. 460.

42 Troeltsch works out his analysis of James's work most thoroughly in Ernst Troeltsch, *Psychologie und Erkenntnistheorie in der Religionswissenschaft* (Tübingen: J. C. B. Mohr, 1905), pp. 5–17. 'Just as William James had distinguished between institutional and personal religion, and concentrated his study of religion solely on the latter, so too Troeltsch distinguished between "objective" and "subjective" religion', Walter E. Wyman, *The Concept of Glaubenslehre: Ernst Troeltsch and the Theological Heritage of Schleiermacher* (Chico, CA: Scholars Press, 1983), p. 26. For an example of James's interpretation of mysticism, see lectures xvi and xvii in William James, *Varieties of Religious Experience: A Study in Human Nature*, Centenary ed. (London: Routledge, 2002), pp. 379ff.

in these 'mystical states of consciousness',[43] or a 'taste for the infinite',[44] the results of this approach was that religion was now firmly rooted in the human subject. In Troeltsch's own words, 'The primary phenomenon [*Urphänomen*] of all religion is mysticism, that is, belief in the presence and influence of supernatural powers and the possibility of an inner connection with them'.[45] With this as the phenomenological ground for his historical investigation of religion, he set out to authenticate these religious experiences according to a set of epistemological heuristics. In so far as Troeltsch recognized the potential for delusion in the subjective experience of mysticism,[46] he was also going to have to recognize this same potential for self-delusion in the historian interpreting the phenomenon itself. First, this was because interpreter and interpreted both are caught within the same historical framework. Second, because 'the unified idea of the essence only exists after all in the thought of the historian summarizing the material',[47] Troeltsch would struggle to adequately extricate the bias of the interpreter from the historical task. 'The most important question is therefore that of the content and the nature [*Wesen*] of the religious *a priori*. It lies in the relationship to absolute substances [*Substanzbeziehung*] effected by the nature of reason, by virtue of which everything real [*Wirkliche*], and in particular all values, are brought into relationship with an absolute substance [*Substanz*] which is their starting point and criterion'.[48] We do not have the space to explicate the totality of Troeltsch's response to the problem this immanent historical ontology posed for his methodology. In brief, however, the potentially deluded and disparate value judgements of the various subjects involved are given a strict ethical mandate to examine their biases critically and honestly.[49] In the end, he will demand that the historian be as ethical

---

43 James, *Varieties of Religious Experience*, p. 379.
44 Friedrich Daniel Ernst Schleiermacher, *On Religion: Speeches to Its Cultured Despisers*, trans. John Oman (Louisville, KY: Westminster John Knox Press, 1994), p. 39.
45 Troeltsch, 'Religion and the Science of Religion', p. 115/GS, p. 493.
46 E. Wyman, *The Concept of* Glaubenslehre, p. 30.
47 Troeltsch, 'What Does "Essence of Christianity" Mean?', p. 141/GS, p. 406.
48 Troeltsch, 'Religion and the Science of Religion', p. 116/GS, p. 494.
49 This epistemological facet of Troeltsch's method draws upon another key influence in his overall approach, Heinrich Rickert's theory of value judgements. Although Troeltsch will often cite his indebtedness to Rickert, cf. Troeltsch, 'What

Introduction

and rigorous as possible when considering the various dispositions influencing their interpretation.[50] As good as Troeltsch's intentions were, however, his criteria for historical authenticity remained contentious and, arguably, the primary reason Karl Barth critiqued him after World War One.[51] Troeltsch was, in the end, left with an irresolvable concession to the idiosyncrasies of the historian's values.[52]

Returning to our focus upon the question 'What is Protestantism?' we arrive at Troeltsch's own answer to this question. After passing through critical fires, the historian returns to the religious phenomena, 'but now however the task is to comprehend this variety as one which arises on the basis of an inner unity and which in its successive phases strives towards a normative goal. This is the task of *the philosophical history of religion*.'[53] Troeltsch will cite Hegel as the 'finest solution of this task',[54] but here we must recall the 'fulfilment of Kant's prophecy that in a hundred years his philosophy

---

Does "Essence of Christianity" Mean?', p. 178 n. 11/GS, pp. 449–50, n. 32. This is not to say that he was not also deeply critical of Rickert's approach; Hans-Georg Drescher, *Ernst Troeltsch: His Life and Work*, 1st Fortress Press ed. (Minneapolis, MN: Fortress Press, 1993), pp. 297ff. For Rickert's own discussion of the values in the formation of historical concepts, see Heinrich Rickert, *The Limits of Concept Formation in Natural Science: A Logical Introduction to the Historical Sciences*, abridged ed. (Cambridge: Cambridge University Press, 1986), pp. 93ff.

50 In Troeltsch's words, 'According to what criterion, however, is this criticism to be carried out? ... When partisan spirit and personal wishes are left in the background, and if one simply gives oneself over to the impression made by the material and attempts to distinguish the specific within the whole and to judge the distortions and the accidental additions and insertions in terms of the whole, then such a problem is soluble, at least to the extent that unprejudiced persons ready to learn may be brought to a sympathetic understanding or at least inducted into the main direction of the conception and evaluation of the essence', Troeltsch, 'What Does "Essence of Christianity" Mean?', p. 142/GS, pp. 407–8. Sykes's discussion of Troeltsch on this point is also insightful: Sykes, *The Identity of Christianity*, pp. 156ff.

51 Troeltsch was a popular public supporter of World War One; Drescher, *Ernst Troeltsch*, pp. 249–52. For Barth's comments on his disillusionment with the theology of this time, see Karl Barth, *The Humanity of God* (London: Collins, 1967), p. 14.

52 Nowhere is this difference more pronounced than in the dispositions of Protestant and Roman Catholic accounts of Christian history. For instance, 'It is only possible for Protestantism, which is based precisely upon the principle that personal insight into what is essential in Christianity is able to evaluate selectively the mass of actual historical manifestations', Troeltsch, 'What Does "Essence of Christianity" Mean?', p. 145/GS, p. 411.

53 Troeltsch, 'Religion and the Science of Religion', p. 117/GS, p. 495.

54 Troeltsch, 'Religion and the Science of Religion', p. 117/GS, p. 495.

would come into its own'.[55] The return to Kant's critique of metaphysics, broadly referred to as neo-Kantianism,[56] meant that even if Troeltsch wanted to maintain Hegelian historicism, 'it must be reached by other logical and methodological paths'.[57] Here we see just how Troeltsch will arrive at a metaphysical essence which arises out of the phenomenological ground of mysticism. As he will say, 'Without any metaphysics it is not possible at all, but it will have to be a metaphysics of *a posteriori* conclusions out of the facts and not a deductive metaphysics of the absolute'.[58] Troeltsch will not begin with the presupposition of Hegel's absolute substance,[59] but rather, out of the ground of religious phenomena he will nonetheless derive the idea of Protestantism, Christianity, and God. In Troeltsch's words,

> The idea of God is admittedly not directly accessible in any other way than by religious belief. Yet it asserts a substantial content [*Sachverhalt*] which must stand in harmony with other forms of scientific knowledge ... it must emerge somehow together with the metaphysical conclusions arising out of the examination of experience and the attempt to unify it in final terms.[60]

---

55 Lewis White Beck, 'Neo-Kantianism', in *Encyclopedia of Philosophy*, ed. Paul Edwards (New York: The Macmillan Company & The Free Press, 1967), pp. 468–9.

56 'Neo-Kantianism is a term used to designate a group of somewhat similar movements that prevailed in Germany between 1870 and 1920 but had little in common beyond a strong reaction against irrationalism and speculative naturalism and a conviction that philosophy could be a "science" only if it returned to the method and spirit of Kant.' Beck, 'Neo-Kantianism'.

57 Troeltsch, 'Religion and the Science of Religion', p. 117/ GS, p. 495.

58 Troeltsch, 'Religion and the Science of Religion', p. 117/ GS, p. 495.

59 'Although Hegel himself never provides a simple definition of the term, one is given by his former philosophical ally, F. W. J. Schelling. According to Schelling, the absolute is that which does not depend upon anything else in order to exist or be conceived', Frederick C. Beiser, *The Cambridge Companion to Hegel* (Cambridge: Cambridge University Press, 1993), p. 4. For an example of the elusive manner in which Hegel understands the notion of absolute substance, or spirit, see Georg Wilhelm Friedrich Hegel, *Phenomenology of Spirit*, trans. A. V. Miller (Oxford: Clarendon Press, 1977), paragraph 25, p. 14. See also M. J. Inwood, *A Hegel Dictionary* (Oxford: Blackwell, 1992), pp. 27ff. We will forgo a more detailed explication of Hegel's thought until the following chapters, where he becomes relevant to Heidegger and Barth who respond to him in more detail.

60 Troeltsch, 'Religion and the Science of Religion', pp. 117–18/GS, p. 496.

Introduction

Here, Troeltsch advocates a metaphysical unity between scientific history and religious history, and in so doing offers a controversial alternative to Harnack's a-metaphysical historical essence. In Troeltsch's view, any talk of 'essence' demands this coinherence between the real facts of history and Protestant identity.[61] Setting aside the potential inner contradictions in Troeltsch's epistemological critique of the phenomenological ground of religious experience, we can nonetheless see how his history of Protestant religion gave rise to a more metaphysically robust notion of historical essence.

Nowhere is this difference between Troeltsch and Harnack clearer than in their understanding of Luther. Whereas Harnack recovered Luther's otherworldly faith as part and parcel of a post-scholastic anti-metaphysical theological framework,[62] Troeltsch tended to psychologize Luther, linking him much more closely with his medieval context, as Catholic and scholastic as he was innovative.[63] It is in this light that we can see how the historical approach to the question 'What is Protestantism?' leads us all the more forcefully back to the 'is' at the heart of that question. Although a number of historical compendiums on Protestantism can be seen to follow either Troeltsch or Harnack's respective strategies for uncovering historical Protestantism,[64] they nonetheless do little to respond to

---

61 As we shall see, this is precisely why Heidegger will condemn Troeltsch, a point we will discuss in more detail in future chapters on Heidegger below. Martin Heidegger, *The Phenomenology of Religious Life* (Bloomington: Indiana University Press, 2004), p. 19, Martin Heidegger, *Phänomenologie des Religiösen Lebens*, vol. 60, Gesamtausgabe (Frankfurt am Main: Klostermann, 1995), p. 27.

62 Harnack, *What is Christianity?*, pp. 270ff/WC, pp. 168ff.

63 Drescher, *Ernst Troeltsch*, pp. 141ff; cf. Ernst Troeltsch, *Protestantism and Progress: A Historical Study of the Relation of Protestantism to the Modern World*, trans. W. Montgomery (Eugene, OR: Wipf and Stock, 1986), pp. 59, 191. Again this is a point he will be chastised for by Heidegger. Heidegger, *The Phenomenology of Religious Life*, p. 19/GS, p. 27.

64 The following is not an exhaustive, but rather illustrative list of historical approaches to the question 'What is Protestantism?' It is therefore a purposely reductive, and nonetheless helpful way to summarize how the history of Protestantism is often deeply, and sometimes uncritically, interwoven within Protestant sensibilities. On behalf of Harnack's approach we find Catholic and Protestant histories of 'the theology of faith', Avery Dulles, *The Assurance of Things Hoped for: A Theology of Christian Faith* (New York: Oxford University Press, 1994), pp. 3–4; the 'spirit and forms of Protestantism', Louis Bouyer, *The Spirit and Forms of Protestantism* (Westminster, MD: Newman Press, 1956), p. 17; 'an appeal to God in Christ, to Holy Scripture, and to the Primitive Church', R. Newton Flew, Francis Fisher and

the fundamental aims of our question 'What is Protestantism?' The reason is that a historical answer to what Protestantism is deflects the inner metaphysical presuppositions which inform any of these respective histories. Hence, the differences between Troeltsch and Harnack's accounts of Protestantism are unmasked as instantiations of metaphysical choices. It is precisely in this manner that the question 'What is Protestantism?' demands further metaphysical reflection if it is to have any impact upon our broader interest in relating it to the critiques of postmodernity evinced by Ward above. We would do well, therefore, to return to the controversial nature of Martin Luther's metaphysics in order to orient ourselves to Heidegger and Barth's own investigations of his thought.

Protestant Metaphysics

There is no question that Luther was critical of medieval scholasticism's penchant for abstract philosophical reflection. His lectures on Paul's epistle to the Romans in the summer of 1516 provide a superb example of Luther's apparent allergy to metaphysics. As he puts it, 'But alas, how deeply and painfully we are ensnared in categories and questions of what a thing is; in how many foolish meta-

---

Rupert Eric Davies, *The Catholicity of Protestantism: Being a Report Presented to His Grace the Archbishop of Canterbury by a Group of Free Churchmen* (London: Lutterworth Press, 1951), p. 15; 'Christianity that is discovered in the Word of God alone', William A. Scott, *Historical Protestantism: An Historical Introduction to Protestant Theology* (Englewood Cliffs, NJ: Prentice-Hall, 1970), p. vi; or more broadly, 'religious ideas', B. A. Gerrish, *The Old Protestantism and the New: Essays on the Reformation Heritage* (Chicago: University of Chicago Press, 1982), p. 1. So too, Troeltsch's demand for a phenomenological approach is still felt in those treatises which deal strictly 'with the data and phenomena of Protestant churches and cultures', Martin E. Marty, *Protestantism*, History of Religion (London: Weidenfeld and Nicolson, 1972), p. ix (interestingly, Marty will set aside the notion of a unifying principle, p. xi); or view 'all these elements of the Protestant development ... as an intelligible whole', John Dillenberger and Claude Welch, *Protestant Christianity Interpreted Through its Development* (New York: Scribner & Sons, 1954), pp. 302ff. In this last case, Dillenberger and Welch try to supplement the outer historical phenomena which provides a primary historical data set from the inner history of memory and imagination which they also seek to uncover. Inner history is that in 'which we as persons are involved so that it has become a part of us', p. 309. This is not strictly the mystical element as in Troeltsch, but certainly could be read in this light.

Introduction

physical questions we involve ourselves!'[65] We have here a clear proscription against an overzealousness for the ontological, and in the opening 'Philosophical Theses' of *The Heidelberg Disputation* of 1518, the anti-scholastic nature of Luther's vitriol can again be heard: 'He who wishes to philosophize by using Aristotle without danger to his soul must first become thoroughly foolish in Christ'.[66] He then continues to critique Aristotle's understanding of the eternal nature of the world to contrast him with Plato whom he finds superior before beginning the proofs for his theses,[67] his *theologia crucis*.[68] It is here, in Luther's theology of the cross, however, that he famously demands that 'a theologian of the cross calls the thing what it actually is'.[69] Luther refocuses his interlocutors' attention upon the physicality of Jesus Christ on the cross, while simultaneously calling metaphysical presuppositions into question. It is in the light of this distance between Luther's polemic against the 'is' of the medieval scholastics and the ontology of the cross he advocates that the historical question 'What is Protestantism?' asks more than a chronology of events. This was precisely Ward's point when he linked Protestantism with nominalism and univocal ontology. In Ward's account, what is at stake in any interpretation of Luther's

---

65 Martin Luther, *Luther's Works*, ed. Jaroslav Jan Pelikan, Hilton C. Oswald and Helmut T. Lehmann, American ed., 55 vols, vol. 25 (Philadelphia, PA: Fortress Press, 1999), p. 361.

66 Luther, *Works*, vol. 31, p. 41.

67 Luther, *Works*, vol. 31, p. 41. A number of examples of Luther against Aristotle could be mentioned at this point. From the outset of the Heidelberg general chapter meeting of the Augustinians of Germany, Luther echoes the *Disputation Against Scholasticism*, which is thought to be an outworking of his commentary on Aristotle's *Physics* in 1517. 'In 1517 Luther was working on a commentary on the first book of Aristotle's *Physics* for the purpose of dethroning the god of the scholastics. Although nothing of this commentary is extant, the *Disputation Against Scholastic Theology* undoubtedly grew out of its preparation', Luther, *Works*, vol. 31, p. 6. In this disputation, Luther again rails against Aristotle. 'Briefly, the whole Aristotle is to theology as darkness is to light. This in opposition to the scholastics', Luther, *Works*, vol. 31, p. 12.

68 Luther's *theologia crucis* can be found in its early form in Luther's 'Sermon on St. Thomas' Day, Ps 19:1, December 21, 1516', Luther, *Works*, vol. 51, pp. 17ff., although it is generally considered to have taken its more mature form in *The Lecture on Hebrews* (1518), Luther, *Works*, vol. 29, pp. 107ff., and its most common citation in *The Heidelberg Disputation* (1518) Luther, *Works*, vol. 31, pp. 35ff. For a 'brief overview in chronological order on the definitions of the concept "theology of the cross"' in the past literature, see Walther von Loewenich, *Luther's Theology of the Cross* (Minneapolis, MN: Augsburg Pub. House, 1976), pp. 169–73, n. 2.

69 Luther, *Works*, vol. 31, p. 53.

thought is the degree to which he was caught up in a modern metaphysics outmoded by postmodernity. In order to respond to Ward's thesis, therefore, we will explore the following two points: (1) the meaning of metaphysics in Luther's context; and, (2) the ambiguous and critical nature of Luther's engagement with this context. Our aim, therefore, is to contribute to the recovery of a more full bodied account of Luther's understanding of metaphysics.[70] In so doing we will demonstrate the reasons why Luther's critique proved such a vital resource for Barth and Heidegger's own critical engagements with the metaphysics of modernity.

First, in order to gain insight into the metaphysical character of Luther's theology his late scholastic context requires some explication. For the sake of space I will limit my comments to the scope of Luther's knowledge of the scholasticism of the fourteenth and fifteenth centuries.[71] What follows is therefore not a definitive account of scholastic metaphysics, but rather, a cursory introduction to the metaphysical issues Luther inherited from his teachers. To this end, we will begin with the disagreement between the *via antiqua* and the *via moderna*, which continued to 'exert vital influence in the Reformation era'.[72]

---

70 See for instance, Risto Saarinen, *Faith and Holiness: Lutheran-Orthodox Dialogue 1959–1994*, 1st Fortress Press ed. (Göttingen: Vandenhoeck & Ruprecht, 1997); Carl E. Braaten and Robert W. Jenson, *Union with Christ: The New Finnish Interpretation of Luther* (Grand Rapids, MI: William B. Eerdman's Publishing Company, 1998); Risto Saarinen, *God and the Gift: An Ecumenical Theology of Giving*, Unitas Books (Collegeville, PA: Liturgical Press, 2005). For a review of the notion of *theosis* in this new Finnish interpretation of Luther, see Veli-Matti Kärkkäinen, 'Salvation as Justification and Theosis: The Contribution of the New Finnish Luther Interpretation to Our Ecumenical Future', *Dialog* 45, no. 1 (2006).

71 'Whereas Luther frequently demonstrates first-hand knowledge of the fourteenth and fifteenth centuries, such as Pierre d'Ailly and Gabriel Biel, such knowledge is conspicuously absent in the case of earlier medieval theologians, such as St. Thomas Aquinas. It must, of course, be pointed out that this is precisely what is to be expected, if Luther was educated within the *via moderna*, characterized by its logico-critical attitudes and epistemological nominalism: the great theologians of the thirteenth century belonged to the *via antiqua*, characterized by an epistemological realism, from which Luther would have been taught to distance himself by his mentors at Erfurt.' Alister E. McGrath, *Luther's Theology of the Cross: Martin Luther's Theological Breakthrough* (Oxford: Blackwell, 1985), p. 73, citing Heinrich Denifle and Albert Maria Weiss, *Luther und Luthertum*, 2nd ed., vol. I (Mainz: F. Kirchheim, 1906), pp. 535–6.

72 Heiko Augustinus Oberman, *The Reformation: Roots and Ramifications* (Grand Rapids, MI: William B. Eerdman's Publishing Company, 1994), p. 9.

Introduction

The term *via moderna*, is now becoming generally accepted as the best way of referring to the movement once known as 'nominalism', which included among its adherents such fourteenth- and fifteenth-century thinkers as William of Occam [1287–1347], Pierre d'Ailly [1350–1420], Robert Holcot [d.1349], and Gabriel Biel [c.1425–1495].[73]

Of these names, Gabriel Biel stands out as an important nominalist antecedent to Luther's time period and one whom he often critiques.[74] Biel 'was appointed to the theological faculty of the newly founded University of Tübingen'[75] in 1484, which effected changes there in two ways. 'First, he succeeded in bringing the *via moderna* to a place of preeminence; and second, he gathered about himself a group of young, enthusiastic students, thus securing his accomplishments for the future'.[76] This had lasting influence upon Luther who studied at one of the strongholds of the *via moderna*, the University of Erfurt. Here he would have been taught by Jodokus Trutvetter from Eisenach [1460–1519] and Bartholomaeus Arnoldi von Usingen [1463–1532] who were both 'instrumental in fostering the *via moderna* at Erfurt'.[77] Inevitably, Luther inherited the arguments of his teachers and, even though he was eventually quite critical of their theology and philosophy, he never fully escaped the context he was trained within. Furthermore, the *via moderna* was a fledgling movement in Luther's early intellectual training, and in order to understand the context out of which it was trying to establish itself, namely the *via antiqua*, we need to go back to a series of positions being debated in light of Aristotle's *Metaphysics*, namely between Averroes [1126–98] and Avicenna [980–1037], and between John Duns Scotus [c. 1266–1308] and William of Occam [1287–1347].

With Aristotle we find the origin of the term 'metaphysics', or as he puts it the 'science which investigates being *qua* being [ὂν ᾗ ὄν] and the properties inherent in it in virtue of its own nature'.[78]

---

73 Alister E. McGrath, *Reformation Thought: An Introduction*, 3rd ed. (Oxford: Blackwell Publishers, 1999), p. 74.
74 Luther, *Works*, vol. 31, p. 9.
75 Heiko Augustinus Oberman, *The Harvest of Medieval Theology: Gabriel Biel and Late Medieval Nominalism* (Durham, NC: Labyrinth Press, 1983), p. 16.
76 Oberman, *The Harvest of Medieval Theology*, p. 17.
77 McGrath, *Luther's Theology of the Cross*, p. 30.
78 Aristotle, *The Metaphysics: Books I – IX*, trans. Hugh Tredennick (Cambridge,

Protestant Metaphysics after Barth and Heidegger

Whereas the other branches of human enquiry tend to 'cut off a part of being and investigate the attributes of this part',[79] metaphysics enquires into the nature of being itself. 'Thus, for instance, the mathematical sciences deal with quantity, the physical sciences with certain definite ways of being, none of which is being as being, but only being as life, as motion, or as quantity'.[80] Hence 'meta' could be justly translated as 'after' in relation to physics,[81] which would fit neatly with most accounts of the compilation of texts which comprise the *Metaphysics* as 'among the latest of all Aristotle's works'.[82] Hence, it is after the philosopher has considered physics and mathematics that fundamental questions about being as being and the origins of beings as such, arise. Although the term metaphysics has become even more broad and multifarious over time,[83] the universal scope of Aristotle's enquiry has provided unending fodder for

---

MA: Harvard University Press, 1980), p. 147/1003a21–5.

79 Aristotle, *Metaphysics*, p. 147/1003a21–5.

80 Etienne Gilson, *Being and Some Philosophers* (Toronto: Pontifical Institute of Mediaeval Studies, 1949), p. 1.

81 The title *Metaphysics* is derived from the Greek title, *TA META TA FUSIKA*, Aristotle, *Metaphysics*, p. 2. For examples of the definition of META as 'after', see Henry George Liddell and Robert Scott, *An Intermediate Greek-English Lexicon, Founded Upon the Seventh Edition of Liddell and Scott's Greek-English Lexicon* (New York: Harper & Brothers, 1889), p. 500.

82 Aristotle, *Aristotle's Metaphysics*, vol. 1, trans. W. D. Ross (Oxford: The Clarendon Press, 1924), p. xv.

83 One of the broadest definitions of metaphysics explains it as 'the philosophical investigation of the nature, constitution, and structure of reality. It is broader in scope than science, e.g., physics and even cosmology ... since one of its traditional concerns is the existence of non-physical entities, e.g., God. It is also more fundamental, since it investigates questions science does not address but the answers to which it presupposes.' Panayot Butchvarov, 'Metaphysics', in *The Cambridge Dictionary of Philosophy*, ed. Robert Audi (New York: Cambridge University Press, 1999), p. 563. For further examples of the consensus on this definition, see E. J. Lowe, *A Survey of Metaphysics* (Oxford: Oxford University Press, 2002), p. v. The breadth of metaphysics here defined allows for a greater appreciation of the varied approaches and strategies at work in metaphysical enquiry. 'Once we discard fashionable contemporary ideologies and study the history of philosophy in detail, it becomes apparent that there are many different types of metaphysics.', Stephen Rosen, 'Is Metaphysics Possible?', *The Review of Metaphysics* 45 (1991), p. 243. The variety this definition of metaphysics accommodates becomes crucial as we notice the ways in which Protestant theologians take up and critique particular metaphysical strategies. In relation to Barth and Luther below, beginning with a broad definition of metaphysics allows for more clarity about how their theologies challenge, incorporate, and in fact are metaphysical.

Introduction

the theologians and philosophers who came after him. For instance, in book VI of his *Metaphysics,* Aristotle will discuss three theoretical philosophies, physics, mathematics and theology.[84] Averroes and Avicenna both try to decipher whether or not 'first philosophy or divine science can be identified with Aristotle's general science of being as being, a difficulty which he himself [Aristotle] recognizes'.[85] Whereas Avicenna argues that the subject of metaphysics must remain the science of being as being, Averroes rejects this view arguing that while no 'science can demonstrate the existence of its subject, he insists that it is in physics rather than in metaphysics that one demonstrates the existence of God, the first mover'.[86] The difference between them came down to whether or not God was a substance and could therefore *be* in the same sense that everything else was, or whether God was something else entirely. Hence physics had no claim on God any more than a metaphysics of being did. Importantly, the positions of both Averroes and Avicenna would have been 'well known to thirteenth- and fourteenth-century Latin scholastics'.[87]

For instance, when we consider one of the main proponents of the *via antiqua,* John Duns Scotus, his arguments tend to offer something from both sides. Although Scotus will deny that God is the subject of metaphysics and consistently side with Avicenna, because 'God is one of the things investigated by the science of metaphysics, it follows that for Scotus God, too, is in some way included within that general notion of being that serves as its subject'.[88] Part of what is at stake in Scotus's decisions upon these matters is his valuation of being as a common universal category, or in Scotus's investigations, the quiddity of being or the nature of its essential properties.[89] In Scotus's terms, 'in "being" there concurs a two-fold

---

84 Aristotle, *Metaphysics*, p. 297/.1026a23–32.
85 John F. Wippel, 'Essence and Existence', in *The Cambridge History of Later Medieval Philosophy: From the Rediscovery of Aristotle to the Disintegration of Scholasticism, 1100–1600*, ed. Norman Kretzmann, Anthony John Patrick Kenny and Jan Pinborg (Cambridge: Cambridge University Press, 1982), p. 385.
86 Wippel, 'Essence and Existence', p. 387.
87 Wippel, 'Essence and Existence', p. 386.
88 Wippel, 'Essence and Existence', pp. 389–90. For Scotus's own discussion of this matter, see John Duns Scotus, *Philosophical Writings: A Selection*, trans. Allan Wolter (Edinburgh: Nelson, 1962), pp. 10ff.
89 '*Quiddity* or *in quid* is generally used by Scotus to refer to an essential or

primacy, namely, a primacy of commonness *in quid* in regard to all concepts that are not irreducibly simple and a primacy of virtuality in itself or in its inferiors regarding all concepts which are irreducibly simple'.[90] In making this distinction between concepts which are irreducibly simple and those which are not,[91] Scotus argues that there is a twofold possibility in which being relates to both kinds of concepts according to commonness and virtuality. Being is both common to reducible concepts and virtual to irreducible concepts. Hence, even with irreducibly simple concepts such as God, metaphysics is necessary. This is not to say that God is reduced to being, but rather that metaphysics is the proper branch of knowledge for discussing God.[92]

However, the manner in which Scotus considered the relationship between being and other concepts, and in particular whether God was the subject of metaphysics, began to change with the arguments of William of Occam, a proponent of the *via moderna*. Chiefly, Occam's critique was animated by his differentiation between the subject and object of a science. For Occam, 'the object of a science is simply any proposition that is demonstrated within that science, but the subject of a science is the subject of such a proposition.

---

substantive form of being'. Duns Scotus, *Philosophical Writings*, p. 165 n. 2. 'A quidditative concept of a thing represents that thing's quiddity. The quiddity of a thing provides the answer to the question, What (kind of thing) is it? It might be tempting to think that a thing's quiddity is simply the set of properties essential to the thing. But Scotus's notion of a quiddity – and thus of a quidditative concept – runs deeper than that. As a first approximation we may say that the quiddity of a thing explains why the thing's essential properties are essential to it.' William E. Mann, 'Duns Scotus on Natural and Supernatural Knowledge of God', in *The Cambridge Companion to Duns Scotus*, ed. Thomas Williams (Cambridge: Cambridge University Press, 2003), p. 243.

90 Duns Scotus, *Philosophical Writings*, pp. 7–8.
91 Duns Scotus, *Philosophical Writings*, p. 166, n. 3.
92 'The *primacy of commonness*, or better, of common predication, which Scotus ascribes to being, simply means that "being" conceived quidditatively or as a noun is predicable of anything that can be grasped by a concept that is not irreducibly simple. The *virtual primacy* that Scotus attributes to "being" in reference to its attributes and ultimate differences does not mean that the formal concept or *ratio* "being" contains these notions in such a way that the latter can be abstracted from the former by an act of intellectual abstraction or analysis as some have claimed. It simply means that these other notions or *rationes* are predicable by a necessary or *per se* predication of some subject that can be designated as "a being" or "a thing".' Duns Scotus, *Philosophical Writings*, p. 167, n. 5.

Introduction

Since a given science, such as metaphysics, includes many propositions with different subjects, it will have many different subjects'.[93] This multiplicity of subjects reflects the *via moderna*'s scepticism about the ability of concepts to refer to universals. 'Occam refuses to admit that in the real world there is anything that corresponds to the universality of a concept'.[94] In his words, 'Neither metaphysics nor philosophy of nature nor mathematics is numerically one piece of knowledge in the same way as this whiteness and this heat and this man and this donkey are each numerically one. Proof: Metaphysics contains many conclusions'.[95] Occam's point is that the argument's conclusions cannot be contained in its subject. He demonstrates this by noting that the object of knowledge represented in its propositions says something more than the subject can contain. Being may be the subject of metaphysics, but this is not to say that it then contains the conclusions of any given metaphysical proposition in advance. In Occam's words, 'It is no part of "a subject" that it should "virtually" contain the whole knowledge of the conclusions, or be something which comes first, and to which everything else is referred'.[96] This comment specifically contradicts Scotist ontology, which implied that the conclusions of an argument could already be virtually contained in the subject of the enquiry itself.

We're now ready to turn to Luther's *theologia crucis,* and it is worth reiterating at the outset the nature of our response to Ward. Chiefly, 'there is no question that Luther was trained as a

---

93 Wippel, 'Essence and Existence', pp. 391–2. Occam puts it this way, 'A science which has only a collective unity has not just one subject; rather it has different subjects according to its different parts. For only that about which something is known can be called a subject of knowledge; yet, in a science that is only collectively one, there are many things about which different things are scientifically known; therefore, such a science has not just one subject ... We must also realize that there is a difference between the object and the subject of knowledge. For the object of knowledge is the whole proposition that is known; the subject, however, is only a part of this proposition, namely the subject-term. For instance, the object of my knowledge that every man is educable is the entire proposition; its subject, however, is the term "man".' William of Occam, *Philosophical Writings: A Selection*, ed. Philotheus Boehner and Stephen F. Brown (Indianapolis: Hackett Publishing Company, 1990), pp. 8–9.
94 William of Occam, *Philosophical Writings*, p. xxvii. For Occam's own argument see pp. 5ff from this same text.
95 William of Occam, *Philosophical Writings*, p. 6.
96 William of Occam, *Philosophical Writings*, p. 9.

nominalist at Erfurt; but the implications of his academic training are still contested and under debate'.[97] Luther's *theologia crucis* innovates, but it is important to note how his innovation works within and against the *via moderna*'s basic framework. This can be seen in both the style and the content of his arguments. Though he clearly makes statements against his nominalist teachers, even as late as 1520, he 'defended himself with an argument derived in both form and content from the nominalistic tradition; "I demand arguments not authorities. That is why I contradict even my own school of Occamists, which I have absorbed completely"'.[98] This is a classic example of Luther's paradoxical relationship to his metaphysical context. On the one hand, Luther distances himself from metaphysical arguments and condemns Biel and the Occamists. On the other hand, much of the mechanism and framework of his arguments are utterly inculcated in their thought. Hence, when we read Luther's many statements against metaphysics and scholasticism, they must be tempered with an understanding of his context. 'Even the reformer has obligations; he too is bound by ties of kin'.[99] As such, 'if we merely conclude that Luther was an "ossified Occamite", we are still left with the problem why Luther was the man who started a Reformation, not Occam, or D'Ailly, or Biel. It will surely be more important, in the long run, to see where Luther *differed from* Occam.'[100] It is precisely here that our response to Ward begins. As we shall see, Luther's relationship to the nominalism of the *via moderna* is ambiguous and critical. It is as we come

---

97 Heiko Augustinus Oberman, *Luther: Man Between God and the Devil* (New Haven, CT: Yale University Press, 1989), p. 120.

98 Oberman, *Luther*, p. 120. Oberman cites the Weimar edition *D. Martin Luthers Werke: Kritische Gesamtausgabe, Briefwechsel* [Correspondence], vol. 6.195 4f. This citation was not included in the English translation of Luther's letters and works cited elsewhere in this essay. The closest thing that can be found to it is: 'But they will never take theology itself away from me or extinguish my love for it, as long as Christ remains gracious to me. I know what scholastic theology did for me, and I know how much I owe it! I am glad that I have escaped from it, and for this I thank Christ my Lord. They do not have to teach it to me, for I already know it. Nor do they have to bring it any closer to me, for I do not want it!' Martin Luther, *Luther's Works*, vol. 14, p. 284.

99 Oberman, *The Reformation*, p. 3. Oberman is here referring to Luther's early criticisms of his teachers in his commentary on Romans in 1515/16.

100 B. A. Gerrish, *Grace and Reason: A Study in the Theology of Luther* (Oxford: Clarendon Press, 1962), pp. 54–5.

Introduction

to understand the nature of this critical ambiguity that a compelling approach to the question 'What is Protestantism?' emerges. So too, we arrive at that aspect of his thinking which made him such a provocative resource for Barth and Heidegger both.

One of the most direct ways in which Luther's ideas demonstrate the critical yet ambiguous relationship to his scholastic contemporaries was in regards to freedom. As he will put it in his *Heidelberg Disputation*, *'free will, after the fall, exists in name only, and as long as it does what it is able to do, it commits a mortal sin'*.[101] This statement cannot help but be read in light of Luther's nominalist training. Free will is cited as a concept in name only. It is not the case that human beings are free as if this would mean they were free in all times, circumstances etc. Rather freedom can be a subject within multiple modes of enquiry – that is, what appears to our natural senses and as it is revealed theologically. In another place Luther states:

> For Scripture does not give man his name in a metaphysical sense, according to his essence (for in this sense the theologians see in man nothing but what is praiseworthy); but Scripture speaks theologically and names him as he is in the eyes of God.[102]

When it comes to the key themes in his *Heidelberg Disputation*, therefore, one of Luther's chief aims is to delineate a theory of knowledge that takes account of humanity's natural *and* theological possibilities. This is all the more important as we face the most controversial of Luther's statements: *'free will, after the fall, has power to do good only in a passive capacity, but it can always do evil in an active capacity'*.[103] Here we find the roots of one of the most oft cited doctrines concerning the capacity of human beings to contribute to their own salvation. As he will go on to say, *'It is certain that man must utterly despair of his own ability before he is prepared to receive the grace of Christ'*.[104] Here, we can see Luther's breakthrough critiquing the *via moderna*'s retention of the possibility of human works to merit salvation in the work of figures

---

101 Luther, *Works*, vol. 31, p. 48.
102 Luther, *Works*, vol. 27, p. 181.
103 Luther, *Works*, vol. 31, p. 49.
104 Luther, *Works*, vol. 31, p. 51.

such as Gabriel Biel, all the while emphasizing that the gift of grace 'is bestowed through the divine liberality, and not through human merit'.[105]

Gabriel Biel's teaching on the distinction between the *potentia Dei absoluta* and *ordinata* within the *via moderna* provides helpful background to Luther's argument.[106] For Biel, 'within the framework of God's absolute power ... God was at liberty to justify man by other means than an infused habit of grace'.[107] In particular Biel 'shows in I *Sent*. d. 17, the habit of grace is not a necessary requirement for a meritorious act *de potentia absoluta*. In II *Sent*. d. 27, however, he deals with this question *de potentia ordinata*, and it is here that we have to look for Biel's actual teaching'.[108] Here Biel argues that the habit of grace is required as a disposition for a human being's 'ultimate acceptation, that is, beatification by God'.[109] What is at stake is the acceptance of a human being's acts and whether they are meritorious.[110] Though God could accept

---

105 McGrath, *Luther's Theology of the Cross*, p. 88. McGrath is here listing out the affinities of Luther's theology and the *via moderna* in his early work, the *Dictata*.

106 Heiko Oberman's magisterial summary of Biel's work is most helpful on these points. 'Apart from cursory references, Biel writes explicitly on God's double *potentia* only in two places: once in the context of justification and infused grace and once in the context of the sacraments and their effects.' Heiko Augustinus Oberman, *The Harvest of Medieval Theology*, p. 36. Here Oberman references Biel's I *Sent*. d. 17 q. I art. 3 H and IV *Sent*. d. I q. I art. 3 [K.] dub. 2. Briefly, Biel understood the distinction 'to mean that God can – and, in fact, has chosen to – do certain things according to the laws which he freely established, that is, *de potentia ordinata*. On the other hand, God can do everything that does not imply contradiction, whether God has decided to do these things [*de potentia ordinata*] or not, as there are many things God can do which he does not want to do. The latter is called God's power *de potentia absoluta*.' Heiko Augustinus Oberman, *The Harvest of Medieval Theology*, p. 37.

107 McGrath, *Luther's Theology of the Cross*, p. 56.

108 Oberman, *The Harvest of Medieval Theology*, p. 166.

109 Oberman, *The Harvest of Medieval Theology*, p. 167.

110 'According to Biel there are only two conditions that have to be met for an act to be worthy of reward. The first is that it should be a laudable act and thus a free act ... [and] the acceptation by God of the act for its reward.' Oberman, *The Harvest of Medieval Theology*, p. 167. This second condition is in turn 'spelled out in a threefold way: (1) the actor should be a friend of God since an enemy of God earns punishment and not reward; (2) the *act* should be "directable" to God. Thus even if one is a friend of God, that is, in a state of grace, indifferent acts or venial sins cannot be considered for reward; (3) as concerns the *rewarder* an acceptation or agreement is required, by which he commits himself to reward certain actors and

Introduction

a person without a habit of grace, Biel maintains this category in his doctrine of justification because it 'allows for a certain form of sinfulness and indifference to coexist with acceptability: partly *iustus*, partly *peccator*.'[111] *Habitus* allows the person to remain a sinful finite being and yet effect and take part in justification and the goodness of the infinite without having to sort out either the goodness or sinfulness of the human being in detail. Thus justification can take place by meritorious acts of human beings on the condition that they are accepted by God. By arguing that a habit of grace is necessary, however, he maintains that 'this is only the case within the context of the eternal decree and not a metaphysical necessity'.[112] Furthermore, even though God's decree was made freely, 'God would act illegally if he did not grant the reward once the conditions in actor and act have been met'.[113]

It is in this light that we can see Luther taking the *via moderna* to its extreme conclusions. If God could accept human beings without their active merit, and if there was some evidence that God did in fact do so, then the role of an active merit could be discarded – especially if it was in fact understood to be a hindrance to salvation, as Luther believed it was.[114] Hence he can say: '*Much less can human works which are done over and over again with the aid of natural precepts, so to speak, lead to that end*'.[115] This had severe implications for the *habitus* of grace which was replaced by Luther's doctrine that the gift of grace was given by the Holy Spirit alone and was all that was required for good works which come after grace is given.[116] Though Luther argues that human works cannot lead to justification, this is not to say that he will abandon the ordinated power of God in human salvation. Luther's argument that human

---

acts. The condignity or equality of deed and reward is not based on any natural or intrinsic goodness of the act, but on this agreement to which God in eternity freely committed himself. This is the only way in which condignity can be established between a temporal act and an eternal reward', Oberman, *The Harvest of Medieval Theology*, pp. 167–8.

111 Oberman, *The Harvest of Medieval Theology*, p. 167.
112 Oberman, *The Harvest of Medieval Theology*, p. 168.
113 Oberman, *The Harvest of Medieval Theology*, p. 168.
114 Luther consistently rails against the arrogance of those who believe in their own potential to merit God's grace. Cf. Luther, *Works*, vol. 31, p. 50.
115 Luther, *Works*, vol. 31, p. 43.
116 Occam was severely chastised by Luther for his disregard of the Holy Spirit's role in salvation as a result. Luther, *Works*, vol. 34, p. 188.

free will can only act in a passive sense is designed to show both the inability of human beings to enact their own justification while maintaining the *potentia Dei ordinata* as an open possibility when the theological subject of the cross was under consideration.

Nowhere are Luther's theological innovations more explicit than in his statements on the cross of Christ itself in theses 19–21 of the *Heidelberg Disputation*, and it is here that we find the most difficult and important delineation of Luther's metaphysical disposition.

> 19 *That person does not deserve to be called a theologian who looks upon the invisible things of God as though they were clearly perceptible in those things which have actually happened [Rom. 1.20]* ...[117] 20 *He deserves to be called a theologian, however, who comprehends the visible and manifest things of God seen through suffering and the cross* ...[118] 21 *A theologian of glory calls evil good and good evil. A theologian of the cross calls the thing what it actually is.*[119]

Although Luther is critical of an attempt to perceive the invisible things of God in the visible world in thesis 19, a clear critique of metaphysical reflection, he nonetheless goes on in thesis 20 to commend the theologian, 'who comprehends the visible and manifest things of God seen through suffering and the cross'.[120] We cannot stress enough how important the difference between these two theses is for what will follow in our explication of Heidegger and Barth. As we shall see, Heidegger and Barth both take particular care with these passages in Luther's thought. Their interpretations hang on the degree to which any emphasis is given to thesis 20, for without it, Luther's demand that the theologian call a thing what it actually is in thesis 21 lacks its Christological focus. There is no cross upon which the theologian can properly fix their gaze. Furthermore, it is this thesis that is linked to the theological realism in Luther's later work, and gives crucial insight into why Luther is said to have written Jesus's '*hoc est corpus*' in chalk on the table when he debated

---

117 Luther, *Works*, vol. 31, vol. 31, p. 52.
118 Luther, *Works*, vol. 31, vol. 31, p. 52.
119 Luther, *Works*, vol. 31, vol. 31, p. 53.
120 Luther, *Works*, vol. 31, vol. 31, p. 52.

Introduction

the Eucharist with Ulrich Zwingli at a castle in Marburg in 1529.[121] For Luther, the cross of Christ reveals the being of God, and this is the chief reason why the 'is' in Christ's statement 'this is my body' could not be understood in a strictly metaphorical sense.

What we mustn't miss at this point in our argument, however, is the metaphysical nuance at work in Luther's claim that 'he who does not know Christ does not know God hidden in suffering'.[122] This addendum to thesis 21 conceals the metaphysically orchestrated truce Luther is developing between natural and theological reason. For on the one hand, 'God is revealed in the cross of Christ. Yet, as the Christian contemplates the appalling spectacle of Christ dying upon the cross, he is forced to concede that God does not appear to be revealed there at all'.[123] For Luther, then, there is no way to get from metaphysical reflection to a revelation of Christ's divinity. God is not apprehensible by human reason when it focuses itself upon the cross. But this is very different from saying that the cross is antithetical to human reason. Luther nonetheless encourages his readers to look with their eyes at the cross, and it is as we face the impossibility of God in the weakness of the man that the theological truth becomes a *real* possibility. As one commentator puts it:

> Though the relation of natural reason and revelation which we have discussed indicates a *diastasis* between reason and faith which the creature can not eliminate, it certainly does not imply a *divorce* between the realms of reason and faith. Far from postulating a double truth, it rather excludes it. Faith is not irrational or contrary to natural reason but rather ungraspable by natural reason. This very conception allows for the reconciliation and harmonization of seemingly contrasting conclusions in science and theology by way of a 'peaceful coexistence.'[124]

Using the argumentative framework of the *via moderna*,[125] Luther is able to disparage human reason in theological matters for the

---

121 Luther, *Works*, vol. 38, p. 66.
122 Luther, *Works*, vol. 31, p. 53.
123 McGrath, *Luther's Theology of the Cross*, p. 161.
124 McGrath, *Luther's Theology of the Cross*, pp. 162–3.
125 This way of configuring natural and theological knowledge is wholly consistent with the *via moderna*. Oberman, *The Harvest of Medieval Theology*, p. 42.

sake of its use in others. Metaphysics and theology could discuss the same subject in different ways. The two neither compete nor are they necessarily doomed to contradict each other – theology simply offers further insight unavailable to metaphysical reflection alone. This helps make sense of how Luther can on the one hand hold that reason is worthless for theology, and yet wholly capable in civil affairs.[126] The difficulty here for future interpretations of Lutheran metaphysics, is on which thesis to put the emphasis. Luther's recovery of the hidden yet revealed God on the cross is a healthy counter to the abstract independence with which metaphysical reflection was carried out in his day (thesis 19) but this *theologia crucis* was largely based upon Luther's radical employment of the methods and metaphysics of the *via moderna* itself (thesis 20). Thesis 19 easily led later interpreters of Luther such as Heidegger to suggest that he advocated a radical divorce between theology and ontology. However, theses 20 and 21 have consistently contributed to the idea that under certain Christological conditions, ontological statements are inevitable as Barth will tend to emphasize. Crucially, however, it is as we uncover these metaphysical nuances in Luther's thought that we can see why he provided such a vital resource for Barth and Heidegger's own negotiations of the philosophical conditions of their own era.

When we return to the question 'What is Protestantism?' the answer which presents itself most compellingly concerns the nature of the 'is' key reformers such as Luther evinced.[127] Protestantism is

---

[126] In Luther's words: 'When the sophists say that the natural endowments are sound, I concede this. But if they draw the inference: "Therefore a man is able to fulfil the Law, to love God, etc.," then I deny the conclusion. I distinguish the natural endowments from the spiritual; and I say that the spiritual endowments are not sound but corrupt, in fact, totally extinguished through sin in man and in the devil. Thus there is nothing there but a depraved intellect and a will that is hostile and opposed to God's will – a will that thinks nothing except what is against God. The natural endowments are indeed sound, but which natural endowments? Those by which a man who is drowned in wickedness and is a slave of the devil has a will, reason, free choice, and power to build a house, to carry on a governmental office, to steer a ship, and to do other tasks that have been made subject to man according to Gen. 1.28; these have not been taken away from man. Procreation, government, and the home have not been abolished by such statements; they have been confirmed. But the sophists twisted them into the spiritual realm', Luther, *Works*, vol. 26, p. 174. For further discussion, see Gerrish, *Grace and Reason*, pp. 69ff.

[127] Though I have focused almost exclusively upon Luther's theology, this is not

Introduction

defined in this sense according to its metaphysical scepticism and ingenuity. It is a movement driven by the fundamental arguments evinced by theologians such as Luther, who radically questioned the human capacity to apprehend the being of God. Nonetheless, this same Luther commended the theologian of the cross, and the Christological ontology this implied. Hence, our analysis above demonstrates that precisely because Protestantism is a metaphysically sceptical tradition, it can neither be reduced to the *via moderna*, nor escape its influence completely. Our aim here was not to exhaust Luther's insights on these matters, but rather to demonstrate why further explication of Protestant metaphysics is so crucial to its identity and future. This utterly overturns the suggestion that postmodernity tolls the bell for Protestantism.[128] Rather, we can now investigate the degree to which Luther's *theologia crucis* may have inspired postmodern critique itself. It is with this in mind that we turn to the work of Karl Barth and Martin Heidegger.

---

meant at the expense of other Reformation figures such as Calvin. Though Calvin and Luther differ in their emphases and approaches to various theological issues, the metaphysics which undergird their theology is largely comparable. For a more thoroughgoing, recent and Reformed account of Calvin's relationship to the metaphysics of late scholasticism, see Richard Muller, 'Scholasticism in Calvin: A Question of Relation and Disjunction', in *The Unaccomodated Calvin: Studies in the Foundation of a Theological Tradition* (Oxford: Oxford University Press, 2000). This study along with this essay here points out how discussions of Luther and Calvin's relationship to late medieval scholastic metaphysics are not as simple as terms like nominalism can capture. As well, see also, Oberman, *The Dawn of the Reformation*, p. 256. Here, Oberman points out both Calvin's difference from and continuity with late medieval scholasticism and even argues that Calvin is more medieval than Luther in some regards. 'Calvin stands in a scholastic tradition which, rooted in St. Augustine, was unfolded by Johannes Duns Scotus and became the central theme in late medieval theology, expressed as God's commitment to the established order, *de potentia ordinata*', Oberman, *The Dawn of the Reformation*, p. 255.

128 McGrath and Marks, *The Blackwell Companion to Protestantism*, p. xv.

PART ONE
Martin Heidegger's Onto-Theology

I

Heidegger's Cross

Being and God

In a 1951 seminar in Zurich, Martin Heidegger was asked the following question: 'May being and God be posited as identical?' His response gives us a number of crucial clues about the kind of future theology which might follow after his work. In the process of interpreting these clues we can raise a number of questions which we will address in the following chapters. Heidegger says this:

> Being and God are not identical and I would never attempt to think the essence of God by means of Being. Some among you perhaps know that I come from theology, that I still guard an old love for it and that I am not without a certain understanding of it. If I were yet to write a theology – to which I sometimes feel inclined – then the word *Being* would not occur in it. Faith does not need the thought of Being. When faith has recourse to this thought, it is no longer faith. This is what Luther understood. Even within his own church this seems to be forgotten. One could not be more reserved than I before every attempt to employ Being to think theologically in what way God is God. Of Being, there is nothing here to expect. I believe that Being can never be thought as the ground and essence of God, but that nevertheless the experience of God and of his manifestedness, to the extent that the latter can indeed meet man, flashes in the dimension of Being, which in no way signifies that Being might be regarded as a possible predicate for God. On this point one would have to establish completely new distinctions and delimitations.[1]

---

[1] Martin Heidegger, 'The Reply to the Third Question at the Seminar in Zürich, 1951', quoted by Jean-Luc Marion, *God without Being: Hors-texte* (Chicago: University of Chicago Press, 1991), pp. 61–2. Marion cites the original German as

Protestant Metaphysics after Barth and Heidegger

This citation is given and expounded upon by Jean-Luc Marion in his *God without Being*, as well as in shorter form by Jacques Derrida in an essay, 'How to Avoid Speaking: Denials'. In the interpretations and comments they offer we find a common agreement concerning the future of theology after Heidegger. In many ways, Heidegger's statement in the Zurich seminar embodies this future in its very manner as an afterthought. This is not a well-polished written statement by Heidegger. Rather, it is a verbal improvisation to the seminar as such, recorded by a listener taking notes. It must therefore be understood in the context of his other writings on the relationship between theology and ontology. As well, it is precisely in contextualizing this passage that we can begin to recognize a coincidence between the physical location of this afterthought as an afterthought, and the manner in which Heidegger's suggestions for theology are always located as afterthoughts to his work overall. Heidegger tells us that he has left theology behind, he is not a theologian, and his suggestion for any future theology thus comes after this leaving theology behind. Neither Derrida nor Marion are particularly concerned with the theology of Heidegger's past, but they do take issue with Heidegger's denial of the category of being and, in their own ways, question whether it is radical enough.

For Derrida, 'Heidegger allows the word being to appear; he does not use it, but mentions it without erasure when he is indeed speaking of theology, of that which he would be tempted to write'.[2] As such, the possibilities for theology after Heidegger are still haunted by being.

---

follows in note 16 on pp. 211–12: 'Wenn ich noch eine Theologie schreiben würde, wozu es mich manchmal reizt, dann dürfte in ihr das Wort "Sein" nicht vorkommen. Der Glaube hat das Denken des Seins nicht nötig. Wenn er das braucht, ist er schon nicht mehr Glaube. Das hat Luther verstanden, sogar in seiner eigenen Kirche scheint man das zu vergessen. Ich denke über das Sein, im Hinblick auf seine Eignung, das Wesen Gottes theologisch zu denken, sehr bescheiden. Mit dem Sein, ist hier nichts anzusuchen. Ich glaube, daß das Sein niemals als Grund und Wesen von Gott gedacht werden kann, daß aber gleichwohl die Erfahrung Gottes und seiner Offenbarkeit (sofern sie dem Menschen begegnet) in der Dimension des Seins sich ereignet, was niemals besagt, das Sein könne als mögliche Prädikat für Gott gelten. Hier braucht es ganz neue Unterscheidungen und Abgrenzungen.' from *Aussprache mit Martin Heidegger* an 06/XI/1951, privately issued edition by the Vortragsausschuss der Studentenschaft der Universität Zürich (Zurich, 1952).

2 Jacques Derrida, 'How to Avoid Speaking: Denials', in *Derrida and Negative Theology*, ed. Harold G. Coward, Toby Foshay and Jacques Derrida (Albany, NY: State University of New York Press, 1992), p. 127.

Heidegger's Cross

It is a theology where being should not be written and yet remains in that very proscription. Derrida therefore draws parallels between the Zurich seminar and Heidegger's other critical statements regarding onto-theology around this time. In particular, Derrida draws attention to the manner in which Heidegger crosses out being in his essay 'The Question of Being'. Derrida is quick to recognize that Heidegger isn't trying to evoke the negation of being as such,[3] but rather he is negating the objectification of being as a thing which approaches human beings. In Derrida's terms, 'One must therefore avoid representing it (*vorzustellen*) as something, an object that stands opposite (*gegenüber*) man and then comes toward him'.[4] This qualification of the objectification of being, however, does not dissuade Derrida from interpreting this cross in terms of a negative theology. As such, when considering any theology without being as Heidegger does in 1951, Derrida critiques Heidegger's crossed out being because he sees it as an example of the kind of procedure Heidegger might follow when considering a theology without being.

Derrida perceives a coinherence between his own interest in negative theology and its relation to Heidegger's negation of the attribution of the category of being to God. As Derrida says,

> Negative theology is everywhere, but it is never by itself. In that way it also belongs, without fulfilling, to the space of the philosophical or onto-theological promise that it seems to break: to record, as we said a moment ago, the referential transcendence of language: to say God such as he is, beyond his images, beyond this idol that being can still be, beyond what is said, seen, or known of him; to respond to the true name of God, to the name to which God responds and corresponds beyond the name that we know him by or hear. It is to this end that the negative procedure refuses, denies, rejects all the inadequate attributions.[5]

Derrida is therefore applying the conditions of negative theology as he has here described them to Heidegger. In so doing, Derrida

---

[3] Martin Heidegger, *The Question of Being* (New York: Twayne Publishers, 1958), p. 83.
[4] Derrida, 'How to Avoid Speaking', p. 125.
[5] Jacques Derrida, *On the Name*, ed. Thomas Dutoit (Stanford, CA: Stanford University Press, 1995), p. 69.

finds Heidegger's crossing out of being to be inadequate. No cross is sufficient on the grounds that it always leaves what it crosses out. No matter how far one takes this method of dealing with the problem of being, crossing it out does not and cannot remove being from the frame of theological thinking. It provides an inadequate erasure ever haunted by the spectre behind the cross. Rather, Derrida favours a *Khora*. 'This is neither an intelligible extension, in the Cartesian sense, a receptive subject, in the Kantian sense or *intuitus derivativus,* nor a pure sensible space, as a form of receptivity. Radically nonhuman and atheological, one cannot even say that it gives place or that *there is* the *khora*'.[6] Derrida thus seeks to go beyond Heidegger's *es gibt Sein,* in so far as it 'too vividly announces or recalls the dispensation of God'.[7] In fact, Derrida deems Heidegger's account to be far too interlocked within the tradition of metaphysical theology to ever presume to escape it. The negative theology which attempts to withdraw from onto-theology and retreat from a metaphysical foundationalism is yet, nonetheless, still caught up in an essentialism which denies it the ability to genuinely move beyond metaphysics. No such overcoming will be possible in Derrida's interpretation of Heidegger.

Derrida's critique of Heidegger's post-ontological theology is similar in kind to that of Jean-Luc Marion. Marion accepts the positive theological possibilities of Heidegger's ruminations on onto-theology and sees in them 'something other than a complete renouncement of (the existence) of God'.[8] For Marion, the radical critiques of onto-theology which can be found in Heidegger's work open up an even more 'paradoxical but radical manifestation of the divine'.[9] And yet, like Derrida, when it comes to the manner in which Heidegger would enact his post-ontological theology Marion finds him wanting. For Marion, Heidegger's manner of articulating the manifestation of the divine nonetheless still limits God ontologically. However, according to Marion, because 'God intervenes only as one being among those that the Being of beings conciliates according to the ontological difference', there is an inevitable

---

6 Derrida, 'How to Avoid Speaking', p. 106.

7 Derrida, 'How to Avoid Speaking', p. 106.

8 Jean-Luc Marion, *The Idol and Distance: Five Studies* (New York: Fordham University Press, 2001), p. 4.

9 Marion, *The Idol and Distance*, p. 4.

Heidegger's Cross

deduction which ties God to being in Heidegger's thought. As such, the point of Heidegger's suggestion for a theology without being demands that God never be invested in ontological categories. Like Derrida, he interprets Heidegger's understanding of the divide between theology and ontology as an inadequate call for a *God without Being*.

Marion devotes himself to an entire book by this title and it is here that he engages Heidegger's comment in the Zurich seminar in 1951.[10] Theology, as much as a theological investigation into the *causa sui* of onto-theology, has made claims upon an ultimate being as such, but this is not what Heidegger means by theology in his work.[11] Herein lies an intriguing suggestion, which we will explore in more detail below, namely, that although Heidegger disassociates being with theology, he does consider theology to have a proper object in faithful existence. 'Theology therefore does not have to do with "God," in whatever sense one understands him. It has to do with the fact (*Faktum/Positivität*) of faith in the Crucified, a fact that only faith receives and conceives'.[12] Marion specifically comments upon the Lutheran affinity with this division between theiology and theology as the reflection upon faithful existence. Strangely, Marion emphasizes the philosophical and decidedly non-theological significance of this Protestant choice in Heidegger's thought.[13] Nonetheless, Marion critiques Heidegger's post-ontological suggestion for theology precisely because of the manner

---

10 Marion, *God without Being*, pp. 62ff.

11 We will discuss this aspect of Heidegger's 'Phenomenology and Theology' below, but Marion will cite Martin Heidegger, 'Phenomenology and Theology', in *The Piety of Thinking*, ed. James G. Hart and John C. Maraldo (Bloomington: Indiana University Press, 1976), p. 11; Martin Heidegger, 'The Question Concerning Technology', in *The Question Concerning Technology and Other Essays* (New York: Harper & Row, 1977), p. 122; Martin Heidegger, *Being and Time*, trans. John Macquarrie and Edward Robinson (New York: Harper Collins Publishers, 1962), p. 30.

12 Marion, *God without Being*, p. 65.

13 Marion, *God without Being*, p. 65. Marion's own Roman Catholicism should be noted at this point. His attempt to make Heidegger's Lutheranism into a strictly 'philosophical decision' will be questioned in the following chapters. He is not writing out of an ecclesial vacuum, and his work bears a number of important reliances upon and affinities with the Roman Catholic magisterial hierarchy. Graham Ward, 'The Theological Project of Jean-Luc Marion', in *Post-secular Philosophy: Between Philosophy and Theology*, ed. Phillip Blond (New York: Routledge, 1998), p. 237.

in which it encloses theology within the confines of an ontological investigation. Luther is therefore no help to Heidegger in so far as the manner in which Heidegger quarantines theology within the confines of faithful existence radically encloses theology within the very ontology it must escape. As Marion concludes: 'Being offers in advance the screen on which any "God" that would be constituted would be projected and would appear – since, by definition, to be constituted signifies to be constituted as a being'.[14]

The Fulfilment of Metaphysics

It is important to note at this point that Derrida's and Marion's interest in Heidegger's account of post-ontological theology stands at the end of philosophy as Heidegger himself understood it. But what kind of end is Heidegger suggesting, and to what extent does it demand the post-onto-theological rigour Derrida and Marion call for? In an essay on 'The End of Philosophy and the Task of Thinking' Heidegger tells us that 'philosophy is metaphysics'.[15] We shall go into this in more detail shortly, but in brief, Heidegger's philosophy enquires into the being of beings, or the manner in which 'Being brings beings to their actual presencing'.[16] When Heidegger speaks of the end of this philosophy, however, he does not mean 'the negative sense as a mere stopping',[17] but rather, 'in contrast, what we say about the end of philosophy means the completion of metaphysics [*Vollendung der Metaphysik*]'.[18] Heidegger's philosophy attempts to reach a place where metaphysics could be fulfilled or completed in so far as philosophy could reflect upon metaphysics more adequately. This completion demanded that Heidegger focus his attentions upon the event of being. One of the most oft-cited later engagements Heidegger would offer in this regard is his 1957,

---

14 Marion, *God without Being*, p. 70.
15 Martin Heidegger, 'The End of Philosophy and the Task of Thinking', in *On Time and Being*, ed. Joan Stambaugh (New York: Harper & Row, 1972), p. 55; Martin Heidegger, *Zur Sache des Denkens*, vol. 14, *Gesamtausgabe* (Frankfurt am Main: Vittorio Klostermann, 1976), p. 69. All German citations are from Heidegger's *Gesamtausgabe* unless otherwise noted.
16 Heidegger, 'The End of Philosophy', p. 56/GS, p. 69.
17 Heidegger, 'The End of Philosophy', p. 56/GS, p. 70.
18 Heidegger, 'The End of Philosophy', p. 56/GS, p. 70.

Heidegger's Cross

'The Onto-theo-logical Constitution of Metaphysics'.[19] Here again we find Heidegger rethinking metaphysics in terms of the problem of ontological univocity and the inevitable onto-theology this univocity implies. 'How does the deity enter into philosophy, not just modern philosophy, but philosophy as such?'[20] This question goes beyond a mere inclination towards a philosophical metaphysics that enquired into the being of beings. It directs Heidegger's attention to the problem which theology would always pose for his project. Heidegger comes to recognize that even in an enquiry into being God is too easily implied as the ultimate ground of that being or as its cause.[21]

In order to elucidate how it is that God enters into philosophy, Heidegger narrates the problematic relationship between being and beings in response to Hegel. According to Heidegger, Hegelian metaphysics became convincingly intertwined with the other sciences. This challenged the difference Heidegger held between them – the difference between beings and being and the difference between his fundamental ontology and all the other sciences. As Heidegger puts it 'the matter of thinking thus is for Hegel thinking thinking itself as Being revolving within itself [*in sich kreisende Sein*]'.[22] The reason is that

> the matter of thinking is for Hegel 'the idea' (*der Gedanke*). 'The idea', developed to its highest essential freedom, becomes 'the

---

19 This was a 'lecture given on the occasion of the 500th anniversary of the University of Freiburg im Breisgau, for the faculty day on June 27, 1957'. Martin Heidegger, 'The Onto-theo-logical Constitution of Metaphysics', in *Identity and Difference*, trans. Joan Stambaugh (Chicago: The University of Chicago Press, 2002), p. 21. The German text is given at the end of this book and will be cited below.

20 Heidegger, 'The Onto-theo-logical Constitution of Metaphysics', p. 55/121.

21 It is important to keep in mind at this point that this essay was a reformatted version of the conclusion to Heidegger's lecture series on Hegel. Heidegger lectured on Hegel's *Science of Logic* in the winter semester 1956. Heidegger's engagement with Hegel was lifelong. Even as early as his 1927 lectures 'Basic Problems in Phenomenology', Heidegger saw the need to differentiate himself from Hegel. As Heidegger puts it, 'This overcoming of Hegel is the intrinsically necessary step in the development of Western philosophy which must be made for it to remain at all alive.' Martin Heidegger, *The Basic Problems of Phenomenology*, trans. Albert Hofstadter (Bloomington: Indiana University Press, 1982), p. 178. However, Heidegger's ultimate 'overcoming' of Hegel would not arrive until much later in the 'The Onto-theo-logical Constitution of Metaphysics'. It is in this essay that Hegel's ontological univocity would be addressed head on.

22 Heidegger, 'The Onto-theo-logical Constitution of Metaphysics', p. 53/120.

Protestant Metaphysics after Barth and Heidegger

absolute Idea' (*Idee*). Near the end of the *Science of Logics* (Lasson edition, Vol. II, 484), Hegel says of the absolute Idea: 'Only the absolute Idea is *Being,* imperishable *Life, self-knowing Truth,* and it is *all Truth'*. Thus Hegel himself explicitly gives to the matter of his thinking that name which is inscribed over the whole matter of Western thinking the name: *Being*.[23]

What Heidegger finds suspect is how Hegel's conception of being conflates any distinction between metaphysics and the other sciences. As Hegel says in *The Science of Logic,* 'Being is the notion implicit only: its special forms have the predicate "is;" when they are distinguished they are each of them an "other," and the shape which dialectic takes in them, i.e., their further specialization is a passing over into another'.[24] This passing over into another ultimately identifies being with nothing or forces us to acknowledge that to say something is, causes being to withdraw back into itself. 'Thus the explication of the notion in the sphere of being does two things: it brings out the totality of being, and it abolishes the immediacy of being, or the form of being as such'.[25] As one commentator puts it, 'since it is wholly indeterminate, being amounts to or "becomes," nothing. But conversely, nothing, since it too is blankly indeterminate, is or becomes being. Thus being and nothing each involves, or is the "unity" of both'.[26] Hegel's conception of being is thus dialectically related to nothing which is sublated as it becomes something or is attributed to a determinate form of being, which Hegel refers to as *Dasein*.[27] Because Hegel begins with a univocal understanding of being, however, *Dasein* never really stands out from being. Being never gives *Dasein* its existence because being has nothing to give. The difference between beings and being collapses. Hence, Hegel's conception of being conceals the very ontological difference Heidegger has been trying to develop in his own work.[28]

---

23 Heidegger, 'The Onto-theo-logical Constitution of Metaphysics', p. 43/108.
24 Georg Wilhelm Friedrich Hegel, 'Dialectic and the *Science of Logic*', in *Hegel: The Essential Writings*, ed. Frederick G. Weiss (New York: Harper & Row, 1974), p. 113.
25 Hegel, 'Dialectic and the *Science of Logic*', p. 113.
26 M. J. Inwood, *A Hegel Dictionary* (Oxford: Blackwell, 1992), p. 45.
27 Inwood, *A Hegel Dictionary*, p. 44.
28 It is important to note that Hegel's ontological univocity is in large part a response to the difference between thinking and being in Kant. Kant could not fully

Heidegger's Cross

Heidegger goes on to explain how being and beings are interrelated with each other in Hegel's thought such that 'we see that *Being* means always and everywhere: the Being of *beings* [*Seiendes des Seins*]'.[29] But this way of conceptualizing the relationship between being and beings misses the vital need metaphysics has to reflect on the difference between them – 'into the active essence of metaphysics'.[30] 'Thus we think of Being rigorously only when we think of it in its difference [*Differenz*] with beings, and of beings in their difference [*Differenz*] with Being'.[31] As such Heidegger believes his only solution to move beyond this problem is to distance himself from metaphysics itself. In other words, he begins to approach thinking in such a way that it will leave the confusion between being and beings behind and focus more specifically upon the difference between them. 'The step back thus moves out of metaphysics into the essential nature of metaphysics'.[32] As is typical, Heidegger begins his task in 'The Onto-theo-logical Constitution of Metaphysics' with a new question: 'If Being here shows itself concurrently as the Being of ..., thus in the genitive of the difference, then the preceding question is more properly: what do you make of the difference if Being as well as beings appear *by virtue of the difference,* each in its own way?'[33] To refute Hegel Heidegger has to separate being from beings without severing them completely. He needs to do this in order to maintain his project's relevance to the ground of the sciences as a topic of enquiry. The only solution is to take the step back from metaphysics, but he cannot do so until there is a clarified distance to take a step back into. That distance is the difference as difference which marks the difference between being and beings in a dynamic way.

The term Heidegger uses to begin his delineation of a difference between being and beings is perdurance [*Austrag*].

---

conceptualize the distance between the thinking subject and its object. For a helpful essay on this topic, see Paul Guyer, 'Thought and Being: Hegel's Critique of Kant's Theoretical Philosophy', in *The Cambridge Companion to Hegel*, ed. Frederick C. Beiser (Cambridge: Cambridge University Press, 1993), pp. 172–210.

29 Heidegger, 'The Onto-theo-logical Constitution of Metaphysics', p. 61/129.
30 Heidegger, 'The Onto-theo-logical Constitution of Metaphysics', p. 72/141.
31 Heidegger, 'The Onto-theo-logical Constitution of Metaphysics', p. 62/129.
32 Heidegger, 'The Onto-theo-logical Constitution of Metaphysics', p. 51/117.
33 Heidegger, 'The Onto-theo-logical Constitution of Metaphysics', pp. 63–4/131.

Being in the sense of unconcealing overwhelming [*entbergenden Überkommnis*], and beings as such in the sense of arrival that keeps itself concealed, are present, and thus differentiated, by virtue of the Same, the differentiation. That differentiation alone grants and holds apart the 'between,' in which the overwhelming and the arrival are held toward one another, are borne away from and toward each other.[34]

Heidegger's understanding of *Austrag* allows him to orient being towards beings in an encircling reciprocity that retains the crucial difference between them. As Heidegger has it, 'The difference of Being and beings, as the differentiation of overwhelming and arrival [*Unter-Schied von Überkommnis und Ankunft*], is the perdurance (*Austrag*) of the two in *unconcealing keeping in concealment* [*entbergend-bergende Austrag*]'.[35] The emphasis upon '*unconcealing keeping in concealment*' cannot be overdrawn enough. Heidegger goes on to demonstrate that if this emphasis is lost, perdurance reverts to a blinding encircling, where 'the onto-theological constitution of metaphysics has its essential origin in the perdurance that begins with the history of metaphysics, governs all of its epochs, and yet remains everywhere concealed *as* perdurance, and thus forgotten in an oblivion which even escapes itself'.[36] This perduring encircling between being and beings provides Heidegger with the mechanism by which to delineate the difficulty of his task as well as demonstrate its possibility. Beings arrive by virtue of their differentiation from being which overwhelms and as such does not conceal itself. The difference between them holds them apart and yet towards each other in a kind of gravitational encircling around each other.

For Heidegger, perdurance thus has a double-edged nature. It is capable both of pointing the way to a step back from metaphysics into its essential nature, as well as concealing that step via its own encircling behaviour. When it fails, however, concealing blinds, which is the activity Heidegger cites in conjunction with the history of metaphysics and the root of Heidegger's critique of the theological intrusion into his project as the ground of metaphysics or an

---

34 Heidegger, 'The Onto-theo-logical Constitution of Metaphysics', p. 65/132–3.
35 Heidegger, 'The Onto-theo-logical Constitution of Metaphysics', p. 65/133.
36 Heidegger, 'The Onto-theo-logical Constitution of Metaphysics', p. 68/136.

Heidegger's Cross

ultimate cause. 'Grounding itself appears within the clearing of perdurance as something that *is,* thus itself as a being that requires the corresponding accounting for through a being, that is, causation, and indeed causation by the highest cause'.[37] It is here that the deity enters in as the *causa sui,* and it is here that the confusion of theology and ontology blocks the path to being as distinct from beings.

> The deity enters into philosophy through the perdurance of which we think at first as the approach to the active nature of the difference between Being and beings. The difference constitutes the ground plan in the structure of the essence of metaphysics. The perdurance results in and gives Being as the generative ground. This ground itself needs to be properly accounted for by that for which it accounts, that is, by the causation through the supremely original matter, and that is the cause as *causa sui.* This is the right name for the god of philosophy. Man can neither pray nor sacrifice to this god. Before the *causa sui,* man can neither fall to his knees in awe nor can he play music and dance before this god.[38]

Heidegger's challenge here is not to an abandonment of a discussion of God, and in that sense theology as such. Rather, he simply wants to free theology from its entanglement with the need to account for an ontological ground for beings. Only as Heidegger is able to show the inadequacy of God as *causa sui,* is he able to employ perdurance as a redemptive pointer towards the step back.

And so we arrive at Heidegger's affirmation of god-less thinking: 'the god-less thinking which must abandon the god of philosophy, god as *causa sui,* is thus perhaps closer to the divine God. Here this means only: god-less thinking is more open to Him than onto-theologic would like to admit'.[39] Which he follows with,

> This remark may throw a little light on the path to which thinking is on its way, that thinking which accomplishes the step back,

---

37 Heidegger, 'The Onto-theo-logical Constitution of Metaphysics', pp. 69–70/138.
38 Heidegger, 'The Onto-theo-logical Constitution of Metaphysics', pp. 71–2/140–1.
39 Heidegger, 'The Onto-theo-logical Constitution of Metaphysics', p. 72/141.

back out of metaphysics into the active essence of metaphysics, back out of the oblivion of the difference as such into the destiny of the withdrawing concealment of perdurance.[40]

Perdurance fulfils the call into the difference between being and beings in a way that does not try to reduce one to the other. If theology has a place in this way of thinking it will of necessity be post-ontological. The a-theological fundamental ontology now becomes an a-theological completion of metaphysics. Or, whatever can be said of God at this point, neither being nor beings can be allowed to interrupt.

In another essay 'On Time and Being', Heidegger himself recognized that 'a regard for metaphysics still prevails even in the intention to overcome metaphysics. Therefore, our task is to cease all overcoming, and leave metaphysics to itself'.[41] Hence, Heidegger does not attempt to overcome metaphysics, but rather, he leaves it as a place holder for his attempts to understand it even more thoroughly. The name he gives to this new stage of his reflection is transcendence. Heidegger puts this most briefly in his essay on 'The Question of Being' as follows: 'Transcendence is metaphysics itself, whereby this name now does not signify a doctrine and discipline of philosophy but signifies that "it" "gives" that transcendence'.[42] Transcendence becomes metaphysics in the arrival of the being of beings. This is not to be understood as a transcendent being which gives beings their being, but rather, that in the very event of giving resides the transcendental meaning of metaphysics. Heidegger denies the doctrinal nature of this association of the word transcendence with metaphysics and it bears noting how metaphysics and transcendence are interwoven at this point in Heidegger's thought. Heidegger is not concerned, primarily, with the identity of God here. Rather, he begins from the logical consequences of his account of the being of beings and then, in representing this event, inserts transcendence as an answer to the question 'What is metaphysics?'[43]

---

40 Heidegger, 'The Onto-theo-logical Constitution of Metaphysics', p. 72/141.
41 Martin Heidegger, *On Time and Being*, trans. Joan Stambaugh (New York: Harper & Row, 1972), p. 24.
42 Heidegger, *The Question of Being*, p. 87.
43 Heidegger, *The Question of Being*, p. 93.

Heidegger's Cross
A-Theological Metaphysics

The question 'What is metaphysics?' finds its most explicit origins in a lecture Heidegger gave by that title in July of 1929. 'What is Metaphysics?' was Heidegger's inaugural address given upon taking up Husserl's chair at Freiburg. It is the hello which immediately followed his goodbye lecture to the theology faculty of Marburg, 'Phenomenology and Theology', in February of 1928, which outlined similar themes. As in 'Phenomenology and Theology', 'What is Metaphysics?' has been interpreted as an exposition of the recently published *Being and Time* to his colleagues. As we shall see, both lectures are interrelated in so far as they demonstrate Heidegger's attempt to free metaphysics from all sciences including theology.

The heart of what Heidegger is trying to do in 'What is Metaphysics?' is justify the independent task of philosophy in contradistinction to the sciences. In order to do so, he elaborates upon the inherent need the sciences have for an alternative philosophy. In his words, 'The scientific fields are quite diverse. The ways they treat their objects of inquiry differ fundamentally'.[44] Where the sciences might rely on metaphysics for an elaboration of their being, they leave open the question of the origins of being.

> What should be examined are beings [*Seiende*] only, and besides that – nothing [*nichts*] ... What about this nothing [*Nichts*]? Is it an accident that we talk this way so automatically? Is it only a manner of speaking – and nothing [*nichts*] besides?'[45]

Far from arguing for nihilism, Heidegger is arguing against nihilism by pointing out the inherent nihilism in the sciences. Nothing goes unquestioned in the sciences, and precisely in questioning this nothing Heidegger sets the context for the potential role his philosophy might play.

Because the truth of metaphysics [*Wahrheit der Metaphysik*] dwells in this groundless ground [*abgründigen Grunde*] it stands

---

44 Martin Heidegger, 'What is Metaphysics?', in *Basic Writings: From Being and Time (1927) to The Task of Thinking (1964)*, ed. David Farrell Krell (San Francisco: HarperSanFrancisco, 1993), p. 94/GS, p. 104.
45 Heidegger, 'What is Metaphysics?', p. 95.

in closest proximity to the constantly lurking possibility of deepest error. For this reason no amount of scientific rigor attains to the seriousness of metaphysics. Philosophy can never be measured by the standard of the idea of science.[46]

Heidegger announces the philosophical pathway he intends to pursue in relation to all sciences. In this account all sciences' metaphysical deficiencies are exposed and this will include theology as well. In the same manner in which Heidegger sets out his a-scientific metaphysics he also evinces an a-theological metaphysics. Here the parallel between 'What is Metaphysics' and 'Phenomenology and Theology' can be seen most clearly. Both essays are based upon their containing the same logic of distinguishing a new kind of metaphysics from theology and the sciences.

Heidegger begins 'Phenomenology and Theology' with an attack on 'the popular understanding of the relationship between theology and philosophy'.[47] For Heidegger, they cannot be understood as competing worldviews as far apart as 'faith and knowledge, reason and revelation'.[48] His difficulty with this oppositional relation between theology and philosophy is that it obfuscates philosophy's radical difference from all other sciences. As he puts it, 'there are two basic possibilities of science: sciences of whatever is [*Seiendes*], or ontic sciences [*ontische Wissenschaften*]; and *the* science of Being [*Sein*], the ontological science [*ontologische Wissenschaft*], philosophy'. In developing his understanding of philosophy, Heidegger directs his listeners to section seven of *Being and Time*.

> Phenomenology is our way of access to what is to be the theme of ontology, and it is our way of giving it demonstrative precision. *Only as phenomenology, is ontology possible*. In the phenomenological conception of 'phenomenon' what one has in mind as that which shows itself is the Being of entities, its meaning, its

---

46 Heidegger, 'What is Metaphysics?', pp. 109–10/GS, p. 22.
47 Martin Heidegger, 'Phenomenology and Theology', in *The Piety of Thinking*, ed. James G. Hart and John C. Maraldo (Bloomington: Indiana University Press, 1976), p. 5/GS, p. 47. The German pagination here refers to Martin Heidegger, *Wegmarken*, vol. 9, *Gesamtausgabe* (Frankfurt am Main: Vittorio Klostermann, 1976).
48 Martin Heidegger, 'Phenomenology and Theology', p. 5/GS, p. 47.

modifications and derivatives. And this showing-itself is not just any showing-itself, nor is it some such thing as appearing.[49]

Philosophy, which in 'Phenomenology and Theology' has become synonymous with the definition of phenomenology in *Being and Time*, is not simply an alternative science that interprets beings as they appear, but rather the being of beings.

When it comes to theology however, Heidegger defines it similarly to other sciences in that they are concerned with beings as they appear as objects. It is important to note that Heidegger does not say God is the object of theology, but rather theology studies Christian existence, or 'faithful existence'.[50] Theology, as a positive science, is

---

49 Martin Heidegger, *Being and Time*, trans. John Macquarrie and Edward Robinson (New York: Harper Collins Publishers, 1962), p. 36/SZ, p. 60. The German pagination here refers to Martin Heidegger, *Sein und Zeit*, 7th ed. (Tübingen: Neomarius Verlag, 1953).

50 Jeff Owen Prudhomme, *God and Being: Heidegger's Relation to Theology* (Atlantic Highlands, NJ: Humanities Press, 1997), pp. 78, 81 and 182, n. 5, see also Heidegger, 'Phenomenology and Theology', pp. 10–11/GS, p. 54. It is interesting to note how Heidegger attempted to clarify the problems with speaking of objectification in a later letter, which he included in the publication along with this essay in *The Piety of Thinking*. This later letter, sent 11 March 1964, gives some pointers to major aspects for a theological discussion concerning 'The Problem of a Non-Objectifying Thinking and Speaking in Today's Theology'. The discussion took place at Drew University in Madison, New Jersey, on 9–11 April 1964 (Heidegger, *The Piety of Thinking*, p. 3). In this letter Heidegger attempts to explain objectification for theology's task. As he says, 'Our everyday experience of things, in the widest sense of the word, is neither objectifying nor a placing-over-against. When, for example, we sit in the garden and take delight in a blossoming rose, we do not make an object of the rose, do not even make it something standing-over-against, i.e. something represented thematically. When in tacit saying *(Sagen)* we are enthralled with the lucid red of the rose and muse on the redness of the rose, then this redness is neither an object, nor a thing, nor a standing-over-against like the blossoming rose. The rose stands in the garden, sways perhaps to and fro in the wind. But the redness of the rose neither stands in the garden, nor can it sway to and fro in the wind. All the same we think it and say of it by naming it. There is accordingly a thinking and saying that in no manner objectifies or places-over-against.' Martin Heidegger, 'The Theological Discussion of "The Problem of A Non-Objectifying Speaking and Thinking in Today's Theology" – Some Pointers to Its Major Aspects', pp. 26–7. He is here referring to a Kantian conception of objectification which places over against. He goes on to discuss the interrelationship of speaking and thinking before developing the ways in which technical science objectifies. 'In what sense do thinking and speaking objectify, and in what sense do they not? Thinking and speaking objectify, i.e., posit as an object something given, in the field of natural-scientific and technical representation. Here they are of necessity objectifying, because scientific-

therefore 'absolutely, not relatively, different from philosophy. Our thesis, then, is that theology is a positive science and as such, therefore, is absolutely different from philosophy'.[51] This is a crucial decision Heidegger is making and one which will have profound consequences for his way of thinking. The philosophy Heidegger is developing depends upon a total division between beings and being, or between the ontic and ontological. Theology thus poses a problem in so far as it might claim to study with Heidegger this ultimate being. In so far as Heidegger closes off this option, he closes off the possibility of drawing upon theological resources as he works through his investigations into the nature of being.

As Heidegger frames his argument, philosophy does not need theology or any other positive science to accomplish its task. Rather theology simply offers an initial orientation which points beyond the ontic to the ontological. Even this pointing, however, is uncovered by a philosophy which explains and clarifies theology's task. 'If faith does not need philosophy, the *science* of faith as a *positive* science does'.[52] Although philosophy does not found theology, theology needs philosophy to help it reflect upon its own scientific character – that is the revelation of the ontic's hidden ontology. 'And so, why philosophy? Whatever is discloses [*enthüllt*] itself only on the grounds of a preliminary [*vorgängigen*] (although not explicitly known), pre-conceptual understanding of what and how it is. Every ontic [*ontische*] interpretation operates within the basic context of an ontology [*Ontologie*], firstly and for the most part hidden [*verborgenen*]'.[53] However, because Heidegger maintains

---

technological knowing must establish its theme in advance as a calculable, causally explicable *Gegenstand*, i.e., as an object as Kant defined the word. Outside this field thinking and speaking are by no means objectifying.' Heidegger, 'The Theological Discussion', p. 28. Hence he can say of theology, 'That task is for theology to place in discussion, within its own realm of the Christian faith and out of the proper nature of that faith, what it is to think and how it is to speak. This task also includes the question whether theology can still be a science – because presumably it should not be a science at all.' Heidegger, 'The Theological Discussion', p. 30. Here Heidegger seems to be referring to the technical definition of science. This differs somewhat from the argument that theology is a science in 'Phenomenology and Theology'. But crucially I do not see it as negating his previous statements on theology as a science necessarily. The two issues speak in conjunction with each other.

51 Heidegger, 'Phenomenology and Theology', p. 6/GS, pp. 48–9.
52 Heidegger, 'Phenomenology and Theology', p. 17/GS, p. 61.
53 Heidegger, 'Phenomenology and Theology', p. 17/GS, p. 62.

Heidegger's Cross

that faith is not only theology's object but its originating source as well, he is quite careful to explain how theology relies on philosophy without being dependent upon it for its origin.[54]

Theology's relation to philosophy is explained by drawing upon the term sublation [*Aufhebung*].[55] Heidegger is very careful here to note theology's independence from philosophy and argues that 'the positive science of faith needs philosophy only in regard to its scientific character, and even then only in a uniquely restricted, though basic, way'.[56] But the nature of sublation tends to give philosophy a much more fundamental relation to theology. A rather lengthy citation will be helpful here in order to explain the meaning of sublation as it is used to articulate Heidegger's conception of how philosophy relates to theology without replacing theology's true object – that is faith.

> We characterized faith as the essential constitutive element of Christianness: faith is rebirth. Though faith does not bring itself about, and though what is revealed [*Offenbare*] through faith can never be founded by way of a rational knowing as exercised by the autonomously functioning reason, nevertheless the sense of the Christian occurrence of rebirth is that one's pre-faith-full [*vorgläubige*], i.e., unbelieving, human existence [*ungläubige Existenz des Daseins*] is sublated *(aufgehoben)* therein ... Hence we can say that precisely because all basic theological concepts, considered in their full regional context, include meanings which are existentially (factually) [*existentiell ohnmächtigen*] powerless, i.e., *ontically* [*ontisch*] sublated *(aufgehoben)*, they have as their *ontological* [*ontologisch*] determinants [*bestimmenden*] meanings which are pre-Christian [*vorchristlichen*] and which can thus be grasped purely rationally.[57]

Heidegger is establishing a subtle and nuanced reconfiguration of a separated relationship between theology and philosophy which allows both to function autonomously, and as such to quell any

---

54 Heidegger, 'Phenomenology and Theology', p. 12/GS, p. 55.
55 This term is used without mention of Hegel who also uses it in a similar way.
56 Heidegger, 'Phenomenology and Theology', p. 17/GS, p. 61.
57 Heidegger, 'Phenomenology and Theology', p. 18/GS, p. 63.

sense in which the two might be understood as competing worldviews. Theology has faith and Christianness as its core ontic orientation, but if it is to reflect critically upon its pre-Christian basis, it will need philosophy to help it uncover its ontological determinants. What exactly is meant by its pre-Christian basis is largely understood here in terms of the analytic of *Dasein*. As Jean-Luc Marion comments upon this aspect in Heidegger's 'Phenomenology and Theology', '"Christianness" becomes the ontic variable of an ontological invariant, *Dasein*. Theology formulates that variable and measures its deviations, just as philosophy proceeds to the analysis of the invariant and identifies it in its possible avatars.'[58] As we already noted, Marion argues that this way of relating theology to metaphysics never fully allows God to escape the onto-theological prison. However, Heidegger himself does not recognize this problem at this point in his thinking, and we must question whether it ever was or should be an escape that is projected by Heidegger. In other words, we must ask about the degree to which Marion's critique actually correlates with Heidegger's own project. Again, for Heidegger, theology is based on faith and the pre-Christian is sublated or taken up into the theological science in a way which requires critical reflection, but does not take away from the divine event as such. However, to keep theology from contradicting philosophy, Heidegger assigns them radically different tasks. Philosophy can clarify the ontological nature of theology as a positive science, but philosophy has no reciprocal need for any clarification from theology. Theology might have interests beyond the ontic existential faith of the believer, but they would not and could not enquire into the being of beings. Rather, this is the task of philosophy in the sense in which Heidegger develops the term. Theology is, thus, utterly divorced from philosophy at this specific point.

The manner in which Heidegger proffers an a-theological metaphysics in his earlier essays of 1928–9 has a number of implications for how we interpret his development after this time. Whereas in 'Phenomenology and Theology' Heidegger sought to delimit theology to an ontic science, in his later essays, Heidegger suggests a theology which might move beyond being altogether. However, because his metaphysical reflections were being justified as a funda-

---

58 Marion, *The Idol and Distance*, p. 208.

Heidegger's Cross

mental enquiry into the sciences, he is not able to draw upon theology as an ontic science in his later work. Whatever theology might be, an investigation into the ontic faithful existence will not suffice. The ambiguity of his later understanding of theology in relation to this earlier one is felt most acutely in Heidegger's essay 'The Way Back into the Ground of Metaphysics' which was written in 1949 as an interpretative addendum to 'What is Metaphysics?' Here, we find him using the image of a tree with roots to describe his earlier essay. What did he mean by his discussion of metaphysics as 'the inquiry beyond or over beings, which aims to recover them as such and as a whole for our grasp'?[59] Importantly, in the metaphorical language of the latter essay metaphysics does not enquire after the roots of the tree (beings as beings), but the ground they grow within (being), which remains concealed in any investigation of the roots themselves.[60] Hence he writes:

> Metaphysics is founded upon that which conceals itself [*dieses Verborgene im ὄν*] here as long as metaphysics studies the ὄν ᾗ ὄν. The attempt to inquire back into what conceals itself [*dieses Verborgene*] here seeks, from the point of view of metaphysics, the fundament of ontology [*Ontologie*]. Therefore this attempt is called, in *Being and Time* (page 13) 'fundamental ontology' [*Fundamentalontologie*]. Yet this title, like any title, is soon seen to be inappropriate ... For what the title 'fundamental ontology' suggests is, of course, that the attempt to recall the truth of Being [*Wahrheit des Seins*] – and not, like all ontology, the truth of beings [*Wahrheit des Seienden*] – is itself (seeing that it is called 'fundamental ontology') still a kind of ontology [*Ontologie*]. In fact, the attempt to recall the truth of Being sets out on the way back into the ground of metaphysics, and with its first step it

---

59 Heidegger, 'What is Metaphysics?', p. 106.
60 The tree and roots analogy is drawn from Descartes, writing to 'Picot, who translated the *Principia Philosophiae* into French, observed: "Thus the whole of philosophy is like a tree: the roots are metaphysics, the trunk is physics, and the branches that issue from the trunk are all the other sciences ..." Sticking to this image, we ask: In what soil do the roots of the tree of philosophy have their hold? Out of what ground do the roots – and through them the whole tree – receive their nourishing juices and strength?' Martin Heidegger, 'The Way Back into the Ground of Metaphysics', in *Existentialism: From Dostoevsky to Sartre*, ed. Walter Kaufmann (New York: Penguin Books, 1989), p. 265/GS, p. 365.

immediately leaves the realm of all ontology [*Indessen hat das Denken an die Wahrheit des Seins als der Rückgang in den Grund der Metaphysik den Bereich aller Ontologie schon mit dem ersten Schritt verlassen*]. On the other hand, every philosophy which revolves around an indirect or direct conception of 'transcendence' [*Transzendenz*] remains of necessity essentially an ontology, whether it achieves a new foundation of ontology or whether it assures us it repudiates ontology as a conceptual freezing [*begriffliche Erstarrung*] of experience.[61]

What we must come to understand is how this addition to 'What is Metaphysics?' clarifies the trajectory of Heidegger's earlier essays in 1928–9. Here he established philosophy as a reflective discipline which enquired into the being of beings, but as Heidegger continued to work through this task in essays like 'The Onto-theo-logical Constitution of Metaphysics' and 'The Question of Being', he began to see the need to look into the event of the encircling relation between being and beings.

Returning to his essay on 'The Question of Being'[62] Heidegger risks 'becoming tedious' for the sake of clarifying again and again just what is gained by his early harbinger enquiry into being in *Being and Time* where 'the indefinability of Being does not eliminate the question of its meaning; it demands that we look that question in the face'.[63] Again, to reiterate, Heidegger is not questioning the beings which the sciences study, but rather the assumption that only nothingness remains beyond beings. This question cannot be answered by objectifying nothing anymore than being. As Heidegger puts it, 'Within the horizon of scientific conception, which only knows being, that which is not being (namely Being) in any way at all can, on the other hand, present itself only as nothingness.'[64] The assumption of nothingness by the sciences, however, conceals the deeper question, 'why is there being at all and not rather Nothingness?'[65]

---

61 Heidegger, 'The Way Back into the Ground of Metaphysics', pp. 276–7/GS, pp. 380–1.
62 Heidegger, *The Question of Being*, p. 93.
63 Heidegger, *Being and Time*, p. 23.
64 Heidegger, *The Question of Being*, p. 97.
65 Heidegger, *The Question of Being*, p. 99, with reference to Heidegger, 'What is Metaphysics?', p. 110.

Heidegger's Cross

Heidegger is quick to point out that he was not arguing for nihilism in his early 1929 essay on the question 'What is Metaphysics?',[66] but rather he questioned the sciences' failure to enquire into the event which gives beings their existence in any sense. As such, in this later essay on 'The Question of Being' Heidegger enacts the strategy of the cross by crossing out both nothingness and being in so far as they represent the same question for the sciences and the same need to challenge any objectification of being. However, in 'The Question of Being' Heidegger goes farther than his earlier essays to point beyond being to the transcendent event of its arrival. It is only when we understand the manner in which this ontological approach to the question of transcendence is understood that Heidegger's own crossing out of being makes any sense. Heidegger does not presume an end to being, but rather the need to enquire into its event-ful-ness all the more fully. As such, he pre-empts the critiques of Marion and Derrida in so far as he did recognize that the fulfilment of metaphysics as he understood it would always be directed toward ontology in what can best be described as an incarnational sense. In many ways, the question, 'What is metaphysics?' is the primary locus of Heidegger's suggestion for a future theological thought pathway. It is in asking this question that the completion of metaphysics can arise, and it is for this reason that he would continue to ask it in his later work. A focus upon transcendence can itself simply play at ontological sleight of hand, thus, being must remain crossed out, a procedure which alerts us to the problem of how being arrives as such.

Here again in these later essays Heidegger recognizes the theological implications of his project, now maintaining his insistence on the need for Christian theology to extricate itself from a crude fixation upon metaphysics as such. He even goes so far as to cite 1 Corinthians 1.20 with this quip, 'Will Christian theology make up its mind one day to take seriously the word of the apostle and thus also the conception of philosophy as foolishness?'[67] The implication being that an onto-theological notion of transcendence is an

---

66 'In which sentence and in which turn of a phrase is it ever said that the nothingness named in the lecture is nothingness in the sense of negated nothingness and as such is the first and last goal of all conception and existence?' Heidegger, *The Question of Being*, p. 99.

67 Heidegger, 'The Way Back into the Ground of Metaphysics', p. 276/GS, p. 379.

idolatrous deity which one can neither pray to nor kneel to worship. And yet, it is precisely in philosophy's directedness towards transcendence that Heidegger believes metaphysics will find its fulfilment. If this is to be a theology, it will be a theology in a new key, unlike what he referred to in 'Phenomenology and Theology' where theology was limited to the science of faithful existence. This understanding of theology does, therefore, differ from Marion's suggestion that Heidegger does not contradict his earlier definitions of theology. If the Christian theology is to accept philosophy as foolishness, and the grounding notion of transcendence which goes with it, then it will accept its task as one which focuses upon the event. It is our contention that Heidegger's thought therefore moves well beyond negative theology, or a strategy of negation as such, and on to something more positive and incarnational.

Contemporary commentators such as Derrida and Marion rightly question what Heidegger means by this enquiry into the event, and the desire to complete metaphysics, just as they are right to question the nature of any theology which might follow after it. However, this is not to say that their understanding of the Heideggerian event of being is consistent with the manner in which Heidegger considers theology more generally. Heidegger's response to the question 'May being and God be posited as identical?' in 1951 suggests that theology might be the proper name for his investigations into the transcendental event. However, he does so under a series of unspoken justifications for leaving theology behind in the first place. 'Some of you perhaps know that I came out of theology' is a statement that demands further enquiry into the precise kinds of theology Heidegger was engaged in, and the reasons why he left this theology behind. Said another way, we are left with a question concerning the manner of Heidegger's crossing.

The Possibility of the Cross

Without going into further detail concerning the alternative to negative theology which Derrida and Marion might offer, I would suggest that we enquire into the justifications upon which they demand Heidegger meet their criteria. In other words, what if it is not a negative theology which Heidegger implies when he crosses being out and calls for a theology without being? What if in fact

Heidegger's Cross

the cross over Heidegger's being invokes a reference to the manner of crossing more generally? What if in fact Heidegger's cross is intentionally obscuring but not erasing being because the problem is not the negation of being as such but rather its incarnation as beings? Derrida would then be right to question Heidegger's cross, but not because of its failure to fully erase. Rather, the question would concern the cross's efficacy to give meaning to the event of being more fully. In other words, what is at stake here is the nature of the *beginning* which Heidegger's speaking of an end of metaphysics always implied. Derrida is right to critique the adequacy of negative theology for always retaining an essentialism of some sort, but the question we are raising is whether he is right to apply this critique to Heidegger. Was Heidegger after a negative theology? Or, like Derrida, was Heidegger also interested in a third possibility?[68] Based on what we have said thus far we can state a key aim of the chapters that follow. Namely, that Heidegger never sought to abolish being from his thinking, but rather, under the procedure of a cross, he sought to refigure the question 'what is metaphysics?' The problem with Heidegger's suggestion is not that it fails to cross being out, but rather that it fails to understand the full theological implications of that cross.

Here, Gianni Vattimo's approach to the post-Heideggerian possibilities for religious thought may offer a further clue as to what we are suggesting is called for after Heidegger. In a collection of essays on religion he writes:

> In religion, something that we had thought irrevocably forgotten is made present again, a dormant trace is reawakened, a wound re-opened, the repressed returns and what we took to be an *Überwindung* (overcoming, realization and thus a setting aside) is no more than a *Verwindung*, a long convalescence that has once again to come to terms with the indelible trace of its sickness.[69]

---

68 Jean-Luc Marion helpfully summarizes Derrida's position concerning a positive, negative and third way of theology in his essay Jean-Luc Marion, 'In the Name', in *God, the Gift, and Postmodernism*, ed. John D. Caputo and Michael J. Scanlon (Bloomington: Indiana University Press, 1999), p. 22.
69 Gianni Vattimo, 'The Trace of the Trace', in *Religion*, ed. Jacques Derrida and Gianni Vattimo (Cambridge: Polity Press, 1998), p. 79.

Protestant Metaphysics after Barth and Heidegger

Vattimo considers religion as a kind of wound which indelibly marks Western culture. It was thought to be gone, stitched up, as secularists such as Marx and Durkheim predicted.[70] The wound which had been thought to have closed over, however, turns out to be infected. Festering within was a problem, a question which had not been overcome, but rather, now returns to haunt the philosopher once again. The nature of that question Vattimo articulates in the terms of an 'indelible trace'. In this inscription we are given a clue as to what kind of religion is being assumed here. The trace is uncovered in the re-presentation of religion, which, in turn is uncovered as that active essence of religion. Religion is experienced in this giving of itself ever again, in the manner in which it arises irrevocably and irreducibly for us. In other words, 'there is a legitimate suspicion that the return may be an (or the) essential aspect of religious experience itself'.[71] The return of religion, which can be felt in the newspapers and high streets,[72] will therefore give way in Vattimo's account of a deeper analysis of the manner in which religion after Heidegger took shape in philosophy of religion more generally. The trace is what can be seen now in the clearing which Vattimo considers after metaphysics, after a theo-logic which gives God the place of *causa sui*, the fundamental ground of fundamentalism as such. In Vattimo's words

> The breakdown of the philosophical prohibition of religion ... [which] coincides with the dissolution of the great systems that

---

70 For Marx, religious opiates, like heroin addictions, would be marginalized once society had alleviated the social problems that lead people to enact such habits of escape; Karl Marx, 'Introduction to A Contribution to the Critique of Hegel's Philosophy of Right', http://www.marxists.org/archive/marx/works/1843/critique-hpr/intro.htm. For Durkheim, although religion's abstract conceptualizations provided the basis for valuable social cohesion, religion would eventually be left behind in favour of civil sensibilities informed by a scientific worldview; Emile Durkheim, *The Elementary Forms of Religious Life* (New York: Alan and Unwin, 1976), pp. 444ff.

71 Vattimo, 'The Trace of the Trace', p. 80.

72 Vattimo refers to this form of return in terms of 'the robust presence in our popular culture of the return of the religious (as a need, in the new vitality of churches and sects, and in the search for different doctrines and practices, the "fashion" for Eastern religions and so forth) is motivated above all by the sense of impending global threats ... and the losing of the meaning of existence, of that true and profound boredom which seems inevitably to accompany consumerism.' Vattimo, 'The Trace of the Trace', p. 80.

Heidegger's Cross

accompanied the development of science, technology and modern social organization, but thereby also with the breakdown of all fundamentalism – that is, of what, so it seems, popular consciousness is looking for in its return to religion.[73]

It is this postmodern character of philosophy of religion which Vattimo focuses upon as he raises the possibility of reflection upon the trace of religion after Heidegger.

Vattimo is quick to point out the religious background to Heidegger's ruminations in *Being and Time,* as he worked out his own pathway through 'problems of historicity, temporality and, in the final analysis, of freedom and predestination.'[74] And here the popular and philosophical return to religion collides in so far as popular culture is caught up within the technoscientific metaphysics which Heidegger reflected upon in his work.[75] Vattimo thus suggests a coinherence between Heidegger's thought and popular culture as follows:

> The common root of the religious need that runs through our society and of the return of (the plausibility of) religion in philosophy today lies in the reference to modernity as an epoch of technoscience, or in Heidegger's words, as the epoch of the world-picture.[76]

For Vattimo, Heidegger sought to clarify the being which comes to fulfilment in technology, and as such, the metaphysical reality which popular culture comes to inhabit. The re-enchantment of the world described by Zygmunt Bauman,[77] would, in the end,

---

73 Vattimo, 'The Trace of the Trace', p. 81.
74 Vattimo, 'The Trace of the Trace', p. 81.
75 Martin Heidegger, 'The Question Concerning Technology'. See also Hubert L. Dreyfus, 'Heidegger on the Connection between Nihilism, Art, Technology, and Politics', in *The Cambridge Companion to Heidegger,* ed. Charles B. Guignon (Cambridge: Cambridge University Press, 1993), pp. 289–316.
76 Vattimo, 'The Trace of the Trace', p. 82.
77 'All in all, postmodernity can be seen as restoring to the world what modernity, presumptuously, had taken away; as a re-enchantment of the world that modernity tried hard to dis-enchant.' Zygmunt Bauman, 'The Re-Enchantment of the World, or How Can One Narrate Postmodernity? (1992)', in *The Bauman Reader,* ed. Peter Beilharz (Oxford: Blackwell Publishers, 2001), p. 191.

exonerate Heideggerian philosophy of religion in so far as it represented religion as magic and mysticism in this new simulacrum of consumer culture. The Disneyization of metropolitan Gothams like New York, predicted by Marshal McLuhan,[78] is just one instantiation of a much deeper trace of the religious as such. Religion thus returns more clearly now today precisely because of the manner in which philosophers like Heidegger recognized the metaphysical artifice of modernity for what it was.

However, the returning is not a return to metaphysical foundationalism. Rather, 'to react to the problematic and chaotic character of the late-modern world with a return to God as the metaphysical foundation means, in Nietzschean terms, to refuse the challenge of the over(hu)man(ity)'.[79] Vattimo's return of religion takes up this challenge, but in a decidedly Heideggerian way that does not denounce metaphysics so much as look beyond it, beneath it, and in so doing begins to find a non-reactive way to engage the trace which is, in the end, being itself. This will mean an acceptance that technology itself is a manifestation of being. 'As Heidegger constantly warns, to look at technology knowing that the essence of technology is not itself technological, and in this way to see it as the most extreme point of arrival of metaphysics and of the oblivion of being in the thinking of the foundation, means precisely to prepare to overcome metaphysics by listening non-reactively to the technological destiny of Being itself.'[80] The trace of the trace recognizes religion in so far as it is for us a return. In this sense the heart of religion is this returning to the trace as it gives itself to us once again. As such, 'It is (only) because metaphysical metanarratives have been dissolved that philosophy has rediscovered the plausibility of religion and can consequently approach the religious need of common consciousness independently of the framework of Enlightenment critique.'[81]

---

78 Some 40 years ago now, sitting in the patio of a New York restaurant, he circled his finger around the skyscrapers above his head and proclaimed: 'of course, a city like New York is obsolete. People will no longer concentrate in great urban centers for the purpose of work. New York will become a Disneyland, a pleasure dome ... You're Gonna Love Gothamland'. Tom Wolfe, 'Pleasure Principles', *New York Times*, 12 June 2005.
79 Vattimo, 'The Trace of the Trace', pp. 82–3.
80 Vattimo, 'The Trace of the Trace', p. 83.
81 Vattimo, 'The Trace of the Trace', p. 84.

Heidegger's Cross

Vattimo locates the return of religion in a post-Heideggerian space which radically critiques the metaphysical foundationalism within which religion was enshrouded in the past Enlightenment era. This trace marks the return itself as the heart of religion. It might follow then, that Vattimo would demand a complete abandonment of metaphysics for this future philosophy of religion which seeks to apprehend the returning, the trace of the trace. Surprisingly,

> however, the fact that the motif of return, and thus of historicity, is essential to religious experience, and not merely accidental, does not mean only or even primarily that the religion to which we wish to return must be characterized by its belonging to the epoch of the end of metaphysics.[82]

And in this one surprise, Vattimo distinguishes himself from Marion and Derrida's own account of the post-Heideggerian possibilities of philosophy of religion. As we have already noted, for Derrida, Heidegger was, in the end, not radical enough. His negative theology left a trace of metaphysical foundationalism which forced him into a dead end, a silence waiting for a mistaken god-event to arrive and for the event of being to happen again. Vattimo however, argues that this form of overcoming metaphysics, this third way 'can only take place as nihilism. The meaning of nihilism, however ... can only think of itself as an indefinite process of reduction, diminution, weakening.'[83] Vattimo recognizes the implications of this form of overcoming, and for his part questions the manner in which this third way would take place. Rather than seeking a null point, a *Khora*, as Derrida does, he refocuses his readers' attention upon the being which still resides under Heidegger's cross. What is the question Heidegger asks? Is it a negative theology at stake? Or is it rather the recollection of being through a reflection upon transcendence as metaphysics? As Vattimo goes on to ask

> Could such a thinking be thought outside the horizon of the Incarnation? If hermeneutics really wishes to continue along the path opened by Heidegger's call to recollect Being (and thus

---

82 Vattimo, 'The Trace of the Trace', p. 84.
83 Vattimo, 'The Trace of the Trace', p. 93.

Ereignis), this is perhaps the decisive question to which it must seek a response today.[84]

What we referred to above as the integral relationship between metaphysics and transcendence is here taken seriously by Vattimo as a question of the incarnation.

Many have considered what comes after Heidegger and more or less accepted Derrida's projections as the standard through which Heidegger must be read. Much can be gained and has been gained through such post-metaphysical readings of religion and philosophical theology as such. However, Vattimo helps us wonder whether the focus of Heidegger's reflections were not reflections at all in a literal sense. Rather, he sought to look through being as if through a translucent window. The goal was therefore to move beyond reflection such that the event itself might be seen and understood. Being was crossed out such that our gaze might become shielded from the blinding light of the event only so that we might look all the more directly through it. 'Therefore, our task is to cease all overcoming, and leave metaphysics to itself'.[85] This is the Heideggerian statement which must be understood in relation to the theological future he projects. What is meant by theology here? 'Phenomenology and Theology', a lecture he dedicated to Rudolf Bultmann,[86] goes some way in giving an answer to this question. However, much is left still unanswered in terms of how this developed later and the theological difference between the late 1920s and the 1950s. Why exactly is theology limited to faith and Christian existence? What kind of theology does Heidegger assume? Is this really Lutheran, as he suggests in his answer to the seminar question? Or Pauline, as he suggests in his addendum to 'What is Metaphysics?' These are questions which must be explored more fully if we are to understand and evaluate the theological nature of Heidegger's work. Hence, a first step in this regard is to investigate the theological roots at the beginning of his thinking. As Hans Jonas rightly comments, Heidegger's thought contains a series of theological proclivities and biases which the

---

84 Vattimo, 'The Trace of the Trace', p. 93.
85 Heidegger, *On Time and Being*, p. 24.
86 Heidegger dedicated the German edition of the publication of this essay to Rudolf Bultmann 'in friendly remembrance of the Marburg years 1923–28'. Heidegger, 'Phenomenology and Theology', p. 169, n. 1.

Heidegger's Cross

theologian would be remiss to overlook. As he puts it, 'the theologian must ask, before he reimports his original product: what have you done with my little ones? ... Can I take them back from you? and what, *if* I take them, will I take *with* them?'[87] In response to such questions we might do well, as Vattimo suggests, to investigate the manner in which Heidegger failed to think through the Incarnation.[88]

---

[87] Hans Jonas, *The Phenomenon of Life: Toward a Philosophical Biology* (Chicago: University of Chicago Press, 1982), p. 243.

[88] Gianni Vattimo, 'The Trace of the Trace', p. 93, cf. Gianni Vattimo, *Belief* (Cambridge: Polity Press, 1999), pp. 38ff. We must make it clear at this point that to accept the need to reconsider this ontological cross does not preclude the *Weakness of God* as John Caputo suggests in light of Vattimo's own 'weak ontology'. Gianni Vattimo, *The End of Modernity: Nihilism and Hermeneutics in Post-modern Culture* (Cambridge: Polity Press, 1988), pp. 85ff, or more explicitly in relation to Vattimo's own 'rediscovery of Christianity' as a 'transcription' of Heidegger's 'weak ontology', see Vattimo, *Belief*, pp. 35ff, and for Caputo's own interpretation of Vattimo's terminology, see John D. Caputo, *The Weakness of God: A Theology of the Event* (Bloomington: Indiana University Press, 2006), p. 7. Contrary to our own thesis here, Caputo tends to run Derrida and Vattimo together, flattening the differences between them. It is not our intention to dismiss the highly thought-provoking interpretations of Heidegger given by either Vattimo or Caputo. Nonetheless, our intention here is different and the favour we have here bestowed upon Vattimo's interpretation of Heidegger is meant to foreshadow the final conclusions we will draw in our own explication of Heidegger's Lutheranism in what follows.

2

Protestant Theology after Heidegger

Heidegger's Theological Influence

Theologians have typically inscribed Heidegger as a secular philosopher whose work opens up new theological directions. This tendency is noted by Laurence Hemming as follows:

> There has been a long-standing intuition that Heidegger's researches must have a profound impact on the question of God as far as it is taken up in theology as a formal discipline. In fact theological appropriations of Heidegger's work have never opened up Heidegger's thought as a question, preferring to reserve for him a place strictly as philosopher. In this sense, rather than raising Heidegger's work as a problem for theologians and for theology in general, it was assumed that an encounter with Heidegger would provide an impetus for fresh theological work.[1]

The difficulty with this way of appropriating Heidegger is that his philosophy consistently intersects and draws upon theology itself. Heidegger's own vocational outlook presents us with a picture of a philosopher with profound theological interests. For instance, in a letter to Karl Löwith, Heidegger states that he is a 'Christian theologian'. This statement is couched in a careful explication of Heidegger's own '*facticity*'. In Heidegger's words, 'in it [facticity] is to be found the historical consciousness, the consciousness of "intellectual and cultural history." And I am all this in the life con-

---

[1] Laurence Paul Hemming, *Heidegger's Atheism: The Refusal of a Theological Voice* (Notre Dame, IN: University of Notre Dame Press, 2002), p. 28.

Protestant Theology after Heidegger

text of the university.'² Heidegger's own testimony from the letter he wrote to Engelbert Krebs probably explains his early sense of vocation best:

> I believe that I have the inner calling to philosophy and, through my research and teaching, to do what stands in my power for the sake of the eternal vocation of the inner man, and *to do it for this alone,* and so justify my existence (*Dasein*) and work ultimately before God.³

But these statements concerning Heidegger's philosophical disposition towards theology must not deceive us into configuring his relationship to theology too one-directionally. The theological aspects of Heidegger's thought are too interwoven into his philosophy to be delineated discretely. Rather, our focus here will be upon the reciprocal intertwining between Heidegger's thought and a uniquely Protestant form of theology.

Our enquiry therefore stands out from those interpretations of Heidegger that tend to gloss over his theological interests as if theology were a unified discipline which Heidegger draws upon to differing effects. Hemming's work exemplifies these tendencies in so far as he reads Heidegger's theology in terms of its relevance for Roman Catholic thought without recognizing the nuanced way Heidegger's construction of Protestant theology shapes his work. A similar problematic emerges in John Macquarrie's interpretation of Heidegger. In his words, 'Heidegger claimed he never left the Catholic church'.⁴ He goes on to talk about Heidegger's influence upon twentieth-century theology citing the Roman Catholic theologian Karl Rahner alongside Tillich and Bultmann as contemporary examples. This is also the case in Theodore Kisiel's work, which explicitly negates the interpretative liberties Heidegger takes when engaging theologians like Luther. Kisiel tends to portray Heidegger

---

2 Theodore J. Kisiel, *The Genesis of Heidegger's Being and Time* (Berkeley: University of California Press, 1993), p. 78.

3 Martin Heidegger, *Supplements: From the Earliest Essays to Being and Time and Beyond,* ed. John Van Buren (Albany, NY: State University of New York Press, 2002), p. 70.

4 John Macquarrie, *Heidegger and Christianity: The Hensley Henson Lectures, 1993–94* (New York: Continuum, 1994), p. 6.

as if he was a paradigmatic example of ecumenicism. 'The "theological heritage" which put the young Heidegger onto the path of thought is thus as much Lutheran as it is Catholic, or simply Christian in the most "primitive" sense of that heritage. "I am a 'Christian theologian'"'.[5] According to Kisiel, in the letter where Heidegger says that he is a Christian theologian, he is explaining to his pupil Karl Löwith how he misunderstood the essence of his thought. Löwith as well as his classmate Oskar Becker both miss the essence of his thought by focusing too much either on the subjective or objective aspect without addressing their interrelationship.[6] Heidegger notes how his own facticity defines what he means by 'Christian theologian', which justifies the sense in which Kisiel reads Heidegger as one for whom both Roman Catholic and Protestant theologies informed him. I do not contest that they both do inform his work, and that his own facticity makes up his particular relation to Christian theology. What we must challenge, however, is the nuanced way that different traditions informed him. It is precisely as we note these differences that the theological implications of his work can be understood more adequately, not to mention compared to other Protestant thinkers like Karl Barth.

Although Heidegger's sporadic ambivalence about his relationship to Roman Catholicism can be found in his thought and is rightly highlighted by Kisiel and Macquarrie, his distance from Roman Catholicism is far more significant than is often allowed. As Hugo Ott comments on this feature of Heidegger's life,

> the issue of his Catholic origins, of the faith of his birth, remained open and entirely unresolved. When the occasion arose the issue would always flare up again. And they still stand, the sombre words that Heidegger wrote in 1935, when he described 'the faith of my birth' as 'a thorn in the flesh'.[7]

The secondary literature is problematic in its engagement with this tension in Heidegger's own life. By exploring the Protestant

---

5 Kisiel, *The Genesis of Heidegger's Being and Time*, p. 115, citing a letter to Karl Löwith on 19 August 1921.
6 Kisiel, *The Genesis of Heidegger's Being and Time*, pp. 77–8.
7 Hugo Ott, *Martin Heidegger: A Political Life*, trans. Allan Blunden (London: HarperCollins Publishers, 1993), p. 121.

nature of his thought we are able to gain important insight into his deconstructive attitude towards metaphysics – an attitude he adopts from some of Protestantism's key progenitors. As such, we must ask about the particularity of Protestantism's influence upon Heidegger, and furthermore we must ask how Heidegger interprets that theological tradition as well.

Early Heidegger – Early Luther

During the course of his first lectureship in Freiburg Heidegger began to take a more critical posture towards his Roman Catholic roots. This did not entail an abandonment of theology altogether. Rather, he began to take a more active interest in Protestant theology. John Caputo refers to this as the first turn in Heidegger's thought.

> For with the turn from Catholicism to Protestantism, the philosophical interests of the young thinker shifted from the questions of logic to those of history, from pure (Husserlian) phenomenology to what he called the 'hermeneutics of facticity' (i.e., concrete life), and from dogmatic theology to the theology of the New Testament. He took his lead not from scholastic theologians like Aquinas, Scotus, and Suarez but from Pascal, Luther, and Kierkegaard, who in turn led him back to Augustine and Paul.[8]

Theodore Kisiel cites a similar sentiment from Heidegger's note to which he affixed his signature in his 1919 *Die Religion in Geschichte und Gegenwart*: 'Faith in the two denominations is fundamentally different, noetically and noematically radically distinct experiences.'[9] What these commentators all demonstrate in their own ways is the central role Protestant theology played in Heidegger's development. Their sentiments are confirmed in Heidegger's oft-cited letter to Engelbert Krebs, the priest who had recently married Heidegger to his wife Elfride. In Heidegger's words, 'Epistemological insights

---

[8] John D. Caputo, 'Heidegger and Theology', in *The Cambridge Companion to Heidegger*, ed. Charles B. Guignon (Cambridge: Cambridge University Press, 1993), pp. 272–3.

[9] Kisiel, *The Genesis of Heidegger's Being and Time*, p. 88, citing p. 1439.

Protestant Metaphysics after Barth and Heidegger

extending to a theory of historical knowledge have made the *system* of Catholicism problematic [*System des Katholizismus problematisch*] and unacceptable to me, but not Christianity and metaphysics – these, though, in a new sense'.[10]

Although it is true that 'Heidegger regarded himself as a member of the Catholic church all his life',[11] he was clear that he also struggled to support a Catholic theological outlook. Nowhere is this more clear than in his appointment as associate Professor in Marburg.

> Husserl wrote to Natorp [at Marburg] about his [Heidegger's] command of a range of material from Aristotle through the neo-Platonists to Augustine, and ... that his knowledge of Catholicity would be important at Marburg for linking up philosophy with Protestant theology, which Heidegger also knows well.[12]

What becomes clear upon his arrival in Marburg is that this interest in Protestantism is earnest, to the point where he gains a reputation as a scholar of Luther. 'Bultmann is said to have described Heidegger (during his time at Marburg) as "our foremost Luther man"'.[13] When it comes to reconstructing the basis for such a reputation we are left with a series of citations and comments which give insight into Heidegger's interpretation of Luther. However, in regard to his own exposition of Luther's thought there is not a great deal of extant discourse from lectures and essays. Having said that, Heidegger does develop a nuanced and critical appropriation of Luther's thought in his course lectures on the phenomenology of religion in 1920–1, which set the tone for his other investigations of Luther in subsequent lectures and writings. Here we can discern

---

10 Heidegger, *Supplements*, p. 69. 'Erkenntnistheoretische Einsichten, übergreifend auf die Theorie geschichtlichen Erkennens haben mir das *System* des Katholizismus problematisch u. unannehmbar gemacht – aber nicht das Christentum und die Metaphysik (diese allerdings in einem neuen Sinne)'. Cf. John D. Caputo, *Heidegger and Aquinas: An Essay on Overcoming Metaphysics* (New York: Fordham University Press, 1982), p. 60.

11 Ott, *Heidegger*, p. 118.

12 Thomas Sheehan, 'Heidegger's Early Years: Fragments for a Philosophical Biography', in *Heidegger: The Man and the Thinker*, ed. Thomas Sheehan (Chicago: Precedent, 1981), pp. 10–11 citing R. I. Natorp 1.II.22.

13 Hemming, *Heidegger's Atheism*, p. 42.

Protestant Theology after Heidegger

how Luther helped Heidegger project a vision of a-metaphysical theology, which foreshadowed the next initial steps he would take towards a-theological metaphysics in his 1928 lecture 'Phenomenology and Theology'.

Heidegger had the following words carved above the door of his house in Freiburg: '*Behüte dein Herz mit allem Fleiß; denn daraus geht das Leben*'. The citation is taken from Proverbs 4.23 in Luther's translation of the Bible. 'Guard your heart with all diligence because from there springs life'. It is thought to have been carved by his wife Elfride, but it offers an allusion to the perennial influence Martin Luther had on Heidegger.[14] Heidegger received a copy of the Erlangen edition of Luther's works in 1921,[15] and there are accounts of his intense study of Luther's works as early as 1920 which are corroborated by his explicit references to Luther in his early lectures from 1919 to 1922. He is even said to have assisted Gerhard Ebeling, who consulted Heidegger for his 1961 work on Luther's *Disputatio de Homine*. 'Karl Jaspers recalled that "in the spring of 1920" he "visited [Heidegger], sat alone with him in his den, watched him at his Luther studies, saw the intensity of his work".'[16] However, although the influence of Luther upon Heidegger has been well documented,[17] what we must consider is

---

14 Van Buren lists the places in Heidegger's *Gesamtausgabe* as Martin Heidegger, *Towards the Definition of Philosophy: With a Transcript of the Lecture Course 'On the Nature of the University and Academic Study'*, trans. Ted Sadler (New Brunswick, NJ: Athlone Press, 2000). GA, p. 56/57 18; Martin Heidegger, *The Phenomenology of Religious Life* (Bloomington: Indiana University Press, 2004). GA, pp. 58, 58, 62, 204–5; Martin Heidegger, *Phenomenological Interpretations of Aristotle: Initiation into Phenomenological Research* (Bloomington: Indiana University Press, 2001). GA, pp. 61, 182–3; Martin Heidegger, *Ontology: The Hermeneutics of Facticity* (Bloomington: Indiana University Press, 1999). GA, pp. 63, 5, 14, 27, 46, 106. See John Van Buren, 'Martin Heidegger, Martin Luther', in *Reading Heidegger from the Start: Essays in His Earliest Thought*, ed. Theodore J. Kisiel and John Van Buren (Albany, NY: State University of New York Press, 1994), p. 439, n. 4.

15 Van Buren, 'Martin Heidegger, Martin Luther', p. 159.

16 Van Buren, 'Martin Heidegger, Martin Luther', p. 159, citing Karl Jaspers, 'On Heidegger', *Graduate Faculty Philosophy Journal* 7 (1978), pp. 108–9.

17 John Van Buren, *The Young Heidegger: Rumor of the Hidden King* (Bloomington: Indiana University Press, 1994), ch. 7 and ch. 16 in particular; Van Buren, 'Martin Heidegger, Martin Luther'; Theodore J. Kisiel, 'The Missing Link in the Early Heidegger', in *On Heidegger and Language*, ed. Joseph J. Kockelmans (Washington DC: University Press of America, 1988); Kisiel, *The Genesis of Heidegger's Being and Time*.

the manner in which Heidegger interpreted the Lutheran critique of metaphysics as a divide between theology and metaphysics altogether. Furthermore, we must raise a question concerning the difference between Luther's reconstruction of the relation between metaphysics and theology and Heidegger's own critique of metaphysics. Although Luther and Heidegger share a fundamental criticism of scholastic metaphysics, they distinctly differ in the constructive relationship between metaphysics and theology. In this sense, Heidegger inherits what he believes to be a key Protestant attitude towards metaphysics in a way that may in fact go beyond Protestant theology itself.

A number of accounts of Heidegger's early work illustrate the way Luther's terminology found its way into Heidegger's thinking. For instance, John van Buren's essay 'Martin Heidegger, Martin Luther' notes how 'Heidegger studied closely here the treatment of the "fall," "care," "anxiety," "death," "flight," and "conscience,"' in passages 'from Luther's *Lecture on Romans,* in his *Heidelberg Disputation,* and in his *Commentary on Genesis'*.[18] But when it comes to his discussion of how Heidegger's 'own deconstructive repetition of Aristotle',[19] is founded upon Lutheran theology, confusion arises. Van Buren cites Ebeling in support of his interpretation of Luther as one for whom philosophy was not an evil and called his followers to 'philosophize well'.[20] But he goes on to cite Luther's 'non-Scholastic appropriation of Aristotle's concepts of *physis, kinesis, dynamis, steresis, etc.*', as if Luther's understanding of philosophy was somehow post-metaphysical in a way akin to Heidegger's thought. He justifies this reading by citing Heidegger's influence upon Ebeling, which is evident in Ebeling's work.[21] In particular Ebeling cites Luther's interpretation of Paul contra Greek metaphysics, 'Luther considers that the way the apostle philosophizes about things is quite different from that of the metaphysicians'.[22] What goes unnoticed, however, is how Luther's critique of

---

18 Van Buren, 'Martin Heidegger, Martin Luther', p. 170.
19 Van Buren, 'Martin Heidegger, Martin Luther', p. 170.
20 Van Buren, 'Martin Heidegger, Martin Luther', p. 169, citing Gerhard Ebeling, *Luther: An Introduction to His Thought,* trans. R. A. Wilson (London: Collins, 1970), pp. 89–92.
21 Van Buren, 'Martin Heidegger, Martin Luther', p. 169.
22 Ebeling, *Luther: An Introduction,* pp. 88–9.

Protestant Theology after Heidegger

metaphysics differed from Heidegger's. Heidegger's interpretation of Luther therefore prefigures the account of Luther and as such, we end up hearing Heidegger again in the explications of Luther being given.

Luther did hold distinctions between civil and ecclesial reasoning,[23] but this division did not necessarily apply to metaphysics in his thinking. Luther was critical of scholastic metaphysics, but, as some more recent commentators have put it, 'Luther's notion of faith does possess some understanding of the structure of being. As noted, Luther says that a Christian can employ some degree of metaphysical understanding when trying to gain this understanding in faith.'[24] What we will come to see is that Heidegger recognized a difference between the early and later Luther which implied a metaphysical aspect to his theology which Luther himself did not resolve. Heidegger commends the early Luther for his critique of scholastic metaphysics, but then goes on to critique the later Luther for returning to metaphysics in a way which Heidegger dismisses. Heidegger therefore divides Luther off into two distinct historical periods. The earlier Luther serves as Heidegger's inspiration, and even though Luther's breakthrough was incomplete, Heidegger carries it out in the more radical a-theological metaphysics he announces in 'Phenomenology and Theology'.

Heidegger appropriated Luther's thought from his early war-emergency lecture of 1919 through to *Ontology: The Hermeneutics of Facticity* in 1923. In his war-emergency lecture 'The Idea of Philosophy and the Problem of Worldview',[25] we find Heidegger developing 'the idea of philosophy as primordial science [*Urwissenschaft*]'.[26] In doing so, he explicates the difficulties

---

23 B. A. Gerrish, *Grace and Reason: A Study in the Theology of Luther* (Oxford: Clarendon Press, 1962), pp. 69ff.

24 Carl E. Braaten and Robert W. Jenson, *Union with Christ: The New Finnish Interpretation of Luther* (Grand Rapids, MI: William B. Eerdman's Publishing Company, 1998), p. 135.

25 This lecture can be found in Martin Heidegger, *Zur Bestimmung der Philosophie*, vol. 56/57, *Gesamtausgabe* (Frankfurt am Main: Klostermann, 1976), which will be cited after the English page numbers below.

26 Martin Heidegger, 'The Idea of Philosophy and the Problem of Worldview: War Emergency Semester 1919' in *Towards the Definition of Philosophy: With a Transcript of the Lecture Course 'On the Nature of the University and Academic Study'* (New Brunswick, NJ: Athlone Press, 2000), p. 18/21.

which arise in conceptualizing how diverse sciences such as mathematics and physics can 'be brought under a common concept'.[27] During this discussion he arrives at theology 'which as the doctrine of God as the Absolute could be called primordial Christianity [*Urchristentum*]'.[28] Even at this early stage Heidegger has begun to think of the difference between what he here is calling primordial science (later he calls this an enquiry into the being of beings or fundamental ontology) and theology. However,

> in neither Protestant nor Catholic theology has a methodologically clear concept of this science so far been achieved; indeed, apart from some incomplete attempts in recent Protestant theology, there is not the slightest awareness that there is a profound problem here ... because [theology] has expected from the sciences of nature and history something (if it understood itself correctly) it had no right to expect, has more than any other fallen victim to the groundless naturalism and historicism of the nineteenth century.[29]

It appears that even at this early stage Heidegger sees an inherent deficiency in theology which needs to be corrected. He gives a slight preference to the attempts made in Protestant theology, but his philosophy is invested in taking theology further than it has heretofore gone. Heidegger mentions Luther as part of his narration of the history of philosophy in this war-emergency essay, but only in passing. Here, Luther is the instigator of a religious consciousness which gained a new position in relation to Descartes' 'radical self reflection of knowledge'.[30] Heidegger believes that high Scholasticism's way of holding philosophy and theology in harmonious tandem conflated them when the original motives and tendencies of their differences were lost in mysticism. 'In this unchecked run-off of original motivations, the two life-worlds come into conflict'.[31] Early on, therefore, we see Heidegger critiquing the relationship between philosophy and theology in a way which will foreshadow his conception of that relation in 'Phenomenology and Theology'.

---

27 Heidegger, 'The Idea of Philosophy and the Problem of Worldview', p. 18/21.
28 Heidegger, 'The Idea of Philosophy and the Problem of Worldview', p. 22/26.
29 Heidegger, 'The Idea of Philosophy and the Problem of Worldview', p. 22/26.
30 Heidegger, 'The Idea of Philosophy and the Problem of Worldview', p. 15/18.
31 Heidegger, 'The Idea of Philosophy and the Problem of Worldview', p. 18/21.

Protestant Theology after Heidegger

Heidegger's early appraisal of Luther is carried forward in Heidegger's lectures of 1920–1, published in English as *Phenomenology of Religious Life*.[32] Here Heidegger demonstrates how a basic differentiation is manifested between primordial Christian religion and metaphysical thinking. It is on the way to recovering 'primordial Christianity [*Urchristentum*]'[33] that an a-metaphysical account of Luther's theology is drawn upon to greatest effect. In these lectures Heidegger is both critical of Luther and inspired by him. The heart of what Heidegger values in Luther can be seen in Heidegger's discussion of Romans 1.20; 'Ever since the creation of the world his eternal power and divine nature, invisible though they are, have been understood and seen through the things he has made. So they are without excuse' (*NRSV*). Heidegger points out that the patristic interpretation of this text was misunderstood as an affirmation of the Greek influences upon Pauline thinking. This letter was 'fundamental for the whole of Patristic "philosophy"', for the orientation of the formation of Christian doctrine in Greek philosophy ... one cannot simply dismiss the Platonic in Augustine; and it is a misunderstanding to believe that in going back to Augustine, one can gain the authentically [*eigentlich*] Christian'.[34] It is important to keep in mind that alongside Heidegger's adaptation of Luther, Augustine is mined for his own elucidation of primordial Christianity. Most notably his notion of *curare* which Heidegger exegetes from chapters 28 and 29 of Augustine's *Confessions*.[35] This requires that Augustine not only be extricated from Platonic thinking, but the interpretations of Ernst Troeltsch and Wilhelm Dilthey as well.[36]

---

32 Martin Heidegger, *The Phenomenology of Religious Life* (Bloomington: Indiana University Press, 2004). Secondary page citations will refer to Martin Heidegger, *Phänomenologie des Religiösen Lebens*, vol. 60, *Gesamtausgabe* (Frankfurt am Main: Klostermann, 1995).

33 Heidegger, *The Phenomenology of Religious Life*, p. 49/60. This is the term Heidegger uses for what he uncovers in Paul's letter to the Galatians. 'Paul wants to say further that he has come to Christianity not through a historical tradition, but through an original experience.' Heidegger, *The Phenomenology of Religious Life*, p. 49/60.

34 Heidegger, *The Phenomenology of Religious Life*, p. 212/281.

35 Heidegger, *The Phenomenology of Religious Life*, pp. 151ff/205ff.

36 Heidegger, *The Phenomenology of Religious Life*, pp. 115ff/160ff. For further commentary on Heidegger's interpretation of Augustine see Theodore J. Kisiel, 'Heidegger on Becoming a Christian', in *Reading Heidegger from the Start: Essays in His Earliest Thought*, ed. Theodore J. Kisiel and John Van Buren (Albany, NY:

Protestant Metaphysics after Barth and Heidegger

Be this as it may, Heidegger believes that the patristic Augustinian reading of Paul's letter is a classic example of Christianity's misunderstanding of the primordial Christianity Paul was trying to express in opposition to Greek thinking. Although Heidegger faults Luther for being too dependent upon Augustine,[37] on the interpretation of Romans 1.20 he thinks Luther is the only theologian to have apprehended Paul's intention.

> Only Luther really understood this passage for the first time. In his earliest works, Luther opened up a new understanding of primordial Christianity. Later on, he himself fell victim to the burden of tradition: then, the beginning of Protestant Scholasticism sets in.[38]

In one sense, therefore, Luther is an untrustworthy interpreter of Paul because he depended upon Augustine, and eventually fell victim to the exact kind of Greek metaphysical inculcation that Heidegger is trying to extricate primordial Christianity from.[39] But in another sense Luther is vindicated in so far as his early theology attempts an anti-Greek, a-metaphysical theology.[40]

In an important passage, Heidegger even goes so far as to cite at length Luther's *Heidelberg Disputation* (1518), theses 19, 21 and 22. Heidegger gives Luther in Latin and then offers his own translation/commentary. Luther's nineteenth thesis in English is as follows: '*That person does not deserve to be called a theologian who looks upon the invisible things of God as though they were clearly perceptible in those things which have actually happened* [*Rom. 1.20*]'.[41] What is interesting is how Heidegger's comments

---

State University of New York Press, 1994), pp. 184ff. and Merold Westphal, *Overcoming Onto-theology: Toward a Postmodern Christian Faith* (New York: Fordham University Press, 2001), pp. 43ff.

37 Heidegger, *The Phenomenology of Religious Life*, pp. 47/67, 115/160.

38 Heidegger, *The Phenomenology of Religious Life*, pp. 213/282.

39 'If one wants to use the aid of a translation, Luther's shouldn't be chosen, for it is all too dependent upon Luther's own theological standpoint'. Heidegger, *The Phenomenology of Religious Life*, p. 48/68.

40 Heidegger, *The Phenomenology of Religious Life*, p. 67/97.

41 Martin Luther, *Luther's Works*, ed. Jaroslav Jan Pelikan, Hilton C. Oswald, and Helmut T. Lehmann, American ed., 55 vols, vol. 31 (Philadelphia, PA: Fortress Press, 1999), p. 52.

on this passage differ from Luther at this point: 'The presentation [*Vorgabe*] of the object of theology is not attained by way of a metaphysical consideration of the world.'[42] But here we have to stop and ask about the anti-metaphysical emphasis Heidegger adds to Luther's thought. Luther's text asks us not to look upon the invisible things of God as though they were clearly perceptible in the things which happen. In a subtle way, Heidegger is implying that Luther recognizes in Romans 1.20 a critique of theologians who believe that they can discern the invisible God in visible things. What's changed in Heidegger is that the invisible things of God are now considered as 'the object of theology', and Luther's critique of their inability to be attained by reflection upon the perceptible things that have happened has been radicalized as the critique of 'a metaphysical consideration of the world'. Heidegger likes the Luther who rages against Aristotle,[43] and reads his *Heidelberg Dissertation* (1518) in that light, but simply dismisses the Luther who sought to redeem Greek thinking in so far as it could be put to the proper service of theology in Luther's commentary on Galatians (1535). Christian theology therefore would be conceived by Heidegger in terms of a-metaphysical religious experience, and it is this direction which Heidegger wishes to take what he sees as Luther's unfinished project.

Heidegger continues to cite Luther in the coming years both in his early lectureships at Freiburg and after his move to Marburg, but he drops the more nuanced critical construction he adduces in his 1920–1 lectures on religious life. In *Phenomenological Interpretations of Aristotle* he again notes how Luther was, in the end, corrupted by Aristotle, and Melanchthon is in part blamed for this re-scholasticization of Lutheran thinking.

> In the assimilation and development, as well as, in some cases, the dismissal of the new motives of Lutheran theology, protestant scholasticism came to be formed. It was immediately nourished, through Melanchthon, by Aristotelian motives as interpreted in a certain way. These dogmatics, bearing essentially Aristotelian directions, constitute the root soil of German Idealism.[44]

---

42 Heidegger, *The Phenomenology of Religious Life*, p. 213/282.
43 Heidegger, *The Phenomenology of Religious Life*, p. 67/97.
44 Martin Heidegger, *Phenomenological Interpretations of Aristotle: Initiation*

Protestant Metaphysics after Barth and Heidegger

But it is clear by *Ontology: The Hermeneutics of Facticity*, that Heidegger has simplified the admission of his debt to the Reformer. 'Companions in my searching were the young Luther and the paragon Aristotle, whom Luther hated'.[45] Here Heidegger's shorthand reference to the early Luther leaves out the more critical appropriation of the complexity of Luther's thinking which Heidegger developed in his 1920–1 lectures.

Furthermore, the loss of this more nuanced reading of Luther is continued as Heidegger distanced himself from his Freiburg Catholicism soon after arriving in Marburg. One wonders whether Luther's inspiration included Heidegger's need to demonstrate that he had moved beyond his Catholic roots.[46] In a lecture he gave for Bultmann's seminar on Saint Paul's ethics 'The Problem of Sin in Luther' (1924) Heidegger comments, 'What is evident from these remarks is how Luther's orientation regarding sin is totally different vis-à-vis Scholasticism, and how he understands Scholasticism as a fundamental antithesis to faith'.[47] This echoes his discernment between Protestantism and Catholicism in his lectures of 1920–1, when he says that they are 'fundamentally different'.[48] What Heidegger demonstrates in his early lectures is that he is critical of both Catholicism *and* Protestantism, but that Protestantism provided a vital corrective. Even so, 'Protestantism is only a *corrective* to Catholicism and cannot stand alone as normative, just as Luther is Luther only on the spiritual basis of Catholicism'.[49] This may give insight into Heidegger's way of holding together his own sense of the two traditions which we noted above.

Heidegger sees a parallel between Luther's corrective relationship to Catholicism and his own understanding of a-metaphysical

---

into Phenomenological Research (Bloomington: Indiana University Press, 2001), p. 7; Martin Heidegger, *Phänomenologische Interpretationen zu Aristotles*, vol. 61, Gesamtausgabe (Frankfurt am Main: Klostermann, 1985), p. 7.

45 Martin Heidegger, *Ontology: The Hermeneutics of Facticity* (Bloomington: Indiana University Press, 1999), p. 4; Martin Heidegger, *Ontologie (Hermeneutik der Faktizität)*, vol. 63, Gesamtausgabe (Frankfurt am Main: Klostermann, 1988), p. 8. This citation can be found in the foreword to the text, but was not given in his actual lecture.

46 Ott, *Heidegger*, p. 121.

47 Heidegger, *Supplements*, p. 110.

48 Heidegger, *The Phenomenology of Religious Life*, p. 236/310.

49 Heidegger, *Supplements*, p. 110.

Protestant Theology after Heidegger

religious experience. As Otto Pöggeler notes, 'to be sure, this distancing from the theological origin signified a radicalization rather than a turning away from theology'.[50] In order to make sense of Luther's later metaphysical writings, however, Heidegger interpreted Luther in terms of his own interest in a primordial science – in what would later be announced as an a-theological metaphysics in 'Phenomenology and Theology' (1928). Clearly, he saw himself recovering and explicating lost interpretations of Protestant theology, even recovering the 'principle of Protestantism' itself in his Luther lecture. In particular, in his lecture on Luther, Heidegger continues to criticize the later Protestant tradition which had lost the Lutheran notion of sin.[51]

Heidegger's interpretation of Luther therefore must be understood as a challenge to Protestant theology at the time, and this explains why Heidegger's interest in recovering fundamental ontology led him to draw upon Protestant theology in the guarded way that he did. This is further evidenced in the other Protestant theologians that Heidegger engages in these early lectures. In many ways, Heidegger's interest in the contemporary Protestant theology of his day may prove to have been more influential in this regard. The reason is that theologians such as Ernst Troeltsch speak more directly to the metaphysical problematics that Heidegger believes to be so crucial for any future theological project. It is in this sense that Heidegger may have looked to the theology of Friedrich Schleiermacher as a kind of proto-phenomenology of religion. Schleiermacher may have been the influence which drew Heidegger to think theology without metaphysics before Luther – possibly even one of the 'incomplete attempts in recent Protestant theology',[52] which we cited above in his war-emergency lecture of 1919.

As with Luther, Heidegger reads Schleiermacher's theology as the paradigmatic recovery of primordial Christianity. His first exposure to Schleiermacher is around 1917, and he even gives a 'lecture to a private group about the problem of that which is religious in Schleiermacher' in August of that year.[53] He had planned to give

---

50 Otto Pöggeler, *Martin Heidegger's Path of Thinking*, trans. Daniel Magurshak and Sigmund Barber (New York: Humanity Books, 1987), p. 265.
51 Heidegger, *Supplements*, p. 110.
52 Heidegger, 'The Idea of Philosophy', p. 22.
53 Pöggeler, *Martin Heidegger's Path of Thinking*, p. 265. Van Buren also

a lecture course in the winter semester of 1919–20 entitled 'The Philosophical Foundations of Medieval Mysticism',[54] but this was cancelled.[55] The notes for this course, however, became the basis for the latter half of *The Phenomenology of Religious Life*. In this winter semester course Heidegger would have presented a favourable reading of the second speech in Schleiermacher's *On Religion*. Amidst explications of Meister Eckhart, Adolf Reinach and Rudolf Otto's *The Holy*, Schleiermacher begins to stand out for Heidegger as an exemplary articulation of a unique conception of religion. In many ways Heidegger is drawing upon the post-Kantian nature of Schleiermacher's work.[56] Like Schleiermacher, Heidegger rejects the reduction of religion to morality and rationality.

> Most often, and also now, one appreciated the expressions, the documents of religion according to the profit they yielded for morals and metaphysics. So the cutting opposition of faith to morals and metaphysics, of piety against morality, is first to be shown.[57]

Heidegger's intention is to demonstrate Schleiermacher's early recognition of how different faith is from metaphysics and morals. Schleiermacher's words from the 1843 edition of his *On Religion* are cited exactly: 'the measure of knowledge is not the measure of piety'.[58] Piety, feeling, the infinite and dependence are all expounded in an articulation of the religious affectation Heidegger believes Schleiermacher evinces.

At this point in his notes, Heidegger does not develop where Schleiermacher's conception of religion will lead. However, if we return to the introduction to the lecture course he gave in 1921, 'Introduction to the Phenomenology of Religion', which comprises the first half of *The Phenomenology of Religious Life*, Heidegger

---

notes Heidegger's interest in Schleiermacher begins in 1917. Van Buren, 'Martin Heidegger, Martin Luther', p. 160.

54 Heidegger, *The Phenomenology of Religious Life*, p. 259.
55 Heidegger, *The Phenomenology of Religious Life*, p. 261.
56 For a more developed analysis of Schleiermacher's relation to Kant, and one which contrasts the way he is misread in light of neo-Kantianism, see Julia A. Lamm, *The Living God: Schleiermacher's Theological Appropriation of Spinoza* (University Park, PA: Pennsylvania State University Press, 1996).
57 Heidegger, *The Phenomenology of Religious Life*, p. 242.
58 Heidegger, *The Phenomenology of Religious Life*, p. 243.

Protestant Theology after Heidegger

announces a point of departure from traditional ways of thinking theology and philosophy together. Heidegger's opening commentary on Troeltsch's philosophy of religion is quite critical of his fourfold approach.

> At issue is to validly determine the essence of religion scientifically. Troeltsch has a fourfold concept of the essence of religion: 1. The *psychological* essence of religion; the genera of its particularity of form. 2. The *epistemological* essence of religion; the a priori of religious reason. 3. The *historical* essence of religion, understood as general typology; the actualization of (1) and (2) in history. 4. The *metaphysical* essence of religion; the religious as principle of every-thing a priori. (Position of religion in the entire complex of reason.)[59]

Troeltsch is said to have 'had no understanding of Luther' and to have believed that the Reformation offered only a continuation of medieval scholasticism. Furthermore, Heidegger argues that Troeltsch's metaphysics of religion depends upon 'the *proof of God*' and therefore are not 'originally Christian, but rather depends upon the connection between Christianity and Greek philosophy'.[60] In brief, Troeltsch is all that is wrong about Protestant theology.[61] Although Heidegger says that he doesn't want 'to establish a critique [of Troeltsch] on the basis of content',[62] it is clear that Heidegger does intend to deconstruct Troeltsch's approach to the study of religion in his lectures. What the ensuing sections of the lecture manifest is that Heidegger *is* familiar with Luther – that is, Heidegger demonstrates the problems a conflation of metaphysics and theology can pose, and he has found ways of conceptualizing a-metaphysical religion with the help of Luther and Schleiermacher. Heidegger, therefore, sets out to

> understand in what way [Troeltsch's] philosophy of religion refers to religion, whether it grows from out of [*herauswächst*]

---

59 Heidegger, *The Phenomenology of Religious Life*, p. 19/26–7.
60 Heidegger, *The Phenomenology of Religious Life*, p. 19/27.
61 It is important to note that Heidegger's critique of Troeltsch implies an unspoken affinity with Harnack. See Introduction above.
62 Heidegger, *The Phenomenology of Religious Life*, p. 19/27.

the meaning of religion, or whether religion is not as much as grasped in the manner of an object [*gegenständlich*] and forced into philosophical disciplines – that is to say, integrated into material complexes [*eingeordnet wird in Sachzusammenhänge*] that already exist in themselves before religion.[63]

According to Heidegger, Schleiermacher's alternative way of orienting individuals towards self-reflection challenges Troeltsch's own appropriation of his work. Heidegger cites Schleiermacher explicitly: 'Thus now everyone can understand each activity of the mind [*des Geistes*] only in so far as he can, at the same time, find it and observe it within himself'.[64] Rather than objectifying religion, Heidegger wants it to reflect upon itself. He seeks the foundation for a phenomenology of religion in the work of theologians rather than in a purely philosophical manner. As such, Schleiermacher's second essay in *On Religion* is justified as 'a prime early example of a proto-phenomenology of religion'.[65] Heidegger begins his notes on Schleiermacher's 'On the Essence of Religion' by emphasizing the 'necessity of a phenomenological attitude toward the religious experience'.[66] As such, religion is articulated as 'the specifically religiously intentional, emotional reference of each content of experience to an infinite whole as fundamental meaning'.[67] Heidegger positively affirms the originary religious experience he discovers in Schleiermacher's work.[68] He even goes so far as to defend and clarify such notions as 'dependence', noting how we mustn't interpret Schleiermacher's conception of dependence as '"dependency as such [*Schlechthinnige Abhängigkeit*]": this interpretive meaning is too raw, it objectifies too much in the direction of a theory of being [*seinstheoretischen*] – specifically that of the reality of nature'.[69] Furthermore, Heidegger cites Reinach's explication of 'the experience of absolute dependence on God',[70] as a valuable contribution to Schleiermacher's similar notion. Heidegger thus draws upon

---

63 Heidegger, *The Phenomenology of Religious Life*, p. 19/27.
64 Heidegger, *The Phenomenology of Religious Life*, p. 242/319.
65 Kisiel, *The Genesis of Heidegger's Being and Time*, p. 89.
66 Heidegger, *The Phenomenology of Religious Life*, p. 241/319.
67 Heidegger, *The Phenomenology of Religious Life*, p. 243/321.
68 Heidegger, *The Phenomenology of Religious Life*, p. 244/322.
69 Heidegger, *The Phenomenology of Religious Life*, p. 250/331.
70 Heidegger, *The Phenomenology of Religious Life*, p. 247/326.

Protestant Theology after Heidegger

Schleiermacher for crucial insight into how a pure religious affection might be grounded in and of itself without metaphysics and without the other scientific disciplines.

Schleiermacher directs Heidegger more forcefully to critique those conceptions of theology which blindly depend upon philosophical notions that do not arise in religion itself. Religion becomes more primordial, and in that sense independent of the other sciences. Given the Protestant conception of an a-metaphysical religion which Heidegger recovered from his interpretation of Luther and Schleiermacher, we must conclude that these insights had direct bearing upon Heidegger's later essays. As we noted in the chapter above, 'Phenomenology and Theology' divides ontology and theology in a way that we can now see is deeply consistent with Heidegger's interpretation of Luther. Although this interpretation went beyond Luther's own position, Heidegger nonetheless considered it to be of crucial importance to his own project. In other words, the heart of an a-metaphysical theology, for Heidegger, is announced as a radical divide between metaphysics and theology which he locates in Protestant thinking. What this demonstrates is that Heidegger already developed a working definition of theology, which his later fundamental ontology can do without. Although 'Phenomenology and Theology' marks Heidegger's own interpretation of the theological implications of *Being and Time's* phenomenological ontology,[71] we must also affirm how deeply it draws upon the results of his earlier appropriation of Protestant theology. As such, we can now more clearly discern just what is at stake in Hans Jonas's call to scrutinize just what Heidegger has done with theology before Protestant theologians re-import their original product.[72]

Protestant Existentialism

The first Protestant theologian to draw upon Heidegger's work explicitly is Rudolf Bultmann. Bultmann's engagement with Heidegger is paradigmatic of an existential interpretation of his

---

71 David Farrell Krell, 'Introduction to "What is Metaphysics?"', in *Basic Writings: From Being and Time (1927) to The Task of Thinking (1964)* (San Francisco: HarperSanFrancisco, 1993), pp. 90–1.

72 Hans Jonas, *The Phenomenon of Life: Toward a Philosophical Biology* (Chicago: University of Chicago Press, 1982), p. 243.

Protestant Metaphysics after Barth and Heidegger

thought which became dominant early on.[73] For our purposes, Bultmann's relationship to Heidegger can be informed by the way in which Paul Tillich is sometimes thought to be related to Heidegger's work. Although Tillich is a pervasive voice in existentialist theology, his relationship to Heidegger is much more ambiguous than Bultmann's. For instance, Tillich is rarely explicit about his reliance upon Heidegger's metaphysical framework. In his three volume *Systematic Theology* there are a total of 11 mentions of Heidegger,[74] most of which tend to either make cursory references to certain aspects of his fundamental ontology (for example finitude as 'thrown into being')[75] or list him among other existentialist philosophers and theologians. These references, however, do not depict Tillich's dependence upon Heidegger's thought, so much as his willingness to demonstrate and illustrate his own theological project in relation to its similarities with others. In other words, there is no special preference for Heidegger's way of framing ontology in Tillich's thought. If anything Heidegger is seen as one of many existentialist thinkers alongside Augustine, Schopenhauer, Schelling and Kierkegaard.[76]

The literature on Tillich is thus rather uncertain about what the relationship between Tillich and Heidegger actually was. Some gloss over it completely with little or no mention,[77] others see it as a structural relationship.[78] Even in a treatise devoted to the role of ontology in Tillich's thought, the author makes it clear that 'no part of [his] purpose in this book [is] to try to trace the heterogeneous elements in his thought about ontology back to these [philosophical] sources'.[79] Even in Wilhelm and Marion Pauck's *Paul Tillich,*

---

73 John Macquarrie gives a helpful overview of existentialism and Christianity in relation to Heidegger and Bultmann in his *An Existentialist Theology: A Comparison of Heidegger and Bultmann* (Westport, CT: Greenwood Press, 1979).

74 Paul Tillich, *Systematic Theology*, 3 vols (London: SCM Press, 1978). Volume one mentions Heidegger five times (pp. 183, 186–7, 208, 217), volume two, three times (pp. 12, 28, 84), and volume three another three times (pp. 62, 217, 247).

75 Tillich, *Systematic Theology*, vol. 2, p. 84, cf. vol. 1, p. 217.

76 Tillich, *Systematic Theology*, vol. 1, pp. 62, 165.

77 David H. Kelsey, *The Fabric of Paul Tillich's Theology* (New Haven, CT: Yale University Press, 1967).

78 Thomas F. O'Meara, 'Tillich and Heidegger: A Structural Relationship', *Harvard Theological Review* 61, no. 2 (1968), pp. 249ff.

79 Alistair M. Macleod, *Paul Tillich: An Essay on the Role of Ontology in His Philosophical Theology* (London: Allen & Unwin, 1973), p. 19.

Protestant Theology after Heidegger

His Life & Thought, the relation to Heidegger is acknowledged but not expounded with any detail.

There are some who feel that had it not been for Heidegger's *Being and Time*, Tillich would never have developed his ontology as he did. In any case, neither in Marburg nor later did the two men become personal friends.[80]

However, when Heidegger *is* mentioned he is referred to as 'one of the chief spokesmen of Existentialism'.[81] Tillich was at Marburg while Heidegger was there, but Tillich's primary interest was Schelling on whom his PhD dissertation at the University of Breslau was based. It could be argued that there is considerable overlap between Schelling and Heidegger. This might explain some similarities between Tillich's thought and Heidegger's. Heidegger himself maintained an interest in Schelling's work throughout his career – for example his lecture on German Idealism in the summer semester of 1929, his lecture on Schelling and the essence of human freedom in the summer semester of 1936, his lecture on Schelling in 1941 and again in 1968 where he lectured on Hegel and the difference between Fichte and Schelling's systems. As Schelling relates being and God in a manner similar to Tillich's position, Heidegger may be rightly seen as a peripheral influence in so far as he was working with Schelling at this time. But there is no concrete evidence that Tillich is somehow a Heideggerian. If there isn't a peripheral role that Heidegger plays in Tillich's thought, the secondary literature's dependence on an existentialist interpretation of Heidegger's *Being and Time* does create the relationship between the two. But that is the key point to make here. The relationship is largely a product of the secondary interpretations of Heidegger's thought as an existentialist, and then backtracking to note the existential quality in Tillich's thought.

What can be said with some certainty is that Bultmann and Tillich have a common existential interpretation of Heidegger's *Being and Time*. Bultmann provides a paradigmatic example of this kind of theology because of his explicit praise of Heidegger's influence upon him, and because he was an early colleague of Heidegger when he

---

80 Wilhelm Pauck and Marion Pauck, *Paul Tillich, His Life & Thought* (San Francisco: Harper & Row, 1989), p. 98.
81 Pauck and Pauck, *Paul Tillich*, p. 95.

arrived in Marburg in 1923. They became friends during their time together in Marburg.[82] Bultmann found the existential quality of Heidegger's analysis of *Dasein* in *Being and Time* to be a helpful supplement to the biblical hermeneutics he had been developing in critique and conversation with neo-Kantian and liberal Protestant theology.[83] Bultmann's hermeneutics eventually developed into what he called 'demythologization', which sought to interpret the Bible's meaning apart from its mythological cosmology. Lessing's 'broad ugly ditch' could be bridged by a universally relevant existential principle.[84] For instance, the being of Paul the apostle could be translated to our own being today because there is a common experience of there-being *(Dasein)* which Paul's letters depict. As Bultmann puts it, 'The real purpose of myth is not to present an objective picture of the world as it is, but to express man's understanding of himself in the world in which he lives.'[85] Even by his own admission, Bultmann consistently defended his use of Heideggerian philosophy to supplement his hermeneutics. As Anthony Thiselton notes, 'It is crucial to Bultmann's own argument, however, to say that *the New Testament itself by its very nature,* invites demythologization.'[86] Be this as it may, this is not to say that we cannot challenge the finality of Bultmann's appropriation of Heidegger's thought. The fact that Heidegger is interwoven into the way existentialism has come to be understood makes it impossible to deny the productive interests of this literature. Furthermore, I believe it perfectly legitimate to allow this work and its interpretation of Heidegger to stand on its own, precisely because existentialist theologians knowingly challenged Heidegger's own understanding of what he was trying to accomplish in *Being and Time*. There is therefore no reason to chal-

---

82 Rüdiger Safranski, *Martin Heidegger: Between Good and Evil* (Cambridge, MA: Harvard University Press, 1998), pp. 134ff.

83 Anthony C. Thiselton, *The Two Horizons: New Testament Hermeneutics and Philosophical Description with Special Reference to Heidegger, Bultmann, Gadamer, and Wittgenstein* (Grand Rapids, MI: W. B. Eerdmans, 1980), pp. 205ff.

84 Gotthold Ephraim Lessing, 'On the Proof of the Spirit and of Power (1777)', in *Philosophical and Theological Writings*, ed. Hugh Barr Nisbet (Cambridge: Cambridge University Press, 2005), p. 87. See also Toshimasa Yasukata, 'Lessing's "Ugly Broad Ditch"', in *Lessing's Philosophy of Religion and the German Enlightenment* (Oxford: Oxford University Press, 2002), pp. 56ff.

85 Hans Werner Bartsch, *Kerygma und Mythos: ein theologisches Gespräch* (London: SPCK, 1964), pp. 5–6, cited in Thiselton, *The Two Horizons*, p. 262.

86 Thiselton, *The Two Horizons*, p. 262.

lenge the way Bultmann is related to Heidegger's work within the secondary literature.

I believe that if Heinrich Ott had taken this attitude in his *Denken und Sein*,[87] he could have avoided the debates that led to the ultimate abandonment of his project. Ott was one of the first to argue that Heidegger's thought may be more akin to the kind of theology Barth was doing than the theology of Bultmann. However, he argued in a way that threatened the followers of Bultmann, who responded quite forcefully to Ott's proposal.[88] Bultmann himself was critical of Ott's thesis and argued that what Heidegger means by transcendence is an '"immanent transcendence", and that Ott has misunderstood this and fallen back into a metaphysical understanding of transcendence'.[89] Other commentators like Eberhard Jüngel repeat Bultmann's critique that Ott had fallen back into metaphysics as well.[90] These critiques of Ott's thesis come down to a primary unwillingness on the part of the theological establishment of that time to let go of their existentialist interpretation of Heidegger. This together with the apparent lack of scepticism in Ott's interpretation of Heidegger made Ott an easy target for dismissal. Ott misunderstood Heidegger's philosophy, and therefore misappropriated Heidegger's theological implications. As Robinson notes,

> Bultmann maintains that the theologian should be basically critical of the later Heidegger ... Although the Bultmannians have not shared in Bultmann's basic reserve with regard to the later Heidegger, Ott has been consistently criticized for his uncritical stance toward Heidegger.[91]

Herein we are introduced to the Bultmannian response to Heidegger's attempts to distance himself from existentialist readings of his

---

87 Heinrich Ott, *Denken und Sein: Der Weg Martin Heideggers und der Weg der Theologie* (Zurich: EVZ-Verlag, 1959).

88 For an account of these debates and their outcome, see James McConkey Robinson and John B. Cobb, *The Later Heidegger and Theology* (New York: Harper & Row, 1963), pp. 63ff.

89 Robinson and Cobb, *The Later Heidegger and Theology*, p. 62.

90 Eberhard Jüngel, 'Der Schritt zurück: Eine Auseinandersetzung mit der Heidegger-Deutung Heinrich Otts', *Zeitschrift für Theologie und Kirche* LVIII (1961), pp. 104–22.

91 Robinson and Cobb, *The Later Heidegger and Theology*, p. 66, n. 145.

thought, and the suggestion by the existentialists that there are two Heideggers. The first Heidegger was attributed to *Being and Time,* and the later Heidegger to the 'Letter on Humanism' and the 'Post-onto-theological Constitution of Metaphysics'.

One Heidegger

Because Heidegger's own rejection of existentialism in the 'Letter on Humanism' touches upon a more thoroughgoing question of the interpretation of his thought, we need to relate ourselves to the debates which surround a distinction which was made between Heidegger I and Heidegger II. In the 'Letter on Humanism' Heidegger opposes the subjective interpretation of *Dasein* which existentialism assumes. Instead, he discusses how a turn (*Kehre*) was at work in the nature of ontology explicated in *Being and Time.*

> The adequate execution and completion of this other thinking that abandons subjectivity is surely made more difficult by the fact that in the publication of *Being and Time* the third division of the first part, 'Time and Being', was held back ... Here everything is reversed. The division in question was held back because thinking failed in the adequate saying of this turning [Kehre] and did not succeed with the help of the language of metaphysics. The lecture 'On the Essence of Truth', thought out and delivered in 1930 but not printed until 1943, provides a certain insight into the thinking of the turning from 'Being and Time' to 'Time and Being'. This turning is not a change of stand-point from *Being and Time,* but in it the thinking that was sought first arrives at the location of that dimension out of which *Being and Time* is experienced, that is to say, experienced from the fundamental experience of the oblivion of Being.[92]

The 'Letter on Humanism' raised a question for previous interpretations of his work. Heidegger now claimed that *Being and Time*

---

92 Martin Heidegger, 'Letter on Humanism', in *Basic Writings: From Being and Time (1927) to The task of Thinking (1964),* ed. David Farrell Krell (San Francisco: HarperSanFrancisco, 1993), pp. 231–2.

Protestant Theology after Heidegger

should be understood in terms of his later lectures and essays. Was Heidegger reinterpreting his work based on a change that had occurred in his thinking after *Being and Time*, or was he correcting the misunderstandings of other interpretations of *Being and Time* by rearticulating more forcefully the main thesis of that text? The question can be taken in two ways. First, what is the difference between Heidegger and his interpreters? Second, what is Heidegger in fact saying of his own work? Did his thought change after *Being and Time* – that is, in his essay 'On the Essence of Truth?' Or is the turn he speaks of an overlooked aspect of his thought which runs through the entirety of his thinking?

Laurence Hemming's *Heidegger's Atheism* raises many of the key issues and cites the accumulative literature surrounding these questions. Hemming deconstructs the mythos of the two Heideggers as they were propagated by both Karl Löwith and William Richardson and I must indicate my indebtedness to his work on this subject.[93] I will not rehearse Hemming's lengthy explication of what the turn is in Heideggerian scholarship, but simply note his answer to the question 'What did Heidegger hold *die Kehre* itself to be?'[94] Hemming is helpful to begin with because of the point he makes concerning the differentiation between the turns and developments in Heidegger's biography and the turn (*die Kehre*) as a descriptive term for the nature of ontology itself.[95] This is not to say that Heidegger's life and thought are inextricable, but that when interpreting this idea of the turn (*die Kehre*) it is helpful to create a distinction. Heidegger's life does in fact influence his thought and vice versa, but this has nothing to do with the turn (*die Kehre*) he is referring to in the 'Letter on Humanism'.

So what is the importance of a unified understanding of Heidegger's thought? We will answer this question by examining two significant proponents of a 'two Heideggers' thesis. Karl Löwith, a student of Heidegger's at Marburg, articulates one of the early accounts of a differentiation between the early and later Heidegger. For Löwith, 'the essential distinction between *Being and Time* and the later writings is focused in a subtle displacement of

---

93 Hemming, *Heidegger's Atheism*, pp. 80ff and 87ff respectively.
94 Hemming, *Heidegger's Atheism*, p. 93.
95 Hemming, *Heidegger's Atheism*, pp. 2 and 81.

emphasis in the relationship between Being and *Dasein*'.[96] By demonstrating that the language Heidegger used in his acceptance speech of his accession to the Rectorship at the University of Freiburg can be differentiated from the Heidegger of *Being and Time,* Löwith sought to clarify his own relationship to Heidegger's work. Two Heideggers are therefore needed for political reasons after World War Two and the way many questioned Heidegger's place in Carl Schmitt's 'translation of "one's ownmost individual *Dasein*" into the "German *Dasein*"'.[97]

In like manner, Richardson compares two Heideggers. Richardson's interest, however, takes its starting place in Heidegger's 'On the Essence of Truth' where Richardson locates the first articulation of a turn (*Kehre*). This presents itself as an insight into Heidegger's development in so far as 'On the Essence of Truth' (1930) was written before the 'Letter on Humanism' (1946). As such, the turning point where Heidegger explicitly rejects existentialist interpretations of his work begins for Richardson 16 years earlier than it does for Löwith. As Richardson puts it,

> The transformation of Heidegger I into Heidegger II is born out of a necessity imposed by the original experience of Being as *finite* (negative). For the shift of focus from There-being to Being (which as far as we can see, characterizes the decisive difference between the two periods) was demanded by the exigencies of the hermeneutic analysis itself, as soon as it became clear that the primacy in the Being-process belongs to Being itself. And when was this? Precisely when the author began to meditate the negativity of truth *as such*.[98]

On the one hand, Richardson thought that *die Kehre* is itself a turn in the biographical history of Heidegger's thought. On the other, it is argued by Heidegger himself in his response to Richardson's work that the turn is inherent in the structure of being. In regards

---

96 Karl Löwith, *Martin Heidegger and European Nihilism*, ed. Richard Wolin (New York: Columbia University Press, 1995), pp. 64–5.

97 Karl Löwith, *My Life in Germany Before and After 1933: A Report* (London: Athlone, 1994), p. 34.

98 William J. Richardson, *Heidegger: Through Phenomenology to Thought* (New York: Fordham University Press, 2003), p. 624.

to Richardson's work, Hemming explicates Heidegger's own prefatory letter to *Heidegger: Through Phenomenology to Thought*, which was taken by Richardson and his publishers as a positive appraisal. What Hemming focuses on, however, is how what was taken as positive in the letter should be read in light of the whole, which is far more critical of 'the endless prattle about the "reversal"'.[99] Hemming, therefore, argues that 'Heidegger does not confirm the validity of the interpretation; he stands it on its head'.[100]

Heidegger admits that the first publication where *die Kehre* was used was in 'The Letter on Humanism',[101] but he goes on to explicitly note that this is not a reversal in the history of his thought.[102] In response to Richardson's account of his work, Heidegger notes how it is quite clear that the idea of a turning (*die Kehre*) was always meant in reference to the nature of ontology. He explicitly states that inherent to his discussion of 'the Whole' in 'The Letter on Humanism'[103] is the inclusion of the headings 'Being and Time' and 'Time and Being' in *Being and Time*.[104]

> *Being and Time* (1957) contains the remark: [This] 'way still remains even today a necessary one, if the question about Being is to stir our There-being'. Contrary [to what is generally supposed], the question of *Being and Time* is decisively ful-filled in the thinking of the reversal.[105]

In other words, *die Kehre* is a way of adding further descriptive content to what was already latent in Heidegger's work prior to where the historical break between a Heidegger I and II is thought to reside. As Heidegger says, 'the reversal is in play within the matter itself. Neither did I invent it nor does it affect merely my thought'.[106]

---

99 Martin Heidegger, 'Vorwort', in *Heidegger: Through Phenomenology to Thought*, ed. William J. Richardson (New York: Fordham University Press, 2003), p. xviii.
100 Hemming, *Heidegger's Atheism*, p. 90.
101 Heidegger, 'Vorwort', p. xvi.
102 Heidegger, 'Vorwort', p. xviii.
103 Heidegger, 'Letter on Humanism', pp. 231–2.
104 Heidegger, 'Vorwort', p. xviii.
105 Heidegger, 'Vorwort', p. xviii.
106 Heidegger, 'Vorwort', p. xviii.

Heidegger's own understanding of his work makes further sense of how, although a developed concept of the turn first appeared in the 'Letter on Humanism', it can be found as early as Heidegger's war-emergency lectures of 1919 (often abbreviated KNS for *Kriegsnotsemester*). This is well documented by Hans-Georg Gadamer,[107] and Theodore Kisiel. Kisiel notes, 'the groundwork for all of Heidegger's later thought after the "turn" was already being laid in KNS 1919'.[108] Heidegger also explicitly discusses the concept of *die Kehre* between 1936 and 1938 in his chapter on 'The Last God' in his *Contributions to Philosophy (From Enowning)*.[109]

> Enowning [*Ereignis*] has its innermost occurrence and its widest reach in the turning [*die Kehre*]. The turning that holds sway in enowning is the sheltering ground of the entire series of turnings, circles, and spheres, which are of unclear origin, remain unquestioned, and are easily taken in themselves as the 'last' (consider, e.g., the turning in the jointure of the guiding-questions and the circle of understanding).[110]

These early uses of *die Kehre* make the issue of a specific one time historical turn in Heidegger's thought irrelevant. Therefore, a strong distinction needs to be made between the development of Heidegger's thought and *die Kehre,* a concept that can be found at various points along that journey as a word Heidegger used to explicate the structure of ontology.

The idea that Heidegger's thought turned [*die Kehre*] according to a historical fault-line muddles any coherent interpretation of the totality of his thought. A much better way of conceptualizing Heidegger's development is to note a series of twists and turns along a consistent pathway which also recovers and returns to lessons learned from previous journeys. Understanding Heidegger according to a consistent development is gaining credibility. Beyond

---

107 Hans-Georg Gadamer, 'Wilhelm Dilthey nach 150 Jahren', in *Dilthey und die Philosophie der Gegenwart*, ed. E. W. Orth (Freiburg: Alber, 1985), p. 159.

108 Kisiel, *The Genesis of Heidegger's Being and Time*, p. 16.

109 Otto Pöggeler, *The Paths of Heidegger's Life and Thought*, trans. John Bailiff (Amherst, MA: Humanity Books, 1998), p. 326.

110 Martin Heidegger, *Contributions to Philosophy (From Enowning)*, trans. Parvis Emad and Kenneth Maly (Bloomington: Indiana University Press, 1999), p. 286.

Protestant Theology after Heidegger

Hemming's work which we mentioned above, John Caputo compares Heidegger's *Habilitationschrift* with his later essays by noting how Heidegger's later work comes full circle and returns to earlier themes that were missed by the interpreters of *Being and Time*.[111]

By describing Heidegger's development in a more consistent manner, however, we are confronting the idea that there are two Heideggers. In this confrontation we are also relegating the existentialist Protestant theological appropriations which have arisen from Heidegger's thought. Although we do not wish to outright reject existentialist theologies due to their merits, the argument here does significantly serve to strengthen those theological approaches which have arisen in relation to an alternative account of Heidegger's thought. It does so because it tends to read the entirety of Heidegger's work as a consistent unity with a series of developments along the way. Central to our interests here is that one of the threads which unites Heidegger's thought is theological. In particular, the ways in which he drew upon Protestant theology early on. It is in this light that we can see that Bultmann and Tillich offer one understanding of Heidegger which exemplified a form of Protestantism foreign to Heidegger's desire to radicalize the division between ontology and theology. As such, although Bultmann and Tillich's theology can stand on their own,[112] they do so in contradiction to Heidegger's understanding of onto-theology.

Heidegger's own self-understanding is deeply critical of the conflation of theology and ontology. This brings us back to the citation we noted in the first chapter, Heidegger's response to the question posed in 1951, 'May Being and God be posited as identical?'

Some among you perhaps know that I come from theology, that I still guard an old love for it and that I am not without a certain understanding of it. If I were yet to write a theology – to

---

111 John D. Caputo, 'Phenomenology, Mysticism and the *Grammatica Speculativa*: A Study in Heidegger's *Habilitationsschrift*', *The Journal of the British Society for Phenomenology* 5, no. 2 (1974), p. 117.

112 In fact, Tillich quite blatantly maintains the 'independent philosophical standing' of *Being and Time*, 'whatever Heidegger may say about it in criticism and retraction', Paul Tillich, *The Courage to Be*, 2nd ed. (New Haven, CT: Yale University Press, 2000), p. 148.

which I sometimes feel inclined – then the word *Being* would not occur in it. Faith does not need the thought of Being. When faith has recourse to this thought, it is no longer faith. This is what Luther understood. Even within his own church this seems to be forgotten.[113]

Heidegger's statement here is consistent with what we would expect based on our explication of Luther which we noted above. God and being are not identical, and being mustn't intrude upon the theological task if one was to follow Heidegger's prescriptions. But here we must now highlight the distinctly Protestant form of theology which he believes to be wholly compatible with his project. He understands Luther as a better Protestant because he divides metaphysics from theology. As we have already seen, however, Heidegger himself recognized the confusion between the early and later Luther on the relation of theology to metaphysics. This raises a question concerning what other critical accounts of onto-theology may arise from Luther's thought at this time, and it is here, most explicitly that we would like to insert Barth into the conversation.

Barth's Heidegger

To say that Heidegger's theological influence goes beyond Tillich and Bultmann is one thing. It is quite another to consider Heidegger's thought in relation to Barth. Before we turn to Barth's understanding of the relationship between theology and ontology and its implications for Protestantism more explicitly, a few comments must be made. As much as it is proposed that Heidegger and Barth are somehow in conversation with each other, there is no substantial evidence that they ever were. There is an unsubstantiated citation circulating that Heidegger read Barth's *Epistle to the Romans*, and that this somehow influenced his own philosophical thought. This is cited in George Steiner's work on Heidegger,[114] but again, it is

---

113 Martin Heidegger, 'The Reply to the Third Question at the Seminar in Zürich, 1951', in *God without Being: Hors-texte*, ed. Jean-Luc Marion (Chicago: University of Chicago Press, 1991), pp. 61–2.

114 George Steiner, *Heidegger*, 2nd ed. (London: Fontana, 1992), p. 73. Graham

Protestant Theology after Heidegger

not substantiated. Furthermore, we will be explicating just how and why Barth is critical of Heidegger's thought in his *Church Dogmatics*. The imperative here is to demonstrate the specifics of that how and why. Barth does in fact critique Heidegger's thought in *Church Dogmatics*, III.3 along the lines of his perceived existentialism. Here Barth argues in terms of a parity between the existentialism of Jean-Paul Sartre and Heidegger. Barth most likely gains this impression of Heidegger early on from conversations with Bultmann which are recounted by Eberhard Busch in *Karl Barth: His Life from Letters and Autobiographical Texts*.[115]

Barth's discussion of Heidegger occurs within his passage on 'The Knowledge of Nothingness' where he discusses Heidegger's lecture 'What is Metaphysics?' in relation to *Being and Time*. As he puts it,

> The initial question concerns (human) existence [*Dasein*]. We are informed that there is a 'basic event' in which all that which is is disclosed to existence [*Dasein*]. The basic event in which this occurs is comprehensively described as the 'affective state'. It is of interest to observe that this basic event is assumed to be identical with metaphysics.[116]

After offering this existentially informed commentary on Heidegger, he immediately follows it with an explication of Sartre's work, *Being and Nothingness*.[117] No mention is made of Heidegger's own critique of Sartre's relationship to his work in his 'Letter on Humanism'. Barth is hardly to be blamed for this, however, as Heidegger's 'Letter on Humanism' was published in 1947 just prior to the years 1948–9 when Barth was preparing *Church Dogmatics* III.3 for publication.[118] Here Barth notes, 'while nothing is the basic concern of

---

Ward cites Steiner in *Barth, Derrida and the Language of Theology* (New York: Cambridge University Press, 1995), p. 80, n. 1.

115 Eberhard Busch, *Karl Barth: His Life from Letters and Autobiographical Texts* (London: SCM Press, 1976), p. 161.

116 Karl Barth, *Church Dogmatics*, ed. G. W. Bromiley and T. F. Torrance, trans. G. W. Bromiley, vol. III.3 (Edinburgh: T. & T. Clark, 1962), p. 335/KD, III.3, p. 385.

117 Karl Barth, *Church Dogmatics*, vol. III.3, pp. 338ff/KD, III.3, pp. 389ff.

118 Busch, *Karl Barth: His Life from Letters and Autobiographical Texts*, pp. 362–4.

both, there is this difference in their respective attitudes towards it. In Heidegger we are concerned with the premise of Sartre, in Sartre with Heidegger's conclusion.'[119]

Barth's criticism of existentialism has sometimes been understood in relation to an interpretation of Barth which portrays him as anti-philosophical. This can be found in John Macquarrie's *An Existentialist Theology: A Comparison of Heidegger and Bultmann*, where he responds to the criticism that because Bultmann's theology relies upon existentialist philosophy it could be condemned outright according to Barthian understandings of purely revealed a-philosophical accounts of theology.[120] Barth's theology would therefore be incompatible with the existentialism of Heidegger because Barth is more post-ontological than he is. As we shall see, this is a distortion of Barth's thought just as much as it is of Heidegger's. In this sense, we must go beyond the existentialist account Barth offers in *Church Dogmatics* III.3 in order to explicate his own breakthrough understanding of what we will refer to as his theological ontology which he evinces in *Church Dogmatics* I.1. It is our contention that Barth understood Heidegger's account of onto-theology as well as Heidegger did, even though he counteracts the conclusions Heidegger came to. In this regard, Luther again will play a crucial role both in Barth's intellectual development, but so too, for our question concerning the future of Protestantism.

---

119 Barth, *Church Dogmatics*, vol. III.3, p. 338/KD, III.3, p. 389.
120 John Macquarrie, *An Existentialist Theology: A Comparison of Heidegger and Bultmann* (Westport, CT: Greenwood Press, 1979), p. 4.

PART TWO
Karl Barth's Theological Ontology

3

Barth's 'God is God'

Barth's Early Christology

In an essay on the interconnection between Barth's earlier and later theology, Eberhard Busch investigates the meaning of Barth's enigmatic tautology 'God is God'.[1] Barth employs this statement as early as a sermon on Genesis 15.6 in 1916 and in both editions of his *Römerbrief* in 1919 and 1922 respectively.[2] Busch goes on to note the possibility of 'a subterranean connection to the Dadaists who, in the intellectually explosive Zürich of 1916, were pounding away at reality with their secret nonsense word-games, such as "Dada is Dada" in order to discern new relations in reality'.[3] During the 1920s Barth's theology would have been read in a broader context of dissatisfaction, and he uses terms specifically designed to overturn and radically affront the previous ways of approaching the theological task. Even though 'God is God' 'makes up the core

---

1 Eberhard Busch, 'God is God: The Meaning of a Controversial Formula and the Fundamental Problem of Speaking about God', *The Princeton Seminary Bulletin* 7, no. 2 (1986), p. 101. For a further discussion of Barth's relation to the political and cultural crisis in the early 1920s, see also Bruce L. McCormack, *Karl Barth's Critically Realistic Dialectical Theology: Its Genesis and Development, 1909–1936* (New York: Oxford University Press, 1995), pp. 209ff.

2 Busch, 'God is God', p. 101. Barth's 'God is God' was probably not even invented by Barth in 1916, but rather 'he took it from the religious socialism of Ragaz and Kutter to which he had a good deal of affinity at the time'. Busch, 'God is God', p. 103. Busch is quick to point out that he has not, however, found any such statement in Ragaz's work. Busch, 'God is God', p. 103.

3 Busch, 'God is God', p. 103. Graham Ward also notes Barth's relation to Dadaism during this time. Ward emphasizes the interconnection between the antihistoricism of Dadaism and Barth's theology during the 1920s. Graham Ward, *Barth, Derrida, and the Language of Theology* (New York: Cambridge University Press, 1995), p. 57. See also Friedrich Gogarten, 'Historicism', in *The Beginnings of Dialectic Theology*, ed. James McConkey Robinson and Jürgen Moltmann (Richmond, VA: John Knox Press, 1968), p. 343.

of only the *early* theology of Barth' this does not dissuade Busch from uncovering the way this statement is transfigured in his later work as well. Barth makes it clear that he viewed the 1920s as his 'apprenticeship'[4] and that at two crucial periods in his development he had to say the same thing in a totally new way. He situates the first change between the first and second editions of his *Römerbrief*,[5] and the second change was with his book on Anselm in 1931 between his *christliche Dogmatik im Entwurf* (1927) and his *Kirchliche Dogmatik* (1932).[6] In each case, however, Barth is always careful to stress continuity and discontinuity, and this has led many interpreters to wonder what precisely changed and what remained the same.[7] It is in response to this conundrum that Busch

---

4 Eberhard Busch, *Karl Barth: His Life from Letters and Autobiographical Texts* (London: SCM Press, 1976), p. 193.

5 Karl Barth, *The Epistle to the Romans*, trans. Edwyn Clement Hoskyns, 2nd ed. (London: Oxford University Press, 1933), p. 2.

6 Karl Barth, *How I Changed My Mind* (Richmond, VA: John Knox Press, 1966), p. 43.

7 Barth's break with his Marburg theology teachers in 1915 is generally accepted across the secondary literature as a defining interval in his development. For Barth's own account, see Karl Barth, *The Theology of Schleiermacher: Lectures at Göttingen, Winter Semester of 1923–24*, trans. Dietrich Ritschl (Grand Rapids, MI: Eerdmans, 1982), pp. 263–4. For a sample of the secondary interpretations of this break in Barth's thinking, see Hans W. Frei, 'The Doctrine of Revelation in the Thought of Karl Barth 1909–1922' (Doctoral Dissertation, Yale, 1956), pp. 87ff; Eberhard Jüngel, *Karl Barth: A Theological Legacy* (Philadelphia, PA: Westminster Press, 1986), p. 25; Thomas Forsyth Torrance, *Karl Barth: An Introduction to His Early Theology, 1910–1931* (London: SCM Press, 1962), p. 38; John Webster, *The Cambridge Companion to Karl Barth* (New York: Cambridge University Press, 2000); Bruce L. McCormack, *Karl Barth's Critically Realistic Dialectical Theology*, pp. 21, 209ff. In regards to the significance of the second shift in Barth's thinking which occurred at his book on Anselm, a more hotly contested debate has ensued. The chief discrepancy is represented by two influential interpretations of Barth's theology, Hans Urs von Balthasar, *The Theology of Karl Barth: Exposition and Interpretation*, trans. Edward T. Oakes (San Francisco: Communio Books, Ignatius Press, 1992), and Bruce McCormack's *Karl Barth's Critically Realistic Dialectical Theology*. In both cases, an attempt is made to account for the development of Barth's theology over the 1920s. Barth's own emphasis upon both change and continuity lies at the heart of the discrepancy between Balthasar and McCormack's theses. On the surface it appears as though their disagreement centres around Barth's employment of dialectic and analogy in his theology. However, our contention is that this focus conceals the ontological strategies Barth's multifarious uses of analogy and dialectic always implied. Although McCormack is right to suggest that Balthasar's depiction of a shift from dialectic to analogy is inadequate, in the end McCormack's account of Barth's development over the 1920s conceals as much as it reveals. The following

Barth's 'God is God'

cites 'God is God' as the location of the interconnection between Barth's early and later work.

Busch's justification for this suggestion is cited in Barth's later 1956 lecture 'The Humanity of God', where Barth reflects upon the continuity of his theological development after his break with the theology of his teachers in 1915:

> He who may not have joined in that earlier change of direction, who still may not be impressed with the fact that God is God, would certainly not see what is now to be said in addition as the true word concerning His humanity.[8]

Barth's statement here, as Busch is quick to point out, raises important questions about the relationship between Barth's Christology, generally associated with his later work, and his early 'God is God'.[9] By investigating this aspect of Barth's theology Busch proposes a tentative thesis: 'the theological principle "God is God" not only did NOT exclude the later christocentric theology but was *and* remained its *premise,* a premise which neither dropped nor even corrected the basic structure of that principle'.[10] The question such a suggestion raises, and one Busch himself answers to some degree, is what influences best explain this coinherence? Our goal in this chapter is therefore to bring this question to bear upon our interest in how Protestant metaphysics was understood in Barth's theology. One of the key ways to do so, as Busch suggests although does not carry through in sufficient detail for our purposes here, is through delineating the influence of Martin Luther upon Barth's early theology.

---

is an attempt to demonstrate the ontological nuance of Barth's development over the 1920s. By looking past McCormack and Balthasar's respective periodizations of Barth's development, a clearer focus upon Barth's theological ontology can begin to take place. For a more detailed account of the debate between Balthasar and McCormack, see Timothy Stanley, 'Before Analogy: Recovering Barth's Ontological Development', *New Blackfriars* 90, no. 1029 (2009), pp. 577–601.

8 Karl Barth, *The Humanity of God* (London: Collins, 1967), p. 42.
9 Busch, 'God is God', p. 102.
10 Busch, 'God is God', p. 102.

Luther Absconditus

What can Barth possibly mean by saying what, on the surface, is a rather meaningless statement, 'God is God'? 'That is to say that the sentence is an explanation that does not explain anything; it is an explanation that works by *refusing* to explain',[11] and this points us precisely towards the apophatic nature of Barth's early theology. Barth's statement leaves us with no God at all. 'God is God means: God is *unknown, hidden,* deus absconditus'.[12] Herein lies the opening for the critiques and misunderstandings of Barth's early theology. Critics were quick to pick up on Barth's emphasis upon the unknowability and total otherness of God in the first two drafts of Barth's *Römerbrief*. For instance, 'the Lutheran Paul Althaus wrote that Barth substituted the revealed God, *deus revelatus,* by a nonrevealed God, *deus absconditus,* substituted "theology of revelation" by a "theology of the unknown God"'.[13] There is every indication that Barth recognized this criticism with some agreement. As he says in his later 1956 *The Humanity of God*,

> We viewed this 'wholly other' in isolation, abstracted and absolutised, and set it over against man ... in such a fashion that it continually showed greater similarity to the deity of the God of the philosophers than to the deity of the God of Abraham, Isaac, and Jacob.[14]

However, it is precisely where Barth recognizes the radical otherness of God as a problem for his theology that Busch is particularly careful to emphasize a Lutheran influence which can easily be overlooked.

For Luther that which lies beyond us is precisely the deus absconditus, the 'hidden God' who remained in a certain sense even for Luther irrevocably and absolutely hidden. And that God should indeed be of no concern to us, Luther said, adding that we should on the one hand turn towards the visible world 'as if there were

---

11 Busch, 'God is God', p. 107.
12 Busch, 'God is God', p. 107.
13 Busch, 'God is God', p. 102.
14 Barth, *The Humanity of God*, pp. 44–5.

Barth's 'God is God'

no God' and on the other, let Christ be sufficient for us as the 'revealed God'. The basic criticism which Barth made of Luther was perhaps Luther took that step with undue haste.[15]

In other words, though Barth emphasized the hiddenness of God, he did so in a way which depended upon the concomitant affirmation that Christ is sufficient for us. Hence, Luther's influence is most forcefully felt in the ambiguity between Luther's hidden *and* revealed God, and Barth begins to think through the implications of this relation in his early theology. As Barth says in the second edition of his *Römerbrief*, 'in Christ Jesus the Deus absconditus is as such the Deus revelatus'.[16]

George Hunsinger's 'What Karl Barth Learned from Martin Luther' offers a helpful clarification of how best to understand Luther's influence upon Barth's early theology. There is no question Barth is Reformed in his basic theological disposition. His theology is deeply marked by his pastoral work as a Reformed minister in Safenwil,[17] and his early appointment as a professor in a newly created chair of Reformed theology at Göttingen gave Barth ample opportunity to work out his Reformed leanings. However, in these lectures Barth is not one to toe a party line. As he says of his lectures at Göttingen, 'I kept having to *approve* and *disapprove* of almost everything'.[18] Hunsinger further explicates the space Barth often traversed between Luther and Calvin's theology as follows: 'Indeed, at certain vital points Barth follows Luther not only, broadly speaking, against Calvin and the Reformed tradition, but also against the main lines of the Lutheran tradition.'[19] As we will note below, Barth would specifically challenge the Lutheranism of Wilhelm Herrmann, his teacher in Marburg.

In the end, Calvin actually comes a close second to Luther in the indexed entries in Barth's *Church Dogmatics*.[20] Although it has been noted that the citations seem to be more frequent in the early

---

15 Busch, 'God is God', pp. 107–8.
16 Barth, *The Epistle to the Romans*, p. 422.
17 Busch, *Karl Barth*, p. 61.
18 Busch, *Karl Barth*, p. 128.
19 George Hunsinger, 'What Karl Barth Learned from Martin Luther', in *Disruptive Grace: Studies in the Theology of Karl Barth* (Grand Rapids, MI: William B. Eerdmans, 2000), p. 282.
20 Hunsinger, 'What Karl Barth Learned from Martin Luther', p. 279.

volumes than in the later ones, we mustn't conclude, as Gerhard Ebeling did,[21] that this indicates a diminished influence of Luther upon Barth. Of course, 'what Barth learned from Luther cannot be appreciated through statistical calculations'[22] alone. Hence, Hunsinger develops an interpretative methodology for deciding what of Barth's theology can be attributed to Luther and what agreement may be concluded between them. As he puts it,

> if an idea can be found in both theologians that has no real precedent before Luther, we may say that Luther has instructed Barth ... moreover, if Barth has followed Luther at junctures where he faced a real choice between Luther and Calvin, we may feel certain that Luther has influenced him strongly at those points.[23]

Hunsinger rightly understands that although Barth 'was a sharp and vigorous critic',[24] his No was often 'contained by a larger Yes',[25] and this can be seen in his treatments of Luther if not something he in fact learned from him.

Hunsinger goes on to cite specific similarities between Luther and Barth's thought, and one of the first to be noted of particular interest to us here is Barth's Christology.

> Not least among the powerful themes that Barth would absorb from Luther is that of 'christocentrism', perhaps the most basic point in all of Barth's theology. Indeed, Barth not only owed this point to Luther, but went on to radicalize it.[26]

Like Busch, and Hans Frei before him,[27] Hunsinger reminds us that this Christocentric emphasis was a focal characteristic of his early theology. Here, Wilhelm Herrmann and Friedrich Schleiermacher played their part, but in the end, 'the real christocentrism that Barth

---

21 Gerhard Ebeling, *Lutherstudien*, trans. R. A. Wilson, vol. 3 (Tübingen: J. C. B. Mohr, 1985), pp. 531–2.
22 Hunsinger, 'What Karl Barth Learned from Martin Luther', p. 280, n. 2.
23 Hunsinger, 'What Karl Barth Learned from Martin Luther', p. 282.
24 Hunsinger, 'What Karl Barth Learned from Martin Luther', p. 280.
25 Hunsinger, 'What Karl Barth Learned from Martin Luther', p. 280.
26 Hunsinger, 'What Karl Barth Learned from Martin Luther', p. 283.
27 Frei, 'The Doctrine of Revelation in the Thought of Karl Barth 1909–1922', p. iv.

Barth's 'God is God'

absorbed was not finally Schleiermacher's but Luther's'.[28] Building on the work of Heiko Oberman, Hunsinger explicates the uniqueness of Luther's Christology contra nominalist, Scotist or Thomistic medieval scholastic influences. 'By contrast, Luther saw justification as "the stable *basis* and not the uncertain *goal* of the life of sanctification"'.[29] In this regard, Hunsinger concludes that 'the centrality of Jesus Christ in this strong soteriological sense is something that Barth most certainly learned from Luther'.[30]

Part of the difficulty in deciding upon Luther's influence on Barth arises as we note the difference between Luther and Calvin's teaching on the two natures of Christ.

> Luther and Calvin both saw Jesus Christ as one person in two natures whose true deity and true humanity were joined by a relationship-in-distinction. However, where Luther would focus on the unity, Calvin would in turn press the distinction. Nowhere would these differences manifest more significantly than at the point of the cross. Remembering the abiding distinction of Christ's deity from his humanity, Calvin insisted on the impassibility of the divine nature. Remembering the real unity of Christ's person, Luther by contrast affirmed the suffering of God. Although Barth respected Calvin's distinction, he moved far closer to Luther. For Barth, the theology of the cross disclosed the suffering of God.[31]

Lutheran Christology was therefore distinct from the Reformed tradition's 'Calvinist extra [extra Calvinisticum]'[32] and the way

---

28 Hunsinger, 'What Karl Barth Learned from Martin Luther', p. 283.
29 Hunsinger, 'What Karl Barth Learned from Martin Luther', p. 286, citing Heiko Augustinus Oberman, *The Dawn of the Reformation: Essays in Late Medieval and Early Reformation Thought* (Grand Rapids, MI: W. B. Eerdmans, 1992), p. 124.
30 Hunsinger, 'What Karl Barth Learned from Martin Luther', p. 286.
31 Hunsinger, 'What Karl Barth Learned from Martin Luther', pp. 287–8. He cites Calvin's *Commentary on Matthew* 24.36 and his *Institutes of the Christian Religion* 4.17.30 and 2.14.2. In Luther's case, he cites his *Heidelberg Disputation* in *Luther's Works* vol. 31, pp. 52–3 as well as Luther's part in the eucharistic controversies ten years later in *Luther's Works* vol. 37, p. 210. Hunsinger, 'What Karl Barth Learned from Martin Luther', p. 288.
32 Karl Barth, *The Theology of the Reformed Confessions, 1923*, trans. Darrell L. Guder and Judith J. Guder (Louisville, KY: Westminster John Knox Press, 2002), p. 202.

they tended to emphasize the difference between the two natures of Christ in Chalcedonian terms.[33] Although Luther would also maintain the teaching of Chalcedon,[34] he would tend to emphasize the unity of the two natures. Although not always fully developed, Luther's Christology would push Barth to stress the wholly otherness of God[35] in a way that would assume his immanence as *deus revelatus*. Furthermore, this unity of natures would become a central problem which Barth explicitly demonstrates in his lectures on Herrmann and Feuerbach which we will explore in more detail below. The key here is to recognize, as Busch does, that Barth's early Lutheranism included his Christological immanence and drew his Reformed theology in that direction. This is a helpful corrective to our understanding of the Christological impulses which were felt in Barth's early interest in the relation between the *deus absconditus* and the *deus revelatus*. Furthermore this offers a helpful insight into the continuity that exists between Barth's early and later theology.

---

33 As the Creed puts it 'our Lord Jesus Christ, at once complete in Godhead and complete in manhood, truly God and truly man'. Henry Bettenson and Chris Maunder, 'The Definition of Chalcedon, 451', in *Documents of the Christian Church* (Oxford: Oxford University Press, 1999), p. 56. Calvin cites Chalcedon positively in *The Institutes of the Christian Religion* (Grand Rapids, MI: William B. Eerdmans Publishing Company, 2001), II, pp. xiv, 4. For further discussion of this aspect of Reformed theology, see Oberman, 'The "Extra" Dimension in the Theology of Calvin', in *The Dawn of the Reformation*, pp. 245ff. It should also be noted that I fully recognize that I am presenting these issues for the most part from the perspective of the Lutheran view and the contemporary context of Barth, who we are arguing would have inherited the Lutheran critiques through his teacher, Wilhelm Herrmann. For the traditional defence of the 'Calvinist certain somewhere' in relation to Christology, see Allen O. Miller and M. Eugene Osterhaven, eds, *The Heidelberg Catechism* (Cleveland, OH: United Church Press,1962), p. 49, Question 48.

34 Martin Luther, *Luther's Works*, ed. Jaroslav Jan Pelikan, Hilton C. Oswald and Helmut T. Lehmann, American ed., 55 vols, vol. 41 (Philadelphia, PA: Fortress Press, 1999), pp. 106ff.

35 Other commentators have argued that Barth inherited this radical otherness from Luther's theology. For instance, John Webster argues 'at the beginning of his theological career, Barth very early came to an account of the magisterial Reformation according to which Luther emphasizes the "vertical", soteriological axis in God's relation to the world, whereas Calvin complements this by stronger humane, moral concerns, a concern with the "horizontal".' John Webster, 'Balthasar and Karl Barth', in *The Cambridge Companion to Hans Urs von Balthasar*, ed. Edward T. Oakes and David Moss (Cambridge: Cambridge University Press, 2004), p. 247. This view is also expressed by Erich Przywara in his 'Gott in uns oder Gott über uns? (Immanenz und Transzendenz im heutigen Geistesleben)', *Stimmen der Zeit* 105 (1923), pp. 347–8.

Barth's 'God is God'

The differentiation between the Reformed and Lutheran understanding on this point clarifies what Barth means when he recalls being branded a Calvinist in early conversations with Adolf von Harnack.[36] In other words, one way to explain Barth's way of resolving the criticisms of the abstractness and wholly otherness of his early theology was to include a profound sense of Lutheran paradox, *deus absconditus* and *deus revelatus,* and the concomitant emphasis upon the ubiquity of God it implied. Such a suggestion must cause us to wonder with Busch, whether Barth's 'God is God' already included an immanence which can best be understood as arising from Lutheran theology, and whether the Reformed pastor from Safenwil was far more Lutheran than his early commentators assumed. As Barth argues in his 'Answer to Professor von Harnack's Open Letter' in 1923:

> You would like (always in connection with the charge of Marcionism) a 'full' answer from me to the question: 'whether God is *decidedly not* all that is said of him on the basis of the development of culture and its insights and morality'. All right. But then let me ask you really to listen to my *full* answer: No, God is '*decidedly not* all that', as surely as the Creator is not the creature or even the creation of the creature. But precisely in this No, which can be spoken with full sharpness only in faith in revelation, the creature recognizes itself as the work and possession of the Creator; precisely in this No, God is known as *God,* as the source and the goal even of the *thoughts* which man, in the darkness of his culture and lack of culture, is accustomed to form of God; precisely this No definitively established by revelation is not without 'the deep, secret Yes under and above the No', which we should 'grasp and hold to with firm faith in God's Word', 'And confess God is right in his sentence on us, so that we then have won'. And thus it is with this No: 'Nothing but Yes is in it, but deep and secretly, and it seems to be nothing but No'. What 'contrast-greedy' person may have said that? Kierkegaard or Dostoevsky? No, Luther! (EA 11, p. 120).[37]

---

36 Busch, *Karl Barth,* p. 115.
37 Karl Barth, 'An Answer to Professor von Harnack's Open Letter', in *The Beginnings of Dialectical Theology,* ed. James M. Robinson (Richmond, VA: John Knox Press, 1968), p. 184.

Thus, Barth is thinking through the relation between God and his creation more carefully, and what we must come to see is how this implies certain ontological convictions which are felt in Luther's Christology. As Barth begins to think through what he means when he says 'God is God' it is the 'is' in that statement which Luther inspires Barth to clarify.

Herrmann's Luther

Barth's application of Lutheran theology did not arise in a vacuum, and we must recall one of the prominent voices Barth's 'God is God' would have been designed to respond to. Part of the reason why the two natures of Christ in both Lutheran and Reformed theology would have been sensitive issues at this time is because of the radicalization of Luther's Christology in the work of Barth's predecessors such as Wilhelm Herrmann. Herrmann was one of the first theologians to capture Barth's early imagination as a student in Berlin, where Barth dreamed of going to Marburg to study with him. As Barth recalls in his 1925 lecture 'The Principles of Dogmatics According to Wilhelm Herrmann', 'The day twenty years ago in Berlin when I first read his *Ethik* I remember as if it were today ... I can say that on that day I believe my own deep interest in theology began'.[38] Hence, after finally arriving in Marburg he did so as 'a convinced "Marburger"'.[39] In many ways Barth's lecture on his teacher gives us Barth's commentary on the theologian which inspired his early interest in the discipline which would engulf his attentions for the rest of his life. So too, this lecture marks Barth's critical attitude towards the appropriations of Lutheran theology which were popularized by his teacher. In many ways, Barth gives us his understanding of the Lutheranism of his teacher and demonstrates why the ambiguities in Lutheran Christology demanded that Barth clarify the ontological relation between God and human being more fully.

In Barth's lecture he highlights Herrmann's engagement with

---

38 Karl Barth, 'The Principles of Dogmatics According to Wilhelm Herrmann (1925)', in *Theology and Church: Shorter Writings, 1920–1928* (New York: Harper & Row, 1962), p. 238.

39 Karl Barth, 'The Principles of Dogmatics According to Wilhelm Herrmann (1925)', p. 238.

Barth's 'God is God'

the neo-Kantianism of Hermann Cohen and Paul Natorp.[40] It is in Marburg that Barth encounters what he refers to as 'a philosophical fervour which is almost priestly'.[41] The neo-Kantianism of Marburg philosophers like Hermann Cohen, as well as theologians such as Wilhelm Herrmann provided prominent examples of pathways through the religious and theological implications of Kant's critique of metaphysics in Barth's context. Our interest here is not to genealogically trace the neo-Kantian origins of Barth's thought. There are a number of studies, which address Marburg philosophy in this regard.[42] However, one of the key debates which raged

---

[40] For more on the relationship between Cohen and Herrmann, see William Kluback, 'Friendship without Communication: Wilhelm Herrmann and Hermann Cohen', in *The Idea of Humanity: Hermann Cohen's Legacy to Philosophy and Theology* (Lanham, MD: University Press of America, 1987).

[41] Karl Barth, *Theology and Church: Shorter Writings, 1920–1928* (New York: Harper & Row, 1962), p. 256. It is important to note that this was not Barth's first encounter with Kant. For instance, he is reading Kant intently before and during the writing of his first *Römerbrief*. Karl Barth and Eduard Thurneysen, *Revolutionary Theology in the Making: Barth-Thurneysen Correspondence, 1914–1925* (Richmond, VA: John Knox Press, 1964), pp. 37–8.

[42] There are some excellent studies available to this effect, not to mention the older standards, Hans W. Frei, 'The Doctrine of Revelation in the Thought of Karl Barth 1909–1922', and Hans Urs von Balthasar, *The Theology of Karl Barth*, which although faulted by more recent literature for their infatuation with Barth's dialectic and analogy, are nonetheless still helpful in uncovering Barth's philosophical beginnings. But also the texts which specifically engage Barth's neo-Kantian Marburg context such as Simon Fisher, *Revelatory Positivism?: Barth's Earliest Theology and the Marburg School* (Oxford: Oxford University Press, 1988), and Johann Friedrich Lohmann, *Karl Barth und der Neukantianismus: die Rezeption des Neukantianismus im 'Römerbrief' und ihre Bedeutung für die weitere Ausarbeitung der Theologie Karl Barths* (Berlin and New York: de Gruyter, 1995). For more general commentary on Marburg neo-Kantianism, see Andrea Poma, *The Critical Philosophy of Hermann Cohen* (Albany, NY: State University of New York Press, 1997); Andrea Poma, *Yearning for Form and Other Essays on Hermann Cohen's Thought* (Dordrecht: Springer, 2006); Judy Deane Saltzman, *Paul Natorp's Philosophy of Religion within the Marburg Neo-Kantian Tradition* (New York: Olms, 1981). See also the introductions in Hermann Cohen, *Reason and Hope: Selections from the Jewish Writings of Hermann Cohen*, ed. Eva Jospe (Cincinnati, OH: Hebrew Union College Press, 1993) and William Kluback, *The Idea of Humanity: Hermann Cohen's Legacy to Philosophy and Theology*, Studies in Judaism (Lanham, MD: University Press of America, 1987). For more general introductions to neo-Kantian thought, see Beck, 'Neo-Kantianism' in *Encyclopedia of Philosophy*, ed. Paul Edwards (New York: Macmillan, 1967); Thomas E. Willey, *Back to Kant: The Revival of Kantianism in German Social and Historical Thought, 1860–1914* (Detroit, MI: Wayne State University Press, 1978).

between the philosophers and theologians in Marburg was the relationship between religion and consciousness. Barth specifically comments on Herrmann's need to shore up a barrier against 'the conception of Kant that ethics, moral idealism or moral earnestness would be the path leading directly to religion'.[43] Cohen and Natorp tended to follow a Kantian line of thought, delimiting religion as a subset of ethics.[44] For his part, Herrmann sets out to respond to the neo-Kantians by articulating the parameters of an autonomous religious consciousness. 'As he wrote in the concluding sentence of *Die Metaphysik,* "When we seek to do theological work, we need not clutch at the goals of metaphysics". The object of Christian faith does not lie within the realm of knowledge of the world. Science and philosophy's methodical knowledge of reality absolutely cannot touch the reality of our God.'[45]

Herrmann's approach was deeply invested in the theology of Ritschl. With Ritschl, the solution to the intertwining of Kant's critique of metaphysics and theology was a radical separation of theology from metaphysics. Theology has to do with the spiritual, and whatever metaphysics is about it does not adequately apprehend what is proper to theological reflection alone.[46] Although in many ways Ritschl was one of the early progenitors of the break between theology and metaphysics after Kant, he nonetheless left a series of ambiguities which would require further clarification.[47] It is in this space that Herrmann would step in both as an early follower

---

43 Barth, 'The Principles of Dogmatics According to Wilhelm Herrmann (1925)', p. 244.
44 It should be noted that Cohen's position was at times different than the position being presented here in Barth. 'In *Der Begriff der Religion im System der Philosophie* Cohen's views on the subject substantially changed. As we have seen, here religion was no longer considered a simple "state of nature", which became part of culture, only inasmuch as it was taken over by ethics: religion is itself a "fact of culture", and, as such, must occupy a position in the system of philosophy. Here too Cohen rejected the "independence" of religion in the system: the system of philosophy was entirely and exhaustively articulated in the three "directions" of consciousness (knowledge, will and feeling) and religion could not constitute an independent fourth direction'. Andrea Poma, *Yearning for Form*, pp. 175–6.
45 Claude Welch, *Protestant Thought in the Nineteenth Century,* vol. II (New Haven, CT: Yale University Press, 1972), p. 45.
46 Albrecht Ritschl, 'Theology and Metaphysics', in *Three Essays* (Philadelphia, PA: Fortress Press, 1972), p. 155.
47 Fisher, *Revelatory Positivism?*, p. 126.

Barth's 'God is God'

of Ritschl as well as a key inspiration for his ideas.⁴⁸ One thing is for sure, 'it was Herrmann who, even more forcibly than Ritschl, made it his goal to exclude every last vestige of metaphysics from theology'.⁴⁹ One of the key ways in which he did so was to take on the philosophical rigour of the neo-Kantians in a way which Barth explicitly cites.

> True religion carries in itself the energy of the moral purpose. It is inextricably bound to the moral will and it will itself be the moral will; but it is neither begotten by it (Kant), nor identical with it (Cohen), nor is it the objectless emotion which accompanies it (Natorp). It has also its own root and its own life.⁵⁰

It is on this basis, this religious mode of consciousness, that Herrmann would establish his theological programme. One of the more interesting aspects of this programme is his understanding of the inner life of Jesus and the implications this had for Herrmann's engagement with the Reformation debates on the two natures of Christ. Barth's critique of Herrmann's 'divergence from Luther' on this point is of particular importance to our understanding of Barth's own early apprehension of Luther's Christology. Herrmann rejected all accounts of the historical Jesus as binding for his a-metaphysical religious experience. Thus Lessing's 'broad ugly ditch'⁵¹ is crossed not through historical critical methodology,

---

48 McCormack, *Karl Barth's Critically Realistic Dialectical Theology*, p. 51.

49 McCormack, *Karl Barth's Critically Realistic Dialectical Theology*, p. 51. This may explain why Heidegger read Ritschl through Troeltsch and found them both to be a metaphysical theology far too dependent on Greek categories; Martin Heidegger, *The Phenomenology of Religious Life* (Bloomington: Indiana University Press, 2004), pp. 14, 17. Heidegger does not in fact cite Herrmann and fails to recognize this alternative theological disposition which arose through and along with Ritschl's thought. It could be argued, however, that Herrmann's position is wholly consistent with Heidegger's depiction of Schleiermacher and, in this sense, Heidegger's own desire to proffer a pure primordial religiosity. See also Chapter 2 above.

50 Barth, 'The Principles of Dogmatics According to Wilhelm Herrmann (1925)', p. 245, citing Herrmann's *Gesammelte. Aufsätze*, pp. 133, 140, 381.

51 Gotthold Ephraim Lessing, 'On the Proof of the Spirit and of Power (1777)', in *Philosophical and Theological Writings*, ed. Hugh Barr Nisbet (Cambridge: Cambridge University Press, 2005), p. 87.

nor the dogmatic teachings of Jesus in the Bible,[52] but rather the actual revelation of Jesus as he confronts us in our contemporary experience. As Herrmann puts it in his *The Communion of the Christian with God*,

> In the Christian fellowship we are made acquainted, not merely with the external framework of Jesus' course amid the fates of life and of His work and history, but we are also led into His presence and receive a picture of His inner life. For this we are certainly dependent in the first instance, upon other men. For the picture of Jesus' inner life could be preserved only by those who had experienced the emancipating influence of that fact upon themselves. The personality of Jesus remained hidden from all others; it could only reveal itself to such as were lifted by it. Hence the picture of his inner life could be preserved in His church or 'fellowship' alone. But, further, this picture so preserved can be understood only when we meet with men on whom it has wrought its effect. We need communion with Christians in order that, from the picture of Jesus which His Brotherhood has preserved, there may shine forth that inner life which is the real heart of it.[53]

Christians encounter the inner life of Jesus in so far as he becomes an actual event in their lives then and there. 'All Christian discourse about the reality of God has its proper locus only within the relation into which God enters when he draws man into active communion with himself, and such communion is mediated exclusively through Jesus Christ'.[54] The inner life of Jesus thus inspires the inner life of the believer, and this interconnection of inner lives would inspire Herrmann to look for ways to simplify if not unify the nature of Christ. Herrmann would therefore reject any doctrine of the two natures of Christ because it caused an unhelpful differentiation to take place in the Christian's religious consciousness, and it is Luther who provides the justification for this move in Herrmann's theology.

---

52 Welch, *Protestant Thought in the Nineteenth Century*, II, pp. 46–7.

53 Wilhelm Herrmann, *The Communion of the Christian with God: A Discussion in Agreement with the View of Luther*, trans. J. Sandys Stanyon (London: Williams & Norgate, 1895), pp. 60–1, Book II, Chapter I, § 13.

54 Daniel L. Deegan, 'The Theology of Wilhelm Herrmann: A Reassessment', *The Journal of Religion* 45, no. 2 (1965), pp. 88–9.

Barth's 'God is God'

It is for these reasons that Barth cites Herrmann's *Systematic Theology* where he delineates the Lutheran critique of Chalcedonian Christology more fully.[55] Be it Lutheran kenosis or the undeveloped carrying forward of Chalcedonianism by the Reformed traditions, Herrmann's point is that Protestant theology requires further theological innovation and clarification. As Herrmann argues,

> Luther continued to employ the inadequate notion of a divine nature in Christ. All he did was to introduce a modification of the Christology of the Early Church, and in this he was followed by the Lutheran orthodoxy to the terms of the Formula of Concord, while the Reformed theology chose to stand by the dogma of Chalcedon.[56]

Herrmann believes that Luther's intention was to move beyond the dogma of the two natures of Christ in so far as he felt that the two 'must be regarded as more closely united than men usually consider them'.[57] However, although Luther recognized the need to correct any overemphasis on the radical distinction between Christ's human and divine natures, Luther would not give up the differentiation. As such, Herrmann argues that although Luther sought to clarify and correct the old dogma, he nonetheless 'bequeathed it as a hidden germ to those generations which should only wean themselves by long mental exercise from the forms of thought employed by the ancient church'.[58]

Herrmann's Christology would face some of Barth's harshest criticisms and the inner life of Herrmann's Jesus would pose one of the main problems. Barth begins by reiterating Herrmann's position as follows, 'That such a man, presenting these spiritual characteristics, lived on earth is "actuality" and this actuality *is* the Christian *revelation*'.[59] Barth's point is to demonstrate that in dissolving the

---

55 Wilhelm Herrmann, *Systematic Theology*, trans. Nathaniel Micklem and Kenneth A. Saunders (London: George Allen & Unwin Ltd, 1927), pp. 142, § 55.
56 Herrmann, *Systematic Theology*, 143, § 55.
57 Herrmann, *The Communion of the Christian with God*, 117, Book II, Chapter IV, § 2.
58 Herrmann, *The Communion of the Christian with God*, 118, Book II, Chapter IV, § 2.
59 Barth, 'The Principles of Dogmatics According to Wilhelm Herrmann (1925)', p. 264.

difference between the two natures of Jesus, the actuality which Herrmann speaks of is in fact a radical reduction of the divine into the human in such a way that his transcendence is totally lost. Interestingly, Barth makes this point by focusing on the 'is' under which Herrmann's notion of revelation stands. For the actuality of Jesus on earth *is* just as we are, and this ontological ambiguity between Jesus and us poses a problem for Barth.

> 'Is?' Yes. *Revelation* stands under the condition that this *is* becomes known in faith. But the *'is'* itself stands under no condition. One need only read in Herrmann's *Dogmatik* the significant (and to him obviously exceedingly important) historical §55 on the Christological dogma to be convinced that he held as a certainty the statement in support of which he could call upon Luther, apparently not without justification: '*In the power of the man Jesus* we apprehend God himself working upon us'. That is monophysite and it is impossible. In the power of *the man Jesus as such* we never 'apprehend' God himself.[60]

Crucially, Barth does not challenge the need to clarify Protestant Christology in his essay on Herrmann, only the manner in which to do so. This leaves us with a question concerning Barth's own approach to Lutheran and Reformed Christology. For Barth the two natures of Christ do not pose a problem to be abandoned, but rather to be worked through all the more vigorously. It is in this sense that we can begin to discern the meaning of Barth's 'God is God' in the Christological way that Busch suggests. Barth's discussions of Lutheran and Reformed Christology often imply ontological relations because Barth needs to clarify more precisely how Jesus 'is' in a way which is appropriate of both God and humanity.

Beyond Feuerbach

Feuerbach is an important figure for Barth in two distinct ways. First, he presents Barth with a radical critique of the anthropocentric tendencies of the theology of his teachers that he was seeking to

---

60 Barth, 'The Principles of Dogmatics According to Wilhelm Herrmann (1925)', p. 264.

Barth's 'God is God'

overcome in the early 1920s. Second, Feuerbach played a positive role in Barth's early thinking by inciting him to consider the merits of a Lutheran Christology which went beyond Herrmann's theological programme and the conflation of human and divine being which it implied. As we will see, responding to Feuerbach thus illuminated for Barth a way to respond to anthropomorphic theology without abandoning an immanent account of the humanity of Christ. The prominent theological voice in Feuerbach's *The Essence of Christianity* is Luther, and this provides a point of contact with Barth's own questions as he began to move beyond Herrmann. It is no coincidence that Barth gives his first significant lecture on Feuerbach in 1920, between the two editions of his *Römerbrief*. Here again, Busch's essay, 'God is God' is helpful in drawing our attention to the clarifications Barth was making in his theology at this time.

> Whatever we humans *want* and *can* call God on our own is 'in truth the human itself', for God is not acknowledged as God in it. It is in *this* context that Barth affirmed Feuerbach's thesis that religion has to do with human projections only.[61]

Here, Feuerbach provides an important insight into some of the guiding questions which led Barth to appropriate Luther's theology in the ways that he did. Feuerbach therefore plays an important part in furthering Busch's argument for the continuity between Barth's 'God is God' and his later Christology in so far as he continues to affirm Feuerbach's thesis throughout the 1920s and on into the 1930s.

Barth both affirms and critiques Feuerbach as a philosopher with critical theological interests, finding in him 'an antithesis which could be grounded only theologically'.[62] Feuerbach appeals to Barth because of his critique of both metaphysical and anthropomorphic projections of God. In both, humanity gets lost in the abstract projection of itself, which in the end distracts it from a more concrete humanism. In Feuerbach's words at the opening of Chapter 2 of his *The Essence of Christianity*, 'The True or Anthropological Essence

---

61 Busch, 'God is God', p. 106, citing Barth, *The Epistle to the Romans*, p. 44.
62 Karl Barth, 'Ludwig Feuerbach (1920)', in *Theology and Church: Shorter Writings, 1920–1928* (New York: Harper & Row, 1962), p. 217.

of Religion', 'In religion man contemplates his own latent nature. Hence it must be shown that this antithesis, this differencing of God and man, with which religion begins, is a differencing of man with his own nature.'[63] Thus in rejecting any religious propensity towards human abstractions Feuerbach seeks to return all the more fully to embrace human beings as they are, in their concrete existence. As Feuerbach has it, 'Think within *existence,* in the world as a part of it; not in the vacuum of abstraction as a solitary monad, nor as an absolute monarch, as an unparticipating God apart from this world'.[64] As a later commentator puts it, 'Feuerbach's purpose is to free religion from its illusion of objective transcendence and to free it for its ultimate purpose: the realization of love among men'.[65]

Feuerbach is not simply a religious cynic. In fact, his criticisms open the door to his own positive proposal, and Barth is quick to pick up on the Lutheran theology Feuerbach's thesis draws upon.[66] In developing the possibility of a true humanism, Feuerbach innovates explicitly upon Luther's Christology. For instance in Chapter 4, 'The Mystery of the Incarnation; or, God as Love, as a Being of the Heart', he says, 'It is the consciousness of love by which man reconciled himself with God, or rather with his own nature as represented in the moral law.'[67] He goes on to cite Luther as follows:

> Such descriptions as those in which the Scriptures speak of God as of a man, and ascribe to him all that is human, are very sweet and comforting – namely, that he talks with us as a friend, and of such things as men are wont to talk of with each other; that he rejoices, sorrows, and suffers, like a man, for the sake of the mystery of the future humanity of Christ.[68]

Feuerbach's point is that God as love must remain the basis for God as man if theology is to fully embrace the human being as he or she is.

---

63 Ludwig Feuerbach, *The Essence of Christianity*, trans. George Eliot (New York: Prometheus, 1989), p. 33.
64 Barth, 'Ludwig Feuerbach (1920)', p. 220.
65 Joseph C. Weber, 'Feuerbach, Barth and Theological Methodology', *The Journal of Religion* 46, no. 1 (1966), p. 27.
66 Barth, 'Ludwig Feuerbach (1920)', p. 217.
67 Feuerbach, *The Essence of Christianity*, p. 50.
68 Feuerbach, *The Essence of Christianity*, p. 50.

Barth's 'God is God'

Love determined God to the renunciation of his divinity. Not because of his Godhead as such, according to which he is the *subject* in the proposition, God is love, but because of his love, of the *predicate*, is it that he renounced his Godhead; thus love is a higher power and truth than deity. Love conquers God. It was love to which God sacrificed his divine majesty. And what sort of love was that? Another than ours? Than that to which we sacrifice life and fortune? Was it the love of himself? Of himself as God? No! It was love to man. But is not love to man human love? Can I love man without loving him humanly?[69]

It is precisely here, in Feuerbach's desire to affirm the human love of God, that Barth embraces him. What we mustn't miss, however, is the way Feuerbach's accentuation of the *human* love of God challenged Barth's early emphasis upon the *deus absconditus* in his first *Römerbrief* and points Barth towards an alternative Christological approach to thinking the relation between God and humanity. Barth, therefore, hears Feuerbach's critique as relevant to his own context and the 'new theology' he was now arguing against. As Barth says, 'it is equally true that the content of his anti-theology demonstrates the crucial importance of one possibility within the problem for the new theology'.[70] And again,

the problem can be seen as a general attack on the methodology of the theology of Schleiermacher and of post-Schleiermacher theology. It is the question of whether and how far religion, revelation, the relation between God and man, can be made understandable as a predicate of man.[71]

By engaging Feuerbach head on Barth is in fact allowing him to clarify – if not justify – his own theological intentions.

Here again it is important to note that the reason Feuerbach's critique of Idealist theology was so pervasive was because he was in fact building upon the full inheritance of Kant's critique of metaphysics. When Barth affirms Feuerbach's critique he is also affirming the totalistic and pervasive nature of Kant's philosophy. In fact,

---

69 Feuerbach, *The Essence of Christianity*, p. 53.
70 Barth, 'Ludwig Feuerbach (1920)', p. 218.
71 Barth, 'Ludwig Feuerbach (1920)', p. 227.

had Feuerbach's argument been made prior to Kant it would have been rejected out of hand as 'purely psychological hypotheses without any metaphysical significance'.[72] However, 'because of Kant's careful investigation in his *Critique of Pure Reason* which limits rational, theoretical knowledge to the phenomenal world, such an easy dismissal of Feuerbach is not possible'.[73] Kant himself recognized the problem of anthropomorphic theology in his *Religion within the Limits of Reason Alone* written near the end of his life (1793),[74] and Barth questions Kant along the same lines as he did Feuerbach, that is on the interconnection between anthropology and theology. Barth therefore accepts the Kantian nature of Feuerbach's critique but then, and this is Barth's genius, applies that critique to Feuerbach's work and finds it wanting. Furthermore, when Barth cites Feuerbach's call to 'think within existence' and the unity between thinking and being,[75] we must note the same attempt in the Neo-Kantianism of Hermann Cohen. As Simon Fisher puts it,

> Cohen, like Heidegger after him, believed that his own philosophy rested upon the insight of Parmenides' cryptic saying, 'to gar auto noein estin te kai einai', and that the 'Eleatic signpost', the identity of being and thinking, was the corner-stone of his system.[76]

Barth recognized that Feuerbach's critique of the abstract nature of theological idealism was also a covert critique of the way abstract being was inevitably reduced to the thinking subject in the neo-Kantian tradition. Barth's interest in Feuerbach would therefore not only demonstrate the futility of Herrmann's theology, but also point out the possibility of a genuine alternative. After Feuerbach, Barth would come to see that the solution to the anthropocentrism of theology would not come through an abandonment of metaphysics, but rather, through its proper attribution in the service of theology.

---

72 Weber, 'Feuerbach, Barth and Theological Methodology', p. 28.
73 Weber, 'Feuerbach, Barth and Theological Methodology', p. 28.
74 Immanuel Kant, *Religion within the Limits of Reason Alone* (London: Open Court Pub. Co., 1960), pp. 156–7.
75 Barth, 'Ludwig Feuerbach (1920)', p. 220, citing Ludwig Feuerbach, 'Philosophie der Zerkunft', pp. 86ff.
76 Fisher, *Revelatory Positivism?*, p. 22.

Barth's 'God is God'

It should come as no surprise, therefore, that Barth's pathway through Feuerbach is to focus in upon his formula, 'God becomes man, man becomes God'. Here we find Feuerbach's most forceful retort to abstract theological idealism. In this regard Barth praises Feuerbach's recovery of Luther's 'enthusiastic overemphasis ... that the deity is to be sought not in heaven but on earth, in the *man*, the *man*, the man Jesus'.[77] The question which arises for Barth is how we speak of man becoming God. Barth is quick to point out how Feuerbach's appropriation of Luther requires qualification,[78] and Barth's lectures on Feuerbach are in large part an attempt to demonstrate the nature of those qualifications. Barth has no problem with this formula as it stands, but rather, all that is at issue is the reversibility of his formula. As Barth puts it,

> To repulse Feuerbach's attack effectively one must be certain that man's relation with God is in every respect, in principle, an irreversible relation ... Therefore it is that the name of Feuerbach has been a thorn in the flesh of the newer theology and perhaps will continue so to be. So long as the irreversibility of the relation with God is not unconditioned and absolutely fixed under all circumstances, there will be no peace in this area.[79]

In Barth's view whatever we say of God must first be said of God and then, and only then, of humanity. Barth is reasserting the radical otherness of God here, and we must hear his emphasis upon the unknowability and hiddenness of God working through his critique of Feuerbach. In Busch's words, '"God is God" indicates that it is not *God* who is denied by this critical thesis but that it actually provides the critical force with which to deny that these human projections are God'.[80] And here we must hear the 'Calvinist certain somewhere' chiming in. As Barth would suggest in 'An Introductory Essay' that would accompany a 1957 edition of Feuerbach's *The Essence of Christianity*, to accept Luther one must always temper

---

77 Barth, 'Ludwig Feuerbach (1920)', p. 230.
78 Barth, 'Ludwig Feuerbach (1920)', p. 230.
79 Barth, 'Ludwig Feuerbach (1920)', p. 231. It should be noted that Luther himself refutes an unqualified reversal as well. Cf. Luther, *Works*, vol. 37, p. 207.
80 Busch, 'God is God', p. 106.

him with Calvin.[81] However, to do so without falling back into the same problem Feuerbach points out, Barth must not only justify how it is that the otherness of God is not an abstraction, but also the inadequacy of Feuerbach's own proposal.

It is for these reasons that Barth brings his most forceful critique to bear upon Feuerbach. And here we can point out the consistency between Barth's 1920 essay on Feuerbach and the revised version which appeared in Barth's lectures on *The History of Protestant Theology in the Nineteenth Century* in 1930. Here, as in the 1920 version, Barth argues that 'like all theologians of his time, Feuerbach discussed man in general, and in attributing divinity to him in this sense had in fact not said anything about man in his reality'.[82] By neglecting humanity's mortality Feuerbach neglected his own mandate and ended up with a generalized humanism abstracted from the human as he or she is on earth as a mortal being 'who must surely die'.[83] Barth sums up the reasons why Feuerbach had not been critiqued in this manner previously by pointing to his own proposal which began with an 'energetic cry' for God.

> But the theology of the time was not so fully aware of the individual, or of wickedness or death, that it could instruct Feuerbach upon these points. Its own hypotheses about the relationship with God were themselves too little affected by them. In this way they were similar to Feuerbach's, and upon this common ground his rivals could not defeat him. That was why the theology of his time found it ultimately possible to preserve itself in the face of him, as it had preserved itself in the face of D.F. Strauss, without summoning an energetic cry of '*God* preserve us!'[84]

Barth's contention is that if Feuerbach had addressed the human being as he or she really is, he would have recognized the need to maintain some form of differentiation between God and humanity.

---

81 Karl Barth, 'Introductory Essay', in *The Essence of Christianity*, ed. Ludwig Feuerbach (New York: Harper and Row, 1957), p. xxiv.

82 Karl Barth, 'Feuerbach', in *Protestant Theology in the Nineteenth Century: Its Background & History* (London: SCM Press, 2001), p. 525. For Barth's comparable conclusion in the 1920 version, see Barth, 'Ludwig Feuerbach (1920)', pp. 235-7.

83 Barth, 'Feuerbach', p. 526.

84 Barth, 'Feuerbach', p. 526.

Barth's 'God is God'

Barth goes on to imply that with all the positive insights Feuerbach offers, he must in the end find that Feuerbach did not significantly embrace concrete humanity sufficiently.

The historical location of Barth's lectures on Feuerbach during the 1920s offers further insight into how we understand the meaning of Barth's 'God is God'. Barth clearly recognizes that no credible theology will be able to speak without facing the challenge of anthropocentricism. After Feuerbach, however, any radical theological exteriority would not, in and of itself, provide the solution to the theological liberalism of his teachers. In this sense, a Calvinist overemphasis upon the divinity of God would not suffice. Hence, Barth would bring Feuerbach's critique of abstract idealism forward as a more full bodied explanation of the problems inherent in the theology and ethics which undergirded the cultural optimism of pre World War One Germany. Whatever we hear in Barth's 'God is God', an abstract idealism it is not. But neither is it a radical immanentism either, and here we would do well to note the polemic quality of Barth's early theology as it differentiated itself from his teachers, most specifically the Lutheranism of Herrmann.

In this context, Luther's *deus absconditus* now points us all the more forcefully to the full concrete humanity of Christ in a way which forces us to wonder how, if at all, we may ever speak of his divinity. As Luther says in his proofs for his *Heidelberg Disputation* in May of 1518, 'He who does not know Christ does not know God hidden in suffering ... Thus they call the good of the cross evil and the evil of a deed good. God can be found only in suffering and the cross'.[85] For Barth, Luther's *deus absconditus* implies that the humanity of Christ depends upon the radical hiddenness of God if it is to be truly God who reveals himself in the man on the cross, *deus revelatus*. Anthropocentric theology is only overcome by radicalizing Christ's finitude, by embracing God's hiddenness in such a way that Christ's divinity becomes impossible without an equally radical revelation. When Barth gives priority to Christ's divinity we must hear this as the reciprocal and deeply Lutheran counterpart of his affirmation of Christ's humanity. Barth's 'God is God' only enacts the desired result in response to Feuerbach if it is heard as Christ's cry of utter abandonment on the cross. In

---

85 Luther, *Works*, vol. 31, p. 53.

this sense, Barth recognizes that the divinity of Christ can only become a paradigm for our own humanity in so far as that divinity is revealed in the radical finitude of Jesus' death. Only, therefore, as Barth emphasizes Feuerbach's inability to embrace human finitude adequately, does the uniqueness of Barth's own theology become clear. This is because the radical finitude of Christ's humanity is the only option which Barth believes can ultimately disbar theology from an anthropocentric basis. As Barth concludes, 'so long as this nail is not firmly fixed, so long as all talk "of God being in man" is not cut off; we have no reason to disagree with Feuerbach'.[86] As such, although God cannot be seen in the human being on the cross, he is revealed there nonetheless. The radical embrace of human finitude, therefore, forces us to cry out all the more forcefully '*God preserve us*'.[87]

Luther in Barth's Reformed Theology

As Barth continues to explore Lutheran and Reformed Christology over the early 1920s, his commitment to clarifying the two natures of Christ in all their ontological significance only intensifies. Barth's Lutheran impulses are carried through in his 1923 *Lectures on the Theology of the Reformed Confessions,* which he gave in his early tenure in the Reformed professorate in theology at the predominantly Lutheran University at Göttingen. Here he is consistently explicating the position of the Reformed confessions in relation to the authority and ecumenicism of the Lutheran *Augsburg Confession*.[88] This is no less true than when Barth discusses the Christology of both. In an explication of the *Bremen Consensus* (1595) on the 'personal union [*unio personalis*]' Barth explores the unique way in which Christ's divine and human natures are interrelated. Contra the Lutheran tradition Barth argues,

> it is not by virtue of the human but of the *divine* nature that Christ is God, eternal, infinite, incomprehensible, and so on. The *human* nature, despite its exaltation, is neither deified nor does it

---

86 Barth, 'Feuerbach (1920)', p. 237.
87 Barth, 'Feuerbach', p. 526.
88 Barth, *The Theology of the Reformed Confessions*, pp. 1ff.

Barth's 'God is God'

participate in the divine being and divine qualities. With regard to his person, one must 'know all things in two ways, omnia duplicia'.[89]

Barth goes on to explicate 'the development of the doctrine of the "glory of the union, the offices, and the character" [*Gloria unionis, office, habitualis*] of Christ's humanity'.[90] But Barth is careful to note the conclusion of this confession, which emphasizes that 'there can be no talk of a mixing of Creator and creature'.[91] This radical differentiation sits at the heart of the 'Calvinist certain somewhere' as it critiqued and responded to what Barth refers to as 'a misreading of the intention of Lutheran doctrine'.[92] Although Barth is quick to note just how close the *Bremen Consensus* comes to Lutheran Christology, when it comes to the 'majestic type', the Reformed confession 'turns aside and refuses to speak the liberating word'.[93] In this type, the 'human nature was said to have what only can be ascribed to the divine, primarily omnipotence, omnipresence, and infinity'.[94] Barth goes on to cite the *Bremen Consensus* explicitly as it critiques the 'senseless paradoxes which the ubiquitists amass without limits, to the great distress and confusion of the church of God'.[95] Barth is clearly questioning the manner in which the *Bremen Consensus* understood the Lutheran doctrine as well as the efficacy of its own Christology. The concern Barth is raising here regards the relation between God and humanity or the very way in which the totally other God is revealed in the humanity of Christ. The way in which Barth highlights the 'Lutheran indignation at the "Calvinist certain somewhere" with the picture of the Reformed Christ absent in heaven'[96] is particularly poignant because Barth gives a general sense of the positive aspects of the Lutheran doctrine here

---

89 Barth, *The Theology of the Reformed Confessions*, p. 183 citing *Bekenntnisschriften der reformierten Kirche* (BSRK) 743, p. 36.
90 Barth, *The Theology of the Reformed Confessions*, p. 183, citing BSRK 746, pp. 14–17.
91 Barth, *The Theology of the Reformed Confessions*, p. 183.
92 Barth, *The Theology of the Reformed Confessions*, p. 184.
93 Barth, *The Theology of the Reformed Confessions*, p. 183.
94 Barth, *The Theology of the Reformed Confessions*, p. 183.
95 Barth, *The Theology of the Reformed Confessions*, p. 183, citing BSRK 746, pp. 9–11.
96 Barth, *The Theology of the Reformed Confessions*, pp. 183–4.

and his dissatisfaction with the Reformed dichotomization between the two natures of Christ.

In another lecture on 'Martin Luther's Doctrine of the Eucharist', in 1923 Barth explicates the Christological implications of Luther's debates concerning the Eucharist. Here, Barth confirms Bernard Lohse's more recent comment that 'not only the particular problems of the Lord's Supper were at issue for Luther, but ultimately the fundamental question of God's presence in the incarnate Christ'.[97] Here a Lutheran understanding of ubiquity plays a crucial part in Luther's doctrinal formulation on the Eucharist. One might assume Luther's doctrine of the Word would follow medieval nominalism according to the *via moderna* at Erfurt where Luther was trained.[98] In fact, Luther's teaching marked a contrast with the Occamite tradition. Luther's innovation gravitated around what we mean when we refer to Christ's presence at the right hand of the Father. Luther's innovation challenged the assumption by Biel and Occam that Christ was located in a particular place,[99] or that the right hand of God could be conceived as a particular place in heaven. In his 1526 sermon 'The Sacrament on the Body and Blood of Christ – Against the Fanatics', Luther argued 'that Christ's body is everywhere because it is at the right hand of God which is everywhere, although we do not know how that occurs'.[100] He argued that because Christ is everywhere the theological problem is not where is Christ, but rather, given that Christ is everywhere, how do we discern his presence properly? The end result was not to blur the lines between theology and, say, politics, but rather to make it all the more clear that although God was everywhere, it was only as God revealed himself that he could be discerned. As Luther says, 'It is certain that man must utterly despair of his own ability before he is prepared to receive the grace of Christ'.[101]

In Luther's doctrine of the Eucharist he emphasizes Christ's ubi-

---

97 Bernhard Lohse, *Martin Luther's Theology: Its Historical and Systematic Development*, Fortress Press ed. (Minneapolis, MN: Fortress Press, 1999), p. 172.

98 Alister E. McGrath, *Luther's Theology of the Cross: Martin Luther's Theological Breakthrough* (Oxford: Blackwell, 1985), p. 30. For more information on the *via moderna* in distinction to the *via antiqua* in late medieval scholastic theology, see Introduction above.

99 Lohse, *Luther's Theology*, p. 174.

100 Luther, *Works*, vol. 36, p. 342.

101 Luther, *Works*, vol. 31, p. 51.

quity precisely in order to teach us to look for him in particular places. As he says, 'where the Word is ... there you will lay hold of him in the right way'.[102] Luther's understanding of the Eucharist therefore cannot help but expect that when Christ says 'This is my body' (*hoc est corpus meus*) in reference to the bread, he means these words realistically and not merely symbolically and he is in this sense challenging the nominalism of his predecessors and contemporaries such as Ulrich Zwingli against whom many of his writings on the Eucharist are directed. Barth specifically picks up on this emphasis upon the Word of Christ amidst his omnipresence and in this sense draws our attention beyond the confines of a strictly Reformed Christology. As Barth puts it, 'Christ, who is truly this bread, is not to be enjoyed until "God speaks the Word thereby, so that you can hear him and recognize him. For what help is it to you if Christ sits in heaven or under the form of bread?"'[103] For Barth, Luther's 'dynamic understanding of the concepts "Word" and "faith" entailed the conclusion *a priori*; so that when the question of the meaning of this sentence was propounded, *est* had to mean, not *symbolizes,* but to all eternity *is*'.[104] Having said that, all Luther is concerned about is *that* Christ is really present in the bread, not *how* this is so. Barth cites Luther as follows: 'Do not scrutinize that miracle, but cling simply to the Word and let it be thine only care how thou canst receive the fruit of this sacrament, the remission of sins'.[105] Thus, Luther does not delve into the scholastic detail at this point, and nor does Barth for that matter at this point in his theological development. Rather, Barth's interest in Luther's doctrine looks past the ambiguity in Luther's ontology in order to focus on the ontological realism Jesus' 'is' implied.[106] Thus, Barth is most interested in the Luther who challenges a purely nominalist understanding of the Word. Here, God 'is' such that he is everywhere hidden and yet wholly revealed in the Word of Christ '*hoc est corpus*'.

---

102 Luther, *Works*, vol. 36, p. 342.
103 Karl Barth, 'Martin Luther's Doctrine of the Eucharist (1923)', in *Theology and Church: Shorter Writings, 1920–1928* (New York: Harper & Row, 1962), p. 76 citing Luther, *Works*, vol. 42, p. 59.
104 Barth, 'Martin Luther's Doctrine of the Eucharist (1923)', p. 110.
105 Barth, 'Martin Luther's Doctrine of the Eucharist (1923)', p. 102.
106 Barth, 'Martin Luther's Doctrine of the Eucharist (1923)', p. 103.

Protestant Metaphysics after Barth and Heidegger

To say that Barth became deeply interested in Lutheran theology during the early 1920s is not to say that Barth ever gave up his Reformed identity or became a Lutheran. Even in his lectures on the Reformed confessions where he is critical of the 'Calvinist certain somewhere' Barth eventually draws his students' attention to a line between the two confessions. As ambiguous as he leaves the decision, there is little question of where his affinities lay. He is more than happy to openhandedly summarize the *Bremen Consensus* against the

> Concordistic-Lutheran view that the heaven into which Christ ascended was not a place distinguished from heaven or hell but rather only the heavenly kingdom and thus everywhere, so that Christ did not have to ascend the width of a shoe, nail, or hair in order to come to the Father.[107]

He even goes so far as to insert a mode of dialectic into the Reformed position as it speaks of Christ's 'presence for us, of the aforementioned givenness of contingent revelation to us, only dialectically, in a twofold manner, "omnia duplicia"'.[108] But this should not dissuade us from noting the distinctively Lutheran attention Barth gives to this doctrine by consistently drawing the 'Calvinist certain somewhere' in the direction of a dialectical relation. As Barth concludes the lecture for that day, 'bearing in mind that there is no clear third option out there, one will have to decide today either for the Lutheran or for the Reformed view, conscious of the problems present in both'.[109] Barth's appropriation of Luther therefore must be seen as he blazed his own trail beyond the inadequacies he found in the contemporary theology in the early 1920s. The ubiquitous realism of Luther's Christology with its dialectic between *deus absconditus* and *deus revelatus* would have been deeply attractive given Barth's own need to work through a radical theological alterity that did not dissolve into idealist abstraction.

---

107 Barth, *The Theology of the Reformed Confessions*, p. 184, citing BSRK 1025, pp. 33–1026, pp. 13, 749, pp. 16–20.
108 Barth, *The Theology of the Reformed Confessions*, p. 184.
109 Barth, *The Theology of the Reformed Confessions*, p. 184.

Barth's 'God is God'
The Difference Luther's Christology Makes

The Lutheran nature of Barth's tautology, 'God is God' brings us to a deeper question concerning the onto-theological nature of that statement. It is one thing to argue that a theological realism informed Luther's Christological ubiquity which resided at the heart of Barth's early proclamation 'God is God', but it is quite another to justify this claim in light of the critical demands of the luminaries which haunted the theological task in Barth's context. Barth was not the first, nor only theologian of his generation approaching Marburg philosophy and theology in new ways. Rather, those like Franz Rosenzweig and Martin Buber could be counted along with Barth's Protestant contemporaries Rudolf Bultmann and Emil Brunner in their interest in the crisis in idealism at this time. Theologians and philosophers alike began to enquire into the possibility that theology itself might pose new-found answers to the inadequacies of pre-World War One philosophy, politics and theology. As we have already noted, Heidegger's early Freiburg lectures were classic examples of this endeavour, but the 'crisis' in German idealism opened doors for other more theologically explicit approaches to clarifying if not rectifying Kant's legacy as well. As Ely Gordon has recently commented regarding Rosenzweig's relation to this context,

> The crisis of confidence in idealism's powers was felt most dramatically among that younger generation of thinkers who came of age just before the First World War. For many of them, German and German Jewish alike, the collapse of the older, academic style of philosophy was heralded as a great victory. The turn to religion seemed to promise a new breakthrough, a reinvigoration of the philosophical discipline.[110]

It is all the more striking, therefore, when we compare Barth's interpretation of Luther during this time to Heidegger's. Heidegger attempted to carry through what he perceived to be Luther's unfinished project, which meant a radical break between ontology and theology. As we noted in the previous chapters, although Heidegger

---

110 Peter Eli Gordon, *Rosenzweig and Heidegger: Between Judaism and German Philosophy* (Berkeley: University of California Press, 2003), p. xxviii.

recognized the ambiguity in his own reading of Luther, he is most interested in the critique of metaphysics which can be located there. Heidegger recognized a need to investigate a radical fundamental ontology. Thus, Luther's critique of metaphysics had to be thoroughly carried through by Heidegger. When Heidegger cites Ritschl as a positive citation of his own understanding of the Lutheran break between metaphysics and theology, we now can see that he is in fact arguing for a post-metaphysical theology wholly consistent with Herrmann, who was a crucial instigator, if not a more comprehensive example, of this impulse in Lutheran theology at the time. It is in this light that we can begin to discern what is at stake in Heidegger's interpretation of Luther. It is our contention that when Heidegger cites theses 19, 21 and 22 of Luther's *Heidelberg Disputation* in his *Phenomenology of Religious Life*,[111] he gives a crucial clue concerning the difference between his approach to theology and Barth's. Although it is true that Luther does critique the theologian 'who looks upon the invisible things of God as though they were clearly perceptible in those things which have actually happened' in thesis 19 of his *Heidelberg Disputation*, Luther goes on in thesis 20 (which Heidegger skipped) to explicitly cite the proper basis of metaphysical theology as follows: 'He deserves to be called a theologian, however, who comprehends the visible and manifest things of God seen through suffering and the cross.'[112] In other words, Christology *is* the proper means by which Luther works out the ontological implications of his theology. It is precisely in his Christology that the intersection of theology and ontology are held together in difference. That is the heart of why it was so important for Luther to maintain the two natures of Christ and why the '*is*' in Jesus's 'This is my body', demanded his attention.

What we have been demonstrating in this chapter is the way in which Barth inherited Luther's infatuation with the 'is' in his Christology. Barth was drawn to Lutheran Christology and the ubiquity and immanence that it implied as the counterpart to a radical affirmation that God alone is God. Introducing Barth's interest in Luther's theology however, must not lead us to conclude that Barth was satisfied with the ontological ambiguities Luther allowed.

---

111 Heidegger, *The Phenomenology of Religious Life*, p. 213.
112 Luther, *Works*, vol. 31, p. 52.

Barth's 'God is God'

Just as Heidegger and Herrmann sought clarification after Luther, so too would Barth. The ambiguities in Luther's Christology would prove wholly inadequate as Barth continued to clarify just what the 'is' in his own declaration that 'God is God' meant under the weight of the developments in the theology of Barth's contemporaries such as Bultmann and Brunner. Was Barth an existentialist? Was he returning to medieval scholasticism and a Heideggerian notion of onto-theology such a move implied? Such questions haunted Barth throughout the 1920s, and were only resolved in his own mind after he finished his book on Anselm's *Proslogion* 2–4, and the ontological proof for the existence of God delineated therein. What we must come to see is how Barth's affirmation that 'God is God' utterly depends on a radical overthrow of Kant's claim that 'to speak of existence or non-existence is *per se* not to speak of God'.[113] Given the influence of Kant upon Barth's contemporaries, it is all the more striking that he concludes his explication of Anselm as follows: 'that anyone could seriously think that it is even remotely affected by what Kant put forward against these doctrines – all that is so much nonsense on which no more words ought to be wasted'.[114] It is to Barth's book on Anselm, therefore, that we now turn for this further clarification of what he would mean by 'God is God'.

---

[113] Barth, *Protestant Theology in the Nineteenth Century*, p. 261.
[114] Karl Barth, *Anselm: Fides Quaerens Intellectum* (London: SCM Press, 1960), p. 171.

4

Returning Barth to Anselm

Barth's Anselm

In the preface to the first edition of Barth's *Anselm: Fides Quaerens Intellectum*, he argues that his newly inspired interest in Anselm was shaped by a guest lecture given by his 'philosopher friend Heinrich Scholz of Münster on the Proof of God's Existence in Anselm's *Proslogion*'.[1] Barth says that it was this lecture which 'produced within me a compelling urge to deal with Anselm quite differently from hither to, to deal directly with the problematical Anselm, the Anselm of *Proslogion* 2–4'.[2] Barth is aware, therefore, that what he writes in 1930 has moved on from his 1926 lectures on Anselm's *Cur Deus Homo*, which he gave in the summer semester as a professor in Münster,[3] and he cites the latter half of his book on Anselm, the specific exegesis of *Proslogion* 2–4, as the locus of that difference.[4] It is these prefatory remarks which echo throughout his later consistent citations of Anselm as a turning point in his thought.[5]

Barth breaks up his book on Anselm into two parts. The first part covers the context of Anselm's theological scheme or method, that is 'the general context of his "proving"'.[6] The primary chal-

---

[1] Karl Barth, *Anselm: Fides Quaerens Intellectum* (London: SCM Press, 1960), p. 7/G1. I will be referring to Ian Robertson's 1958 translation of the second edition of Barth's *Fides Quaerens Intellectum* and will give the page numbers for *Gesamtausgabe* volume 13 Karl Barth, *Fides Quaerens Intellectum* (Zürich: Theologischer Verlag, 1981).

[2] Barth, *Anselm*, p. 7/G1.

[3] Eberhard Busch, *Karl Barth: His Life from Letters and Autobiographical Texts* (London: SCM Press, 1976), p. 169.

[4] Barth, *Anselm*, p. 8/G3.

[5] Karl Barth, *Church Dogmatics*, ed. G. W. Bromiley and T. F. Torrance, trans. G. W. Bromiley, vol. III.4 (Edinburgh: T. & T. Clark, 1962), p. xii; Karl Barth, *How I Changed My Mind* (Richmond, VA: John Knox Press, 1966), pp. 42–3.

[6] Barth, *Anselm*, p. 8/G3.

Returning Barth to Anselm

lenge Barth faces in this first section on Anselm's theology is to interpret what Anselm means by proof. Barth is thereby attempting to extricate Anselm's understanding of proof from Aquinas and Kant's critiques of it, not to mention the engagements with Anselm contemporary to Barth's own theology by F. Christian Baur or J. Bainvel.[7] This context, however, provides the gateway to the second half of the book which explicates Anselm's *Proslogion* 2–4 in greater detail. When scholars assess Barth's 1930 book on Anselm we might assume that they would pay close attention to this latter exegesis of Anselm's proof given that Barth cites this part of the book as the reason for returning to Anselm in the early 1930s. In fact, however, this half of Barth's book has been consistently overlooked. This oversight can best be explained by Barth's preface to the second edition, which commends Hans Urs von Balthasar's recognition that Barth's book on Anselm provided a 'vital key' to his theology.[8] Balthasar's interpretation of Barth focused on a shift from dialectic to an analogical way or method of theology.[9] As a result, scholarly debate concerning just what was significant about Anselm has often emphasized the introductory first section of the book, which delineates the context of Anselm's method, and not the general and special existence of God that Barth develops in the second part.

For instance, Jeffrey Pugh's *The Anselmic Shift* focuses upon Barth's introductory description of his approach to Anselm.[10] Pugh stands at the heart of the agreement with other commentators who also mark Anselm as a significant turning point in Barth's approach to the theological task.[11] In so doing, however, he rehearses the focus upon the assumed shift from dialectic to analogy which is thought to have taken place at this point in Barth's theological development,

---

7 Barth, *Anselm*, p. 8, cf. n. 1/G n. 3.
8 Barth, *Anselm*, p. 11/G6.
9 Hans Urs von Balthasar, *The Theology of Karl Barth: Exposition and Interpretation*, trans. Edward T. Oakes (San Francisco: Communio Books, Ignatius Press, 1992), p. 93.
10 Jeffrey C. Pugh, *The Anselmic Shift: Christology and Method in Karl Barth's Theology* (New York: P. Lang, 1990), pp. 93–118.
11 Hans W. Frei, 'The Doctrine of Revelation in the Thought of Karl Barth 1909–1922' (Doctoral Dissertation, Yale, 1956), pp. 193–4; Eberhard Jüngel, *Karl Barth: A Theological Legacy* (Philadelphia, PA: Westminster Press, 1986), pp. 41ff; Henri Bouillard, *The Knowledge of God* (London: Burns & Oates, 1969), pp. 63ff.

and does not give significant attention to the structure of the ontological relations Barth develops in the latter half of the book. Bruce McCormack, one of the more recent and influential commentators on Barth's theological development, follows suit in focusing on the first section of Barth's Anselm book. In his case, however, he does so in order to refute the emphasis upon an analogical shift that Balthasar argued can be located there.[12] In so doing, McCormack gives the impression that there is no significant difference between Barth's 1926 and 1930 lectures and thus de-emphasizes the significance of Anselm in development.[13] Although we will address McCormack's justifications for contradicting Barth's own self-assessment of his book on Anselm in our conclusions below, the question we are raising at the outset here is whether or not a more thorough engagement with Barth's exegesis of *Proslogion* 2–4 might give crucial insight into the onto-theological nature of the 'vital key' he referred to in his preface.

Presuppositions

Although the first part of Barth's book on Anselm does provide an insightful context for Anselm's theology overall, Barth in fact explains the significance of this context more clearly in the presuppositions to the second half of the book on the *Proslogion* itself. First, Barth clarifies the revealed name Anselm uses to designate God in *Proslogion* 2: '*aliquid quo nihil maius cogitari possit*'.[14] 'In German it can be paraphrased: "Etwas über dem Grösseres nicht gedacht werden kann". (Something beyond which nothing greater can be conceived.)'[15] The initial translation serves to orient the reader to the nature of the text itself as well as pointing to its unique function in Anselm's argument. As Barth says,

> we are dealing with a concept of strict noetic content which Anselm describes here as a concept of God. It does not say that God

---

[12] Bruce L. McCormack, *Karl Barth's Critically Realistic Dialectical Theology: Its Genesis and Development, 1909–1936* (New York: Oxford University Press, 1995), p. 421.
[13] McCormack, *Karl Barth's Critically Realistic Dialectical Theology*, p. 423.
[14] Barth, *Anselm*, p. 73/G75.
[15] Barth, *Anselm*, p. 74/G75.

is, nor what he is, but rather, in the form of a prohibition that man can understand, who he is.[16]

Anselm's name for God is in this sense a negative statement. It outlines the conditions and parameters any true positive statement of God's existence will have to follow. In other words, it depends upon a second assumption: 'the prior "givenness" (credible on other grounds) of the thought of the *Existenz* of the essence [*Wesen*] of God which with his help is to be raised to knowledge and proof'.[17]

---

16 Barth, *Anselm*, p. 75/G77.
17 Barth, *Anselm*, p. 75/G77. I have, wherever possible, left the different words Barth uses for existence, that is *Existenz, Dasein* and *daseiend* in German thus assuming a certain familiarity with these terms in philosophical English. As well, I have made more consistent translation of *Wesen* as essence, *Wahrheit* as truth and *Gegenständlichkeit* as objectivity. It should be noted that Barth does not clarify whether or not he is following a particular usage of any of these terms according to any previous authors. Given that Kant tended to use *Dasein* and *Existenz* invariably and synonymously, our argument here is that Barth is doing something different than Kant in his book on Anselm; Howard Caygill, 'Existence', in *A Kant Dictionary* (Oxford: Blackwell Publishing, 1995), p. 184. Having said that, his use of *Dasein* does not follow Heidegger's precisely and is closer in its use of *Existenz* to Karl Jaspers's terminology in his 1932 work *Philosophy*, trans. E. B. Ashton (Chicago: University of Chicago Press, 1969). Given that Barth's book on Anselm was written before the publication of this book, and to my knowledge Barth had no relation to Jaspers during this time, it seems safe to say that it was not Jaspers who was the inspiration for Barth's language here either, although Barth does engage Jaspers's use of *Existenz* in *Church Dogmatics* III.2, pp. 113ff in a relatively positive light and Barth did teach as a colleague of Jaspers's in Berne from 1948 onwards; Busch, *Karl Barth*, p. 351. A better suggestion concerning where Barth derived his use of his existential terminology, and this is the one we are assuming here, is that Barth may have shared Jaspers's interest in Hegel's use of these terms. For instance, it seems likely that Barth may have, at least at the back of his mind, Hegel's use of *Existenz* as follows: '*Existenz*, on Hegel's account, is a determination of essence. In the Logic it follows the category of ground: the notion of a ground develops into that of a condition (a *sine qua non*), and when the totality of conditions is realized the thing or matter (*Sache*) emerges into existence. The existent (*das Existierendes*) is a thing (*Ding*) with many properties.' M. J. Inwood, *A Hegel Dictionary* (Oxford: Blackwell, 1992), pp. 94–5. This contrasts with *Dasein* in Hegel as follows: '*Dasein*, Hegel says, is being (*Sein*) with determinacy (*Bestimmtheit*), an immediate determinacy (in contrast to an underlying essence), that is, a quality. (Hence *Dasein*, in this context, is usually translated as "determinate being").' Inwood, *A Hegel Dictionary*, p. 94. Determinate existence or objective existence is more or less what we believe Barth is after in his use of *Dasein* below, and this discussion of Hegel's terminology at least offers some context to what Barth may have been thinking. The problem with attributing *Dasein* to God is precisely Barth's problem in his book on Anselm.

Protestant Metaphysics after Barth and Heidegger

The name of God therefore provides the rule by which we might speak of the unique existence of God and come to demonstrate God's existence along the lines of Anselm's *Proslogion*.

It bears noting at this point what Barth developed previously in the first part of the book and the way commentators have tended to focus upon the more complicated and nuanced notion of *ratio* as Anselm understands it. 'What does *ratio* mean in Anselm?'[18] By asking this question Barth is in essence asking about the nature of 'the knowing *ratio* peculiar to man',[19] and the way in which Anselm applies *ratio* to both the knower and known objects. Here Barth distinguishes between the ontic *ratio* and the noetic *ratio* with the former referring to the known and the latter to the knower. But Barth recognizes here a peculiar use of *ratio* unique to faith and it is in this sense that the notion of *ratio* becomes important to Barth. For Barth, Anselm goes beyond human knowledge when he speaks 'of the *ratio fidei* or of the *ratio* of the words and acts of God, of the *ratio* of their possibility and necessity'.[20] It is in relation to this *ratio fidei*, that Barth interrelates the ontic and noetic *ratios*. Hence,

> if an ontic *ratio* were to be proved by means of the knowing *ratio* of the human faculty of making concepts and judgements, after the object of faith is given by revelation, then this conception would not be correctly interpreted until we take into account that Anselm recognizes a third and ultimate *ratio*, a *ratio veritatis*.[21]

Truth itself, therefore, is described here in terms of its inherent rationality. What we mustn't miss, however, is Barth's emphasis upon the way the object of faith becomes given in revelation as an *ontic ratio* in such a way that its proper interpretation is secured by a *ratio veritatis*. The object of faith is being discussed here after

---

Inwood's discussion of *Dasein, Daseiendes* and *Existenz* in Hegel in fact will track closely with Barth's use of these terms in his book on Anselm, and so we will promote this affinity in our translations below. Having said that, Barth does not cite Hegel in any sense, which leaves us with the presumption that all such conversations concerning what Barth means by *Existenz, Dasein* and *daseiendes* comes down to Barth's own development of these terms.

18 Barth, *Anselm*, p. 44/G44.
19 Barth, *Anselm*, p. 44/G44.
20 Barth, *Anselm*, p. 45/G45.
21 Barth, *Anselm*, p. 45/G45.

it has been revealed, and it therefore assumes a differentiation between the existence of God as an object for our thinking and the existence which is properly attributable to God in and for himself. What mustn't be missed at this point in Barth's argument is the way in which God is being discussed in terms of the *ratio veritatis*.[22] As Barth goes on to say, 'it is not because it is *ratio* that it has truth but because God, Truth, has it'.[23] Thus all *rationes* are relative to God himself.[24]

Barth had, as has been noted by scholars such as Eberhard Busch, already developed the possibility whereby the radical otherness of God could be articulated as a constitutive reality early on in the 1920s – such as Barth's enigmatic proclamation 'God is God'.[25] What Barth is establishing here in his Anselm book in the early 1930s, however, is the difference between the existence of God himself and the way in which God becomes known according to the ontic and noetic *rationes*. If we were to say, as McCormack does, that 'ontic *ratio* stands at the beginning and at the end of the *intellectus fidei*. It is that which is sought, but it is also that which gives rise to the search in the first place',[26] then we must also emphasize that Barth has left open at this point in the first half of his book on Anselm's context, the existence of the Truth which stands beyond all knowing. Although Anselm believes that the *ratio fidei* is identical with the *ratio veritatis,* Barth is quick to add that 'even here decision enters into it, not as to whether it is *ratio veritatis* but whether it can be recognized as such'.[27] It is this *recognition* of the *ratio veritatis* in the ontic *ratio* of the object of faith that Barth is focusing upon in the first section of his book on Anselm. He is not trying to finalize the ontological nature of the Truth, but rather to bracket the ontological nature of that Truth off and to demonstrate the need to explicate further its unique existence, an existence which is not identical with the ontic *ratio* itself.

---

22 Barth, *Anselm*, p. 45/G45.
23 Barth, *Anselm*, p. 45/G45.
24 Barth, *Anselm*, p. 48/G47.
25 Eberhard Busch, 'God is God: The Meaning of a Controversial Formula and the Fundamental Problem of Speaking about God', *The Princeton Seminary Bulletin* 7, no. 2 (1986).
26 McCormack, *Karl Barth's Critically Realistic Dialectical Theology*, pp. 430–1.
27 Barth, *Anselm*, p. 47/G46–47.

Protestant Metaphysics after Barth and Heidegger

As we return to Barth's presuppositions to his exegesis of Anselm's *Proslogion*, he deals more specifically with the importance of his discussion of the ontic and noetic *rationes* by developing Gaunilo's critique of Anselm's name for God. Gaunilo maintains that the name of God is in itself a blinding symbol which cannot provide the

> truth in relation to God. Whether it be the word *Deus* or Anselm's formula – the word itself could not provide him with a knowledge of God unless some extension of what the word is meant to denote were also given to him from another source.[28]

Barth's contention here is that Gaunilo has misunderstood the noetic nature of Anselm's name for God. Of course, Anselm himself would agree that God remains hidden in the ontic objectification of God and that God is always incomprehensible. What Anselm has done with his particular name of God, however, is first to lay 'down a rule of thought which, if we follow it, enables us to endorse the statements about the essence [*Wesen*] of God accepted in faith (example, the statement of his incomprehensibility) as our own necessary thoughts'.[29] This is why it is so important to Barth that we begin with the noetic nature of Anselm's name before moving on to its ontic objectification. When we make this distinction we can see that Anselm's name for God isn't trying to produce knowledge of God out of a vacuum, but rather he provides this statement as an axiom, as a guiding rule of thought from which the argument for the existence of God could properly follow.[30]

In delimiting Anselm's *aliquid quo nihil cogitari possit* as a rule for knowing God, Barth is explicitly demonstrating the need for that something greater than what can be conceived. It is in this sense that Barth interprets Anselm's procedure for attributing existence to God and this brings us to the second introductory clarification Barth makes in the presuppositions he offers before he delves into the *Proslogion* itself. Here he justifies his interpretation of Anselm's use of *esse* in the *Proslogion* in terms of '*existere* or *subsistere*'.[31] By interpreting *esse* in terms of *existere* Barth means to emphasize

---

28 Barth, *Anselm*, p. 79/G81.
29 Barth, *Anselm*, p. 80/G82.
30 Barth, *Anselm*, p. 81/G82.
31 Barth, *Anselm*, p. 90/G91.

Returning Barth to Anselm

the way the recognition of that than which nothing greater can be conceived demands a notion of existence *over against* thought. In explaining this relationship Barth explicates Gaunilo and Anselm's discussion of a painter's creation. The painter thinks of what he will paint and then paints it into existence. By applying this analogy to Anselm Gaunilo presumes that he has discredited his argument because Anselm makes the move from the mind to reality without qualifying how the exterior reality is established.[32] In response, Anselm contends that what Gaunilo overlooks is that there is more going on here than mere painter and painted in his proof. What Anselm attributes to the mind is that than which nothing greater can be conceived. If, therefore, anyone presumes that they have thought of what is greater, they will naturally have to admit that its existence goes beyond their cognition.[33] The structure of Anselm's name for God precludes any reduction to the mind alone. We do not presume that the painter could dream up a unicorn and then because he painted it that unicorns do in fact exist. Rather, the thought and the object of thought have to correspond to a third form of existence, and here Barth argues that Anselm's name of God corresponds to a special mode of 'thought, and if known and proved then it has to be specially known and proved'.[34] This special mode of thought and proving presumes therefore a special mode of questioning which asks not just what is *thought,* but *what* is thought.[35]

Here we must engage a longer citation where Barth deepens his discussion of the painter and painting in terms of three circles which demonstrates further what this special proving entails.

> It asks whether and to what extent this object [*Gegenstand*], as surely as it is the object of thought [*Gegenstand des Denkens*], at the same time stands over against [*entgegensteht*] thought [*Gedacht*] and is itself not to be reduced [*aufzulösen*] to something that is merely thought [*bloßes Gedachtes*]; it asks whether and to what extent, while belonging to the inner circle of what is thought

---

32 Anselm, *The Major Works,* ed. Brian Davies and G. R. Evans (Oxford: Oxford University Press, 1998), p. 106.
33 Anselm, *The Major Works,* pp. 113–15.
34 Barth, *Anselm,* p. 92/G93.
35 Barth, *Anselm,* p. 92/G93.

[*Gedachten*], it also 'protrudes' [*heraustritt*] into the outer circle of what is not only thought [*Nichtnurgedachten*], but exists independently of thought [*dem Denken gegenüber selbständig Seinden*]. For Anselm, on this *ex-sistere* of the object [*Gegenstandes*] depends nothing less than its true-being [*Wahrsein*]. Its being in truth [*Das Sein in der Wahrheit*] is for Anselm, as it were, the third and last outer circle by which the existence [*Dasein*] and within the existence [*Daseins*], the existence in thought [*Gedachtsein*], must be enclosed if a thought [*Gedachtsein*] ...[36] is to be true [*wahr sein soll*]. The object [*Gegenstand*] then is first of all in truth [*Wahrheit*], then following from that it exists [*ist er da*], then as a consequence of that it can be thought [*gedacht sein*]. Without the middle step of existing [*Daseins*] what is thought [*Gedacht*] could not truly be [*nicht wahr sein*].[37]

Because of the way in which God is named as that than which nothing greater can be conceived, the noetic character of that name demands an ontic referent which can be apprehended only as that greater beyond even itself. Barth consistently refers to this ontic referent in terms of *Dasein, ist da,* etc. But this greater object cannot subsist as an ontic objectification. Rather it only is [*ist da*] in relation to the necessity of the thought [*Gedacht*] of that than which nothing greater can be conceived. If this were not the case, then Gaunilo would be right and the artist's creation would never fully extricate itself from the artist's mind. Barth therefore differentiates the objective being [*Dasein*] of the object of thought from its true being [*Wahrsein*] which is presumed beyond the ontic objectification. It is here, precisely in the distance and relation between the ontic object and its true being, that Barth establishes his proof for the unique existence of God in his exegesis of *Proslogion* 2–4.

Barth takes the time in his presuppositions to orient his readers to the ontological language games that he will be playing throughout

---

36 I have specifically removed the following: 'that is an object that is thought' from this citation because it is an addition to the German text that the translators seem to have added for clarification. In fact, this addition only confuses the point by referring to the object of thought out of place in Barth's concise ordering of the relation between the object of thought, its existence in thought alone and its true being.

37 Barth, *Anselm*, p. 92/G93–4.

his exegesis of the *Proslogion*. As he says in one of the more concise examples of those games, '*Existenz* means in general the *Dasein* of an object [*Gegenstandes*] without regard to whether it is thought of as existing [*daseiend*]'.³⁸ This brief statement sums up the basic contours of Barth's interpretation of Anselm's proof. Hence, when discussing the general *Existenz* of God in relation to *Proslogion* 2, Barth uses *Dasein* in every translation of Anselm's argument in order to emphasize its existence over against thought. When he turns to the specific *Existenz* unique to God in *Proslogion* 3, he switches and uses *nicht-daseiend* to indicate the negative prohibition against attributing the general concept of existence [*Existenz*] to God without qualifying it as the *Dasein* which is impossible not to be [*nicht-daseiend*]. Needless to say that these language games are wholly lost in the English translations, and this no doubt has contributed to the oversight of the importance of what Barth is doing in the second half of his book on Anselm.

Proslogion 2–4

Given that we have already outlined the ontological differentiations which make up the heart of Barth's presuppositions to Anselm's *Proslogion* 2–4, our goal here is simply to demonstrate the way these presuppositions work themselves out in his exegesis of these passages more explicitly. It is in this light that we must pay close attention to Barth's use of language in his translation of *Proslogion* 2, the first part of which Barth gives as follows: '*quod vere sit Deus* (I 101, 2) That God truly exists [*Daß Gott in Wahrheit da sei*]'.³⁹ Barth's interest is in the true existence of God, and how Anselm's proof delineates the pattern to arrive at it. To begin with, then, Barth again points out that Anselm's use of *esse* must in fact mean *existere* which correlates with Barth's use of *Dasein*, or a kind of determinate or objective being which clarifies the general concept of existence [*Existenz*] in relation to the thought alone. In order to explain more precisely why this must be so, Barth comments on Anselm's use of *vere* which outlines his approach to the general (*Prosl.* 2) and special (*Prosl.* 3) proofs for God's existence more specifically.

---

38 Barth, *Anselm*, p. 97/G99.
39 Barth, *Anselm*, 100/G103.

Protestant Metaphysics after Barth and Heidegger

In reference to *Proslogion* 2 Barth says,

> God does not exist [*ist da*] only in thought [*Denken*] but over against thought [*Denken gegenüber*]. Just because he exists [*da ist*] not only 'inwardly' but also 'outwardly' (*in intellectu et in re*), he (from the human standpoint) 'truly' exists [*ist*], exists [*ist da*] from the side of truth [*Wahrheit*] and therefore really [*wirklich*].[40]

Here, Barth explicitly draws attention to the relation between an inward and outward existence from the human standpoint. It is this inner and outer aspect of *Dasein* which Barth demonstrates in his explication of *Proslogion* 2, and this also lays the heuristic pattern that the rest of the proof will follow. Hence, Barth then goes on to explain the way in which this general understanding of *Dasein* opens up a proper assessment of *Proslogion* 3 which explores the special manner in which we can attribute existence [*Existenz*] to God, and God alone, as an existence [*Dasein*] which is uniquely different from all other existents.[41] The two proofs are therefore deeply dependent upon each other.

In Barth's view, the goal of *Proslogion* 2 is to explicate the *general* sense of existence which Anselm's name for God, 'something beyond which nothing greater can be conceived' implies.[42] As he says, this name 'conceals no declaration about the essence [*Wesen*] of God and still less about God's *Existenz*. The formula simply repeats the injunction inculcated on the believer's thinking'.[43] Barth is using *Existenz* in order to explain the problem with presuming an uncritical conception of existence upon Anselm's proof. Barth's prohibition is therefore not against the attribution of existence to God, but rather his concern is with attributing existence to God in a way which does not take account of the manner which Anselm's name for God dictates. This is a relation Barth attempts to clarify with his use of *Dasein* and Anselm's *existit*. It should be noted at this point that the German *Existenz* is derived from the Latin *existentia*, which 'is the existence of something in contrast to its *essentia*

---

40 Barth, *Anselm*, p. 101/G103.
41 Barth, *Anselm*, p. 101/G103.
42 Barth, *Anselm*, p. 102/G105.
43 Barth, *Anselm*, pp. 102–3/G105.

Returning Barth to Anselm

or nature'.[44] In Barth's interpretation of Anselm's *Proslogion*, however, he gives the impression that *Existenz* has lost this differentiation from essence, and Barth seeks to recover the stand-out character of *existentia* by developing the meaning of *Dasein*. It is as he gives a proper account of how *Dasein* is attributable to God that a proper understanding of how God is related to the general concept of *Existenz* can follow.

No more apparent is the need for this differentiation between *Dasein* and *Existenz* in *Proslogion* 2 than in Barth's discussion of the fool's ability to deny the *Existenz* of God. The fool's denial of God is referred to again more fully in Barth's explication of *Proslogion* 4, but at this point Barth wants to refute the fool's mistake and demonstrate the basis upon which *Proslogion* 4 can stand. Anselm's enquiry into the fool is really an enquiry into whether the object of Anselm's name for God is in fact first a true object. Barth is therefore trying to clarify what Anselm's approach means for the concept of *Existenz* as 'the inconceivable existence [*transmentalen Existenz*] of God'.[45] It is the believer's different attitude towards this transmental *Existenz* that determines his or her understanding of its relation to whatever we mean when we apply the general concept of *Existenz* to existing things. As the believer accepts the need he or she has to know the inconceivable God as that than which nothing greater can be conceived, then they reflect 'two different modes of human existence [*Existenzweisen*]'.[46] The problem of how the *insipiens* is able to say what Anselm deems impossible is resolved therefore, through this differentiation. Barth responds to the fool's ability to say in his heart that there is no God by demonstrating the unqualified notion of God's *Existenz* which the fool's rejection depends upon. As such, the fool does not follow the procedure indicated by the name of God which demands the differentiation between the general concept of *Existenz* and the *Dasein* which is given to us according to Anselm's faithful way of knowing.

Barth's discussion of the relationship between the fool and Anselm's proof opens up more fully into the heart of *Proslogion* 2 at the point at which Anselm argues: '*Et certe id quo maius*

---

44 Inwood, *A Hegel Dictionary*, p. 94.
45 Barth, *Anselm*, pp. 103–4/G106.
46 Barth, *Anselm*, p. 105/G108.

cogitari nequit, non potest esse in solo intellectu'.[47] Barth translates Anselm at this point as follows: 'And certainly "that than which nothing greater can be conceived" cannot exist [*da sein*] only in knowledge'.[48] Barth is therefore building on what he has previously said concerning the reasons why Anselm begins with the thought of God's being [*Gedachtsein*] and the way this thought implies an ontic object [*Dasein*]. Barth believes that the significance of this portion of Anselm's *Proslogion* is rooted in the recognition that if we are to discuss the existence of God, we will have to do so in relation to all other existing things as we know them. In other words, when we say God exists outside the mind, we are confronted with the comparison between how we know other things which also exist outside the mind. This is the first [*zunächst*] time that this aspect of Anselm's proof of God's existence is raised in which 'things which are different from God also exist [*existiert*]',[49] and it is in this sense that Barth refers to *Proslogion* 2 as a proof of the *general* existence of God.

Barth summarizes what Anselm is proving in *Proslogion* 2 according to the necessary pathway from our own understanding of God's existence purely in the mind to the way in which Anselm's name for God demands an objective existence which beckons beyond itself. Anselm's text is as follows: '*Existit ergo procul dubio aliquid quo maius cogitari non valet, et in intellectu et in re*' and Barth translates it in his usual way: 'Thus objectively as well as in knowledge there does undoubtedly exist [*ist da*] "something than which nothing greater can be conceived"'.[50] Thus, the point of *Proslogion* 2 is to demonstrate the general sense in which objective ontic *Dasein* as well as existence in the mind alone [*Gedachtsein*] can be attributed to God. As Barth concludes his comment on *Proslogion* 2, he draws specific attention to the translation given in other German commentaries on this text. Importantly, the German translation Barth cites uses *existiert*. This gives Barth opportunity to draw attention to his own use of *Dasein* and what he is doing in his own explication of Anselm's proof by pointing out the problem with leaving existence in an ambiguous state of expression. As he says,

---

47 Barth, *Anselm*, p. 123/G126.
48 Barth, *Anselm*, p. 123/G126.
49 Barth, *Anselm*, p. 123/G126.
50 Barth, *Anselm*, p. 127/G130.

Returning Barth to Anselm

It follows from the whole content of the chapter that the emphasis of the sentence is not on this *existit*, which in itself is ambiguous, but on what explains it – *et in intellectu et in re*. Not till then does the *existit* become unambiguous.[51]

Hence, the name of God in *Proslogion* 2 is the place to begin because it is in this name that the meaning of objective existence can be properly understood, and this is why Barth spends so much time delineating the different senses of existence implied by that name.

In Barth's interpretation, developing the meaning of the notion of *Dasein* as the ontic objective existence allows him to be more true to the logic of Anselm's proof. By explicating the manner in which God becomes there for us in a determinate objective sense [*Dasein*] Barth is able to emphasize more clearly what previous commentators did not when they attributed *Existenz* to Anselm's proof in a more univocal sense. With different nuances in German, Barth is attempting to more appropriately capture what Anselm's name for God implies in terms of its objective existence beyond thought. *Dasein* already implies this existence over-against-thought and better captures what Barth believes Anselm is after in *Proslogion* 2. In short, all Barth believes Anselm has been proving here in *Proslogion* 2 is the general sense in which this objective existence [*Dasein*] is attributable to God in a way which is beyond mere existence in the mind alone. *Existenz* thus becomes, for Barth, the overarching concept against which he develops the general sense in which *Dasein* clarifies the ambiguous uses of *esse/existit* in Anselm.

Barth concludes *Proslogion* 2 precisely where *Proslogion* 3 will begin. That is, all Barth sought to establish with the first proof was that due to the nature of the name for God, any attribution of objective existence would have to go beyond thought alone. Thus, God's existence was being discussed in terms of the manner in which *Dasein* captured its nature as over-against thought. Barth was quick to point out, however, the negative nature of this proof.[52] It did not say anything unique or specifically positive about God's existence, but rather, left a vacuum out of which a positive and

---

51 Barth, *Anselm*, pp. 127–8/G131.
52 Barth, *Anselm*, p. 128/G131.

specific attribution of existence would have to follow. Although God must be beyond thought and share in existence with all other existents, God's existence must, in the end go beyond all other existents if God is to remain God. It is in this vacuum that Barth begins his explication of *Proslogion* 3 as follows: '*Quod non possit cogitari non esse*. That he could not be conceived [*gedacht*] as not existing [*nicht-daseiend*]'.[53] Note the use of present participle *daseiend* here. In using this term Barth emphasizes the present active sense in which we can attribute existence to God which relates to existing things. As Barth goes on to say, 'this heading denotes the second, more specific meaning of *vere sit*: God exists [*ist da*] in such a way (true only of him) that it is impossible for him to be conceived as not existing [*nicht-daseiend*]'.[54] It is in this sense that Barth can then narrow what he means by the general concept of the *Existenz* of God to the special sense in which it is proved in *Proslogion* 3.[55]

When Barth asks how *Proslogion* 3 is anything 'more than a mere repetition or underlining of this result from *Prosl.* 2?'[56] his answer follows the contours of the linguistic differentiations he has been making throughout his exegesis of Anselm's argument throughout.

Answers: in *Prosl.* 2 the concept of existence [*Begriff von Existenz*] was expressly the general concept of existence [*Dasein*] in thought [*Denken*] and in objectivity [*Gegenständlichkeit*]. On that basis it was proved that it is impossible to conceive of God if his existence [*Dasein*] in thought [*Denken*] and in objectivity [*Gegenständlichkeit*] are denied.[57]

The concept of *Existenz* articulated in *Proslogion* 2, was expressly the general concept of *Dasein* in *Denken* and in objectivity [*Gegenständlichkeit*].[58] God's existence has to be clarified beyond a general concept of *Existenz*. That is why Barth introduces *Dasein* in the first place. It is only therefore as *nicht-daseiend*, in so far as God alone is impossible not to be, that Barth argues that a

---

53 Barth, *Anselm*, 132/G135.
54 Barth, *Anselm*, 132/G135.
55 Barth, *Anselm*, 132/G135.
56 Barth, *Anselm*, 132/G135.
57 Barth, *Anselm*, pp. 132-3/G136.
58 This was translated as 'reality' in Robertson's version.

positive attribution of *Existenz* to God can be proved. It is under these conditions alone that Barth can now say that 'the limitation [*Restriktion*] on the concept of existence [*Existenzbegriffs*] – *esse in intellectu et in re* – with which it was applied to God in *Prosl.* 2, now disappears'.[59] The reason this positive attribution of *Dasein* to God comes about depends upon this negative *nicht-daseiend* which makes up the heart of *Proslogion* 3: It is this aspect of the proof that is 'not a repetition but a vital narrowing of the result of *Prosl.* 2'.[60] Barth therefore continues his discussion of the existence of God as that special *Existenz* which arises in the aftermath of Barth's clarification of how *Dasein* is properly attributable to God alone as *nicht-daseiend*.

One of the more interesting ways in which Barth develops the nuance of his attribution of *Dasein* to God is through Gaunilo's critique of Anselm's argument at this point.[61] Gaunilo thinks it would have been better if Anselm had said, 'we cannot know God as existing [*nicht-daseiend*] or possibly not existing [*nicht daseiend*]'.[62] Barth finds Gaunilo's 'possibly' quite troublesome because Gaunilo here assumes he is taking the more humble ground by assuming the limits of human knowledge. In Barth's view, Gaunilo has taken the place of Descartes in so far as he questions his own existence and all other things, and in like manner assumes an interconnection between his doubt of his own existence and God's.[63] If we could possibly hypothesize our own non-existence and the non-existence of all other things, then in what sense can we make axiomatic claims upon the existence of God? 'Do I exist [*Ob ich bin*]? Does God exist [*Ob Gott ist*]? What thinking [*Denken*] could decide these conclusively? Be my knowledge [*Wissen*] in all these points ever so sure, pure thinking [*reines Denken*] as such is here as free as it is insufficient to make this decision'.[64] Barth then cites Aquinas' conclusion concerning Anselm's proof by concluding along this train of thought, 'we can conceive of God as not existing

---

59 Barth, *Anselm*, p. 134/G137.
60 Barth, *Anselm*, p. 135/G138.
61 Barth, *Anselm*, p. 135/G138.
62 Barth, *Anselm*, p. 135/G138.
63 Barth, *Anselm*, p. 137/G140.
64 Barth, *Anselm*, p. 137/G140.

[*nicht-daseiend*]'.⁶⁵ Here again we must emphasize how Barth is resurrecting the critiques of Gaunilo and Aquinas in order to specifically point out the problem of interpreting Anselm's argument in a univocally ontological sense.⁶⁶

Anselm's response to Gaunilo specifically engages the confusion between the question of human and divine being and the special sense in which *Proslogion* 3 attributes existence to God and God alone. As Barth argues,

> The statement, 'God cannot be conceived as not existing' [*Gott kann nicht als nicht-daseiend gedacht werden*], can only have one subject [*Subjekt*], 'God'. For all existing beings [*Daseiende*]⁶⁷ apart from God can be conceived as not existing [*Nicht-daseiend*].⁶⁸

Here Barth makes it clear that 'there is no analogous [*analogen*] statement (Anselm is not Descartes) concerning man's own existence [*Dasein*]'.⁶⁹ It is through the unqualified sense in which Gaunilo thinks existence in an undifferentiated way that Barth prohibits analogy. As we will see in *Proslogion* 4, Barth makes more positive statements about analogical relations which will be important for our conclusion. Suspending that conversation, however, Barth here uses analogy as a foil against which he seeks to ensure that what we are attributing to God here in *Proslogion* 3 is a unique form of existence. Again, this is what is unique and special about *Proslogion* 3 as opposed to *Proslogion* 2. In the latter, Barth developed the difference between existence in thought alone and the existence of objects. However, in the former, the uniqueness of God's exist-

---

65 Barth, *Anselm*, p. 137/G140.
66 Many scholars have addressed the accuracy of Barth's various interpretations of Aquinas and the degree to which univocal Being is rightly attributed to him. See, for instance, Eugene F. Rogers, *Thomas Aquinas and Karl Barth: Sacred Doctrine and the Natural Knowledge of God*, Revisions (Notre Dame, IN: University of Notre Dame Press, 1995), p. 64. See also Fergus Kerr, *After Aquinas: Versions of Thomism* (Malden, MA: Blackwell Publishers, 2002), pp. 35–6. Or for an interesting interpretation of Aquinas' understanding of Truth and its implications for his analogical ontology, see John Milbank and Catherine Pickstock, *Truth in Aquinas*, Radical Orthodoxy series (London: Routledge, 2001), p. 34.
67 This was translated as 'that exists', which misses the substantive use of *Daseiende* here.
68 Barth, *Anselm*, p. 138/G141.
69 Barth, *Anselm*, p. 139/G142.

ence comes to the fore beyond thought and object and makes up what form of existence can be attributed to God as a subject unto himself.

The relation between *Proslogion* 2 and 3 becomes the basis upon which Barth establishes the necessity of his own interpretation and clarification of Anselm's proof. All roads lead to this conclusion. The heart of Anselm's proof is often overlooked precisely because it is assumed that in proving the existence of the object of faith, Anselm did not in fact go much farther in his proof for the unique existence of God in *Proslogion* 3. But if God exists in such a way that he cannot fail to be, then Barth achieves a positive attribution of existence to God in such a way that it only applies to God. It is from this point, then, that existence is properly attributed to other existing things as well. Gaunilo is right in so far as he questions his own existence and all other existing things. But in so far as God is God, i.e. God exists such that he cannot not exist, then his existence takes on its special character.

Furthermore, God's existence becomes the only certain existence through which the existence of all other existing things becomes a real possibility. God's existence gives [*gibt*] all other existing things their existence. As Barth says:

> The reason why there is [*gibt es*] such a thing as *Dasein* is that God exists [*da ist*]. With his *Dasein* stands or falls the *Dasein* of all essences [*Wesen*] that are distinct from him. Only fools and their theological and philosophical supporters, the Gaunilos, could think that the criterion of general *Dasein* is the criterion of God's *Dasein* and could therefore either not get beyond *Prosl.* 2 or take *Prosl.* 3 as conditioned by *Prosl.* 2. Whereas it is all the other way round: it is the *Dasein* of God that is the criterion of general *Dasein* and if either of these two chapters of Anselm is ultimately or decisively conditioned by the other, then it is *Prosl.* 2 by *Prosl.* 3, and not *vice versa*.[70]

Barth's condemnation of the fools who miss the uniqueness of *Proslogion* 3 cannot be emphasized enough at this point. Barth is clearly stating that anyone who presumes a simple reiteration of

---

70 Barth, *Anselm*, pp. 154-5/G157-8.

the proof in *Proslogion* 2 with *Proslogion* 3 will fundamentally misunderstand the latter's impact. It is not enough to presume that beyond objective existence there remains post-ontological Truth, or a realism which does not take seriously just how its reality exists in relation to our own.[71] Hence, the existence of God, precisely because it is that conception which cannot not exist, becomes the condition upon which we can credibly attribute existence to all other existing things.[72]

When Barth comes to *Proslogion* 4 therefore, he turns to the fool's statement '*Gott ist nicht da*',[73] and in so doing points to those later fools who came after Anselm and presumed to have overcome his argument (that is Kant towards whom Barth addresses his closing remarks). Barth addresses the fool's denial through two questions: '1. How far can he say what he can in no sense conceive? 2. How far can he conceive what he can in no sense say?'[74] The problem is that in denying that which is greater than he can conceive, the fool presumes a verdict upon something which is beyond the power of his judgement. The only validity the fool can claim for his denial, therefore, is that no such distinction between the fool's existence and God's existence exists. Thus Barth can say that, 'the assertion and the denial of the Existence [*Existenz*] of God do not take place ... on the same plane at all'.[75] In other words, the fool makes a statement about God's existence on a different level than the judgement of that existence. This occurs when inaccurate statements are made about the existence of God, which means that the judgement pronounced on that existence does not apply.[76]

Barth eventually works his way back to Anselm's starting point, the knowledge of God's existence in the mind as that than which nothing greater can be conceived. He takes us back to Anselm's frustrated plea with the *insipiens* to face the existence which must, of necessity, be greater than what he can conceive. 'Even if every conceivable physical and moral property were raised to the nth degree, that could quite well be nothing more than the sum total of

---

[71] Barth, *Anselm*, pp. 155–6/G158–9.
[72] Barth, *Anselm*, pp. 155–6/G158–9.
[73] Barth, *Anselm*, p. 162/G165.
[74] Barth, *Anselm*, p. 162/G165.
[75] Barth, *Anselm*, p. 163/G166.
[76] Barth, *Anselm*, p. 163/G166.

Returning Barth to Anselm

the predicates of a purely conceptual essence [*Wesen*]'.[77] There is, in other words, no escape for the existence the fool speaks of. It is inevitably trapped in his own mind of docetic conceptualities. Here Barth inserts one of those tantalizing citations of analogy which a number of later commentators would spend so much time upon when interpreting Barth's theological development.

> The fact that *id quod Deus est* is synonymous with God himself makes this analogical, 'speculative' understanding of his reality [*Wirklichkeit*] into true knowledge of his essence [*Wesen*][78] and that creates the fully efficacious, indeed over-efficacious substitute for the missing (and necessarily missing) experiential knowledge of him.[79]

Analogy thus functions as a stand-in for existential experience and the presumption that human ontology must be the referent for our significations of God. In an undeveloped alternative way, analogy is here said to meld the *Deus est,* properly understood in terms of the rest of Anselm's proving, with God himself such that the two are irreducibly intertwined. Of course, this is not, strictly speaking, a new use of analogy, but rather a new approach to the way in which Barth means 'God is God' after this time. This may explain Barth's refusal to designate Anselm's argument as 'ontological' and his attempt to sidestep Kant's critique of Anselm's proof.[80] We must emphasize all the more, however, that Barth is not refuting the ontological designation in favour of a post-ontological theology. We must not be so quick to jump to Heideggerian conclusions. Rather, in the context of all that has come before, Barth is contrasting a univocal ontology with the ontological difference which Anselm clarified theologically.

Kant's discussion of Anselm's argument follows a use of ontological language which Barth has here gone beyond. Kant tended to use *Dasein* and *Existenz* interchangeably in reference to the analytic attribution of existence to God. Kant's concern comes down

---

77 Barth, *Anselm*, p. 167/G170. Robertson chose to translate *Wesen* at this point as 'being' which is highly confusing given the rest of Barth's language here.
78 Here Robertson translated *Wesen* as Nature.
79 Barth, *Anselm*, p. 167/G170.
80 Barth, *Anselm*, p. 171/G174.

to whether our attribution of existence to God is an analytic or synthetic proposition.[81]

> If it is the former, then with *Dasein* you add nothing to your thought of the thing; but then either the thought that is in you must be the thing itself, or else you have presupposed a *Dasein* as belonging to possibility, and then inferred that *Dasein* on this pretext from its inner possibility, which is nothing but a miserable tautology.[82]

Kant's contention here is that '*Sein* is not a real predicate',[83] and however and whatever we say when we say God exists cannot impart any possibility beyond what is already inherent to God. The reason Barth says that no words ought to be wasted on Kant's critique of this argument is because, as Barth has shown, he believes that when Kant denies the existence of God he adopts the same position as the *insipiens*. If we follow Anselm's proof what we find is that the attribution of existence to God is utterly distinct from the attribution of existence to all other things. If we presume that there is only one form of existence which is attributable to both God and humans univocally, then we could come to the conclusions Kant did. This would have devastating consequences for Barth's own early articulation 'God is God'. But this is precisely what Barth recognizes is not the case. The 'is' in his early statement required the qualifications he gained through his exegesis of Anselm. It is in this same sense that we must be careful not to repeat his mistake by assuming an unqualified understanding of existence upon Barth's theology at this time. Barth's theology does in fact develop these ontological nuances at this point and explains why he would consistently cite the importance of his book on Anselm.

---

81 For a discussion of the difference between Kant's analytic and synthetic propositions, see Charles Parsons, 'The Transcendental Aesthetic', in *The Cambridge Companion to Kant*, ed. Paul Guyer (Cambridge: Cambridge University Press, 1992), pp. 75–6.

82 Immanuel Kant, *Critique of Pure Reason*, ed. Paul Guyer and Allen W. Wood (Cambridge: Cambridge University Press, 1998), p. 566/A97/B625. I have inserted the German here from the online Project Gutenberg text version. Immanuel Kant, 'Kritik der reinen Vernunft (1787)', ed Gerd Bouillon. (Project Gutenberg, 2004), http://www.gutenberg.org/dirs/etext04/8ikc210.txt.

83 Kant, *Critique of Pure Reason*, p. 567/A99/B627.

Returning Barth to Anselm

By qualifying the proof of God's *Existenz* as that *Dasein* which cannot fail to be [*nicht-daseiend*], Barth effectively sets out a pattern for considering the being of God from which he never wavers after this time. Put briefly, Barth starts with a strong prohibition against attributing a general category of *Existenz* to God. In so doing, he articulates the difference between *Dasein* in human thought and objectivity and the attribution of *Dasein* to God. However, if God's *Existenz* is going to be proved, it will have to be in the same manner in which all other things are there for us [*Dasein*] in thought and objectivity. This was the thrust of *Proslogion* 2, and the question it raised for *Proslogion* 3. What was gained in *Proslogion* 3, therefore, was a robust clarification of the *Dasein* of God as a being which cannot fail to be [*nicht-daseiend*]. The relationship between this divine *Dasein* and the *Dasein* in objective thought is now interpreted according to an ontological reversal. The whole of the proof demonstrates that the difference between human and divine *Dasein* is utterly and irreducibly one directional. Hence, not even analogy (much less dialectic) will be sufficient in so far as similarity is still implied in dissimilarity. *Proslogion* 2 and 3 are utterly necessary to each other, but, again, to reiterate Barth's emphasis on this point, it is *Proslogion* 3 which conditions *Proslogion* 2. Only as God cannot fail to be [*nicht-daseiend*] can the category of *Dasein* be attributed to God, and this is what Barth gains from Anselm's manner of proving the *Existenz* of God.

Barth's Ontological Development

At first glance, what Barth has done in his book on Anselm is quite subtle and its significance could be easily missed. In order to highlight the ways it has been missed in the past we turn to Bruce McCormack's summary dismissal of Barth's Anselm book. We have not the space to rehearse McCormack's argument more generally here, but the details of his specific critiques of those who cite Anselm's significance bear mentioning. McCormack lists five possible reasons why Anselm has been deemed of significance for Barth's theology, and by exploring these we gain an overview of the secondary literature more broadly. This will allow us to make further comments upon the implications Barth's account of onto-theology has for contemporary theologians working in his wake.

Protestant Metaphysics after Barth and Heidegger

First, citing Michael Beintker, McCormack takes on the argument that in Barth's commentary on Anselm 'Truth makes itself *objective* for us without becoming ensnared in the network of the Cartesian subject–object polarity'.[84] Because McCormack locates this extrication from Cartesian subject–object relations earlier, it therefore cannot be deemed a significant shift at Anselm. McCormack himself would wholeheartedly agree that Truth stands over against and beyond all human noetic capacities. What both Beintker and McCormack failed to do, however, was account for the unique existence of that Truth.[85] That is what Barth deems so important. This is, for all intents and purposes, one of the most significant oversights in the literature on Barth's Anselm book more generally. When commentators have noted the theological realism,[86] eschatological realism[87] or *Realdialektik*[88] in Barth's thought, they too easily overlook the specific way Barth came to understand the difference between how that reality is known by us as an object [*Dasein*] and how that objective existence could be attributed to God alone as true existence [*Wahrsein*]. If we are to understand what Barth himself pointed to in Anselm, we must go beyond the assumption, as Barth himself did, 'that theological assertions, if true, are true because there is some sort of objective order that they conform to, independently of our ability to recognise them as true'.[89] To say that God is God, or God is Truth fails to account for the ontological progress Barth makes through his account of Anselm.

---

84 McCormack, *Karl Barth's Critically Realistic Dialectical Theology*, p. 434; Michael Beintker, *Die Dialektik in der 'dialektischen Theologie' Karl Barths: Studien zur Entwicklung der Barthschen Theologie und zur Vorgeschichte der 'Kirchlichen Dogmatik'*, Beiträge zur evangelischen Theologie; Bd. 101 (München: C. Kaiser, 1987), p. 191.

85 In our reading, the distinction between the object of faith [*Dasein*] and the unique existence of God [*Existenz*] is not emphasized or developed to any degree in Beintker. Rather, he stops with the relation between objective being [*Dasein*] and being in thought alone [*Gedachtsein*]. See Beintker, *Die Dialektik in der 'dialektischen Theologie' Karl Barths*, pp. 187–91.

86 Graham White, 'Barth's Theological Realism', *Neue Zeitschrift für systematische Theologie und Religionsphilosophie* 26 (1984), pp. 54–70.

87 Ingolf U. Dalferth, 'Karl Barth's Eschatological Realism', in *Karl Barth: Centenary Essays*, ed. Stephen Sykes (Cambridge: Cambridge University Press, 1989), pp. 14–45.

88 McCormack, *Karl Barth's Critically Realistic Dialectical Theology*, p. 432.

89 White, 'Barth's Theological Realism', p. 57.

Returning Barth to Anselm

Second, again citing Beintker, McCormack notes:

> With the turn to a position which can proceed from the objectivity and knowability of the Truth in the *ratio fidei*, the necessity for the thought-form of dialectic on the noetic plane falls away. Here logic takes the place of dialectic.[90]

Because McCormack deems the Anselm book along with Barth's later theology to be inherently dialectical, this argument itself falls away. McCormack's second point is therefore closely related to his third. Namely, the long influential view of Balthasar that 'with the Anselm book, Barth turned "from dialectic to analogy"'.[91] Without rehearsing the details of McCormack's argument here we can in fact take his point further. To say that Barth gains a set of analogical relations in Anselm, as Balthasar seems to suggest,[92] not only overlooks the fact that Barth discusses analogical relations in his theology before this time, in his *Göttingen Dogmatics* for instance,[93] but also that his discussion of analogy in his explication of Anselm's *Proslogion* 2-4 is insufficiently developed.

What then can be made of Barth's various references to analogy in his commentary on Anselm? Barth mentions analogical relation between God's existence and all other existence on five occasions but they differ in emphasis and in no way give a clear picture of what precisely he means by analogy. Rather, Barth's emphasis is upon the attribution of existence to God, and it is in this sense that he applies analogy in both a positive and negative sense. In terms of the latter, Barth commends Anselm for not being content to simply uncover 'formal analogies',[94] or where he discusses 'that than which nothing greater can be conceived' as something which we do not know analogically, but rather which points out precisely that it cannot be known analogously,[95] or lastly where he argues that

---

90 Beintker, *Die Dialektik in der 'dialektischen Theologie' Karl Barths*, p. 188, cited in McCormack, *Karl Barth's Critically Realistic Dialectical Theology*, p. 436.
91 McCormack, *Karl Barth's Critically Realistic Dialectical Theology*, p. 437.
92 Von Balthasar, *The Theology of Karl Barth*, pp. 143-5; McCormack, *Karl Barth's Critically Realistic Dialectical Theology*, p. 437.
93 Karl Barth, *The Göttingen Dogmatics: Instruction in the Christian Religion*, ed. Hannelotte Reiffen, vol. 1 (Grand Rapids, MI: W. B. Eerdmans, 1991), p. 94.
94 Barth, *Anselm*, p. 67/G67.
95 Barth, *Anselm*, p. 112/G115.

Anselm offers no analogous relationship between a statement about his own existence and God's.[96] In terms of the former positive references to analogy, however, Barth discusses the way the unique existence of God advocated by Anselmic theo-logic makes the 'analogical speculative understanding of his reality [*Wirklichkeit*] into true knowledge'.[97] The point being that Anselm's argument in some way redeems an analogical understanding of God which would in all other cases be inadequate. As Bouillard has noted, this makes Barth's use of analogy a kind of negative counter against other forms of analogy, namely his understanding of the Catholic doctrine of *analogia entis* in his *Church Dogmatics*.[98]

In other words, if we assume that the priority and point of Barth's explication of Anselm's theology is to demonstrate the efficacy of a shift to analogy, then we are faced with a series of negative comments coupled with a vacuous affirmation designed to follow the logic of Anselm's name for God. If, however, we presume that the priority of Barth's book is upon the ontological difference Anselm's *Proslogion* evinces, then a much clearer picture emerges concerning why Barth would have cited this book as one of the most significant in his theological development. The emphasis upon analogical relations as a turning point characteristic of Barth's book on Anselm can be best understood, therefore, according to particular commentators such as Hans Urs von Balthasar whose own Roman Catholic heritage took its cues from Erich Przywara, who renewed *analogia* as a primary locus of the theological task.[99]

If we return to Balthasar's own discussion of Anselm's influence upon Barth, we find that he does briefly explicate the difference between God's Existence [*Existenz*] and God as an ontic object of

---

96 Barth, *Anselm*, p. 139/G142.
97 Barth, *Anselm*, p. 167/G170.
98 Bouillard, *The Knowledge of God*, p. 115.
99 We will discuss Przywara's influence upon Barth in more detail in the next chapter. For another account of this interconnection, see Stephen Wigley, 'The von Balthasar Thesis: A Re-Examination of von Balthasar's Study of Barth in the Light of Bruce McCormack', *Scottish Journal of Theology* 56, no. 3 (2003), pp. 351–2. Wigley's account argues that Balthasar's approach may have skewed Barth's development to fit his own interest in analogy, but in so far as it illuminates Balthasar's interest and provides a point of discussion with Barth then it serves its purpose and is an important theological contribution which demands engagement. Wigley, 'The von Balthasar Thesis', p. 345.

Returning Barth to Anselm

faith [*Dasein*]. Although he makes little of it, he does in fact cite a specific use of *Existenz* in relation to the event of God's self-revelation which comes close to what we are arguing was Barth's intention throughout his book on Anselm. In Balthasar's words,

> Whatever is thought [*gedacht*] is thought [*gedacht*] from this event [*Ereignisses*]. This shows that, rooted in this event, the very thought of the concept of God [*Gottesbegriff*] ('greater than which cannot be conceived' as the name and pointer for the intended incomprehensible content) would be a contradiction unless we assented to the existence [*Existenz*] of such a content. And this existence [*Existenz*] is not merely a *de facto* [*faktischen*] existence (which means it might also *not* exist [*dasein*] in the factual order) but divine and absolute.[100]

Here Balthasar refers *Dasein* to the factual order in a way which sets up his later discussion of the relative and absolute being of God. Importantly, he tends to somewhat blur the distinction between divine and human being that we have been arguing was at the heart of Barth's explication of Anselm's *Proslogion*. As Balthasar says:

> Only because there is absolute Truth [*Wahrheit*] and absolute existence [*Dasein*] are there relative truth [*Wahrheit*] and relative existence [*Dasein*]; the latter are completely 'real and true existence [*Dasein*]' and real and true truth [*Wahrheit*] but analogous being [*Sein*] and analogous truth [*Wahrheit*].[101]

This language was most likely used to support Balthasar's argument for the importance of the analogous relation between the *Dasein* which is attributable to God alone and all other objective *Dasein*. As we have discussed above, it is only as it is impossible for God not to exist [*nicht daseiend*], however, that Barth positively attributes *Dasein* to God, and in this sense constitutes a proof of God's *Existenz*. Although Balthasar is, strictly speaking, correct in noting the interconnection Barth's use of *Dasein* was meant to

---

100 Von Balthasar, *The Theology of Karl Barth*, p. 144/G56.
101 Von Balthasar, *The Theology of Karl Barth*, p. 144/G57. I have adjusted the translation of *Dasein* from 'being' to existence in order to better suit our other translation of *Dasein* in Barth's Anselm book.

imply, he does not spend significant attention upon the nuances Barth worked out in the Anselm book. As a result, those who followed his commentary tended to focus upon analogy rather than ontology. In this sense, the secondary literature which follows after Balthasar makes little of the ontological distinctions.[102] This may explain why McCormack, in the end, inherited Balthasar's discussion of Anselm in the way that he did. The importance he failed to grasp was not simply the emphasis upon analogy, but the ontological development that discussion concealed.

Fourth, McCormack takes note of the belief that 'In the Anselm book, Barth stressed for the first time that ontic necessity and rationality have an ontological priority over noetic necessity and rationality.'[103] Here McCormack rightly points out, this time in agreement with Beintker,[104] that the priority of the reality of God pre-dates the Anselm book. We would agree with McCormack that the significance of Anselm cannot be granted according to an *unqualified* understanding of how ontology precedes epistemology, or the way Barth discusses an ontic necessity and rationality over a noetic one as has been maintained by Ingrid Spieckermann, Eberhard Jüngel and T. F. Torrance.[105] As we have already demonstrated, if we understand ontic priority to mean that theological realism precedes human noetic capacities, then Barth's 1920s tautology, 'God is God', is the proper location for this aspect of his theology. Our contention, however, is that to do so is to miss the distinction between the ontic object of faith [*Dasein*] and the positive attribution of *Existenz* to God as *nicht daseiend* in Barth's book on Anselm. This is a far more important contribution to his development than these commentators have allowed. To say that God exists is much different than articulating the unique existence of God such that no confusion could be made between God's objective

---

102 Hans W. Frei, 'The Doctrine of Revelation in the Thought of Karl Barth 1909–1922', pp. 6–7, 178; Beintker, *Die Dialektik in der 'dialektischen Theologie' Karl Barths*, pp. 187–91; Jüngel, *Karl Barth*, pp. 42–3.
103 McCormack, *Karl Barth's Critically Realistic Dialectical Theology*, p. 438.
104 Beintker, *Die Dialektik in der 'dialektischen Theologie' Karl Barths*, p. 188.
105 McCormack, *Karl Barth's Critically Realistic Dialectical Theology*, p. 438; Jüngel, *Karl Barth*, p. 42; Ingrid Spieckermann, *Gotteserkenntnis: ein Beitrag zur Grundfrage der neuen Theologie Karl Barths* (München: Chr. Kaiser, 1985), pp. 228–9; Thomas Forsyth Torrance, *Karl Barth: An Introduction to His Early Theology, 1910–1931* (London: SCM Press, 1962), pp. 182–3.

Returning Barth to Anselm

Dasein as it is revealed to us and God's *Existenz* in and for himself. To argue that an ontic priority develops in Barth's discussion of Anselm leaves open the question of which ontology? It is our contention that when Barth denies the attribution of 'ontological' to Anselm's proof while simultaneously maintaining the ontological differentiations between *Existenz, Dasein* and *nicht-daseiend*, he is in fact progressing beyond a univocal understanding of being. Our explication of Anselm's *Proslogion* does significantly move on from the ontology Barth understood in terms of 'God is God' before this time. It was in this sense that Barth began to differentiate himself from Brunner and it was precisely because this aspect of the discussion was lost in his No! to Brunner that he consistently pointed his readers to Anselm where his understanding of the difference between our existence and God's was much more explicit.[106]

Fifth, when McCormack, therefore, critiques Barth's own claim that, 'in *Fides Quaerens Intellectum*, [he] overcame every last remnant of the attempt to ground, support, or justify theology by means of existential philosophy',[107] he concretizes the way he misses the importance of Anselm's proof for Barth. The political reasons McCormack cites for Barth's critique of his contemporaries cannot be extricated from Barth's concern that an unqualified onto-theology was discernable in Brunner's theology, and even his own. When McCormack claims that Barth's intentions were never to have grounded his theology existentially he misses the significance of the need Barth felt to clarify the relation between ontology and theology. McCormack dismisses the importance of this clarification and in so doing misses what was of central concern to Barth at this time. 'Now I must make myself clear!'[108] Barth may well have always intended the radical Truth of God's existence from early on in his theology, but what drove him forward was a clear articulation of the existence of that Truth.

The way McCormack cites the previous engagements with Anselm allows us to note their inadequacy. In this sense, McCormack is

---

106 Barth, *How I Changed My Mind*, pp. 42–3.
107 McCormack, *Karl Barth's Critically Realistic Dialectical Theology*, p. 438.
108 Karl Barth, 'No! Answer to Emil Brunner', in *Natural Theology: Comprising 'Nature and Grace' by Professor Dr. Emil Brunner and the Reply 'No!' by Dr. Karl Barth*, ed. Peter Fraenkel (London: Geoffrey Bles, 1946), p. 73, translation in Jüngel, *Karl Barth*, p. 41.

able to clarify and push our own enquiry farther. Our justification for Anselm's significance ultimately leads us to Barth's 1956 lecture *The Humanity of God,* where he stated:

> we were wrong exactly where we were right, that at first I did not know how to carry through with sufficient care and thoroughness the new knowledge of the *deity* of God which was so exciting both to myself and to others.[109]

Our own investigation into the point at which Barth located his adjustment of where his early 'God is God' went wrong presumes a judgement upon McCormack's contention that Barth exaggerates the uniqueness of his 1930 book on Anselm in order to distance himself from his theological contemporaries like Gogarten, Bultmann and Brunner.[110] Barth's desire to distance himself from his theological contemporaries is, strictly speaking, accurate. But the reasons and manner in which he did so cannot be degraded to a 'personality quirk',[111] or mere exaggeration. There were much more ontological reasons why he differed from these theologians, and he felt a need to clarify his thought to make those differences more pronounced. What we have demonstrated here is that Barth held higher criteria for the articulation of the ontological relations his theology implied than later theologians have often demanded. Furthermore, the *way* Barth came to understand the existence of God in his book on Anselm is far more significant than the analogical relations later scholars would infer from that understanding. In this sense, Barth's early affirmation that 'God is God' implied an ontological priority that Barth became wholly dissatisfied with as the existentialism of his fellow dialectical theologians became more pronounced in the 1930s.

By taking Barth's disposition towards his book on Anselm we can regain some of his ontological sensitivities. Our suggestion is that this is precisely what is needed if we are to recover Barth's own self-understanding of the change that he referred to in the early 1930s. So too, by investigating the ontological nuances of Barth's theological development we gain crucial insight into the ways in

---

109 Karl Barth, *The Humanity of God* (London: Collins, 1967), p. 44.
110 McCormack, *Karl Barth's Critically Realistic Dialectical Theology,* pp. 442–7.
111 McCormack, *Karl Barth's Critically Realistic Dialectical Theology,* p. 442.

Returning Barth to Anselm

which Protestant metaphysics were transfigured in Barth's thought. Our statements here, therefore, imply that Barth may in fact have been far more honest about the clarity he gained in his thinking in the early 1930s and the way Anselm helped him gain that clarity than McCormack has allowed. This clarity, however, would lead us to those commentators who have recognized the ontological sensitivity in Barth's theology. The recent commentators closest to our own position here on the ontological difference in Barth's Anselm book are Graham Ward and Merold Westphal. Both in their own ways can help us clarify just what has been gained in our own argument.

Ward's explication of Barth's Anselm book, albeit brief, does comment on the ontological differentiations he gained there. Ward rightly points out that Barth did not learn a theological method from Anselm, but rather he came to understand how 'the being of objects in the world and the existence of God are not the same. One is not quantitatively different from the other – they are dipolar.'[112] The term dipolar, however, misleadingly gives the impression that the two forms of being are related dialectically in Barth's thought, and Ward goes on to discern a 'dialectic of being' which he correlates to Heidegger's ontological difference.[113] Here we must raise a question concerning the relationship between Barth and Heidegger which Ward's account implies. To this end, it will be helpful to return briefly to Heidegger's 1928 lecture 'Phenomenology and Theology' where he develops the difference between 'the two basic possibilities of science: sciences of whatever is, or ontic [*ontische*] sciences; and *the* science of Being [*Sein*], the ontological science, philosophy'.[114] Barth's use of ontic in his Anselm book shares a structural similarity to Heidegger's in so far as ontic refers to the apprehensible being of things as they become known to us and the prohibition Barth articulates against attributing a general unqualified existence [*Existenz*] to God. The difference between them, however, arises in so far as Heidegger gives primacy to his ontological

---

112 Graham Ward, *Barth, Derrida, and the Language of Theology* (New York: Cambridge University Press, 1995), p. 101.
113 Ward, *Barth, Derrida, and the Language of Theology*, pp. 100–1.
114 Martin Heidegger, 'Phenomenology and Theology', in *The Piety of Thinking*, ed. James G. Hart and John C. Maraldo (Bloomington: Indiana University Press, 1976), p. 6.

science and in this sense cuts theology off from his desire to look Being in the face.[115] It was this dichotomization of ontology and theology at this early stage in Heidegger's career which would set up his later 1956 critique of 'The Onto-theo-logical Constitution of Metaphysics'.[116] At no point in Barth's theological development, however, does he develop an alternative science of Being, or ontology of ontology in the way Heidegger does. Heidegger's concern is to ensure that the deity does not enter into philosophy and as such does not concern himself to attribute true existence to God. Barth on the other hand, is primarily concerned with the proper attribution of the category of existence to God. Said another way, Barth's interest in Anselm's way of theology is an attempt to clarify the 'is' in his 'God is God'.

Although Ward is one of the few contemporary commentators to note the ontological difference Barth gained in Anselm, he fails to clarify the difference between Barth and Heidegger's form of post-ontological theology in a satisfactory way. Ward's insight into Anselm is therefore difficult to extricate from those other comparisons between Barth and Heidegger which locate Barth's critique of onto-theology at the first edition of his *Römerbrief* and early lectures in the 1920s. For instance, Merold Westphal locates Barth's fundamental critique of metaphysics 'developed along the lines of a physics',[117] at his 1920 lecture 'Biblical Insights, Questions and Vistas'.[118] It is in this light that he presumes that 'we can understand Barth's critique of liberal Protestant theology best if we see it as a critique of onto-theology that differs from Heidegger's in coming several decades earlier and in having a much broader scope'.[119] By locating ontological difference in Barth's early articulation 'God is

---

115 Martin Heidegger, *Being and Time*, trans. John Macquarrie and Edward Robinson (New York: Harper Collins Publishers, 1962), p. 23.

116 As Heidegger puts it, 'the god-less thinking which must abandon the god of philosophy, god as *causa sui*, is thus perhaps closer to the divine God. Here this means only: god-less thinking is more open to Him than onto-theo-logic would like to admit'. Martin Heidegger, *Identity and Difference*, trans. Joan Stambaugh (Chicago: The University of Chicago Press, 2002), p. 72.

117 Karl Barth, *The Word of God and the Word of Man*, trans. Douglas Horton (London: Hodder and Stoughton, 1928), p. 68.

118 Merold Westphal, *Transcendence and Self-Transcendence: On God and the Soul* (Bloomington: Indiana University Press, 2004), p. 145.

119 Westphal, *Transcendence and Self-Transcendence*, p. 145.

Returning Barth to Anselm

God' however, Westphal rehearses the mistake McCormack made, which failed to note the nuance of what was in fact new in Barth's Anselm book. Westphal does not, as it turns out, spend any significant time on Anselm as a result.[120] When Westphal claims that ontological difference can be located earlier on, therefore, he fails to note the difference between the theological critique of ontotheology which Barth maintained with his 'God is God' in the early 1920s, and the ontological difference he would work out in his Anselm book in 1930. Ward on the other hand locates ontological difference at 1930, but fails to account for the development in Barth's theological ontology, which makes it difficult to differentiate his account of Barth's ontology from Westphal's.[121]

Such accounts of the similarity between Barth and Heidegger have led to a consistent correlation between contemporary theologians like Jean-Luc Marion and Barth. As we noted in Chapter 1, Marion suggests a post-ontological theology or a *God without Being*. For Marion, God is not bound to metaphysics any more than he is to any other philosophical system. He stands as the infinite ineffable beyond concept and representation. In his view, 'the destruction of onto-theology's conceptual idols ... would clear a space for the "icon", that is, a space for the 'negative theophany'.[122] In response to the idol of ontologically corrupted theology, Marion answers with the infinite distance of the icon.[123] Given the affinity often assumed between Barth's critique of conceptual idolatry in the secondary literature, critics of Marion such as John Milbank have in fact depicted his theology as a kind of Heideggerian Barthianism.[124]

---

120 Westphal, *Transcendence and Self-Transcendence*, p 168, 72.

121 In other words, in Ward's account Westphal appears to be correct in citing Barth's later understanding of ontological difference at an earlier point in Barth's thought.

122 Jean-Luc Marion, *The Idol and Distance: Five Studies* (New York: Fordham University Press, 2001), p. xviii. It should come as no surprise then that he will interpret Anselm's argument as non-ontological in order to disassociate it from Kant's damnation. Jean-Luc Marion, 'Is the Ontological Argument Ontological? The Argument according to Anselm and Its Metaphysical Interpretation according to Kant', in *Flight of the Gods: Philosophical Perspectives on Negative Theology*, ed. Ilse Nina Bulhof and Laurens ten Kate (New York: Fordham University Press, 2000), pp. 78ff.

123 Marion, *The Idol and Distance*, p. 8.

124 John Milbank, *The Word Made Strange: Theology, Language, Culture* (Oxford: Blackwell Publishers, 1997), p. 37. This interpretation is somewhat encouraged by Marion's own citation of Barth's theology as 'an ontic science of faith,

Protestant Metaphysics after Barth and Heidegger

Milbank's comment is somewhat explained by his sometimes reductive treatment of Barth's theology as anti-philosophical.[125] Because Milbank is determined to overcome metaphysics with a robust theological domestication of ontology, he challenges any strict delineation between metaphysics and theology. Rather, theology 'must evacuate philosophy, which is metaphysics, leaving it nothing ... to either do or see'.[126]

However, by returning Barth to the theological account of ontology he develops in his Anselm book we must emphasize how Barth's theology differs from Marion's and Heidegger's revulsion against ontological theology. What we have been arguing is that Barth's theology is far from a strictly post-ontological account. Rather, Barth is developing a notion of ontological difference that is inherently theological and in this sense will reject any radical difference between theology and ontology. Barth's goal is, in the end, to affirm that God *is* God, albeit in a more nuanced way than he did in the early 1920s. In this sense, we are confirming the interpretations of those commentators who understand Barth's theology to be a critical form of metaphysical theology. For instance, in Stanley Hauerwas's Gifford Lectures, *With the Grain of the Universe,* he discusses Barth's theology in a complementary if not positive relation to John Milbank's 'Only Theology Overcomes Metaphysics'.[127] This interpretation echoes Fergus Kerr's sentiments in his essay on Barth in *Immortal Longings,* where he discusses Barth's eschatol-

---

whose perfect independence remains exactly ontic, and which, in that very measure, must be subject to the ontological "correction" of *Dasein*'. Jean-Luc Marion, *God without Being: Hors-texte,* (Chicago: Chicago University Press, 1991), p. 69. For another account of what is at stake between Barth and Milbank, see Neil Ormerod, 'Milbank and Barth: A Catholic Perspective', in *Karl Barth – A Future for Postmodern Theology?,* ed. Christiaan Mostert and Geoff Thompson (Adelaide: Australian Theological Forum, 2000).

125 John Milbank, Catherine Pickstock and Graham Ward, *Radical Orthodoxy: Suspending the Material* (New York: Routledge, 1999), p. 33, n. 1. Here Milbank critiques Barth's interpretation of Kant as the basis of his anti-philosophical attitudes.

126 Milbank, *The Word Made Strange,* p. 50.

127 Stanley Hauerwas, *With the Grain of the Universe: The Church's Witness and Natural Theology: Being the Gifford Lectures Delivered at the University of St. Andrews in 2001* (Grand Rapids, MI: Brazos Press, 2001), p. 189, citing Milbank, *The Word Made Strange,* pp. 36–52. I would suggest that Hauerwas is right and that Milbank and Barth have far more in common than Milbank's citations of Barth would lead his readers to believe.

Returning Barth to Anselm

ogy. Here Kerr confirms the Lutheran theologian Robert Jenson's thesis that Barth puts 'the historical event of Jesus' existence in the place formerly occupied by changeless "Being"'.[128] The common theme among this body of literature is that Barth's theology is a deeply ontological form of theology. They therefore support the idea that what is at stake in Barth's theology goes beyond an affirmation of philosophical realism and is much broader in its metaphysical implications. It is for these reasons that we would refute the reduction of Barth's thought to a Heideggerian form of ontological difference. Crucially, however, for our thesis here, by returning Barth to Anselm we can return to the question 'What is Protestantism?' with an alternative account of the 'is' at its centre.

---

128 Robert W. Jenson, *Alpha and Omega: A Study in the Theology of Karl Barth* (New York: Nelson, 1963), p. 140, cited in Fergus Kerr, 'Karl Barth's Christological Metaphysics', in *Immortal Longings: Versions of Transcending Humanity* (Notre Dame, IN: University of Notre Dame Press, 1997), p. 193, n. 90.

5

The Being of the *Church Dogmatics*

The Difference of *Church Dogmatics*

Barth's first attempt at dogmatic theology occurred as a lecture series from 1924–5 as a professor in Göttingen. Here, Barth would move on from his lectures on Reformed and Lutheran confessions which he gave in the previous year and begin to blaze his own trail. In his own words,

> I found myself so to speak without a teacher, all alone in the vast field. I knew that the Bible had to be the master in Protestant dogmatics. And it was clear to me, as to other scholars of the time that in particular we had to take up the Reformers again ... Nevertheless, it was also clear that a return to this orthodoxy (to stick to it and to do the same sort of thing) was impossible.[1]

It was Barth's desire to get back to the revelation of the Word of God in the scriptures that is most strongly felt in his early dogmatics. Here Barth discusses the *Deus dixit* as the intervening Word of God himself who has spoken 'so that the correlation of God and faith is not destroyed or restricted by the interposition of a truth that we humans have rationally or irrationally established'.[2] His discussion of Christology also emphasizes more profoundly his preference for the divine alterity implied by the Calvinist way of framing the problem, which he had left more open ended in his 1923 lectures on the Reformed tradition.[3] Furthermore, Barth is

---

1 Eberhard Busch, *Karl Barth: His Life from Letters and Autobiographical Texts* (London: SCM Press, 1976), p. 154, citing H. Heppe, *Dogmatics* (London: Allen & Unwin, 1950), p. 5.

2 Karl Barth, *The Göttingen Dogmatics: Instruction in the Christian Religion*, ed. Hannelotte Reiffen, vol. 1 (Grand Rapids, MI: W. B. Eerdmans, 1991), p. 10.

3 Barth, *The Göttingen Dogmatics*, pp. 159–60. For Barth's discussion, see Karl

The Being of the Church Dogmatics

clearly aware of the problem Kant's critique of metaphysics posed for his theology at this time, and notes how any attempt to reflect upon the Word of God in and of itself 'confuses dogmatics with a metaphysics that has become impossible since Kant'.[4] However, rather than confronting Kant's critique head on with a radical affirmation of the being of God, Barth begins working with categories which strip his theology of the ontological nuance he will develop later, after Anselm.

With the publication of the 1927 *Die christliche Dogmatik im Entwurf* Barth went even further in his desire to erase the category of being from his account of God. This was Barth's own flirtation with a 'non-ontological'[5] account of the Word of God in the reductive terms of *Deus dixit*.[6] Commenting on this version of Barth's dogmatics, Hans Frei notes how Barth 'was speaking of God in terms which avoid any implication of knowledge of transphenomenal being, of being as that which it actually is'.[7] Frei's implication is that Barth had not yet solidified how to speak of the existence of God without some confusion with human existence. Frei presumes that this was because Barth had not yet made the shift from dialectic to analogy,[8] and based on our discussion in the previous chapters, we now can see that it was in fact the ontological relations inherent in Anselm's *Proslogion* 2–4 which enhanced Barth's ability to think through the ontological nature his early theology always implied. We could, therefore, agree with Bruce McCormack and Michael Beintker's assessment that the Göttingen lectures and *christliche Dogmatik* are very similar to each other.[9] However,

---

Barth, *The Theology of the Reformed Confessions*, 1923, trans. Darrell L. Guder and Judith J. Guder (Louisville, KY: Westminster John Knox Press, 2002), p. 184.

4 Barth, *The Göttingen Dogmatics*, 10.

5 This is a term adopted by Frei. 'Barth's much more radical realism in this volume is non-ontological. He tried, at that time, to speak of God as one who is related to his creation as absolute origin [*Ursprung*]'. Hans W. Frei, 'The Doctrine of Revelation in the Thought of Karl Barth 1909–1922' (Doctoral Dissertation, Yale, 1956), p. 189.

6 As Barth will say in the opening paragraph, 'There are Christian dogmatics, because there is Christian speech [*Es gibt christliche Dogmatik, weil es christliche Rede gibt*]'. Karl Barth, *Die christliche Dogmatik im Entwurf*, ed. Gerhard Sauter (Zürich: Theologischer Verlag, 1927), p. 1.

7 Frei, 'The Doctrine of Revelation', p. 190.

8 Frei, 'The Doctrine of Revelation', p. 197.

9 Bruce L. McCormack, *Karl Barth's Critically Realistic Dialectical Theology: Its*

when it comes to the *Church Dogmatics,* we find McCormack's conflation of all of Barth's dogmatic attempts at prolegomena to be unsatisfactory. From the opening pages it is clear Barth gained a confidence in speaking of the existence of human beings in relation to the being of God which is markedly absent from the previous drafts. Hence, in the opening paragraphs of Barth's first volume he could confidently say that 'the question of truth [*Wahrheit*], with which theology is concerned throughout, is the question as to the agreement of the Church's distinctive talk about God with the being of the Church [*Sein der Kirche*] ... namely, Jesus Christ'.[10] It is our contention that the difference between Barth's 1932 *Church Dogmatics* and his previous drafts of dogmatics in 1925 and 1927 can best be understood in the ontological terms he gained through his exposition of Anselm. As such, his first two attempts at dogmatics represent a difficulty Barth would later overcome in his mature theological ontology in the *Church Dogmatics*.[11]

This discussion of the ontological nature of Barth's *Church*

Genesis and Development, 1909–1936 (New York: Oxford University Press, 1995), p. 375; Michael Beintker, 'Unterricht in der christlichen Religion', in *Verküdigung und Forschung: Beihefte zur 'Evangelische Theologie'*, ed. Gerhard Sauter (Munich: Kaiser Verlag, 1985), p. 46.

10 Karl Barth, *Church Dogmatics*, ed. G. W. Bromiley and T. F. Torrance, trans. G. W. Bromiley, vol. I.1 (Edinburgh: T. & T. Clark, 1962), p. 4/KD I.1, 2. For Barth's original German edition we are citing here, see Karl Barth, *Die Kirchliche Dogmatik*, vol. I.1 (Zurich: Evangelischer Verlag, 1964). All future citations will be abbreviated as CD and KD respectively.

11 It should be noted how our periodization differs from McCormack on this point. First, McCormack contends that Barth's theology was always post-metaphysical in principle. However, he recognizes the metaphysical nature of the first volume of Barth's *Church Dogmatics* just as we are suggesting here. However, he refers to it as 'a *moment*' in his thinking. Bruce L. McCormack, 'Karl Barth's Historicized Christology: Just How "Chalcedonian" Is It?' in *Orthodox and Modern: Studies in the Theology of Karl Barth* (Grand Rapids, MI: Baker Academic, 2008), p. 212. Our contention here is that Barth always referred to his dogmatics as a whole and that he had hit on a consistent starting place from the first volume onward. His work throughout the 1920s demonstrates this desire to come to terms with the being of God in a more consistent manner than he had considered it in either of his Romans commentaries or the first attempts at dogmatics. We are therefore utterly rejecting McCormack's notion that the first volumes are metaphysical moments until Barth finally realized the error of his ways and developed a truly post-metaphysical theology in *Church Dogmatics*, volume II.2. McCormack, 'Karl Barth's Historicized Christology', pp. 213ff. We will discuss McCormack's Christology in more detail in the next chapter.

The Being of the Church Dogmatics

Dogmatics returns us to Barth's own consistent reflections upon Anselm's significance. This, as we saw in Barth's Anselm book, was answered in terms of an ontological difference between divine and human being, and the irreversible manner in which the divine being became the condition for human being. What we must now come to see is how Barth began to consider the knowledge of this divine being according to the ontological difference in God's self. It is here that the Anselmic pattern to Barth's theology is most evident at this time. Of course, Barth is not Anselm and the Anselm book is not a stand-in for the position Barth developed in his *Church Dogmatics,* but he does consistently cite the Anselm book's importance for his understanding on these matters. For instance, in Barth's 1938 essay 'How I Changed My Mind',[12] as in the 1958 'Preface' to the second edition of his *Anselm: Fides Quaerens Intellectum,* Barth laments the limited number of commentators who recognized how much of a 'vital key, if not the key' Anselm became for 'that whole process of thought' that had impressed him in his *Church Dogmatics* 'as the one proper to theology'.[13] Such comments, however, must be heard as the reverberation of Barth's citations in the *Dogmatics* themselves. In the 'Preface' to volume I.1, Barth cites the 'pressing nature of his book on Anselm' as the reason for the delay in producing this new revised edition before going on to defend his consistent desire to begin his dogmatics 'at the very point where the fable of "unprofitable scholasticism" and the slogan about the "Greek thinking of the fathers" persuade us to stop'.[14] Of course, Barth had been defending his scholasticism since his *christliche Dogmatik,* but this shouldn't dissuade us from noting the particularly metaphysical accent the scholasticism of his *Church Dogmatics* would take on at this point. Here again, Frei makes this point in connection with Barth's Anselm book, which he believes to be 'absolutely indispensable for a knowledge of the revolution in his thought between the two editions of *The Doctrine of the Word of God*'.[15] As we approach Barth's mature theological ontology, therefore, we must allow what

---

12 Karl Barth, *How I Changed My Mind* (Richmond, VA: John Knox Press, 1966), p. 43.
13 Karl Barth, *Anselm: Fides Quaerens Intellectum* (London: SCM Press, 1960), p. 11.
14 CD I.1, p. xiv.
15 Frei, 'The Doctrine of Revelation', pp. 193–4.

we have gained from our explication of the Anselm book in the previous chapter to be heard. By bringing forward the details of our discussion of Barth's Anselm book, we can now clarify just what exactly Barth means by the interrelation between the *Sein* of the Church and the existence of individual believers. In so doing we can address our central question concerning the transfiguration of Protestant metaphysics in Barth's theology, and how it differs from Heidegger's.

Prolegomena to Any Future Protestant Metaphysics

Barth's first volume of his *Church Dogmatics* begins with an introduction to the task of dogmatics before moving on to a discussion of prolegomena to dogmatics. One might assume that prolegomena would come before any description of the task of dogmatics itself, but it is Barth's particular agenda to allow the 'pro' in prolegomena 'to signify the first part of dogmatics rather than that which is prior to it'.[16] Barth's introduction can therefore begin with a forceful affirmation of theology's call to self-examination. 'It puts to itself the question of truth, i.e., it measures its action, its talk about God, against its being as the Church [*Sein als Kirche*] ... namely, Jesus Christ, God in His gracious revealing and reconciling address to man.'[17] Thus the Church's talk about God stands under the condition of the Church's being, Jesus Christ, and here we are confronted with an ontological imperative unlike the beginning of any of Barth's other enquiries into dogmatics. Barth opens his *Church Dogmatics* with an onto-theological riddle which beckons his readers to enquire just how this being can be related to the existence of the human beings who participate in any particular ecclesial community.

What becomes clear as Barth progresses through his introductory comments to his section on 'The Possibility of the Dogmatic Prolegomena' is the totalistic nature of Barth's critique of the ontology of modern and Enlightenment approaches to dogmatics. Barth summarizes such prolegomena in the following terms: 'the Church and faith are to be understood as links in a greater nexus of being

---

16 CD I.1, p. 42/KD I.1, 41.
17 CD I.1, p. 4/KD I.1, 2.

The Being of the Church Dogmatics

[*Seinszusammenhang*]'.[18] It is this nexus of being that Barth finds so troubling. Barth isn't necessarily critiquing ontological univocity here. As we will note in a moment, the ontological nexus of which he is speaking includes certain degrees of ontological difference. Rather, Barth is challenging any radical *differentiation* between ontology and theology and the ontological *prius* this could imply. As Barth says,

> This nexus of problems, however, is that of an ontology [*Ontologie*], and since Descartes this necessarily means that of a comprehensively explicated self-understanding of human existence [*Daseins*] which may also at a specific point become the pre-understanding of an existence [*Daseins*] in the Church or in faith, and therefore the pre-understanding and criterion of theological knowledge.[19]

Although Descartes is mentioned as an originator of the problem, Barth has a number of targets in mind here. For instance, earlier on in his discussion of 'The Necessity of Dogmatic Prolegomena', he critiques Brunner's emphasis upon the problem of the existence of God as a separate pre-theological task.[20] Barth's contention with Brunner is that the existential nature of his approach to dogmatics represents an example of why 'the task of giving an explicit account of the way of knowledge taken in dogmatics can and must be an inner necessity grounded in the matter itself'.[21] What should be emphasized here is that Barth's critique of Brunner does not simply want to cut off any discussion of divine being or existence from the dogmatic task, but rather that divine and human being cannot be interrelated without critical theological qualification.

Barth would try to articulate this same onto-theological critique in his later 1934 'No!' to Brunner's 'Nature and Grace'. One of the difficulties which arises when interpreting this debate is that it attempts to enact an approach to theology which has overcome a concern with the themes of the Enlightenment with the themes of the 'Bible itself'. Hence, the debate can appear to be of a post-

---

18 CD I.1, p. 36/KD I.1, 35.
19 CD I.1, p. 36/KD I.1, 35–6.
20 CD I.1, p. 26/KD I.1, 25.
21 CD I.1, p. 34/KD I.1, 33.

ontological and purely theological nature. This façade is in large part propagated by Brunner,[22] but is not significantly challenged by Barth who seems to accept the terms of the debate on purely theological grounds. On this level, Barth faults Brunner because of the way he divides revealed from natural theology according to a fragmented *imago dei*.[23] Barth categorically rejects Brunner's division between a formal and material *imago* (and the point of contact it announces) as an apostate representation of *humanitas*. Barth says,

> What he calls the purely formal side of humanity is evidently full of material. And the material is the capacity for a sinless knowledge of sin, the capacity to do on earth subjectively, *per analogiam*, what God does in heaven *per essentiam*![24]

Barth's point has as much to do with the ontological nature of God, the divine *essentia*, as it does with the strictly noetic way in which Barth's argument for pure revelation is sometimes read.[25] What we are suggesting is that Barth's earlier critique of Brunner in the 1932 *Church Dogmatics* further illuminates Barth's contention with Brunner and why Barth would always draw attention to his Anselm book and not his debate with Brunner when marking out the contours of his own theological task at this time.[26] What Barth is doing in his *Church Dogmatics*, like his Anselm book, is delineating the ontological relations between God's being and human being and the inadequacy of attempting to appropriate existence to the

---

22 Emil Brunner, 'Nature and Grace', in *Natural Theology: Comprising 'Nature and Grace' by Professor Dr. Emil Brunner and the Reply 'No!' by Dr. Karl Barth*, ed. Peter Fraenkel (London: Geoffrey Bles, 1946), p. 17.

23 Brunner, 'Nature and Grace', pp. 23-4.

24 Karl Barth, 'No!' Answer to Emil Brunner', in *Natural Theology: Comprising 'Nature and Grace' by Professor Dr. Emil Brunner and the Reply 'No!' by Dr. Karl Barth*, ed. Peter Fraenkel (London: Geoffrey Bles, 1946), p. 121.

25 In the process of his critiques of Brunner's position, Barth will focus his attack upon Brunner's conflation of the human capacity for words (*Wortmächtigkeit*) as a capacity for revelation (*Offenbarungsmächtigkeit*) Barth, 'No!', pp. 78-9. This appears naïve to Brunner and commentators on the debate. Cf. John Baillie, 'Introduction', in *Natural Theology: Comprising 'Nature and Grace' by Professor Dr. Emil Brunner and the Reply 'No!' by Dr Karl Barth*, ed. Peter Fraenkel (London: Geoffrey Bles, 1946), p. 9; Emil Brunner, 'Nature and Grace', p. 25.

26 Barth, *How I Changed My Mind*, pp. 42-3.

The Being of the Church Dogmatics

former through a differentiation in the existence in the latter. No ontological differentiation within the *imago dei* would ever provide the proper means of attributing existence to God as Barth would formulate it from his Anselm book onwards. This is precisely the problem Barth is raising in the prolegomena to his dogmatics in terms of a nexus of being [*Seinszusammenhang*].

Barth goes on to trace this ontological nexus back to Schleiermacher and De Wette's understanding of 'human existence as a sum of capacities or tendencies or activities of human self-consciousness, and within this to discover at the central point, in the form of feeling or direct self-consciousness, an original disposition'.[27] Again, however, Barth's interpretation of Schleiermacher's 'form of feeling' is simply a preamble to open up a more profound critique of his own contemporaries' understanding of dogmatic prolegomena, in this case, Bultmann and Heidegger. As Barth says,

> The understanding of existence [*Daseinsverständnis*] here presupposed was, of course, far too naïve both formally and materially in relation to the real problems of human existence [*Existenz*]. This modern ontology [*Ontologie*], better instructed theoretically by Kierkegaard and practically by world war and revolution, interprets human existence [*Dasein*] not merely secondarily but from the very outset as history, and materially not so much as capacity but rather as 'being projected into nothingness [*Hineingehaltensein in das Nichts*]'.[28]

Barth's citation of Heidegger's 'What is Metaphysics?' is of particular interest to us here. He cites Heidegger as a progression beyond Schleiermacher in so far as he recognized the ontological *prius* Schleiermacher's prolegomena implied. As we have seen in Chapter 1, Heidegger's 'Phenomenology and Theology' pushed ontology further by totalizing its role as a science of the being of beings.[29] So too, he demonstrated the nihilist quality of the sciences in his 'What is Metaphysics?' For Heidegger, the sciences failed to address the

---

27 CD I.1, p. 36/KD I.1, 36.
28 CD I.1, pp. 36–7/KD I.1, 36, citing Heidegger's 'Was ist Metaphysik?' p. 20.
29 Martin Heidegger, 'What is Metaphysics?', in *Basic Writings: From Being and Time (1927) to The Task of Thinking (1964)*, ed. David Farrell Krell (San Francisco: HarperSanFrancisco, 1993), p. 95.

nothingness which haunted its enquiry into beings.[30] It is in light of this 1929 lecture by Heidegger that Barth notes an interconnection between Heidegger's radical ontology and Bultmann's attempt to 'find in it the ontologically existential [*existenzial*] possibility of the existential [*existenziellen*] event of faith'.[31] Barth's point is that 'the methodological relationship of Bultmann's conception to that of Schleiermacher and De Wette should not be overlooked'.[32] The shared ontological nexus of the modern liberal theological tradition falls on this one onto-theological problem. Although Barth does not explicate Heidegger's fundamental ontology in any detail at this point, Barth does in fact critique the break between ontology and theology that Heidegger's thought implied early on. As such, Barth predicts where Heidegger's divide would lead if carried through.[33]

By beginning with an a-theological ontological differentiation Barth argues that an inevitable choice would be forced whereby theology would need to either be fully identified with fundamental ontology, or it would become limited as an ontic science. As Barth says of those theologians who adopted this ontological–ontic nexus,

> Dogmatic prolegomena on the basis of this conception obviously consist first in the demonstration that in a general ontology [*Ontologie*] or anthropology there is actually a place for this ontic [*ontische*] factor, for the being of the Church [*Sein der Kirche*] or faith, and that human existence [*Dasein*] is practicable also as believing existence [*Dasein*]. They then consist in the concrete historical reminder that his particular ontic [*ontische*] factor is in fact present as an event and it is thus the object of ontic [*ontische*] science. They finally consist in the establishment of the rules suggested by this ontological–ontic [*ontologisch-ontischen*] foundation for this science, and therefore for the criticism and correction of Christian utterance.[34]

---

30 Heidegger, 'What is Metaphysics?', p. 95.
31 CD I.1, p. 37/KD I.1, 36.
32 CD I.1, p. 37/KD I.1, 36.
33 See our discussion of Heidegger's 'The Onto-theo-logical Constitution of Metaphysics' and 'On Time and Being' in Chapter 1.
34 CD I.1, p. 37/KD I.1, 36.

The Being of the Church Dogmatics

Thus, Barth recognized very early on what the outcome of this existential theology must be. General ontology makes room for the ontic human being. In this form of prolegomena the *Sein* of the Church functions on the same plane as human *Dasein*, which is reducible to believing *Dasein*. It is on this basis then that ontology always attempts to correct the ontic nature of the theological being of the Church or believing existence because it precedes them in a 'prior' if not primary way.[35] Thus the rules of the ontological–ontic difference predetermine any differentiation between the being of God and human being and as a result all theological utterance is ultimately not determined by divine being, but by this ontological–ontic nexus. 'In the words of Schleiermacher, "the statements made at this point cannot themselves be dogmatic too"'.[36] It is in this sense that Barth critiques Protestant metaphysics in so far as 'the statements of such prolegomena have instead the character, in part, of statements borrowed from metaphysics'.[37] Given Barth's own use of metaphysical and ontological terminologies, we must read such critique as the critique of the independent superiority of metaphysics in and of itself, and the a-theological nature of the form of prolegomena they imply.

Barth's critique of the modern ontological–ontic difference ultimately opens up the logical possibility of his own form of theological prolegomena.[38]

> Is there an existentially ontological [*existenzial-ontologisches*] *prius* to this ontically existential [*Ontisch-Existenziellen*] factor? If this presupposition is granted, then prolegomena of this kind are possible. This presupposition, however, does not have a neutral but a highly theological character.[39]

For Barth the resolution to this ontic-existential problem will not come through a general neutral enquiry into ontology. Rather, it

---

35 CD I.1, p. 37/KD I.1, 37.
36 CD I.1, p. 37/KD I.1, 37, citing Schleiermacher's *Glaubenslehre* I.1.
37 CD I.1, p. 37/KD I.1, 37.
38 It is here that we can see just how different Barth's theology is from Marion's citation of it as 'an ontic science of faith, whose perfect independence remains exactly ontic, and which, in that very measure, must be subject to the ontological 'correction' of *Dasein*'. Jean-Luc Marion, *God without Being: Hors-texte* (Chicago: University of Chicago Press, 1991), p. 69.
39 CD I.1, p. 38/KD I.1, 37.

169

demands a theological enquiry. Barth is here sounding the exact problem Heidegger would later face in his 1957 lecture 'The Onto-theo-logical Constitution of Metaphysics'. In Heidegger's words, 'how does the deity enter into philosophy, not just modern philosophy, but philosophy as such?'[40] The ontological difference Heidegger had presupposed would consistently be confronted by the pervasive interconnection between ontology and theology, and here, 25 years earlier, Barth broaches the same question in his own way. What we must be careful to note, however, is the difference between their answers to this onto-theo-logical problematic. Whereas Heidegger divorced theology from ontology, Barth, in fact, takes the relation between ontology and theology up in a radical way.

Barth's chief problem with the ontological–ontic nexus is that its

> presupposition is that the being of the Church [*Sein der Kirche*], Jesus Christ, is no longer the free Lord of its existence [*Daseins*], but that He is incorporated into the existence of the Church [*Daseins der Kirche*], and is thus ultimately restricted and conditioned by certain concrete forms of the human understanding of his revelation and of the faith which grasps it.[41]

By returning to his primary focus upon the being of the Church, Barth is able to demonstrate the horizon his own theology is aiming for. In other words, he returns to the enigmatic and yet, at this point in his argument, undefined notion of the being of the Church, Jesus Christ. In so doing, Barth moves on from the modern liberal conception of the ontological–ontic nexus, to present his understanding of the Roman Catholic way of conceptualizing the onto-theological problem. Barth only briefly touches upon his understanding of the Catholic *analogia entis* at this point, but it is clear that Barth understands it to be another false answer to the question of the relationship between the being of the Church and human existence. Here, the difficulty is not the radical divide of theology from ontology, but rather, the way in which the former is so integrated into

---

40 Martin Heidegger, *Identity and Difference*, trans. Joan Stambaugh (Chicago: The University of Chicago Press, 2002), p. 55.

41 CD I.1, p. 40/KD I.1, 40.

The Being of the Church Dogmatics

the latter that the former becomes 'constantly available'.[42] We will suspend our conversation concerning Barth's critique of *analogia entis*, and the meaning of his alternative, *analogia fidei*, for later in this chapter. For now, however, it bears importance in so far as it provides one of the boundaries against which Barth articulates his own position, which Barth gives as follows:

> The only possibility of a conception of dogmatic knowledge remaining to us on the basis of an Evangelical faith is to be marked off on the one hand by the rejection of an existential ontological [*existential-ontologischen*] possibility of the being of the Church [*Sein der Kirche*] and on the other hand by the rejection of the presupposition of a constantly available absorption of the being of the Church [*Sein der Kirche*] into a creaturely form, into a 'there is' [*es gibt*]. On the one side we have to say that the being of the Church [*Sein der Kirche*] is *actus purus*, i.e., a divine action which is self-originating [*selbst anfangende*] and which is to be understood only in terms of itself and not therefore in terms of a prior anthropology. And on the other side we have also to say that the being of the Church is *actus purus*, but with the accent now on the *actus*, i.e., a free action and not a constantly available connection, grace being the event of personal address and not a transmitted material condition.[43]

Barth's own position here stands between the two options he has thus far discussed. He is attempting to avoid both the foundation of an ontological nexus as well as any absorption of divinity into creaturely ontology, all the while maintaining that God *is* in fact the God under discussion in his dogmatics. Here we must be particularly careful to note what Barth is not saying. He is not saying that his own theological project will be strictly theological at the expense of ontology. Barth is not saying that God and being are to be radically extricated from each other in a post-ontological sense. Such a division has been the justification for reading Barth along Heideggerian lines. As Jeffery Robbins puts it, 'What Barth and Heidegger share in common ... is their mistaken notion that the quality of thought

---

42 CD I.1, p. 41/KD I.1, 40.
43 CD I.1, p. 41/KD I.1, 41.

is distinguished by its purity'.[44] In this light, Barth's *actus purus* implies a radical break between God and being, and as such 'philosophical theology is undesirable ethically, because it sets humans in the place of God by forgetting the infinite qualitative difference'.[45] However, given what we already noted in our discussions of the ontological nature of Barth's theology in the previous chapters, we must be careful not to confuse the way Barth sought to engage Kant's metaphysics with the a-metaphysical theology of Herrmann. It has been our consistent goal therefore to demonstrate the particular ways in which Barth understood the relation between ontology and theology such that the two always implied each other.

Although it is strictly true to say, as Eberhard Jüngel does, that 'Barth thinks as a theologian',[46] he goes too far when he goes on to say that 'for Barth "thinking as a theologian" can mean nothing other than "thinking consistently and exclusively as a theologian"'.[47] Jüngel's reasons for this theological exclusivity may have more to do with the polemical context in which he is writing in his day, where, as he would put it, the word '"ontological" in the world of so-called Barthians nowadays triggers complete phobia'.[48] Jüngel is in many ways working against this taboo by explicating in detail the ontological nuance Barth's theology implies, but in attempting to respond to this taboo he ends up with an inadequate portrayal of that ontology. For instance, he explicitly says in agreement with what we are arguing here that Barth will 'not yield to a revulsion against the idea of being as such' but rather seeks to 'take up the concept ... with complete impartiality'.[49] This is in reference to an important passage in the second volume of Barth's dogmatics where he is dealing with the reality of God most explicitly. Jüngel goes on to argue that 'the concept of being which is taken up in all impartiality must immediately be adequately specified, both theologically and ontologically, if it is to be suitable for responsible

---

44 Jeffrey W. Robbins, *Between Faith and Thought: An Essay on the Ontotheological Condition* (Charlottesville, VA: University of Virginia Press, 2003), p. 37.

45 Robbins, *Between Faith and Thought*, p. 26.

46 Eberhard Jüngel, *God's Being Is in Becoming: The Trinitarian Being of God in the Theology of Karl Barth* (Grand Rapids, MI: W. B. Eerdmans, 2001), p. 9.

47 Jüngel, *God's Being Is in Becoming*. We discussed this aspect of McCormack's thought above in Chapter 4 as well as below in Chapter 6.

48 Jüngel, *God's Being Is in Becoming*, p. 129.

49 Jüngel, *God's Being Is in Becoming*, p. 76, citing CD II.1, p. 360.

The Being of the Church Dogmatics

speech about God's being'.[50] But then, in a footnote thereafter Jüngel argues that it is because of this that 'ontological statements in theology do not imply a theological ontology'.[51] This is utterly confused and marked more by the controversies and taboos in Barthianism than in Barth's theology itself. It makes little sense to say that Barth is not explicitly arguing for a theological ontology. Rather, it is only in reading Barth closely, as Jüngel in fact does, that we can decide the merits of that theological ontology. It is precisely Barth's ability to apprehend the standpoint of philosophers like Kant and Heidegger that allows him to engage and criticize their thought in order to bring about both theological and ontological clarifications. It is to Barth's credit that he, just as profoundly as Heidegger, was able to see the way one always implied the other. Barth does not attempt to talk past his philosophical contemporaries with an elitist theology any more than offer a purely ontological critique to his theological contemporaries. Barth did not attempt to go under or beyond the philosophers, but rather he goes through their arguments in order to investigate the ways in which their philosophy uncovered theological issues and problems which could push his own theology forward.

Hence, when interpreters of Barth's thought cite its exclusively theological nature without denoting the way Barth's understanding of the theological task is inherently ontological, they leave open the possibility, if not ambiguous impression, that Barth's theology is in fact post-ontological in a Heideggerian sense, that is that he sought to supersede or cross ontology out of the theological task. In the *Church Dogmatics,* it is precisely Barth's ability to disagree with Heidegger on his own terms that allows him to speak of the possibility of a *philosophia Christiania*.[52] His very reason for calling theology a science is because he doesn't want to give the impression that 'for all the radical and indissoluble difference in the understanding of the term, theology ... believes in the forgiveness of sins, and not in the final reality of a heathen pantheon'.[53] When understood in the context of the ontological nature of Barth's theology, *actus purus* does not exclude philosophy but rather, grounds it all the

---

50 Jüngel, *God's Being Is in Becoming*, pp. 76–7.
51 Jüngel, *God's Being Is in Becoming*, p. 77, n5.
52 CD I.1, p. 5/KD I.1, 4.
53 CD I.1, p. 11/KD I.1, 10.

more fully in the being of the Church, Jesus Christ.⁵⁴ Barth is, therefore, excluding particular ontological options precisely in order to present his own understanding of how it is that Jesus Christ truly *is* God in a way that would be satisfactory to both philosopher and theologian alike.

In this light, *actus purus* indicates Barth's focus upon the possibility of God's revelation and how it is that we know that when we speak of God it is God that is, in fact, under consideration. Just as with the early Protestants, Barth recognizes the impossibility of avoiding 'decisive references to the contents of Christian utterance concerning God ... e.g. the doctrine of reconciliation, the Holy Spirit, faith, or the Church'.⁵⁵ It is Barth's great achievement to construct cohesively his own dogmatic task in such a way as to capture this early Protestant spirit. But so too, Barth's aim goes beyond scholasticism to the Roman Catholicism and modernism of his own period, and the need for 'a comprehensive elucidation of context'.⁵⁶ Barth's explication of the Word of God in his contemporary context will therefore 'treat the doctrine of the Trinity and the essentials of Christology in this connection'.⁵⁷ What mustn't

---

54 Some commentators have referred to this aspect of Barth's thought as actualism. George Hunsinger lists this aspect of Barth's theology as the first and one of the more 'pervasive' motifs of his theology. George Hunsinger, *How to Read Karl Barth: The Shape of His Theology* (Oxford: Oxford University Press, 1991), p. 30. 'It is present whenever Barth speaks, as he constantly does, in the language of occurrence, happening, event, history, decisions, and act.' Hunsinger, *How to Read Karl Barth*, p. 30. Another prominent interpretation of this aspect of Barth's theology can again be found in Eberhard Jüngel's *God's Being Is in Becoming*. Jüngel's title presents us with the interconnection between act, ontology and Trinity in Barth's theology. In particular, his use of 'becoming [*werden*]' focuses his interpretation and translation of the actualistic nature of Barth's theology. Although Barth does use the language of becoming in a few places (Cf. CD I.1, p. 427/KD I.1, 448), it is not the primary linguistic convention of his discussion of actualism. Our explication will therefore pay closer attention to the terminology Barth appropriates for being and existence. Whereas in his book, *Anselm: Fides Quaerens Intellectum*, Barth developed a relationship between *Existenz* and *Dasein*, in the *Church Dogmatics*, he will develop the use of *Sein* in terms of different modes as he works out his own pathway through onto-theo-logical problematics. However, Jüngel's emphasis on 'becoming' does alert his readers to the unfamiliar nature of Barth's use of ontological terminology, and is helpful in understanding the uniqueness of Barth's thought on these matters. Jüngel, *God's Being Is in Becoming*, p. xxv.

55 CD I.1, pp. 43–4/KD I.1, 43.
56 CD I.1, p. 43/KD I.1, 43.
57 CD I.1, p. 44/KD I.1, 43.

The Being of the Church Dogmatics

be missed are the ontological implications of Barth's explication and his contention that 'the question of truth, with which theology is concerned throughout, is the question as to the agreement of the Church's distinctive talk about God with the being of the Church'.[58] The elucidation of this agreement becomes the driving force throughout the first volume of Barth's dogmatics. It is in this regard that the parallels between Barth's *Church Dogmatics* and his book on Anselm are the most striking. Just as with his *Anselm: Fides Quaerens Intellectum*, Barth's starting place is designed to delineate the onto-logic that the latter half of the book will follow. It is in this sense that Barth's discussion of the Word always foreshadows a more precise affirmation of the being of the Church, Jesus Christ.

The Word of God

Barth begins his explication of the first chapter of the *Church Dogmatics*, 'The Word of God as the Criterion of Dogmatics' with a problem:

> Not all human talk is talk about God. It could be and should be. There is no reason in principle why it should not be. God is the Lord from whom and to whom we exist [*sind*]. Even the realities and truths distinct from Him and us which usually form the concrete occasion and subject of human speech exist [*sind*] from Him and to Him. Hence there is no genuinely profane speech. In the last resort, there is only talk about God. Yet serious reflection on human talk about God must take as its starting-point the fact that this is not at all the case, that it is quite impossible to interpret human talk as such as talk about God.[59]

Barth's problem arises as he fluctuates between a description of how it ought to be and how it is. What we are in fact saying about God does not and cannot begin by assuming that it is in fact speech about God. Quite the opposite is the case. The problem arises in so far as Barth wants to get ahead of himself and say what is at this

---

58 CD I.1, p. 4/KD I.1, 2.
59 CD I.1, p. 47/KD I.1, 47.

point still impossible to say, that God alone is Lord and creator of our existence. We are, in so far as God is. The interconnection here between word and being is the crucial relation which drives the problem forward. For if it is the case, as Barth eventually demonstrates, that all that we are is from God and participates in God, then in what sense can anything we say be other than talk about God? To say that the Word of God is a criterion of dogmatics, naturally implies a relation between our words and God's. For it really to be the case that all talk is ultimately about God as Barth suggests, then the relation between Word and words must ultimately be determined by a relation between divine and human being.[60] In this sense, the crucial question we will be asking Barth at this point concerns the nature of the Word and what it effects in its address to human beings? In other words, what does the Word do to bring the ontological relations into focus? As we shall see, it is Barth's answer to these questions which justifies the logic of his concluding chapter on revelation and the doctrine of the Trinity.

In section five of the *Church Dogmatics* Barth refigures the question of the nature of the Word of God in order to avoid the attempt to locate the Word in a nature that we might know or comprehend as our own. 'God and His Word aren't given to us in the same way as natural and historical entities'.[61] It is not that he will not discuss the nature of the Word of God but, and this is the crucial qualification, it can only be discussed indirectly.[62] God speaks and 'in this divine telling there is an encounter and fellowship between His nature and man but not an assuming of God's nature into man's

---

60 This is an aspect of Barth's theology which we feel was overlooked in Graham Ward's account of Barth's theology. As he puts it, 'Who talks? And whence comes such talk? ... there are two possible answers to both questions: human beings or God.' Graham Ward, *Barth, Derrida, and the Language of Theology* (New York: Cambridge University Press, 1995), p. 13. For Ward, there are two words being spoken here and some form of relationship has to be established. His suggestion is that Barth relates these two activities dialectically in a 'paralogical journey towards the horizon of an eschatological dawn', Ward, *Barth, Derrida*, p. 16. He is right to identify two words in Barth's discussion, but our contention is that he does not adequately affirm Barth's articulation of the human word's proper ontological grounding in the being of the Church, Jesus Christ. As such he develops a dialectic between word and Word in a way that runs counter to what we will be arguing was Barth's intention.
61 CD I.1, p. 132/KD I.1, 137.
62 CD I.1, p. 132/KD I.1, 137.

The Being of the Church Dogmatics

knowing, only a fresh divine telling'.[63] The discussion of the nature of the Word of God is therefore transformed into a discussion of the nature of faith and human divine encounter. However, unlike the previous drafts which delved into an existential account of human preaching and understanding,[64] Barth now focuses upon the Lord God whose Word, 'aims at us and smites us in our *Existenz*'.[65] Death may be dumb and unable to question our existence, but the Word in fact does what death cannot do.

The Word of God applies to us as no human word as such can do, and as death does not do, because this Word is the Word of our Creator, of the One who encompasses our *Existenz* and the end of our *Existenz*, by whom it is preserved by this Word, and without it would not exist [*nicht wäre*].[66]

In this way Barth has moved on from a dialectic between human existence in and of itself and divinity in and of itself. There can be no 'co-positing [*mitgesetzt*]' between God and human being as he put it in the first edition, in a way akin to Schleiermacher's feeling of absolute dependence.[67] God and human beings do not co-posit their existence alongside each other, rather, God reigns supreme over human beings. Furthermore, this supremacy implies a sovereignty which does not depend upon human beings. God must be able to be God without the condition of created human beings.[68]

---

63 CD I.1, p. 132/KD I.1, 137.
64 Barth will clarify the difference between his previous *die christliche Dogmatik* where he tended to favour a 'phenomenological treatment and existential treatment' of the Word of God, and his later *Church Dogmatics*. CD I.1, p. 125/KD I.1, 128. He will go on to justify the changes he made of this draft in light of Gogarten's critique of the anthropological confusion this existential/phenomenological treatment implied. CD I.1, p. 127/KD I.1, 130.
65 CD I.1, p. 141/KD I.1, 146. The parallel between the descriptions of the Word as over against thought here in the *Church Dogmatics* and in his book on Anselm should not be missed.
66 CD I.1, p. 142/KD I.1, 146.
67 CD I.1, p. 140/KD I.1, 145.
68 Hence Barth will say, 'Only when we are clear about this can we estimate what it means that God has actually, though not necessarily, created a world and us, that his love actually, though not necessarily, applies to us, that His Word has actually, though not necessarily, been spoken to us.' CD I.1, p. 140/KD I.1, 144.

Protestant Metaphysics after Barth and Heidegger

By emphasizing the sovereignty of God's Word, Barth isn't trying to abstract God, making his relation to the world a relative impossibility. Rather, as God alone is God, Barth goes on to argue how this God speaks to human beings concretely and not as a 'general Truth'.[69] At this point in section five, however, Barth's emphasis is upon the Lordship and otherness of God. No human word can promise 'the specific and definitive coming of this Other [*Anderen*]'.[70] 'Again, what God says to us specifically remains His secret which will be disclosed in the event [*Ereignis*] of His actual speaking.'[71] The cornerstone of Barth's understanding of the point of contact between divine and human being is located in this event and the ontological impact it actualizes in human beings. Hence Barth says, 'The claim of the Word of God is not as such a wish or command which remains outside the hearer without impinging on his existence [*Existenz nicht tangierte*].'[72] Rather, Barth goes on to say that

> the judgement of God as such creates not only a new light and therewith a new situation, but also with the new situation a new man who did not exist [*existierte*] before but who exists [*existiert*] now, being identical with the man who has heard the Word.[73]

The Word therefore enacts an ontological change in twofold form. In the first sense it alerts human being to the *nihil*; the Word smites the existence of the human in order that, second, he or she may be made aware of the true existence which is possible. Genesis is echoed: the Word hovers over the chaos bringing life into true existence.[74]

---

69 CD I.1, p. 140/KD I.1, 145.
70 CD I.1, p. 142/KD I.1, 147.
71 CD I.1, p. 143/KD I.1, 147.
72 CD I.1, p. 152/KD I.1, 158.
73 CD I.1, p. 153/KD I.1, 158.
74 The account we are offering here therefore provides a stark contrast to those commentators who would see a qualitative difference between divine and human being in Barth's thought at this point in his development. Such was the thesis of Peter Halman Monsma, *Karl Barth's Idea of Revelation* (Somerville, NJ: Somerset Press Inc., 1937), p. 153. It is Monsma's failure to account for the ontological relations in Barth's thought that leads him to be confused by the manner in which Barth clearly does speak of the Lordship and primacy of God in relation to his part in the human world. Monsma, *Karl Barth's Idea of Revelation*, pp. 199–200.

The Being of the Church Dogmatics

According to the creative power of the Word, Barth delimits the secular world apart from the Church. Because it is God who holds the world to account, however, there can be no talk of the Church standing in judgement of an autonomous secular sphere.

> It is not at all true that the Church is outside with God and the world is inside without God. Things can be seen thus only if the Bible and the Church are seen apart from the revelation that constitutes them or if the revelation itself is understood, with Schleiermacher, only as the distinctive beginning of the religion that is our own.[75]

How could the Church hold the world to account? The Church has no power in and of itself. It is only the actualization of the God who brings it into being. It is in this sense, and this sense alone, that Barth understands the interim nature of the secular world.[76]

> Not in the light of nature but in the light of grace, there is no self-enclosed and protected secular sphere, but only one which is called into question by God's Word, by the Gospel, by God's claim, judgement and blessing, and which is only provisionally restrictedly abandoned to its own legalism and its own gods.[77]

The ontological nature of the Word's act in the world, the event upon which it brings new life into being, must face honestly that it is in *this world* that the Word is in fact spoken. As such, a secular realm raises the problem of *how* the Word of God *is* all the more sharply.

For Barth, 'the speech of God is and remains the mystery of God supremely in its secularity'.[78] The relation between God and the secular world cannot therefore be resolved by demarcating a line between God's Word and the ways in which it manifests itself to us

---

75 CD I.1, p. 155/KD I.1, 160.
76 The idea that Barth embraced 'the idea of a valid secular autonomy' must therefore be challenged. John Milbank, 'The Programme of Radical Orthodoxy', in *Radical Orthodoxy?: A Catholic Enquiry*, ed. Laurence Paul Hemming (Aldershot: Ashgate, 2000), p. 34.
77 CD I.1, p. 155/KD I.1, 160-1.
78 CD I.1, p. 165/KD I.1, 171.

as an event. Rather, it is precisely in this secularity that God's Word is truly understood as mystery.

> The Church is also in fact a sociological entity ... Jesus is also in fact the Rabbi of Nazareth who is hard to know historically and whose work, when He is known, might seem to be a little commonplace compared to more than one of the other founders of religions and even compared to some of the later representatives of his own religion. Nor should we forget that theology also, in so far as it uses human speech, is in fact a philosophy or a conglomerate of all kinds of philosophies.[79]

There is no other way in which God becomes God for us except shrouded in this secularity. It is this phenomenon that Barth describes in terms of the Word's mystery. The Word does not at first appear to us to be the Word of God. 'The veil is thick.'[80] 'We see through a mirror dimly', as Saint Paul says in 1 Corinthians 13.12. Barth discusses this passage in particular because it highlights the twofold nature of the problem. Not only do we see in a mirror which is itself an indirect reflection, but we see dimly. As Barth says in relation to this passage of scripture, 'first the Word of God meets us in a form that is to be distinguished from its content, and secondly the form as such is an enigma, a concealing of the Word of God'.[81] The problem goes beyond saying that God is hidden. Rather, God speaks in a way that hides himself. Again citing Saint Paul, Barth delves into an important excursus on the relation between the wisdom of the world and the folly of Christ in 1 Corinthians 1.18—2.10. Barth's interpretation of Paul's thought again highlights the way in which Christ crucified 'is indeed the power and wisdom of God, by which God turns the wisdom of the world into folly, but which as such, from the world's standpoint, can only be μωρία [foolishness]'.[82]

Here we would do well to recall Heidegger's citation of 1 Corinthians 1.20 in his 1949 essay 'The Way Back into the Ground of Metaphysics', which was written as an interpretative addendum

---

79 CD I.1, p. 165/KD I.1, 171.
80 CD I.1, p. 165/KD I.1, 171.
81 CD I.1, p. 166/KD I.1, 172.
82 CD I.1, p. 167/KD I.1, 173.

The Being of the Church Dogmatics

to 'What is Metaphysics?' Here Heidegger asks, 'will Christian theology make up its mind one day to take seriously the word of the apostle and thus also the conception of philosophy as foolishness?'[83] Barth too is dealing with this question, but in a way that prefigures Heidegger's question and takes it to different conclusions. As we already noted in the previous chapters, Heidegger attempts to quarantine philosophy from theology. However, as we can see here, Barth in fact wants to demonstrate how theology and philosophy are inextricably interwoven in so far as the Word of God consistently reveals itself in the hiddenness of philosophy. It is precisely because it is Christ crucified as the Jewish Rabbi from Nazareth that we can always ensure that it is in fact God alone who must do the revealing here. God's Word refuses any direct apprehension of human existence precisely in order to give it to us all the more truly.

It is this Christological understanding of the onto-theological problem which differentiates Barth from Heidegger. This is no more clear than in Barth's reference to Luther's *Heidelberg Disputation* (1518) in conjunction with 1 Corinthians 1.18—2.10. As Barth puts it, 'Luther opposes a *theologia crucis* to a *theologia gloriae,* i.e., a direct or only relatively indirect desire for knowledge of God.'[84] It is not that philosophical or strictly secular forms are set in opposition to God, but rather the predicament is that God is in fact incarnated in this secular form in such a way that we must face both his secularity and divinity simultaneously. Unlike the division between the early and later Luther, which Heidegger would develop in his *Phenomenology of Religious Life,*[85] Barth argues that this is 'not just a principle of the younger Luther, but a principle of his whole theology'.[86] In another passage Barth cites Luther's *Commentary on Galatians* (1535) in relation to the claim that Barth's theology borders on *speculatio Maiestatis*. According to Barth, Luther isn't critiquing our ability to recognize and understand 'the incarnate

---

83 Martin Heidegger, 'The Way Back into the Ground of Metaphysics', in *Existentialism: From Dostoevsky to Sartre,* ed. Walter Kaufmann (New York: Penguin Books, 1989), p. 276.
84 CD I.1, p. 167/KD I.1, 173.
85 Martin Heidegger, *The Phenomenology of Religious Life* (Bloomington: Indiana University Press, 2004), pp. 67, 213.
86 CD I.1, p. 167/KD I.1, 173.

Word in all seriousness as God's Word'.[87] It is not an attack 'on acknowledging its invisible majesty'.[88] Rather,

> it is an attack on the attempt to evade the necessity of believing by trying to get a direct or only relatively indirect knowledge of God apart from the secularity and the resultant mystery of the incarnate Word. When Luther points to the crib of Bethlehem and the cross of Golgotha, he is not saying that direct knowledge of God is possible and actual here in this very secular phenomenon as such.[89]

Barth therefore argues that, in order to maintain the mystery of God in his secular revelation, Luther points to 'the total secularity, i.e., the hiddenness of the Word, and therewith the sole reality of indirect knowledge, and therewith the distinction whose elimination can only be thought of as in process and never completed, and therefore the immanent Trinity'.[90] Luther is not advocating a radical divide between philosophy and theology here as Heidegger suggested. Rather, Barth believes Luther is advocating a radical theology which has the power to bring the secular into a participatory relationship. The problem with *speculatio Maiestatis* is not its secularity, but its lack of faith. 'Here in the *humanitas Christi* we are to seek and find everything. We seek and find this, but we seek and find; we do not see and have directly.'[91]

Barth therefore consistently argues for the coincidence of God's Word and its secular form in order to demonstrate the impossibility of our recognizing it as God's Word apart from a decisive act of God, as he tears an 'untearably thick veil, i.e. His mystery'.[92] This secures both the mystery of God as well as the revelation of God's Word without creating opposition between God and the secular world. Barth is quick to realize that if this were not the case, God would in fact be utterly irrelevant to our own existential concerns. 'If God did not speak to us in secular form, he would not speak to

---

87 CD I.1, p. 173/KD I.1, 179.
88 CD I.1, p. 173/KD I.1, 179.
89 CD I.1, p. 173/KD I.1, 180.
90 CD I.1, p. 173/KD I.1, 180.
91 CD I.1, p. 173/KD I.1, 180.
92 CD I.1, p. 168/KD I.1, 174.

The Being of the Church Dogmatics

us at all.'⁹³ If this were the case, then we really would be left waiting for a God to come and save us as Heidegger suggested towards the end of his life.⁹⁴ Rather, for Barth, God has already come in an utterly mysterious secularity. It is precisely because the mystery of the Word of God is so pervasive, the veil so thick, that we can be assured that our knowledge of this Word is given by God.⁹⁵

This further explains Barth's response to the criticisms Erich Przywara SJ made concerning Barth's early *christliche Dogmatik*. Barth conceptualized God and human being as if the two were oppositionally related in an ontologically unqualified way in his early work, and it is for these reasons that Przywara accused Barth of pantheism. Barth could emphasize the radical transcendence of God as prominently and persistently as he wanted. Przywara's contention remained that 'all the fullness of the divine life is thus reduced to the one address, and in the last resort the final pantheistic correlation-theology [*Korrelationstheologie*] of Protestant Liberalism is simply reversed'.⁹⁶ It is for these reasons that Barth agrees not to go in the direction Gogarten asked him to go.⁹⁷ Barth's solution to the problem is to draw 'a sharp distinction between the Trinity of God as we may know it in the Word of God revealed, written and proclaimed, and God's immanent Trinity'.⁹⁸ Human beings can participate in God's revelation, but this participation is conditioned from without. In other words, Barth can say that he agrees with Gogarten that theology must not 'speak of man in himself, in isolation from God',⁹⁹ but this is not to say that the relation between God and human being can be conceived by any other way than by speaking of 'God in Himself, in isolation from man'.¹⁰⁰ The Trinitarian nature of God therefore justifies the manner in which Barth thinks through the relation between God and human being according to participation

---

93 CD I.1, p. 168/KD I.1, 175.
94 Martin Heidegger, '"Only a God Can Save Us": The *Spiegel* Interview (1966)', in *Heidegger: The Man and the Thinker*, ed. Thomas Sheehan (Chicago: Precedent, 1981), p. 57.
95 CD I.1, p. 169/KD I.1, 175.
96 CD I.1, p. 172/KD I.1, 178.
97 See above.
98 CD I.1, p. 172/KD I.1, 179.
99 CD I.1, p. 172/KD I.1, 179.
100 CD I.1, p. 172/KD I.1, 179.

and not divinization.[101] Man does not become God, rather, God becomes man. Barth is therefore destabilizing the basis of the parity between God and human beings. The problem isn't with God in himself, but rather the dialectic between God and humanity according to Kierkegaardian terms.[102] Hence, Barth's claim that the relation between God and the secular world is not oppositional demands that human being is negated, 'smited' and challenged by the Word. This is not pantheism precisely because the created secular world is not given a claim to existence in and of itself. Only in God and according to the decision of God is the secular world to be considered really real. By denying an opposition between two ontological realms, Barth is able to discuss all the more freely how it is that God can in fact speak to us. This occurs only in so far as the secular world is returned to a divine participation in God by his grace.

Barth continues to emphasize that it is God alone who unveils himself in a veiling that utterly bars theology from developing a dialectic between God and the secular world. Rather, 'the speech of God is and remains the mystery of God in its onesidedness'.[103] It is in the sole and miraculous act of God that this unveiling veiling takes place and this means that there can be 'no thought of synthe-

---

101 We would agree with McCormack on this point. Bruce L. McCormack, 'Participation in God, Yes; Deification, No: Two Modern Protestant Responses to an Ancient Question', in *Orthodox and Modern: Studies in the Theology of Karl Barth* (Grand Rapids, MI: Baker Academic, 2008).

102 Kierkegaard accounts for the difference between divine and human being in terms of an absolute paradox whereby the difference between divine and human being cannot be resolved from the side of human being. As he puts it, 'That God has existed in human form, has been born, grown up, and so forth, is surely the paradox *sensu strictissimo*, the absolute paradox'. Søren Kierkegaard, *Concluding Unscientific Postscript to Philosophical Fragments*, trans. David F. Swenson and Walter Lowrie (Princeton, NJ: Princeton University Press, 1968), pp. 194–5. It should be noted that Barth goes beyond Kierkegaard, whom he associates with Heidegger's nexus of being (CD I.1, p. 36), and the inward existentialism of the Pietists (CD I.1, p. 20). For further comment on Barth's critique of pietism, see Eberhard Busch, *Karl Barth & the Pietists: The Young Karl Barth's Critique of Pietism and Its Response* (Downers Grove, IL: InterVarsity Press, 2004). When Kierkegaard qualifies the absolute difference between the divine and human, he only exacerbates the problem of dialectically relating a self-grounded human being to divine being. Barth's rebuttal of both Kierkegaard (and Hegelian) dialectic arises in so far as he refuses to give human being a dialectical standing in relation to God. Barth will not give human being claim over the dialectic, nor will he so differentiate the human being from the divine being [paradox] that no genuine knowledge of the reconciliation is possible.

103 CD I.1, p. 174/KD I.1, 180.

The Being of the Church Dogmatics

sis. Faith means recognizing that synthesis cannot be attained and committing it to God and seeking and finding it in Him. Finding it in God we acknowledge that we cannot find it ourselves'.[104] When discussing the how of God's Word therefore, Barth's emphasis upon mystery is ultimately an acknowledgement of the hearer's limits.[105] Echoing his book on Anselm, Barth argues that whenever we speak of God, if it is to be God that we are truly speaking of, he must always be greater than that which we can conceive. This implies again that any connection between the Word of God and human words will be created solely by the Word itself. Barth's emphasis counters the previous draft's existentialist account of the hearer. In this later draft, Barth concludes section five by stating that 'theology cannot be in controversy with the autonomies of this world'.[106] Here again Barth points beyond the how of the Word of God to the Spirit which makes this Word a possibility for us to hear.[107] In this hearing, however, the conditions of our hearing also have to change. It is in this sense that all language might be talk about God in so far as all things become what they most are in God. Although Barth discusses the Holy Spirit's part in the event of God's revelation at this point, he will ultimately suspend that discussion until he deals more thoroughly with the doctrine of the Trinity. At this point he is therefore delimiting the trajectory that doctrine will follow. In this regard, section six continues Barth's desire to foreground his discussion of the Trinity, by concretizing the Word of God's relation to our knowledge. It is here that the distinctive title of Barth's dogmatics as *Church Dogmatics* becomes clear.

Thus far, Barth has discussed the nature of the Word of God in its threefold form as preached, written and revealed in order to emphasize a divine onesidedness which demands that we come to terms with the secularity of the Word. The one-sided nature of the Word of God therefore challenges an ontological dialectic between divine and human being in and of itself. In discussing the nature of the Word, he therefore sets out the parameters for how this divine Word acts in the mystery of its secularity. These are the parameters which guide his discussion in section six of 'The Knowledge of the

---

104 CD I.1, p. 175/KD I.1, 182.
105 CD I.1, p. 176/KD I.1, 183.
106 CD I.1, p. 186/KD I.1, 193.
107 CD I.1, p. 186/KD I.1, 194.

Word of God'. Given that the nature of the Word was already discussed in terms of the way or manner in which it acts in the world, much has already been implied for what Barth says concerning how we know this Word. Barth is as much going to clarify what he said in the previous sections as he will develop those ideas further.

He begins therefore by reiterating the peculiar and specific nature of the existence of human beings in the Church. If we are to take it for granted that it is possible for human beings to know the Word of God then particular assumptions must be made concerning the nature of those human beings. Barth makes it clear that he is not starting with a general existentialism which becomes the dialectical counterpart to a divine ontology. Rather, to know the Word of God, Barth assumes 'a specific sphere of human existence, namely, the sphere of the Church'.[108] Barth begins with a most forceful reaffirmation of the importance of an ecclesial existence which differs from a general affirmation of human being. This ecclesial existence is the basis upon which Barth claims any place to begin his discussion of our knowledge of the Word of God. Without this ecclesial existence, Barth makes it clear that 'the whole concept of the Word of God would have to be called a figment of the imagination, and Church proclamation, including dogmatics, would have to be called a pointless and meaningless activity'.[109] The question Barth raises then is how does the active event of the Word of God become known in the Church? Barth's answer to this question is that the concept of the Church provides a location for a specific form of human existence. The Church does not contain Christian people in and of itself, rather, people become a Christian Church in so far as they are marked by a 'necessary and inward determination'.[110] The truth of the existence of the Word of God now becomes true for people as well. Thus, the Church is a condition for the knowledge of the Word of God only in so far as it marks this event whereby the ontological nature of the Word is actualized in people. There is no way to extricate the Church from this event. 'Knowing, they are affected by the object known. They no longer exist without it, but with it.'[111] There is an ontological change which is necessary to the

---

108 CD I.1, p. 187/KD I.1, 195.
109 CD I.1, pp. 187–8/KD I.1, 195.
110 CD I.1, p. 188/KD I.1, 195.
111 CD I.1, p. 188/KD I.1, 195.

The Being of the Church Dogmatics

knowledge of God and this drives forward Barth's explication of what he means by knowledge of the Word of God.[112]

As Barth turns to explicate the relation between the Word of God and human beings, he returns to the Christological nature of God's Word.

> The Word of God, Jesus Christ, as the being of the Church [*Sein der Kirche*], sets us ineluctably before the realization that it was and will be men who are intended and addressed and therefore characterized as recipients but as also themselves bearers of this Word.[113]

The ontological nature of the Church will therefore raise an anthropological question in so far as Barth develops the meaning of this Christological being of the Church. Barth's contention is that this question cannot be subsumed under an anthropological assessment of human religious experience. Such was the manner in which Barth believes Schleiermacher interpreted Christianity 'within the framework of a general doctrine of man'.[114] It's not that Barth is averse to the concept of religious experience in and of itself.[115] Rather, Barth's contention is that the Word of God determines human being in such a way that human existence is returned to the moment of its creation *ex nihilo*.

> It will also be the limitation of his *Existence* by the absolute 'out there' [*Außerhalb*] of his Creator, a limitation on the basis of which he can understand himself only as created out of nothing and upheld over nothing.[116]

The knowledge of the Word of God is therefore the acknowledgement of the human person's ontological lack. It is in this acknowledgement, however, that the possibility of an ontological renewal becomes possible as well.[117]

---

112 CD I.1, p. 188/KD I.1, 196.
113 CD I.1, p. 191/KD I.1, 199.
114 CD I.1, p. 192/KD I.1, 200.
115 CD I.1, p. 193/KD I.1, 201.
116 CD I.1, p. 194/KD I.1, 202.
117 CD I.1, p. 194/KD I.1, 202.

Protestant Metaphysics after Barth and Heidegger

If human beings can know the reality of the Word of God, then they must participate in this reality. Given that this participation depends upon a creative act by God upon human beings, Barth has no objection to a discussion of the human experience of this Word. But here again, Barth is absolutely explicit that divine and human being do not coexist [*Zusammensein*] on the same level.[118] The contrast between a human being determined and renewed by God and a self-determined human being cannot be related according to dialectic [*Dialektik*].[119] There is no space in which this dialectic can take place precisely because unredeemed human being is in fact in conflict with the true being which can only be determined by God.

> Precisely as self-determination [*Selbstbestimmung*], it is subject to determination [*Bestimmung*] by God. In this relation of total subjection and need *vis-à-vis* determination [*Bestimung*] by God it cannot possibly replace this, as Pelagius wished, or co-operate with it, as the Semi-Pelagians wished, or be secretly identical with it, as Augustine wished.[120]

We do not decide upon ourselves, God does. Our determination is not identical with God's, but depends upon God's determination. This is not to say that human beings are in a state of 'total receptivity or passivity',[121] but rather, that there is no spectator seat from which we can judge God's own decision upon us.[122]

Barth describes the chief mark of this divine determination of human existence in terms of acknowledgement [*Anerkennung*].[123]

---

118 CD I.1, p. 200/KD I.1, 208.
119 CD I.1, p. 200/KD I.1, 208.
120 CD I.1, p. 200/KD I.1, 208.
121 CD I.1, p. 200/KD I.1, 209.
122 Barth's answer to his own awareness that he is implying a kind of anthropological passivity is that it is precisely in their self-determination that human beings are determined by God. It is the entire human being in all of his or her feeling, will and intellect that is at stake here, and there can be no place that human beings can claim apart from God. Nor can they assume that this self-determination is God. Nor can they gain a vantage point upon which to decide for themselves God's own determination, his own decision upon the obedience or disobedience of the human being. Rather, 'we may quietly regard the will and conscience and feeling and all other possible anthropological centers as possibilities of human self-determination and then understand them in their totality as determined by the Word of God which affects the whole man'. CD I.1, p. 202/KD I.1, 211.
123 The German term *Anerkennung* is related to its verbal form *anerkennen*

The Being of the Church Dogmatics

As Barth says regarding this term: 'I am aware of no word relatively so appropriate as this one to the nature of the Word of God whose determinative operation is our present concern'.[124] In fact, Barth goes on to summarize section five according to the meaning he gives for this term. Acknowledgement includes knowledge, but goes beyond a human *ratio,* to include the manner in which 'the determination of man's existence ... is determined by God's person'.[125] Whatever this determination accomplishes, however, acknowledgement indicates that the human being agrees and submits to this Word.[126] In this sense, Barth notes the way this Word brings human beings into obedience. This is therefore not a form of 'persuasion between equals'.[127] God's Word bends human beings, bringing them 'into conformity with itself'.[128] In so far as it is God's choice to come to human beings, human beings are then given the choice to respond in faith to God's decision or not to. The choice for human beings, however, cannot contravene this rule of faith. Barth refers back to section five's discussion of the secularity of the Word precisely to emphasize that 'apart from this ambivalence ... there is no experience of God's Word'.[129] Human beings do therefore act in acknowledging the mystery of the Word of God, but this acknowledgement implies 'a yielding of the man who acknowledges'.[130]

Barth's understanding of revelation consistently demonstrates

---

which derives its meaning from the legal sense of to judge or find a person guilty. It therefore 'suggests overt practical, rather than merely intellectual recognition ... Thus, *Anerkennung* involves not simply the intellectual identification of a thing or person (though it characteristically presupposes such intellectual recognition), but the assignment to it of a positive value and the explicit expression of this assignment.' M. J. Inwood, *A Hegel Dictionary* (Oxford: Blackwell, 1992), p. 245. '*Anerkennung* and *anerkennen* overlap the meanings of "recognition" and "to recognize", and of "acknowledgement" and "to acknowledge", but do not coincide with either pair. *Anerkennen* is a sixteenth-century formation, on the model of the Latin *agnoscere* ("to ascertain, recognize, acknowledge"), and based on the (thirteenth-century) legal sense of *erkennen* ("to judge, find (e.g. a person guilty)"), rather than its older sense of "to know, cognize". It thus suggests overt, practical, rather than merely intellectual recognition.' Inwood, *A Hegel Dictionary*, p. 245.

124 CD I.1, p. 205/KD I.1, 214.
125 CD I.1, p. 205/KD I.1, 214.
126 CD I.1, p. 205/KD I.1, 214.
127 CD I.1, p. 206/KD I.1, 215.
128 CD I.1, p. 206/KD I.1, 215.
129 CD I.1, p. 207/KD I.1, 216.
130 CD I.1, p. 207/KD I.1, 217.

that there is no possible discussion of human knowledge of the Word of God that does not account for the ontological determination of human beings in their concrete existence. Barth is not trying to eliminate 'the intimate personal experience of faith'.[131] Rather, he seeks to establish the true basis upon which faith can in fact be a real experience for human beings. As Barth turns to 'The Word of God in Faith' in the last subsection of section six, he draws specific attention to the question of faith. 'Thus it is in faith, as the possibility given in faith, that we have to understand the knowability of the Word of God.'[132] In this regard, however, faith and acknowledgement are interwoven in so far as faith is the act of acknowledgement by a concrete individual human being. Here, Barth cites Anselm's *Proslogion* 1 in order to deepen what he means by the referential character of faith, that is how it is that this act of faith by the human being is not limited to his or her own imagination.[133] Rather, he returns to the prayerful starting point Anselm assumes when confronted by the mystery of God.

> In the closest material relation to the famous proof for the existence of God immediately following, there is brought up here in the form of a prayer the problem whether God is present at all to the thinker who sets out to understand and explain the existence and nature of God.[134]

Prayer becomes that starting place whereby the act of faith finds its proper object beyond itself. Because its object is utterly enshrouded in mystery, faith can only expect this object. 'It is by this external object that Christian faith lives.'[135]

It is in this context that Barth discusses just how close he comes to the Roman Catholic doctrine of *analogia entis*. Here we must remember that Barth's understanding of *analogia entis* was deeply influenced by Erich Przywara, SJ. It should be noted, however, that Przywara's account of *analogia entis* does not necessarily represent the view of all Roman Catholic theology on this matter. Rather,

---

131 CD I.1, p. 209/KD I.1, 218.
132 CD I.1, p. 229/KD I.1, 241.
133 CD I.1, p. 230/KD I.1, 242.
134 CD I.1, p. 230/KD I.1, 242.
135 CD I.1, p. 232/KD I.1, 244.

The Being of the Church Dogmatics

although Przywara saw his understanding of analogy as 'presupposed' by all Catholic theology, he nonetheless 'was certainly aware that he was using this expression in a very idiosyncratic sense'.[136] For instance, in his 1927 *Religionsphilosophie katholischer Theologie*,[137] Przywara is working out a way beyond the rationalism and radical immanentism of the neo-Kantianism of Herrmann Cohen or 'religion within the limits [*innerhalb*] of humanity'.[138] Przywara sought to offer an alternative solution to the understanding of religion as 'the relation [*Beziehung*] between absolute God and relative man'.[139] Relative man would be understood in a way which opens him ever upward which never reduces that openness to being itself. Rather, human being finds itself in an openness which implies similarity to the being it opens itself to, and yet, in the very openness, dissimilarity is implied regarding what human being cannot provide in and of itself. Thus, Przywara's *analogia entis* was utterly modern in its affirmation of the phenomenology of being articulated in the work of Husserl and, later, Heidegger.[140] It is fair

---

136 Henry Chavannes, *The Analogy between God and the World in Saint Thomas Aquinas and Karl Barth* (New York: Vantage Press, 1992), p. 4. As one commentator puts it, 'Przywara insisted repeatedly in debate that the *analogia entis* is presupposed by all types of Catholic philosophy and is not limited to any one school of Catholic thought. He developed his "*analogia entis* metaphysics" as his own synthesis of classical, scholastic and modern philosophical ideas in the spirit of Aquinas'. Niels C. Nielsen Jr., 'Przywara's Philosophy of the Analogia Entis', *Review of Metaphysics* 5 (1952), pp. 600–1.

137 Translated into English as Erich Przywara, *Polarity: A German Catholic's Interpretation of Religion*, trans. Alan Coates Bouquet (London: Oxford University Press, 1935), For the German original see, Erich Przywara, 'Religionsphilosophie katholischer Theologie (1927)', in *Religions-Philosophische Schriften* (London: Johannes-Verlag, 1962), Hereafter cited as RKT.

138 Przywara, *Polarity*, p. 25/RKT397. For Przywara, even modern emphases upon a transcendent 'experience of infinity [*Erkenntnis der Unendlichkeit*]', Przywara, *Polarity*, p. 23/RKT396, inevitably reduce to a 'camouflaged rationalism [*versteckter Rationalismus*]', Przywara, *Polarity*, p. 26/RKT398, and a conflation of human and divine being. In the opening paragraphs of the second section of *Religionsphilosophie katholischer Theologia*, Przywara puts forward the heart of his own way forward: 'As a decisive feature in the groundwork of the Catholic religion, running through its treatment of essence and existence, we may descry the following: that the relationship between God and creation is one which is *open upwards* [*nach oben offense*]'. Przywara, *Polarity*, p. 29/RKT400.

139 Przywara, *Polarity*, p. 22/RKT395.

140 'Przywara accepted Husserl's phenomenological analysis as conclusive proof that human knowledge has its first basis in and is directed to a comprehension of be-

to say, therefore, that the understanding of *analogia entis* that Barth gained through his interactions with Przywara[141] 'has only the most distant connection with Thomist doctrine'.[142]

Barth inserts his critique of *analogia entis* at this point in his *Church Dogmatics* in so far as he recognizes that for faith to be faith, it must remain open to the radical otherness of its object. As such, there must be some manner in which a 'point of contact' [*Anknüpfungspunkt*] is created between human beings and this object.[143] The object cannot be apprehended or domesticated by a capacity inherent to the human being. Hence, Barth says that

> in faith there takes place a conformity of man to God. We do not say a deification but a conformity to God, i.e., an adapting of man to the Word of God. In faith, as he really receives God's Word, man becomes apt to receive it.[144]

Here again Barth critiques Emil Brunner's conception of the image of God which provides the point of contact in a manner wholly inconsistent with what Barth means here. Barth challenges any sense in which a common being can be assumed between God and humanity. What is at stake is not that human beings are in some sense brought into conformity with God's being, but rather, the manner in which this conformity is understood.

> Not a being which the creature has in common with the Creator for all their dissimilarity, but an act that is inaccessible to any mere theory, i.e., human decision, is in faith similar to the decision of God's grace for all its dissimilarity.[145]

---

ing in its richness and depth ... and insists with Heidegger on the temporal, existential givenness of all knowledge in its particularity'. Niels C. Nielsen Jr., 'Przywara's Philosophy of the Analogia Entis', p. 602, cf, Erich Przywara, 'Drei Richtungen der Phänomenologie', *Stimmen der Zeit* CXV (1928).

141 Most notably Barth invited Przywara to 'a "solemn seminar" where he could present everything he had to say about the analogy of being ... in February of 1929'. Thomas F. O'Meara, *Erich Przywara, S.J.: His Theology and His World* (Notre Dame, IN: University of Notre Dame Press, 2002), p. 103.

142 Chavannes, *The Analogy between God and the World*, p. 150.

143 CD I.1, p. 238/KD I.1, 251.

144 CD I.1, p. 238/KD I.1, 251.

145 CD I.1, p. 239/KD I.1, 252.

The Being of the Church Dogmatics

Barth contrasts *entis* with *actus* precisely in order to ensure that human beings do not assume that they can contravene the necessity of faith, that is the need to expect God's grace from beyond themselves. If there is to be an analogy in this sense, it is in so far as God's act of grace can be thought to be analogous to the human faith which is created in the human being by God's grace. Citing Augustine, Luther and Calvin, Barth argues that faith presumes an ontological redemption in human beings that they all described in one way or another as *deificatio*. Barth's clarification is that

> neither in Augustine nor in Luther is there anything about a deification in faith in the sense of a changing of a man's nature into the divine nature. What makes the expression possible is the *apprehensio Christi* or *habitatio Christi in nobis* or *unio hominis cum Christo* that takes place in real faith according to the teaching of Gal. 2.20.[146]

Faith is, as such, a kind of limit case which bars human beings from claiming an ontological stasis between themselves and God at any point. The pre-fall notion of an *imago dei* cannot provide the basis for our knowledge of the Word of God because no such remnant can secure a point of contact that we could take any confidence in when discussing this Word of God. The analogical relation Barth develops here is ultimately then, one of faith.

Analogia fidei provides the contrast to *analogia entis* precisely at this point of contact by ensuring that human beings do not assume that their act of faith is in anyway independent from God's act of grace. *Analogia fidei* is a disruption to any form of *analogia entis,* and not a comparable analogical set of relations. As Henri Bouillard puts it,

> When Barth substitutes *analogia fidei* for *analogia entis* he is not opposing, as one might think, two formal conceptions of analogy. He wishes to affirm that there is a resemblance between man and God only through Jesus Christ, and that the correspondence

---

146 CD I.1, p. 240/KD I.1, 253.

between human discourse and the divine reality is only assured by the grace of revelation.[147]

This explains why Barth does not develop the concept of analogy in much detail. It is rather the notion of faith that Barth is discussing at this point in his *Dogmatics,* and it is precisely here that we must recognize the similarity between Barth's approach to true being, and Heidegger's. As we discussed in Chapter 1, Heidegger's cross was meant to foster understanding of the being of beings. By leaving metaphysics to itself, he sought to understand the being of beings all the more fully. For Heidegger, being was crossed out not excluded; it was obscured not discarded. It is our contention that this is the same strategy that Barth is employing when he considers the revelation of the being of God. However, Barth's understanding of the cross is far more vibrant theologically than Heidegger's, and this is in no small part because of Barth's more ontologically rich interpretation of Luther. By speaking of faith analogically, Barth intends to obscure the Word of God in order to enact a reversal in the epistemological capacity of the human being. It is a self-determined human being which Barth is speaking of here, not a 'passive apathetic contemplation in faith'.[148]

> Man believes, not God. But the fact that man is the subject in faith is bracketed as a predicate of the subject God, bracketed in the way that the Creator encloses the creature and the merciful God sinful man, i.e. in such a way that man remains subject, and yet man's I as such derives only from the Thou of the subject God.[149]

If the human being is to understand the true nature of its existence, therefore, then it must face honestly the manner in which its true being arrives from beyond itself. As Barth concludes in section six, 'The Word of God becomes knowable by making itself known ... The possibility of knowing the Word of God is God's miracle on

---

147 Henri Bouillard, *The Knowledge of God* (London: Burns & Oates, 1969), p. 115.
148 CD I.1, p. 245/KD I.1, 258.
149 CD I.1, p. 245/KD I.1, 258.

us just as much as is the Word itself or its being spoken'.[150] If it is to be the case that this Word is truly known then God must create this possibility. This demands in Barth's mind that God in some constitutive way restores the human being to its created glory. As we shall see, this is precisely what Barth will argue is at the heart of the redemptive power of Christ in his discussion of the revelation of the Trinitarian God.

The Revelation of God

The second chapter and latter half of the first volume of Barth's *Church Dogmatics* gravitates around one central locus, the Trinitarian nature of God's revelation. All that has come before has led up to this point. Whatever is meant by the being of the Church, Jesus Christ, will come into full fruition in this latter chapter. There is no accounting for our knowledge of God without exploring the way in which this God makes himself known. If we are to know this God as truly God, then Barth has delineated why God must initiate and actualize this knowledge. In this second chapter of the book, therefore, Barth interrelates the question of our knowledge of God with a second question which draws attention to the need to delineate the revelation of God more clearly. As Barth puts it, 'how does it come about, how is it actual [*wirklich*], that this God reveals himself?'[151] Furthermore, Barth is quick to recognize that when asked in this manner, a third question is inevitable as well. If God is to remain God in our knowledge of him, then we must also ask, 'What does this event do to the man to whom it happens?'[152] Because of the nature of human knowledge, the revelation of God must constitute a change in the human being it encounters. Barth is adamant that these questions be answered in relation to each other precisely because the 'Revealer, is identical with his act in revelation and also identical with its effect'.[153] Thus, Barth sets out to discuss God's revelation in a threefold way in terms of a Revealer, revelation and effect, and it is in this sense and based on the line of

---
150 CD I.1, p. 246/KD I.1, 260.
151 CD I.1, p. 296/KD I.1, 311.
152 CD I.1, p. 296/KD I.1, 312.
153 CD I.1, p. 296/KD I.1, 312.

questioning this threefold investigation of revelation implies that Barth draws specific attention to the triune nature of God.[154]

Before Barth's exploration of the threefold enquiry into revelation in the *Church Dogmatics,* however, he stops to comment upon his treatment of this topic in the *christliche Dogmatik.*

> In the first edition of this book (p. 127) I referred to these three questions and then continued with the words: 'Logically they are quite simply questions about the subject, predicate and object of the short statement: God speaks'. '*Deus dixit*'.[155]

Barth defends this statement on the grounds that he did not intend to give the impression that the doctrine of the Trinity could be derived from the subject–object relations implied by God's speech, but rather that this formula naturally follows from the dogma of the Trinity.[156] Barth therefore does not abandon his interest in the speech of God, but he is giving the reasons why he might give a more substantive account of the Trinity than he did in the first draft. What we must come to see is the manner in which Barth clarified the substantive precedence of the triune God with a more full bodied ontology. As such, Barth demonstrates how the encounter with God's speech raises a crucial problem concerning his existence. Asked as a question: how is it possible to arrive at the existence of God from his act in the world? As his critics rightly commented, to say that God speaks does not necessarily solve the problem of how the hearer can be sure that it is God who has in fact spoken.[157]

Barth's recognition of the coinherence of the doctrine of the Trinity and revelation does not necessarily resolve the problem of the hearer's recognition of divine speech. Barth does not, however, attempt to resolve this issue strictly in terms of the noetic capacities of the rational subject. Rather, he does so in terms of the ontological consistency which triune revelation demands. As Barth puts it,

> It does not seem possible, nor is any attempt made in the Bible, to dissolve the unity of the self-revealing God, His revelation and

---

154 CD I.1, p. 303/KD I.1, 319.
155 CD I.1, p. 296/KD I.1, 312.
156 CD I.1, p. 296/KD I.1, 312.
157 CD I.1, p. 296/KD I.1, 312.

The Being of the Church Dogmatics

His being revealed into a union in which the barriers that separate the above three forms of His divine being [*Gottseins*] in revelation are removed and they are reduced to a synthetic fourth and true reality [*Eigentliches*].[158]

If God truly is to be God there can be no differentiation between the three questions of who God is, how he is and what he effects without a concomitant emphasis upon the unity and interdependence between the three. There can be no fourth actual thing behind or beyond the revelation of God, and here Barth gives in brief his framework for working through this problem: 'Thus the same God who in unimpaired unity is the Revealer, the revelation and the revealedness, there is also ascribed in unimpaired differentiation within Himself this threefold mode of being [*dreifache Weise von Sein*]'.[159] God is one being, one ontological deity, who reveals himself in three ways. Barth is attempting to make the final move beyond a dialectic between God and the world to a differentiation between God and God. In a positive citation of C. J. Nitsch's *System der christlichen Lehre,* Barth notes that 'so long as theism only distinguishes God and the world and never God from God, it is always caught in a relapse or transition to the pantheistic or some other denial of absolute being'.[160] Barth's response to Przywara's critique of his own pantheism, as we noted above,[161] has to be read in this light. Barth is not denying absolute being, but rather addressing the question of being in terms of the doctrine of the Trinity. So too, the distance between God and his speech and the potential metaphysical or conceptual basis our understanding of his speech implies is closed in so far as the Revealer and his revelation are in fact the one Trinitarian God. As such, Barth's *Deus dixit* is not abandoned, but ontologically enriched. 'From the standpoint of the comprehensive concept of God's Word it must be said that here in God's revelation God's Word is identical with God Himself.'[162]

As Barth takes account of the mediated nature of this Word, 'first through the prophets and apostles who receive it and pass it on, and

---

158 CD I.1, p. 299/KD I.1, 315.
159 CD I.1, p. 299/KD I.1, 315.
160 CD I.1, p. 302/KD I.1, 318.
161 CD I.1, p. 172/KD I.1, 178.
162 CD I.1, p. 304/KD I.1, 321.

then through the human person of its expositors and preachers',[163] he has to make it clear that there can be no ontological difference between these mediated words and the Word of God. This means that the words of the prophet are not, in and of themselves, the Word of God any more than the words of the preacher. 'They must become [revelation]. Revelation does not have to become it'.[164] Crucially, Barth argues in this same passage that for the Word of God to be the revelation of God in human words there must be no ontological difference between the words becoming the Word and the Word itself. The difference between God in himself and the Word is a differentiation in God's self which is marked by a different mode of the divine being. This is why Barth says that 'God's revelation has its reality [*Wirklichkeit*] and truth [*Wahrheit*] wholly and in every respect – both ontically [*ontisch*] and noetically [*noetisch*] – within itself'.[165] The temptation Barth is avoiding here is the assumption that God's being must become a different kind of being altogether if it is to interact with our own.

Here Barth's rejection of Heidegger's ontic–ontological divide is rehearsed in Barth's own Trinitarian terms.[166] For to allow such a divide to remain would inevitably fall into a form of pantheism as this autonomous human being is divinized, or atheism, as the apophatic distance between divine and human being makes real knowledge of God impossible. Thus, Barth realizes that by affirming that God is in fact the same God for us in revelation, he can avoid the possibility of trying to answer his question concerning who God is in terms of 'another higher or deeper ground'.[167] It is because of Barth's denial of any ontological difference between divine and revealed being, that Barth can conclude, 'the fullness of the original [*ursprünglichen*] self-existent [*selbst-wesenden*] being [*Seins*] of God's Word reposes [*ruht*] and lives in it'.[168] Just as in Anselm, Barth is delineating the unique way in which existence can be attributed to the object which the human being encounters beyond itself. This divine existence comes at the expense of, or as

---

163 CD I.1, p. 304/KD I.1, 321.
164 CD I.1, p. 305/KD I.1, 322.
165 CD I.1, p. 305/KD I.1, 321.
166 CD I.1, pp. 36–7/KD I.1, 36
167 CD I.1, p. 305/KD I.1, 321–2.
168 CD I.1, p. 305/KD I.1, 322.

The Being of the Church Dogmatics

a negative prohibition against attributing human being to divine being. Revelation does not change, but rather we do. In one sense then, we can see how the ontic–ontological divide understood in a Heideggerian manner is relativized by the being of God in its three modes. However, this is not to say that there is no ontological difference between divine and human being, but that this difference will be understood in terms of different modes, first and foremost in terms of the being of Christ. We will suspend a more thoroughgoing investigation into the nature of Christ's being for the following chapter.

At this point, however, it is important simply to note that Barth is not trying to make an ultimate claim upon God here by rooting the Trinity in revelation. God is not the triune God 'only in his revelation and only for the sake of his revelation'.[169] Rather it is that 'we arrive at the doctrine of the Trinity by no other way than that of an analysis of the concept of revelation',[170] and in this analysis we are inevitably starting from an ontic and noetic level. Hence, when discussing the manner in which God reveals himself, Barth rehearses the mystery and hiddenness of God who yet is able to reveal himself in concealment.

> The God who reveals Himself here can reveal Himself. The very fact of revelation tells us that it is proper to Him to distinguish Himself from Himself, i.e., to be God in Himself and in concealment, and yet at the same time to be God a second time in a very different way, namely, in manifestation, i.e., in the form of something He Himself is not.[171]

Notice here that it is a differentiation in God now, and not an ontic–ontological differentiation. As Barth discusses in an extended subtext in terms of the Old Testament, God says, 'I am that I am' to Moses, and in so doing God maintains his mystery and hiddenness. Precisely in this name God shrouds himself in an ontological riddle which resists reduction to whatever we might mean when we speak of existence in an ontic or noetic sense. 'Under this name, which in

---

169 CD I.1, p. 312/KD I.1, 329.
170 CD I.1, p. 312/KD I.1, 329.
171 CD I.1, p. 316/KD I.1, 334.

itself and as such pronounces His mystery, God does reveal Himself to His people'.[172]

Barth's ontological understanding of the mystery of revelation directly informs his understanding of Christ. 'The lordship discernible in the biblical revelation consists in the freedom of God to differentiate Himself from Himself, to become unlike Himself and yet to remain the same ... being not only God the Father, but also ... God the Son'.[173] God's freedom therefore dictates that he is not subject to the form of the *humanitas Christi*. If it is the case that 'revelation in the Bible means the self-unveiling, imparted to men, of the God who by nature cannot be unveiled to men',[174] then Jesus' humanity cannot be the limit of God. Whatever is happening in this revelation, and Barth is arguing that revelation is a kind of happening [*Ereignis*], we cannot assume that Jesus' humanity is revelation for us. The *Deus revelatus* is the *Deus absconditus*. 'Only when we have grasped this as the meaning of the Bible do we see the full range of its statement that God reveals Himself, i.e., that He has assumed form for our sake'.[175] As such, the form does not present human beings with an immediately apprehensible divinity. Jesus' humanity is not an ontic medium between divine and human being. If Jesus is to be the revelation of God then God's act of revelation must never be taken for granted in that human form. Rather,

> God's self-unveiling remains an act of sovereign divine freedom. To one man it can be what the Word says and to another true divine concealment. To the same man it may be the former to-day and the latter to-morrow. In it God cannot be grasped by man or confiscated or put to work.[176]

Barth goes to great lengths to demonstrate this point from passages in the Bible. For instance, all who saw Jesus and heard him did not recognize and acknowledge him as God. It was only a few for whom Jesus was in fact the revelation of God. Crucially Barth comments on the ontological implications of this biblical phenom-

---

172 CD I.1, p. 318/KD I.1, 335.
173 CD I.1, p. 320/KD I.1, 338.
174 CD I.1, p. 320/KD I.1, 338.
175 CD I.1, p. 321/KD I.1, 338.
176 CD I.1, p. 321/KD I.1, 339.

The Being of the Church Dogmatics

enon, 'this reconciling action [*Handeln*] of God is the *being* [*Sein*] of God in Christ, but it is this reconciling *action* [*Handeln*] that is the being [*Sein*]'.[177] God's being can only be apprehended as an action in Christ. The ontological acts in such a way that it never gives way to the ontic. If anything, Barth is implying that the ontic must give way to the action of God in this form. Thus, the ontic existence which we objectify in thought, which we might claim to know, can never be the condition for our attribution of existence to God. Barth's way of securing this principle is to re-emphasize the mystery of God in Christ. As he says, 'the mysteries of the world are of such a kind that some day they can cease to be mysteries. God is always mystery'.[178] But, an interest in the mystery of God does not dissuade Barth in any sense from clarifying the ontological relations that it must inevitably imply. If God really exists, and he really does reveal himself, then he must not sacrifice his mystery to do so.

After addressing how revelation arrives in the person of Christ as both *revelatus* and *absconditus* simultaneously, Barth then moves on to how it is possible that this revelation actually is imparted [*zuteilwerden*] to human beings. Barth's use of *zuteilwerden* has the connotations of allocation and apportionment: to become apportioned or to be given something which one did not have and could not provide on their own. Barth has been working under the premise that the freedom of God must be maintained in the form in which God takes in Christ. If the *humanitas Christi* cannot guarantee divine revelation in and of itself, then the act which confirms God's being in Christ must also make some form of impact upon the human being to whom this divine being is revealed. In other words, Barth is keen to demonstrate just how it is that the revelation of God implies both the Son, but also the Holy Spirit as well. It is in this context that Barth deals with the problem of the historical nature of the biblical representation of revelation. For if it is the case that God acted not only in Jesus but upon those who recognized him as divine revelation, then it might be assumed that one might apprehend revelation by proxy through an apprehension of an historical event and not necessarily through an ontological transformation in all instances of revelation.

---

177 CD I.1, p. 323/KD I.1, 341.
178 CD I.1, p. 321/KD I.1, 339.

A question is being asked here: why couldn't we apprehend the historical event and in so doing apprehend revelation which took place in history?[179] In response Barth draws a connection between a historical apprehension of revelation and an abstract metaphysics of God. As he puts it, 'God in His incomprehensibility and God in the act of His revelation is not the formula of an abstract metaphysics [*Metaphysik*] of God, the world, or religion which is supposed to obtain at all times and in all places'.[180] The critique here is of an abstract metaphysics in so far as it is comparable to an abstract history that supposes that the theologian might find a shortcut to the revelation of God through metaphysics or historical analysis. Rather, metaphysics and history for Barth must centre themselves around the concrete event of revelation.

> The divine self-unveiling which [the Bible] records, with the holiness which it ascribes to God in this act, is not imparted [*wird zuteil*] to man but to such and such men in very definite situations. It is a very specific event and as such it is incomparable and cannot be repeated.[181]

Because history cannot become a source of revelation abstracted from the concrete need human beings have to become imparted with divine revelation, Barth can comment upon the mythological or unhistorical aspects of the Bible.[182] As Barth turns to discuss the biblical context and support for his position, he finds that

> what the Bible is trying to say here is obviously that there is no disposition [*Disposition*] in man at all ... In the New Testament the puzzle or the solution of the puzzle of this inconceivably fac-

---

[179] This Barth asks in order to critique Troeltsch's historical theology explicated in the introductory chapter above.
[180] CD I.1, p. 325/KD I.1, 344.
[181] CD I.1, p. 326/KD I.1, 344.
[182] Barth therefore refers to these elements in the Bible as saga in order to maintain the truth of the divine encounter which they depict. Saga is related to *die Sage* or legend in German, but more importantly to *sagen* or to say. It echoes the speech of God, that directs the attention beyond the story itself. For Barth, 'Saga or legend can only denote the more or less intrusive part of the story-teller or story-tellers in the story told.' CD I.1, p. 327/KD I.1, 345.

The Being of the Church Dogmatics

tual presence of real men at God's revelation is expressed by the concept of πνευμα.[183]

It is therefore by God's spirit that the knowledge of God in Christ on the cross is truly possible. As one commentator on the role of the Holy Spirit in Barth's thought puts it, 'As the one transition both from Father to Son and from Christ to the Christian, the Holy Spirit is Himself the coincidence between God's being both inside and beyond Himself'.[184] For Barth, 'without God's being historically revealed in this way, revelation would not be revelation'.[185]

In concluding his discussion of the root of the doctrine of the Trinity, Barth refocuses his attention to the pinnacle on the horizon, the doctrine of the Trinity itself. Revelation in its veiling, unveiling and impartation simply expounded the proper trajectory of our gaze.[186] Saying that revelation is the root of the doctrine of the Trinity is not, however, to say that it is the doctrine itself. In Barth's words 'the doctrine of the Trinity has not yet encountered us directly'.[187] Just as Barth's explication of the knowledge of God was designed to open up a proper discussion of the revelation of God, Barth's discussion of the revelation of God opens up the possibility of a proper discussion of the Trinity itself. Barth therefore projects the need to delve more deeply into

> the concept of the one essence [*Wesens*] of God and of the three persons or modes of being (*Seinsweisen*) to be distinguished in this essence [*Wesen*], and finally the polemical assertion, which we touched on only briefly, that God's triunity [*Dreieinigkeit*] is to be found not merely in His revelation but, because in His revelation, in God Himself and in Himself too, so that the Trinity is to be understood as 'immanent' and not just 'economic'.[188]

---

183 CD I.1, p. 331/KD I.1, 350–1.
184 Philip J. Rosato, *The Spirit as Lord: The Pneumatology of Karl Barth* (Edinburgh: T. & T. Clark, 1981), p. 120.
185 CD I.1, p. 331/KD I.1, 350.
186 CD I.1, p. 332/KD I.1, 351.
187 CD I.1, pp. 332–3/KD I.1, 351.
188 CD I.1, p. 333/KD I.1, 351–2.

As we will see, Barth's threefold discussion of revelation provides the roots out of which will grow the triune God whose threefold modes of being will clarify the economic interrelation God has with his creation as well as the relation he has in and with himself. There are not two Gods here, but one, and the whole of Barth's first volume leads us to this end.

The Triune Being of God

As Barth finally is able to turn to the doctrine of the Trinity proper, he introduces the following title: 'The Triunity of God [*Gottes Dreieinigkeit*]'. As is his custom, Barth begins each section with a short summary of what is to follow, and here we are given the climax towards which the *Church Dogmatics* has been building:

> The God who reveals Himself according to Scripture is One in three distinctive modes of being [*Seinsweisen*] subsisting in their mutual relations: Father, Son, and Holy Spirit. It is thus that He is the Lord, i.e., the Thou who meets man's I and unites Himself to this I as the indissoluble Subject [*unauflösliche Subjekt*] and thereby and therein reveals Himself to him as his God.[189]

Barth's discussion of the knowledge of God and the revelation of God ultimately depends on the discussion Barth evinces in this section. To that end, Barth defends his notion of *Seinsweise* and the three manners or modes in which God *is* God. It is Barth's delineation of this *is*, therefore, which provides his own way through the problem of attributing existence to God, and here we would do well to briefly remind ourselves of what we learned from Barth's Anselm book in the previous chapter.

The first thing to take account of is the difference between the ontological language Barth applies in his Anselm book and the Trinitarian ontology he develops in his *Church Dogmatics*. In the former, as we argued in the previous chapter, Barth began to delineate the importance of differentiating between an ontic object of faith and the *Dasein* which was unique to God alone. This *Dasein*

---

189 CD I.1, p. 348/KD I.1, 367.

The Being of the Church Dogmatics

could refer to all objects, but only to God in so far as it could not fail to be. Anselm's proof of the *Existenz* of God was therefore clarified in terms of this unique *Dasein,* or *nicht-daseiend.* It was on the stability of this *Dasein,* therefore, that Barth would argue all other *Dasein* found its true being. However, the *Church Dogmatics* differs from the Anselm book in that Barth is now employing the Trinitarian language of the different modes of God's being [*Seinsweise*] and this supersedes his discussion of *Dasein* and *nicht-daseiend.*[190] The general category of *Existenz* still remains in the *Church Dogmatics,* but the uniqueness of divine being is now articulated in terms of *Seinsweise.* This brings us to a second more positive affirmation of the similarity between the theological ontology set out in the Anselm book and that in the *Church Dogmatics.* Namely, that Barth is still firmly establishing the ontological priority of divine being which gives human beings their existence. Human beings do not exist in such a way that their existence can provide insight into the divine existence. As a result, Barth does not attribute any dialectic between divine being and created being in and of itself. It is this lack of dialectic between Creator and creation that makes up the heart of Barth's understanding of God's relation to the world. In this sense, there is a clear structural parity between the ontological difference Barth articulates in both books.

This is not to say that dialectic plays no part in Barth's account of triunity.[191] Rather, the three-in-oneness or *Dreieinigkeit* implies a dialectic in God between his unity in Trinity and his Trinity in unity. In both emphases Barth is attempting to delineate a more profound truth concerning his dogmatic account of who God is. For instance, by emphasizing the unity in Trinity, Barth draws particular attention to the need to respond to particular heretical formulations of the Trinity. Barth begins with the irony of the early anti-Trinitarian movements' critique of the early doctrine of the Church. In an extended footnote, Barth introduces the qualms he has with Arius, Origen and Sabellius. Although each sought a more monotheistic formulation of God's deity, they each failed in so far

---

190 Barth, *Anselm,* pp. 155–6/G158–9.
191 We would therefore agree with interpreters such as Graham Ward that Barth's theology maintains a dialectical structure at times, even if we maintain no dialectic of being is present in Barth's *Church Dogmatics.* Cf. Ward, *Barth, Derrida, and the Language of Theology,* p. 16.

as they ended up with an even worse conflagration of that unity. Hence, by honouring Christ as the most glorious creature of the one God, Arius's followers

> did violence to the divine unity by the very adoration they thought they should pay this creature, and the more so the more seriously the adoration was intended.[192]

So too, when the Subordinationist Christology of Origen introduced a 'graduation; the idea of a hierarchy, a variable measure of divine substance' into the essence of God, or the Adoptionist Monarchians argued 'their human Christ, who is endowed with special divine power and finally exalted to divine dignity', they in fact committed the same error as Arius.[193] These semi-divine accounts of Christ do damage to the unity they sought to protect.[194]

The same is true of the Modalist Monarchians such as Sabellius whom Barth will associate with Schleiermacher in the modern period. Barth's contention is that

> they did indeed assert the substantial equality of the Trinitarian 'persons' but only as manifestations behind which God's one true being is concealed as something other and higher, so that one may well ask whether revelation can be believed if in the background there is always the thought that we are not dealing with God as He is but only with a God as he appears to us.[195]

Such an account of the triunity of God cuts wholly against Barth's account of the revelation of God as the pathway into a true encounter with the being of God. Hence, Barth sees the Adoptionists and Modalists committing either one of two errors. 'Inevitably – and we must see this if we are to understand the sharpness with which the Church has fought it – all antitrinitarianism is forced into the dilemma of denying either the revelation of God or the unity of God'.[196] Barth's interest is of course to demonstrate how revelation can be

---

192 CD, I.1, p. 352/KD I.1, 372.
193 CD I.1, pp. 352–3/KD I.1, 372.
194 CD I.1, p. 352/KD I.1, 372.
195 CD I.1, p. 353/KD I.1, 372.
196 CD I.1, p. 352/KD I.1, 371.

The Being of the Church Dogmatics

real revelation of the one God, and it is in this sense that Barth's use of *Seinsweise* comes into its own. If 'revelation and revealing must be equal to the revealer',[197] then God must be in such a way that it is always the same divine being who encounters us. If it is not the real being of God in the Father, Son and Holy Spirit, 'then this means that God in his revelation is not really God'.[198]

Barth further delineates his intra-Trinitarian dialectic of the three modes of God's being as he turns to emphasize triunity in terms of *Trinity* in unity [*Dreiheit in der Einheit*]. To say that God is one must eventually open up to the manner in which a dogmatic account of his threeness might properly unfold. Barth therefore treats the traditional dogmatic use of the term 'person' and its merits for his own understanding of triunity. Part of the difficulty Barth faces is that the term person

> was never adequately clarified when first introduced into the Church's vocabulary, nor did the interpretation which it was later given and which prevailed in the mediaeval and post-Reformation Scholasticism as a whole really bring this clarification, nor has the injection of the modern concept of personality into the debate achieved anything but fresh confusion.[199]

Barth's preference for the three modes of God's being is based upon this need to clarify the notion of person and bring it into a more adequate meaning for his own dogmatics. Barth's discussion here shifts emphasis from the meaning of person to the meaning of ontology. As Barth rehearses the Trinitarian discussion of persons in Thomas and Augustine the importance of substantive and essential language comes to the fore again and again.[200] In his desire to apprehend a more adequate, if not clear Trinitarian dogma, Barth therefore abandons the language of persons, not only because it adds little to the accounts of the past, but because *Seinsweise* expresses 'better and more simply and clearly the same thing as is meant by "person"'.[201]

---

197 CD I.1, p. 353/KD I.1, 372.
198 CD I.1, p. 353/KD I.1, 372.
199 CD I.1, p. 355/KD I.1, 374–5.
200 CD I.1, pp. 355–9/KD I.1, 375–8.
201 CD I.1, p. 359/KD I.1, 379.

Seinsweise allows Barth to claim that 'in all three modes of being God is the one God both in Himself and in relation to the world and man'.[202] Barth has set himself the task, therefore, of demonstrating how it is that three modes are of one being in God. It is one *Sein* that Barth's concept of *Seinsweise* implies, and if God is revealing himself in this world as really God then those modes of being cannot change in his revelation. God is a unity even and most importantly in his revelation. Hence, Barth says that

> God is One, but not in such a way that as such He needs a Second and then a Third in order to be One, nor as though He were alone and had to do without a counterpart, and therefore again – and this will be of decisive significance in the doctrine of creation and man and also in the doctrine of reconciliation – not as though He could not exist without the world and man, as though there were between Him and the world and man a necessary relation of reciprocity. In Himself these limits of what we otherwise regard as unity are already set aside. In Himself His unity is neither singularity nor isolation.[203]

God's unity, the very essence of his existence, is such that there can be no constraint upon God. Just as God reveals himself such that no second deity is required beyond himself, so too, he requires no supplement in the created order. As such, the problem of attributing existence to God, or the relation between ontology and theology, must be turned on its head. Being must be given to the creation in each instantiation of God's revelation as the Creator, the Reconciler and the Redeemer. The response to the Adoptionists and the Arians is that Jesus *is* God and as such Christ's being as God remains and is truly God. So too, in response to the Modalists there is no revealed being of God that is in any way different from God as he is in and for himself.

Hence, although Barth does account for the importance of drawing 'a sharp distinction' between the immanent and economic trinities when delineating how it is that we can know this God in his revelation,[204] when it comes to his discussion of the triunity of God,

---

202 CD I.1, p. 360/KD I.1, 380.
203 CD I.1, p. 354/KD I.1, 374.
204 CD I.1, p. 172/KD I.1, 179.

The Being of the Church Dogmatics

the character of this distinction comes into sharper focus. Although our knowledge of God depends upon the revelation of God, and in this sense demands that we begin with a distinction between the God who reveals himself before we begin a dogmatic discussion of God in and for himself, it nonetheless remains paramount that in our discussion of the God who reveals himself we nevertheless come to see that this is the same God who is in fact in and for himself. There is no God behind God, just as there is no existence which can be divinized apart from God. All things flow from God's being and as such when God makes himself known to us, we must come to say that this is in fact one God in three modes of being.

Triunity [*Dreieinigkeit*] is therefore a conflation [*Zusammenfassung*] of the two formulae unity in trinity and trinity in unity.[205] 'In practice, however, this concept of "triunity" can never be more than the dialectical union and distinction in the mutual relation between the two formulae that are one-sided and inadequate in themselves'. [206] By focusing upon the triunity of God, Barth is able to draw specific attention both to the inadequacy of the formulations he has offered up to this point, but also to a more thorough-

---

205 CD I.1, p. 368/KD I.1, 389.
206 CD I.1, p. 369/KD I.1, 389. It should be noted that this dialectic corresponds to the argument George Hunsinger makes for the Chalcedonian character of Barth's Christology contra Charles Waldrop's assessment that Barth's Christology is basically Alexandrian in character. Briefly, their debate concerns Barth's ability to affirm the humanity of God properly without sacrificing his divinity and vice versa. Whereas the Alexandrian Christology emphasized Christ's divinity and in its extreme forms can become Docetic, the Antiochian Christology emphasized Christ's humanity and in its extreme forms can become Nestorian in its character. George Hunsinger, 'Karl Barth's Christology: Its Basic Chalcedonian Character', in *Disruptive Grace: Studies in the Theology of Karl Barth* (Grand Rapids, MI: William B. Eerdmans, 2000), p. 134. Waldrop's evidence for arguing the Alexandrian interpretation of Barth revolves around the factors in his thought which emphasize the oneness of Jesus Christ with God. The most important of these are Barth's identification of Jesus Christ's act and being with the act and being of God. Charles T. Waldrop, *Karl Barth's Christology: Its Basic Alexandrian Character* (New York: Mouton Publishers, 1984), p. 199. However, as Hunsinger rightly points out, Barth's thought only gives the appearance that a choice must be made because of the way he purposely uses terminology relative to both. As he puts it, 'The reason why a non-Chalcedonian Christology has been imputed to Barth, one way or the other, would seem to be rooted mainly in a failure to appreciate that he employs a dialectical strategy of juxtaposition. The discussion is always jinxed when one or the other prong in Barth's two-sided dialectic is seized upon in isolation as if it could stand for his Christology as a whole.' Hunsinger, 'Karl Barth's Christology', p. 137.

going account of participation and what he will refer to, following John of Damascus, as the 'perichoresis (*circumincessio*, passing into one another) of the divine persons. This states that the divine modes of being mutually condition and permeate one another so completely that one is always in the other two and the other two in the one'.[207] *Perichoresis* facilitates Barth's desire to maintain both emphases upon the unity and trinity without compromising one or the other. God can be both three and one precisely because his three modes of being 'in-exists [*inexistieren*]' within themselves.[208] Barth therefore explicitly regards *perichoresis* as 'an important form of the dialectic needed to work out the concept of "triunity"'.[209]

This leads Barth to conclude that 'God's essence [*Wesen*] and work are not twofold but one. God's work is His essence [*Wesen*] in its relation to the reality which is distinct from Him and which is to be created or is created by Him.'[210] If God is to be one God in three modes, then there can be no ontological distinction between the way God acts in the world and his essential nature. This means that as God is in himself, he also must be as he reveals himself to be. God acts in the world in such a way that is wholly consistent with who he is regardless of the world's existence. For God to be God he cannot have any need which cannot be satisfied in his own being. As such, 'God gives Himself entirely to man in His revelation, but not in such a way as to make Himself man's prisoner'.[211] God is free because his existence does not change in his self-giving and most particularly in his becoming human.

This presents us with the crucial importance of the interpretation we have been developing here. Chiefly, that human existence is smitten in its encounter with God. Human existence as we know it dissolves into the phantasm that it always was in its independence from divine being. As Barth will later say in his treatment of 'God the Son':

> Obviously, the dogma of Christ's deity snaps any correlation between the divine revelation and human faith. The cycle of reli-

---

207 CD I.1, p. 370/KD I.1, 390.
208 CD I.1, p. 370/KD I.1, 391.
209 CD I.1, p. 371/KD I.1, 391.
210 CD I.1, p. 371/KD I.1, 391.
211 CD I.1, p. 371/KD I.1, 391.

The Being of the Church Dogmatics

gious psychology, the theory of two accessible elements of truth in a unity of tension, and all such well-meant inventions no matter what we call them, can never lead us to what this dogma is seeking to say. And if everything that cannot be grasped by these instruments is for that reason illegitimate metaphysics, then certainly this dogma is metaphysics of that kind. But on the basis of the three points made above we may simply turn the tables and say that the illegitimate metaphysics in which the Reformers obviously did not indulge consists in absolutizing the correlation that we suppose we can attain and survey and understand, in regarding it as the reality in which God has as it were delivered Himself up to man and human thought and speech, instead of remembering that our being in this relation may always be pure illusion, and our thought within it and speech about it may always be pure ideology, if they are not grounded in God Himself and continually confirmed by God Himself.[212]

Improper metaphysics arises as we contemplate being apart from divine revelation. But being is the heart of theology precisely because it is as God reveals himself that we come to truly understand our own existence. And here the echoes of Luther's *Heidelberg Disputation* can be heard once again. Just as Luther critiques the theologian 'who looks upon the invisible things of God as though they were clearly perceptible in those things which have actually happened' in thesis 19 of his *Heidelberg Disputation*, Luther goes on in thesis 20 (which Heidegger skipped) to explicitly cite the proper basis of metaphysical theology as follows: 'He deserves to be called a theologian, however, who comprehends the visible and manifest things of God seen through suffering and the cross.'[213]

We can now understand the full onto-theological implications Barth draws from this statement. Barth recognizes that a proper metaphysics rooted in the being of God is absolutely vital to theology. This being of God on the cross, the God hidden in suffering, is the one God whose being created us, redeems us and reconciles us. As Eberhard Jüngel puts it, 'the taking up of humanity into the event of the knowledge of God is grounded in the taking up

---

212 CD I.1, p. 422/KD I.1, 443–4.
213 Luther, *Works*, vol. 31, p. 52.

of humanity into the event of the being of God'.[214] God's being as Creator therefore cannot be separated from the act of salvation, and as such, the doctrine of the Triunity of God as Creator, Reconciler and Redeemer provides the necessary relation within which salvation can be discussed.

> He can meet us and unite Himself to us, because He is God in His three modes of being as Father, Son and Spirit, because creation, reconciliation and redemption, the whole being, speech and action in which He wills to be our God, have their basis and prototype in His own essence, in His own being as God. As Father, Son and Spirit God is, so to speak, ours in advance.[215]

Ontological difference is now understood in terms of a modality in divine being, and it is precisely as the Word confronts the confused inadequacy of ontic human being that true divine being comes into proper focus. Barth does not establish dialectic between divine and human being as a dialectic between our fallen ontic state and the ontological being of God, but rather, divine being in its one-sidedness determines human being. This is not to say that Barth's theology is anti-metaphysical any more than it is post-ontological. Rather Barth's negative metaphysical statements all contradict any attempt to divorce theology from ontology. This is the problem he addressed in direct opposition to the Heideggerian framing of the onto-theological problem.

The being of the Church, Jesus Christ, directly challenges what has increasingly become a dominant post-Heideggerian conception of onto-theology by demonstrating the possibilities of the true being of the human person, redeemed and returned to its ontologically complete status. The being of the Church is Jesus Christ, and it is here that we must press Barth further and ask about the nature of this difference between Father and Son. As Graham Ward puts it, what is Barth's 'teaching on the humanity and divinity of Christ such that, on the one hand Christ is coequal and not subordinate to the Father-God, and, on the other, he embraces the full nature of what it is to be human'?[216] In brief, Ward is right to highlight the

---

214 Jüngel, *God's Being Is in Becoming*, p. 75.
215 CD I.1, p. 383/KD I.1, 403–4.
216 Graham Ward, 'Barth, Modernity, and Postmodernity', in *The Cambridge*

The Being of the Church Dogmatics

manner in which Barth's theology implies that Christ has to be in such a way that he is both fully divine and fully human. Otherwise there is no basis upon which to speak of Christ as a human being. According to the Trinitarian relations we have explicated above, Christ is coequal with God, and yet his being is ontologically and distinctly human. In Barth's view ontological difference is inevitably a theological question, and as such our participation in being will always imply God's being, especially, and most particularly in the being of the Church, Jesus Christ. The theological ontology Barth develops in his *Church Dogmatics* therefore raises a question first and foremost about the humanity of God. Here Heidegger's cross haunts us still, and it is to the cruciform shape of Barth's ontology that we now turn in the next chapter.

Companion to Karl Barth, ed. John Webster (Cambridge: Cambridge University Press, 2000), p. 293.

6

The Humanity of God

Christological Differences

In a recent essay in *Modern Theology*,[1] George Hunsinger sets out 25 theses designed to clarify and defend what he refers to as a 'traditionalist' account of the relationship between election and the Trinity in Karl Barth's mature theology. Hunsinger responds to 'revisionist' accounts proffered most notably by Bruce McCormack in his essay 'Grace and Being' in the *Cambridge Companion to Karl Barth*,[2] and his response to Edwin Chr. Van Driel in the *Scottish Journal of Theology*.[3] Both of these essays depict Barth's later doctrine of election from volume II.2 onwards in the *Church Dogmatics*, as a groundbreaking innovation, which demanded a revision of his account of the triunity of God. In brief, if Barth's Jesus is both the subject and the object of election, then the economic triunity of God must logically (not temporally) precede his immanent triunity.[4] In other words, in order to avoid undue 'speculation',[5] McCormack suggests that it is the act of God to elect Jesus of Nazareth that constitutes the triune structure of God in and for himself. As such, the *logos asarkos* speculated upon by the Reformers is not only the *logos incarnandus*, but God's determination to be incarnated implies a certain ontological contingency of God in relation to his creation in a way that demands further clarification

---

[1] George Hunsinger, 'Election and the Trinity: Twenty-Five Theses on the Theology of Karl Barth', *Modern Theology* 24, no. 2 (2008), pp. 179–98.

[2] Bruce L. McCormack, 'Grace and Being: The Role of God's Gracious Election in Karl Barth's Theological Ontology', in *The Cambridge Companion to Karl Barth*, ed. J. B. Webster (New York: Cambridge University Press, 2000), pp. 92–110.

[3] Bruce L. McCormack, 'Seek God Where He May Be Found: A Response to Edwin Chr. van Driel', *Scottish Journal of Theology* 60, no. 1 (2007), pp. 62–79.

[4] McCormack, 'Grace and Being', pp. 101–3.

[5] McCormack, 'Grace and Being', p. 95.

if not a reversal: that is: the doctrine of election must precede the doctrine of the Trinity.

Hunsinger responds to this thesis (and others which follow similar lines)[6] as follows: (1) Barth always affirms the logical priority of the immanent triunity of God when considering election; and that therefore, (2) God is God regardless of whether he created the world or not; as such, (3) 'the Son *incarnatus* is not external but internal to the pre-existing eternal Son', or in Barth's words, 'without ceasing to be the Word, he nevertheless ceased to be only the Word'.[7] What this amounts to then is that when Barth comes to God's eternal election, it is always the immanent Trinitarian sense that is emphasized, in so far as 'the primal decision of election takes place "within his triune Being"'.[8] Hunsinger forcefully argues and supports these points with explicit citations from Barth's *Dogmatics* in order to demonstrate how and why Barth never recognized the problem in the way the revisionists recommend (and, therefore, never changed his mind) precisely because even as late as 1942 'he still clearly regarded the Trinity as ontologically prior to, and presupposed in, the pre-temporal act of election',[9] that is the revisionists are grossly misreading Barth.

With McCormack and Hunsinger both, the interest in Barth's theological ontology provides a critical insight into the problems they are addressing in Barth's work. In McCormack's case, he recognizes the manner in which Barth will address the pre-existent *logos asarkos* and the divine Word *incarnandus,* via his account of the Trinitarian modes of being. McCormack rightly recognizes that Barth was not avoiding speculation as an 'end in itself'.[10] Rather,

> what was really at stake ... was divine ontology. How is it possible for God to *become,* to enter fully into time as One who is

---

[6] Kevin Hector, 'God's Triunity and Self-Determination: A Conversation with Karl Barth, Bruce McCormack and Paul Molnar', *International Journal of Systematic Theology* 7, no. 3 (2005), pp. 246–61.

[7] Hunsinger, 'Election and the Trinity', p. 184, citing Karl Barth, *Church Dogmatics*, ed. G. W. Bromiley and T. F. Torrance, trans. G. W. Bromiley, vol. I.2 (Edinburgh: T. & T. Clark, 1962), p. 149. We will refer hereafter in this chapter to the *Church Dogmatics* as CD, and the German *Die Kirchliche Dogmatik* as KD.

[8] Hunsinger, 'Election and the Trinity', p. 186, citing CD II.2, p. 76.

[9] Hunsinger, 'Election and the Trinity', p. 187.

[10] McCormack, 'Grace and Being', p. 96.

subjected to the limitations of human life in this world, without undergoing any *essential* (i.e. ontological) change?[11]

I would suggest that this is the most important question McCormack asks in regard to Barth's understanding of election and the Trinity. How we configure the relationship between human and divine being has drastic implications for Christology. McCormack is absolutely right to recognize that for Barth there is no ontological rift in God 'between His being [*Sein*] and essence [*Wesen*] in Himself and His activity and work as Reconciler of the world created by Him'.[12] But it is precisely here that the issue is complicated by McCormack's way of configuring the relationship between divine and human being as such, and we must take a moment to explain how McCormack reads Barth's theology in terms of *Realdialektik*.

For McCormack *Realdialektik* apprehends the ontological difference between the being of God and human created being. For Barth's early work, the problem was how to affirm the total otherness of God in contradiction to the cultural Protestantism of his teachers such as Wilhelm Herrmann. In fact *Realdialektik* acts as a unifying medium between two forms of dialectic which McCormack inherits from Michael Beintker's work: (1) the Hegelian supplementary form; and, (2) the Kierkegaardian complementary form.[13] In McCormack's interpretation, Barth's theology will be understood according to a stable onto-logic which prevails from its early stages in the first and second *Römerbrief* through to the mature theology of his *Church Dogmatics*. This challenges the dominant view propagated after Hans Urs von Balthasar's influential interpretation of Barth's work,[14] which argued that something significant developed

---

11 McCormack, 'Grace and Being', p. 96.
12 CD IV.1, p. 184/KD IV.1, 201. Barth specifically mentions an 'absolute paradox' in this regard.
13 Michael Beintker, *Die Dialektik in der 'dialektischen Theologie' Karl Barths: Studien zur Entwicklung der Barthschen Theologie und zur Vorgeschichte der 'Kirchlichen Dogmatik'*, Beiträge zur evangelischen Theologie; Bd. 101 (München: C. Kaiser, 1987), pp. 38–9.
14 Hans Urs von Balthasar, *The Theology of Karl Barth: Exposition and Interpretation*, trans. Edward T. Oakes (San Francisco: Communio Books, Ignatius Press, 1992), pp. 116–17, 124. A critique of this account can be found in Bruce L. McCormack, *Karl Barth's Critically Realistic Dialectical Theology: Its Genesis and Development, 1909–1936* (New York: Oxford University Press, 1995), p. 3. For a summary of the discrepancy between them, see Timothy Stanley, 'Before

The Humanity of God

with Barth's book on Anselm in the early 1930s. McCormack's thesis is even more radical, however, in that it challenges Beintker and Balthasar's distinction between the first and second *Römerbrief*, which they maintain exhibits two different forms of dialectic, the first being Hegelian and the second more Kierkegaardian. In contrast, McCormack sees a deeper coinherence between the two. This explains why he will argue that even

> In *Romans* I, both the *realdialektische* relationship between 'real history' and 'so-called history' as well as the *realdialektische* relationship between 'real humanity' (in Christ) and the 'unreal humanity' (in Adam) are of the supplementary type. In both cases, what is in view is a relationship in which 'real reality' overcomes 'unreal reality'.[15]

Hence, after McCormack, the autonomous reality of God is established from the outset of Barth's thought and as a result the idea that there is some need to apprehend the ontological development in Barth's theology according to dialectic and analogy (as is the case with Balthasar) is unnecessary because Barth's ontology is stabilized from the point his theology becomes dialectical. Thus, McCormack's title takes two of its primary terms, dialectical and realist, and instantiates them as the *Realdialektik* in Barth's theology from 1919 onwards.

McCormack therefore interprets the difference between divine and human being dialectically, that is, oppositionally and requiring some form of resolution which Barth effects in a number of ways. This explains why McCormack argues that there can be no rift on an 'ontic' level[16] when Christ takes on flesh. As such, this ontic humanity of Christ constitutes and determines the eternal in Christ. McCormack gives human being a status which demands that Christ has to overcome a rift to become human. This dialectical presupposition is what forces him to overstate the contingency of divine being in his account of election. For McCormack, Christ

> takes this human experience into his own life and extinguishes its power over us. But he is not changed on an ontological level by

---

Analogy: Recovering Barth's Ontological Development', *New Blackfriars* 90, no. 1029 (2009), pp. 577–601.
15 McCormack, *Karl Barth's Critically Realistic Dialectical Theology*, p. 163.
16 McCormack, 'Grace and Being', p. 96.

this experience for the simple reason that his being, from eternity, is determined as a being-for this event.[17]

McCormack appears to have Barth in an ontic bind here. If he says that the human Jesus' acts are really divine acts eternally and essentially, as Barth says he wants to do, then it must be the case that the electing Christ who is also the elect Christ is eternally so. If Barth then wants to turn around and say that Christ could be otherwise than as we find him in the act on the cross, then we have an acting God who plays a part, but is a mere symbol without ontological pertinence.[18] Barth contradicts himself. God's being must be constituted by this act in Jesus, or we merely have a phantom and are not in fact dealing with the real God here in crib or on cross.

Did Barth need to reverse his theology and put election before the Trinity to avoid speculation and avoid a modalism which hides Christ behind the shadow of Jesus? In order to answer this question we must return to Hunsinger's response to McCormack and the revisionist accounts of Barth's theology. In many respects Hunsinger takes us a long way towards recovering Barth's intentions and demonstrates that whatever the logical coinherence of McCormack's theses, they are simply not consistent with Barth's theology. Hunsinger's theses in *Modern Theology* are broken into two parts, the first of which offers a series of concrete citations from Barth's theology with explanations as to why they clearly contradict the revisionist account of Barth. The second attempts to explain more precisely why Barth said and meant what he did. Regarding the first section, there are two main points which are particularly relevant here. Hunsinger begins: 'Barth nowhere says that God's being is *constituted* by God's act. He says only that God's being and act are inseparable'.[19] According to Hunsinger, when McCormack argues that God's act in Jesus is in fact constituting his being eternally, he misunderstands Barth's actualistic ontology. In Barth's words in CD IV.1, 'The whole being [*Sein*] and life of God is an activity, both in eternity and in worldly time, both in Himself as Father, Son and Holy Spirit, and in His relation to man and all creation'.[20] The

---

17 McCormack, 'Grace and Being', p. 98.
18 McCormack, 'Grace and Being', p. 97.
19 George Hunsinger, 'Election and the Trinity', p. 180; he cites a number of passages in Barth to this effect (CD IV.1, p. 7, IV.2, p. 345, IV.1, p. 561).
20 CD IV.1, p. 7 (revised translation in Hunsinger).

The Humanity of God

point is not to suggest that act forces being, or vice versa, but rather that for God, no unqualified distinction can be made between the two. McCormack's concern that if Jesus' act on the cross is not eternally constitutive then Jesus is a mere shadow of God utterly misses Barth's point, which is to neutralize any attempt to prioritize or force either act or being in either direction. The goal is not to be able to definitively say something about God in eternity based on his acts, retrospectively overreaching our epistemological much less ontological bounds. Rather, Barth is able to appropriate an axiomatic quality to the manner in which Jesus did in fact act for us. As such, God will always be free to do whatever he wants and act however he chooses precisely because what we have in act is what we have, not because it determines or constitutes God in and for himself based on what we can see or apprehend. God is God, precisely in his acts as we have them. No more and no less can be made of this than what we actually have been given to know by God.

So too, and this is the second point we will highlight from Hunsinger's first section of theses, when Barth argues that the Trinity is *determined* [*Bestimmung*] by God's free decision of election, Hunsinger takes this to mean that 'the Trinity is ontologically prior to and logically presupposed by the pre-temporal act of election. For Barth something can be "determined" only if it already exists'.[21] Just as God is not constituted by his acts, so too determination implies again the coinherence of act and being such that being is presupposed in the determination. Precisely in so far as Barth speaks of the determination of God to be for us in election, he therefore presupposes logically the Trinitarian being which determines. When Barth is pressed to explain himself on this point, he will give primacy to the actualistic being of the Trinitarian God as the foundation for how we understand his acts towards us, and not vice versa. This is best seen in Barth's consistent and thoroughgoing affirmation that God is God in his Trinitarian modes of being regardless of whether the world had been created or not. From CD I.1 in 1932 Hunsinger cites

> God would be no less God if He had created no world and no human being. The existence [*Dasein*] of the world and our own

---

21 Hunsinger, 'Election and the Trinity', p. 181.

existence [*Dasein*] are in no sense vital to God, not even as the object of His love ... His love has its object in Himself.[22]

And from I.2 in 1938, '... Father, Son and Holy Spirit would be none the less eternal God, if no world had been created'.[23] Hunsinger makes it clear that from volume I.1 of the *Church Dogmatics* in 1932 through to IV.2 in 1953,[24] God is God in his Trinitarian modes of being and without remainder. In terms of IV.2 in 1953,

> The triune life of God ... is the basis of his whole will and action also *ad extra* ... It is the *basis [is begründet]* of his *decretum et opus ad extra* ... of election of the human being to covenant with himself; of the determination [*Bestimmung*] of the Son to become human, and therefore to fulfill the covenant.[25]

This is an explicit and late refutation of the revisionist thesis. Even in a 1968 interview, Barth responds to the 1932 passage cited above: 'Ist doch herrlich, nicht?' [Splendid, isn't it?][26] Hunsinger effectively establishes the case that after 1932 Barth never retracted or changed his mind to suppose that election should or could (or would if Barth had the guts or time) precede the Trinity in his *Dogmatics*. The revisionist account simply is not consistent with Barth's theology. In Barth's own words, Hunsinger clearly reaffirms the primal liberation of the Trinitarian God, but this does not explain why. Why is this the case in Barth's thought? Don't the revisionists at least have justification to suggest that Barth's theo-logic demands the supplement they are offering? However, as we face the eternal Son's incarnation all the more bluntly, Hunsinger focuses upon the crucial issue here, the humanity of God. How does Barth understand the relationship between the Word of God in his Trinitarian mode of being eternally and Jesus of Nazareth? What we have here again is not simply a matter of logical priority but a matter of the

---

22 CD I.1, p. 139, KD I.1, 144. He goes on 'And so one cannot say that our existence [*Existenz*] as that of the recipients of God's Word is constitutive for the concept of the Word'.
23 CD I.2, p. 135/KD I.2, 148.
24 George Hunsinger, 'Election and the Trinity', pp. 180–1.
25 CD IV.2, p. 345/KD IV.2, 386
26 Karl Barth, *Gespräche 1964–1968* (Zurich: Theologischer Verlag Zürich, 1997), p. 286.

The Humanity of God

very being of God as God. Here, we can accept that from his commentary on Romans in 1919 onwards, Barth sought to affirm that utter otherness of God. As we noted in Chapter 3, this can even be seen as early as what some have referred to as Barth's Dadaist remark from 1915, 'God is God'.[27] But what does it mean to say God is God? How did Barth move beyond the meaningless babble to actually say something distinct about who God really is? The Christological manner in which Barth will appropriate this little word 'is' must not be overlooked precisely because confusion rests at the heart of commentary upon Barth's theology.

The Being of Jesus Christ

We will begin where Hunsinger does, with the relationship between the *logos asarkos* and the *logos ensarkos*. It should be noted that this concern for the flesh of Christ corresponds to a series of similar differentiations, i.e. the *logos incarnandus* and *incarnatus*, *anhypostasis* and *enhypostasis*, and ultimately the difference between the immanent and economic accounts of the Trinity as such. Hunsinger puts it as follows:

> The eternal Son is the *logos asarkos*. And yet the Son is so infinite that he can (and does) become *ensarkos* without ceasing to be *asarkos*. The *logos asarkos* represents the Son in his primary objectivity; the *logos ensarkos* in his secondary objectivity. The Son is always hidden from us in his first mode of being (*asarkos*), but manifest to us in his second mode of being (*ensarkos*). These two modes of being represent the 'double structure' of the eternal Son.[28]

Before focusing upon Hunsinger's description of Christ's two natures according to two modes of being, it may be helpful to revisit the sixteenth- and seventeenth-century debates of the Lutheran and

---

27 Barth employs this statement as early as a sermon on Genesis 15.6 in 1916 and in both editions of his *Römerbrief* in 1919 and 1922 respectively. Eberhard Busch, 'God is God: The Meaning of a Controversial Formula and the Fundamental Problem of Speaking about God', *The Princeton Seminary Bulletin* 7, no. 2 (1986), p. 101.

28 Hunsinger, 'Election and the Trinity', p. 191.

Reformed traditions, or the polemical attribution of *extra Calvinisticum* to the Reformed by the Lutherans. Whereas the Calvinists stressed the sovereign Logos at all times *ad extra* the enfleshed Christ, the Lutherans stressed the full divinity of the flesh, which they logically carried through to mean the ubiquity of the flesh. In Luther's words: 'If they should poke their heads into heaven ... they would find no one but Christ laid in the crib and in the woman's lap, and so they would fall down again and break their necks.'[29] Although Barth will side with the Reformed position, he does not do so at the expense of the Lutheran. Barth offers a sensitive discussion of the merits of both positions as follows:

> They did not want the reality of the *logos asarkos* abolished or suppressed in the reality of the *logos ensarkos*. On the contrary, they wished the *logos asarkos* to be regarded equally seriously as the *terminus a quo* [starting point], as the *logos ensarkos* was regarded as the *terminus ad quem* [end point] of the incarnation.[30]

Hunsinger interprets Barth's Christology on this point in terms of two modes of being implying Barth's use of *Seinsweise* to coordinate the Chalcedonian emphasis upon the Nicene *homoousios* and later Fathers' use of *hypostasis*. For Barth, one being with different modes best describes not only the Trinitarian relations, but the double structure of the eternal Son, and the particular manner in which Barth considered it according to *anhypostasis* and *enhypostasis*.

A number of essays have concerned themselves with the degree to which Barth's thought is his own innovation or a genuine representation of an ancient *anhypostatic-enhypostatic* formula as it can be found in Leontius of Byzantium or Lutheran scholasticism.[31] Given that our interest here is in what Barth had to say, we will

---

29 CD I.1, p. 418/KD I.1, 439, citing *Schol. in libr. Gen. on Gen. 28*, W.A., 9, p. 406, l. 11.

30 CD I.2, p. 169/KD I.2, 185.

31 Matthias Gockel, 'A Dubious Christological Formula? Leontius of Byzantium and the *Anhypostasis-Enhypostasis* Theory', *Journal of Theological Studies* 51, no. 2 (2000), pp. 515–32; U. M. Lang, 'Anhypostatos-Enhypostatos: Church Fathers, Protestant Orthodoxy and Karl Barth', *Journal of Theological Studies* 49, no. 2 (1998), pp. 630–57; F. LeRon Shults, 'A Dubious Christological Formula: From Leontius of Byzantium to Karl Barth', *Theological Studies* 57, no. 3 (1996), pp. 431–47.

The Humanity of God

forgo a judgement on whether or not his views on this matter were consistent with the ancient Church. As Hunsinger points out in another essay, there is a Chalcedonian grammar at work in Barth's theology even if, in the end, it is only Chalcedonian in spirit rather than letter.[32] When it comes to this double structure of the eternal Son, therefore, what we are dealing with is the heart of the debate between Hunsinger and the revisionists precisely because it is here that we must decide whether Jesus really is God even and most particularly in his enfleshment. For Barth, this is the point at which his theological ontology rises or falls. It is the point at which he can either say that God is God or not. For our purposes here we will address Barth's discussion of this double structure of Christ's being in *Church Dogmatics* I.2 and IV.2 respectively. This will demonstrate consistency in Barth's position throughout his work to counteract the revisionist suggestion that Barth changed his later work.

Barth's interpretation of the meaning of the Reformation attempts at Chalcedonianism takes him into some of his most difficult statements on the relation between divine and human being as such. Barth's goal here is to affirm the unity of divine and human being in Christ, while not opening the door to an affirmation of created being as the basis or equal counterpart in this unity. Barth begins as follows:

> The unity of God and man in Christ is, then, the act of the Logos in assuming human being [*menschliches Sein*]. His becoming, and therefore the thing that human being [*menschliches Sein*] encounters in this becoming of the Logos, is an act of God in the person of the Word. Therefore God and man, Creator and creature cannot be related to each other in this unity as in other men or in creation generally.[33]

What we have then is the beginning of a differentiation between what Christ's flesh *is* in all its ontological fullness, and what we are. Importantly, the difference Barth is developing here never gives

---

32 George Hunsinger, 'Karl Barth's Christology: Its Basic Chalcedonian Character', in *Disruptive Grace: Studies in the Theology of Karl Barth* (Grand Rapids, MI: William B. Eerdmans, 2000), pp. 131–47.

33 CD I.2, p. 162/KD I.2, 177.

human being as we experience it on its own terms apart from God any significant weight.

Earlier in this volume Barth makes this point explicitly against any *analogia entis*.[34] For Barth, the flesh of Christ is itself the point at which Christ confronts human beings in their particularity. God did not become man in general in John 1.14, but flesh. As Barth puts it,

> man's interpretation of himself as 'flesh' is not one to be gained in advance, but only to be derived from the revealed Word and verdict of God ... We are liable to die, and if nevertheless we live in the midst of death, it is because here and now we are already encountering an eternal redemption through Him. This is the meaning of being flesh.[35]

Here we are presented with the faith which contradicts and negates any attempt to begin from human being and arrive at the meaning of divine being. Of course, Barth recognizes that God must speak in a way that we can understand, in words that we will recognize in a person that identifies itself to us,[36] but Barth will not do so under the conditions of our human being as it is. Human being, as Barth consistently points out as he introduces these topics, is confused about itself. Its being only comes into coherency when in contact with the being of Jesus Christ.

> Man who is flesh, man the creature, the sinner liable to death, has these qualities. To behold this man is to behold what is alien, puzzling, insoluble, that which is not yet transparent, that which stands over against us as object (*Gegen-Stand*).[37]

Although not mentioned here, Barth develops *analogia fidei* elsewhere as a negative counter to *analogia entis*.[38] It is not an alterna-

---

[34] CD I.2, p. 43/KD I.2, 48.
[35] CD I.2, p. 40/KD I.2, 44.
[36] 'If God's revelation is the way from veiling of the eternal Word to His unveiling, from crib and cross to resurrection and ascension, how can it possibly be anything else than God's becoming man, His becoming flesh?' CD I.2, p. 43/KD I.2, 48.
[37] CD I.2, p. 42/KD I.2, 47.
[38] We noted this in the previous chapter, but again, as Henri Bouillard puts it,

The Humanity of God

tive set of analogical relations worked out to rival Thomas, but rather, the point at which human beings recognize their ontological frailties, where the Word of God 'aims at us and smites us in our *Existenz*'[39] to use Barth's phrase from *Church Dogmatics* I.1. *Analogia fidei* is therefore similar to Heidegger's cross[40] in so far as it obscures human being in order to enact a reversal in the knowing subject. It demands faith at the point at which true being might become manifest, and in this case the point at which flesh comes to be properly and ultimately defined in terms of the flesh of Jesus. As Barth concludes: 'We are not saying too much when we say that really and originally only Jesus Christ is man who is flesh, and then derivatively and secondarily those who in faith are one flesh with Him.'[41] This explains why Barth favours the use of the Word becoming [*ward*] flesh over assuming [*Annahme*] flesh,[42] precisely in order to guard against any notion with which we might presume human flesh as it is as the basis of what the Word assumed. The entire point of what Barth is trying to do in his theology is preserve the revelatory quality of the incarnation, that it was a divine veiling and unveiling according to the principles of revelation and faith. Revelation, to be unveiled, must be veiled precisely in the flesh, but the flesh will become what it is for us, only in so far as it is perfected in Christ who becomes it for us.

This is all the necessary preamble to arrive at Barth's account of *anypostasis-enhypostasis* as a clarification and deepening of what is meant by the two modes of Christ's being here. In Barth's words:

> *Anhypostasis* asserts the negative. Since in virtue of the ἐγένετο, [became] i.e., in virtue of the *assumptio* [assumption], Christ's human nature has its existence [*Dasein*] – the ancients said, its subsistence – in the existence [*Dasein*] of God, meaning in the

---

'When Barth substitutes *analogia fidei* for *analogia entis* he is not opposing, as one might think, two formal conceptions of analogy. He wishes to affirm that there is a resemblance between man and God only through Jesus Christ, and that the correspondence between human discourse and the divine reality is only assured by the grace of revelation.' Henri Bouillard, *The Knowledge of God* (London: Burns & Oates, 1969), p. 115.

39 CD I.1, p. 141/KD I.2, 146.
40 See Chapter 1 above.
41 CD I.2, p. 44/KD I.2, 49.
42 CD I.2, p. 160/KD I.2, 175.

mode of being [*Seinsweise*] (*hypostasis*, 'person') of the Word, it does not possess it in and for itself, *in abstracto*. Apart from the divine mode of being [*Seinsweise*] whose existence [*Dasein*] it acquires it has none of its own; i.e., apart from its concrete existence [*konkreten Dasein*] in God in the event of the *unio*, it has no existence [*kein eigenis Dasein*] of its own, it is ἀνυπόστατος [anhypostatic].[43]

First, this is a negative term. Barth here identifies the second person of the Trinity as having a *Dasein* which exists solely in terms of its mode of being in and with the Trinity as such.[44] It cuts against any attempt to locate Christ's being in our world in the terms of an assumption in this sense. Rather, there is an event, a becoming, which is required in whatever we must mean by assumption. Barth is affirming what many commentators assume his theology must affirm, that God is totally other and that his being is unique in and for itself. Such is the presupposition of Graham Ward in his recent comments on this aspect of Barth's theology. For Ward, '*Anhypostasis* safeguards two theological axioms for Barth: first, the utter uniqueness of this unity and, second, the lack of a point of contact between God and human beings in creation'.[45] We would agree in so far as the divine reality and 'form'[46] which Barth attributes to Christ is unique, whole and complete in and of himself. But the *anhypostatic* leads onto the *enhypostatic* and here is where the trouble lies.

For Ward, as for McCormack, the *enhypostatic* sounds a dialectical chord in Barth's theology. Ward in fact begins with the *enhypostatic* affirmation of the flesh which Christ assumes, which creates the dialectical problem for his interpretation of Barth on this matter.[47] By beginning with human being as we are, with human

---

43 CD I.2, p. 163/KD I.2, 178.

44 Barth refutes those who rejected the hypostatic doctrine as being without personality by pointing out that the use of *impersonalitas* as a stand-in for *anhypostatic* was in no way meant at the expense of what we mean by personality today. In other words, personality is inherently implied in both terms, and one should not presume a modern meaning onto the ancient terminology. CD I.2, p. 164/KD I.2, 180.

45 Graham Ward, *Christ and Culture* (Malden, MA: Blackwell Publishing, 2005), p. 11.

46 CD I.2, p. 146/KD I.2, 161.

47 Ward, *Christ and Culture*, p. 10.

The Humanity of God

being which Christ must assume, Ward begins precisely where Barth does not. The whole thrust of Barth's thought at this point is to negate our human being as a confused and inadequate point of contact. McCormack too understands the doctrine along dialectical lines in Barth's thinking:

> In that God takes to God's Self a human nature, God veils God's Self in a creaturely medium. He enters 'the divine incognito' – a situation of unrecognizability. Outwardly (and inwardly!), He is a human being like any other.[48]

Of course, Barth will affirm that Christ is a human being truly and in the flesh. But as we already noted, his flesh becomes the basis for our understanding of the flesh and not vice versa. Let us look at what Barth says regarding the enhypostatic union.

> In virtue of the ἐγένετο [became], i.e., in virtue of the *assumptio* [assumption], the human nature acquires existence [*Dasein*] (subsistence) in the existence [*Dasein*] of God, meaning in the mode of being [*Seinsweise*] (*hypostasis*, 'person') of the Word. This divine mode of being [*Seinsweise*] gives it existence [*Dasein*] in the event [*Ereignis*] of the *unio* [union], and in this way it has a concrete existence [*konkretes eigenes Dasein*] of its own, it is ἐνυπόστατος [enhypostatic].[49]

Note the similarity to the anhypostatic statement. The flesh is identified with the divine mode of being of the Word. But just as the anhypostatic has no concrete existence of its own, the enhypostatic does. Here we have the positive affirmation of the *Dasein* of Christ as that being who is there for us in such a way that he alone can be, and yet nonetheless as we are, as created beings with concrete existence. He becomes such as we are meant to be in relation and participation with our Creator.[50]

---

48 McCormack, *Karl Barth's Critically Realistic Dialectical Theology*, p. 327.
49 CD I.2, p. 163/KD I.2, 178.
50 Barth affirms these two modes of Christ's being by re-emphasizing the ontological language. As Barth puts it, 'Understood in this its original sense, this particular doctrine, abstruse in appearance only, is particularly well adapted to make it clear that the reality attested by Holy Scripture, Jesus Christ, is the reality of a divine

God and Us

Given that the difference between Christ's two natures is considered according to two modes of the same divine being, it is all the more important for Barth to stress the difference between creation and Creator. Said another way, because God's being now includes human being, the difference between Christ and all other human beings requires careful qualification. One of the ways Barth does so is through his explication of created time. Interestingly, Barth cites Heidegger's explication of 'our' time as we have it positively.[51] But this is not created time, as it was originally given at creation, or a time which would give us insight into the truth of the time God has for us. Rather, Barth refers to human unredeemed time as 'lost time'[52] as a second time after the time of the Garden of Eden. Barth then goes on to suggests that whatever we find in the revelation of the being of God in Christ, it must be a third time.[53]

> But this different time is the new, the third time, which arises and has its place because God reveals Himself, because He is free for us, because He is with us and amongst us, because in short, without ceasing to be what He is, He also becomes what we are. God's revelation is the event of Jesus Christ. We do not understand it as God's revelation, if we do not state unreservedly that it took place in 'our' time. But, conversely, if we understand it as God's revelation, we have to say that this event had its own time; in this event it happened that whereas we had our own time for ourselves as always, God had time for us, His own time for us – time, in the most positive sense, i.e. present with past and future, fulfilled time with expectation and recollection of its fulfilment, revelation time and the time of the Old Testament and

---

act of Lordship which is unique and singular as compared with all other events, and in this way to characterise it as a reality [*Wirklichkeit*] held up to faith by revelation. It is in virtue of the eternal Word that Jesus Christ exists [*existiert*] as a man of flesh and blood in our sphere, as a man like us, as an historical phenomenon. But it is only in virtue of the divine Word that He exists [*existiert*] as such'. CD I.2, p. 165/KD I.2, 180.

51 CD I.2, p. 46/KD I.2, 51.
52 CD I.2, p. 46/KD I.2, 51.
53 CD I.2, p. 46/KD I.2, 51.

The Humanity of God

New Testament witness to revelation – but withal, His own time, God's time; and therefore real time.[54]

In the present of our time God breaks in. The theological ontology which undergirds Barth's depiction of the revelation of God brings with it the possibility of real time as well. This being, is the condition and grounds for the plurality of times Barth will discuss.

'The Word became flesh' also means 'the Word became time …' It does not remain transcendent over time, it does not merely meet it at a point, but it enters time; nay, it assumes time; nay, it creates time for itself.[55]

Barth depicts God as the 'Lord of time',[56] because he is the infinite eternal God. The act of creation is evoked precisely here, and Barth emphasizes all the more that even in our redeemed participation in the being which Christ makes possible, the flesh through which we come to know the true meaning of flesh, ontological participation never contravenes the contingent nature of our createdness. As our being is received, so too is time, and this is itself the heart of what it means to be created. It is in this sense that Barth would continue his reference to that 'infinite qualitative difference'[57] between God and man. However, Barth would understand that difference in his *Church Dogmatics* in a more ontologically nuanced way than he did in the second edition of his *Römerbrief*.[58] In a manner wholly consistent with his book on Anselm, God alone exists such that he cannot fail to be. It is on the basis of his ontological uniqueness that the relationship between time and eternity will be understood as given to us.

---

54 CD I.2, p. 49/KD I.2, 54. Interestingly, here Barth notes how his understanding of time here does far better justice to John 1.9 than the 'permanently transcending time' he evinced in both of his *Römerbriefe*.
55 CD I.2, p. 50/KD I.2, 55.
56 'But the special thing about the time of Jesus Christ is that it is the time of the Lord of time. Compared with our time it is mastered time and for that very reason real, fulfilled time'. CD I.2, p. 52/KD I.2, 57.
57 CD II.2, p. 577, CD IV.1, p. 364. As well there are examples where Barth speaks of God as qualitatively infinitely greater than us (e.g. CD I.2, p. 677) and of a qualitative distinction which is established in revelation (e.g. CD I.1, p. 488).
58 Karl Barth, *The Epistle to the Romans*, trans. Edwyn Clement Hoskyns, 2nd ed. (London: Oxford University Press, 1933), p. 10.

As Barth turned to discuss 'The Misconception of Nothingness', in his later *Church Dogmatics* III.3, we find him reiterating the contingent nature of creation. Here, Barth explicates the ambiguous 'twofold character and aspect of creaturely existence'.[59] Creation hangs over nothingness, and in the context of the existence of creation is 'the frontier of nothingness'.[60] This is not to say that creation is nothing, but rather,

> it belongs to the essence of creaturely nature, and is indeed a mark of its perfection, that it has in fact this negative side, that it inclines not only to the right hand but also to the left, that it is thus simultaneously worthy of its Creator and yet dependent on Him, that it is not 'nothing' but 'something', yet 'something' on the very frontier of nothingness, secure, and yet in jeopardy.[61]

For Barth, therefore, creation, even in perfected goodness, is created with nothing as its horizon, and this contingency is included precisely within the definition of what it means to be a creature. Unredeemed human beings are not nothing, but rather, utterly confused concerning their relation to nothingness, and therefore will be unable to resolve this confusion by addressing themselves to the nothingness 'either theoretically or practically with Marcion or Schopenhauer'.[62] Rather, fallen human beings must look to the person of Jesus Christ for clarity concerning their true being precisely because Christ's enfleshed mode of human being *is* simultaneously the divine being which cannot fail to be. Whereas we are onesidedly contingent both temporally and ontologically, Christ's humanity is in such a way that it not only flows from the plenitude of divine being, but is in fact that same divine being in all its fullness. As Barth puts it in a section on 'Given Time', in volume III.2,

> In our disintegrating being in a lost time [Jesus] finds His true and genuine being in the time created by Him and given to man. Because we are the men loved by God from all eternity, He places

---

59 CD III.3, p. 295/KD III.3, 335.
60 CD III.3, p. 295/KD III.3, 335.
61 CD III.3, p. 296/KD III.3, 335.
62 CD III.3, p. 299/KD III.3, 340.

The Humanity of God

our being in time in the light and under the promise of the true and genuine being in time actualised in this One.[63]

Christ therefore is that one human being who really *is* fully God and fully human. But he is in such a way that only he can be as both the source and arrival of this true human being.

Barth's attempt to differentiate Christ's being from our own ontological confusion must be emphasized all the more forcefully when we consider Christ's two natures as two different modes of being. When we presume that the creation only comes into focus and gains its true value in Barth's theology according to the Christ who was made flesh, then we must simultaneously carefully interpret how this maintains an infinite difference between us and the God who cannot fail to be. In this sense, McCormack is right to point out the importance of incarnated being for Barth, but this is not to say that because Christ is eternally human we must also accept that his election implies that his death on the cross binds him to the unredeemed created order. As such, what we are confirming here is Hunsinger's theses in so far as he too highlighted Barth's use of the Christological modes of being as *asarkos* and *ensarkos*. However, as Hunsinger concludes in Barth's own words from CD II.2, 'Of course, the fact that Jesus Christ is the Son of God does not rest on election'.[64] How could it be otherwise if Jesus' twofold mode of being is the criterion for human being, and not the reverse?

Furthermore, Barth's understanding of the incarnation does not instantiate a dialectic between divine and unredeemed human being, and as a result he therefore does not have to be concerned with resolving this difference. Rather, when Barth comes to consider Christ's relation to the created world, he will develop the *anhypostasis–enhypostasis* formula which instantiates two modes of Christ's one being. In other words, Barth maintains that *Seinsweise* is just as appropriate to the three modes of God's being as Father, Son and Holy Spirit, as it is to Christ's being as the *incarnandus* and *incarnatus*. This use of two Christological modes of being is carried

---

63 CD III.2, pp. 519–20/KD III.2, 626.
64 CD II.2, p. 107, revised English translation in Hunsinger, 'Election and the Trinity', p. 196.

throughout his dogmatics and is again affirmed, along with *anhypostatis* and *enhypostatis*, in *Church Dogmatics* IV.2 as follows:

> The particularity of Jesus Christ, and therefore of the history between God and man which took place in Him, and therefore of the determination [*Bestimmung*] of His human essence [*Wesens*] by the grace of God, emerges at once and comprehensively when we look first to the origin [*Ursprung*] of His being [*Seins*] as the Son of Man, of His human existence [*Dasein*]. It is not a matter of the Virgin Birth. This does not constitute, but only indicates, the grace of His particular origin.[65]

God is eternally determined to be the Son of Man, but this in no way constrains his freedom because the humanity of God is God's first and foremost as an event within himself. What happens in the crib or on the cross does not constitute, but simply indicates.

We would therefore agree with McCormack that Barth does not affirm divinization, but rather participation,[66] in order to maintain the distinctive antithesis to created human being as an abstract self-defined concept. Barth is, in a sense, more radical than Eastern Orthodox tradition in so far as he assumes, in advance,[67] that God's humanity is the basis upon which we can speak adequately of our participation in the divine. Ward's critique that Barth did not develop a sufficient understanding of the *sacramentum mundi*[68] therefore fails to account for the implications of this participation. It is not that the bread and wine cannot participate in the divine, but that they do so only in so far as God gives this as a possibility to them. This takes us back to the distinctive language of the *Church Dogmatics'* being of the church, Jesus Christ. From the

---

65 CD IV.2, p. 90/KD IV.2, 99.

66 Bruce L. McCormack, 'Participation in God, Yes; Deification, No: Two Modern Protestant Responses to an Ancient Question', in *Orthodox and Modern: Studies in the Theology of Karl Barth* (Grand Rapids, MI: Baker Academic, 2008). Barth challenges any notion of *theosis* in CD IV.2. Cf. CD IV.2, p. 81.

67 'He can meet us and unite Himself to us, because He is God in His three modes of being as Father, Son and Spirit, because creation, reconciliation and redemption, the whole being, speech and action in which He wills to be our God, have their basis and prototype in His own essence, in His own being as God. As Father, Son and Spirit God is, so to speak, ours in advance.' CD I.1, p. 383/KD I.1, 403–4.

68 Ward, *Christ and Culture*, p. 10.

The Humanity of God

very outset in CD I.1, Barth critiques the ontological difference understood in a Heideggerian sense[69] in so far as it presumes an ontic–ontological presupposition for the being of the Church, Jesus Christ.[70] In response Barth argues that only in so far as Jesus really is the ontologically complete human being in his twofold mode can the true being of the Church become a real possibility. The Church does not exist of its own accord, but only in so far as Christ exists does the Church find its ontological possibility.

It is in this light that we can clarify the ambiguity which Richard Roberts attributed to Barth's treatment of time and being in his *A Theology on Its Way*. Roberts found that, for Barth, 'God's being and his time were co-posited in the event of revelation'.[71] He interpreted Barth's actualism as a form of ontological exclusivism which is never allowed to exist in real time. This ontological exclusivity led to a completely baseless Christology which 'hovers above us like a cathedral resting upon a cloud'.[72] In this view, Barth's Christology distances God entirely from real human being.[73] Roberts is not alone in this concern that Christ's humanity is sacrificed by Barth's overemphasis of his divinity,[74] but Roberts is one of the more adept at recognizing the metaphysical implications of Barth's theology.[75] However, Ingolf Dalferth offers a helpful response to Roberts's criticisms in a way which supplements what we have been arguing above. In 'Karl Barth's Eschatological Realism', Dalferth demonstrates why Barth's emphasis upon the new time of Christ cannot become the basis for a total dismissal of his Christology as Roberts

---

69 CD I.1, p. 36/KD I.1, 35. See Chapter 5.
70 CD I.1, p. 40/KD I.1, 40.
71 Richard H. Roberts, *A Theology on Its Way?: Essays on Karl Barth* (Edinburgh: T&T Clark, 1991), pp. 67–8.
72 Roberts, *A Theology on Its Way?*, p. 57.
73 Roberts himself recognizes the sometimes reductive nature of his interpretation of Barth but justifies it due to the acute need to respond to the danger that Christian theology might withdraw 'into the illusory security of a *disciplina arcani*'. Roberts, *A Theology on Its Way?*, p. 78.
74 Cf. Donald Macpherson Baillie, *God Was in Christ: An Essay on Incarnation and Atonement* (London: Faber and Faber, 1948), p. 53; John Macquarrie, *Jesus Christ in Modern Thought* (London: SCM Press, 2003), pp. 14, 288; Alister E. McGrath, *The Making of Modern German Christology, 1750–1990*, 2nd ed. (Grand Rapids, MI: Zondervan, 1994), pp. 142–3.
75 He considered Barth's theology to be 'a reworking of metaphysical theology, albeit in "biblical" guise'. Roberts, *A Theology on Its Way?*, p. 57.

suggests. Dalferth's essay is important because it recognizes that Barth's understanding of time cannot be understood as a stand-in for his ontology. As well, Dalferth argues that what Roberts misses is the integrative or, as Dalferth calls it, 'the interiorizing operations of Barth's theology'.[76] Dalferth goes on,

> [Barth] does not attempt as his critics have complained, 'to preserve Christian theology from the indifference and hostility of a secular world' through 'a profound ontological exclusiveness'. Rather he unfolds in a painstaking and detailed way a theological perspective of universal inclusiveness which incorporates and reconstructs the shared and public reality of our world within theology.[77]

The interiorizing power of Barth's theological ontology therefore offers a profound corrective to the interpretations which depict Barth's Christology as baseless. To suggest that Barth's theology never touches down in the real world is to suppose that we can give the world a value higher than it has in its ontological participation within the being of God himself. For Barth, the world as we experience it, as a creation hanging over nothingness, is simply not enough. It is not that human existence as we have it is excluded from the event of the incarnation, but that it is understood on the terms of this event. In Barth's words:

> That the Word was made 'flesh' means first and generally that He became man, true and real man [*wahrer und wirklicher Mensch*], participating in the same human essence [*Wesens*] and existence [*Daseins*], the same human nature and form, the same historicity that we have. God's revelation to us takes place in such a way that everything ascribable to man, his creaturely existence [*Existenz*] as an individually unique unity of body and soul in the

---

[76] Ingolf U. Dalferth, 'Karl Barth's Eschatological Realism', in *Karl Barth: Centenary Essays*, ed. Stephen Sykes (Cambridge: Cambridge University Press, 1989), p. 30.

[77] Dalferth, 'Karl Barth's Eschatological Realism', p. 30, citing Richard H. Roberts, 'Barth's Doctrine of Time: Its Nature and Implications', in *Karl Barth: Studies of His Theological Method*, ed. Stephen Sykes (New York: Oxford University Press, 1979), p. 145.

The Humanity of God

time between birth and death, can now be predicated of God's eternal Son as well.[78]

What more can be said at this point, than that this is a cross which, like Heidegger's, crosses being out, obscures it (*absconditus*), precisely in order to reveal its truth all the more fully (*revelatus*). It is to this comparison between Barth and Heidegger's respective crosses that we now turn in our concluding chapter.

---

78 CD I.2, p. 146/KD I.2, 161

Conclusion

Protestant Metaphysics after Karl Barth and Martin Heidegger

When asked in a posthumously published interview, 'Can the individual man in any way still influence this web of fateful circumstances?' Heidegger replied:

> Philosophy will be unable to effect any immediate change in the current state of the world. This is true not only of philosophy but of all purely human reflection and endeavor. Only a god can save us. The only possibility available to us is that by thinking and poeticizing we prepare a readiness for the appearance of a god, or for the absence of a god in [our] decline, in so far as in view of the absent god we are in a state of decline.[1]

It is interesting to note that here, at the end of his life, one of the most prolific philosophers of the twentieth century evinces the ineffectualness of 'all purely human reflection'. Heidegger's philosophical pathway led him ultimately to 'a telling silence'.[2] On the one hand this silence offers hope in so far as it recognizes that preparations for salvation are possible. On the other hand, however, as Heidegger's interviewers themselves pointed out,

> the rest of us ... must constantly make decisions. We must adapt ourselves to the system in which we live, must seek to change it,

---

[1] Martin Heidegger, '"Only a God Can Save Us": The *Spiegel* Interview (1966)', in *Heidegger: The Man and the Thinker*, ed. Thomas Sheehan (Chicago: Precedent, 1981), p. 57.

[2] Martin Heidegger, *Identity and Difference*, trans. Joan Stambaugh (Chicago: The University of Chicago Press, 2002), p. 73/142.

Conclusion

must scout out the narrow openings that may lead to reform, and the still narrower openings that may lead to revolution.[3]

It is here that Gianni Vattimo's suggestion, that Heidegger's later work implied an account of the incarnation which he did not in fact develop, is the most relevant.[4] Surely, what is most needed from the philosopher is an account of how being manifests itself for us, and the mechanisms by which we may effect real change in our world. The cross which Heidegger placed over being in his later work,[5] was simply devoid of such productive inspiration. However, this is not to preclude necessarily that our account of the incarnation must again be limited by a post-Heideggerian horizon, as with Vattimo's own 'weak ontology'.[6] Rather, once we have accepted that this theological turn is an authentic interpretation of Heidegger's thinking, then we open ourselves to a much wider range of possible responses to Heidegger's way of framing the onto-theological problem.

As we have seen, Heidegger's phenomenological investigations throughout the early 1920s exploited the ambiguity in Luther's ontology by dividing his early from his later work. Heidegger liked the Luther who raged against Aristotle[7] and read thesis 19 of his *Heidelberg Disputation* (1518) in that light, but simply dismissed Luther's '*theologian of the cross [who] calls the thing what it actually is*'.[8] Although not the only way to interpret Luther on these matters, Heidegger never contravened this basic principle in his philosophy: God and being do not go together. It is this divide

---

[3] Heidegger, '"Only a God Can Save Us"', p. 60.

[4] Gianni Vattimo, 'The Trace of the Trace', in *Religion*, ed. Jacques Derrida and Gianni Vattimo (Cambridge: Polity Press, 1998), p. 93; cf. Gianni Vattimo, *Belief* (Cambridge: Polity Press, 1999), pp. 38ff.

[5] Martin Heidegger, *The Question of Being* (New York: Twayne Publishers, 1958), p. 83.

[6] Gianni Vattimo, *The End of Modernity: Nihilism and Hermeneutics in Postmodern Culture* (Cambridge: Polity Press, 1988), pp. 85ff; cf. Vattimo, *Belief*, pp. 35ff. Cf. John D. Caputo, *The Weakness of God: A Theology of the Event* (Bloomington: Indiana University Press, 2006), p. 7.

[7] Martin Heidegger, *The Phenomenology of Religious Life* (Bloomington: Indiana University Press, 2004), p. 67/97.

[8] Martin Luther, *Luther's Works*, ed. Jaroslav Jan Pelikan, Hilton C. Oswald, and Helmut T. Lehmann, American ed., 55 vols., vol. 31 (Philadelphia, PA: Fortress Press, 1999), p. 53.

which Heidegger puts forward in his lecture, 'Phenomenology and Theology', in 1928, where he sought to investigate the being of beings phenomenologically. Here, theology was inculcated in the ontic realm which demanded Heidegger's own ontological clarification. Later, as Heidegger faced Hegelian univocity in his 'The Onto-theo-logical Constitution of Metaphysics', in 1957, he found that no such pure theology free of ontology was possible and, therefore, began to develop alternative strategies to clarify the meaning of being. This is the context for the cross that Heidegger placed upon being. In order to face being, Heidegger needed to prohibit any direct apprehension of it. Crucially, however, what we must emphasize at this point, is that as Heidegger's ontological investigations progressed, his post-ontological conception of theology always remained the same. In keeping with this, the theological possibilities he alluded to in his later work never accept the category of being within the theological task. This is not to say that Heidegger ever wished to be a theologian. Rather, that he never questioned the theology which his ontology always implied, namely, his own post-ontological interpretation of Lutheran theology.[9] Our contention is that it was this divide between theology and ontology which disbarred any significant transition from *absconditus* to *revelatus* in his thinking, and ultimately explains the silence which haunts his later work.

What, in the end, does Heidegger's account of onto-theology mean for Protestant theology today? Our suggestion is that we must avoid answering this question in terms of Heidegger's appropriation in contemporary phenomenology of religion,[10] much less the

---

9 Martin Heidegger, 'The Reply to the Third Question at the Seminar in Zürich, 1951', in *God without Being: Hors-texte*, ed. Jean-Luc Marion (Chicago: University of Chicago Press, 1991), pp. 61–2.

10 I will list here a selection of influential contemporary essays and compilations: John D. Caputo, *Radical Hermeneutics: Repetition, Deconstruction, and the Hermeneutic Project* (Bloomington: Indiana University Press, 1987), pp. 153ff; John D. Caputo, 'Introduction: Who Comes after the God of Metaphysics?', in *The Religious*, ed. John D. Caputo (Malden, MA: Blackwell, 2002), pp. 1–22; Francis Schüssler Fiorenza, 'Being, Subjectivity, Otherness: The Idols of God', in *Questioning God*, ed. John D. Caputo, Mark Dooley, and Michael J. Scanlon (Bloomington: Indiana University Press, 2001), pp. 341–70; Regina M. Schwartz, *Transcendence: Philosophy, Literature, and Theology Approach the Beyond* (New York: Routledge, 2004); Kevin J. Vanhoozer, *The Cambridge Companion to Postmodern Theology* (Cambridge: Cambridge University Press, 2003); Merold Westphal, *Postmodern*

Conclusion

existentialism of Bultmann. Rather, by returning to the Protestant theology which influenced Heidegger's understanding of onto-theology in the first place, we can uncover alternative strategies and lost insights into the onto-theological problem. Hence, although it is true to say that a Protestant disposition towards metaphysics influenced Heidegger's account of onto-theology, Protestant theologians mustn't be limited by Heidegger's understanding of ontological difference and the theological strictures such difference creates. Although some recent scholarship has begun the process of recovering a more full bodied account of Luther's understanding of metaphysics,[11] our contention has been that it is equally important to investigate alternative accounts of Lutheran theology arising contemporary with Heidegger's development. This is particularly true as these scholars come to terms with the ambiguities inherent in Luther's ontology.[12] It is vitally important to recover the ontological nuance in Luther's thought, but so too, the manner in which other prominent Protestant theologians such as Barth reappropriated Luther in response to their own theological and philosophical problematics.

When we disagree with the suggestion that postmodernity spells the end of Protestantism,[13] therefore, we do not mean to challenge

---

Philosophy and Christian Thought (Bloomington: Indiana University Press, 1999); Merold Westphal, *Overcoming Onto-theology: Toward a Postmodern Christian Faith* (New York: Fordham University Press, 2001); Merold Westphal, *Transcendence and Self-Transcendence: On God and the Soul* (Bloomington: Indiana University Press, 2004); Mark A. Wrathall, *Religion after Metaphysics* (Cambridge: Cambridge University Press, 2003).

11 See, for instance, Risto Saarinen, *Faith and Holiness: Lutheran–Orthodox Dialogue 1959–1994*, 1st Fortress Press ed. (Göttingen: Vandenhoeck & Ruprecht, 1997); Carl E. Braaten and Robert W. Jenson, *Union with Christ: The New Finnish Interpretation of Luther* (Grand Rapids, MI: William B. Eerdman's Publishing Company, 1998); Risto Saarinen, *God and the Gift: An Ecumenical Theology of Giving*, (Collegeville, MN: Unitas Books, Liturgical Press, 2005). For a review of the notion of *theosis* in this new Finnish interpretation of Luther see, Veli-Matti Kärkkäinen, 'Salvation as Justification and Theosis: The Contribution of the New Finnish Luther Interpretation to Our Ecumenical Future', *Dialog* 45, no. 1 (2006), pp. 74–82.

12 See for instance, Dennis Bielfedlt, 'The Ontology of Deification', in *Caritas Dei: Beiträge zum Verständnis Luthers und der gegenwärtigen Ökumene*, ed. Oswald Bayer, Robert W. Jenson and Simo Knuuttila (Helsinki: Luther-Agricola-Gesellschaft, 1997), pp. 90–113.

13 Alister E. McGrath and Darren C. Marks, *The Blackwell Companion to Protestantism* (Oxford: Blackwell, 2004), p. xv. Graham Ward, 'The Future of

Protestantism's roots in the early modern period, nor its various and vibrant contributions to modern development.[14] Rather, we are simply emphasizing and further delineating the manner in which certain features of Protestant thinking have influenced postmodern critique. This is all the more important in so far as Luther is increasingly cited at the origins of the post-metaphysical dehellenization of religion in the West. For instance, Pope Benedict XVI depicts Protestantism as follows,

> Dehellenization first emerges in connection with the postulates of the Reformation in the sixteenth century. Looking at the tradition of scholastic theology, the Reformers thought they were confronted with a faith system totally conditioned by philosophy, that is to say an articulation of the faith based on an alien system of thought. As a result, faith no longer appeared as a living historical Word but as one element of an overarching philosophical system. The principle of *sola scriptura*, on the other hand, sought faith in its pure, primordial form, as originally found in the biblical Word. Metaphysics appeared as a premise derived from another source, from which faith had to be liberated in order to

---

Protestantism: Postmodernity', in *The Blackwell Companion to Protestantism*, ed. Alister E. McGrath and Darren C. Marks (Malden, MA: Blackwell, 2004), p. 453.

14 Beyond those cited in Ward, 'The Future of Protestantism: Postmodernity', a number of others could be acknowledged here, for example Taylor's explication of the secularization of spiritual life, or 'the affirmation that the fullness of Christian existence was to be found within the activities of this life, in one's calling and in marriage and the family'. Charles Taylor, *Sources of the Self: The Making of the Modern Identity* (Cambridge, MA: Harvard University Press, 1989). A point not unnoticed by Frederick Engels, in his 'Origin of the Family, Private Property, and the State', http://www.marxists.org/archive/marx/works/1884/origin-family/cho2d. htm. II.4. However, this is not to say that Taylor will 'treat the distinctions between the Catholic and Protestant contributions to the theistic heritage as being of great significance', as noted by Tracey Rowland in *Culture and the Thomist Tradition: After Vatican II* (London: Routledge, 2003), p. 89. Furthermore, it is not the only Protestant feature of modernity as such. In an almost opposite fashion, for instance, Hegel will cite the inward turn as the Protestant principle, its highest expression being the work of Frederick Jacobi and Friedrich Schleiermacher. Cf. Georg Wilhelm Friedrich Hegel, *Faith & Knowledge*, trans. Walter Cerf and H. S. Harris (Albany, NY: State University of New York Press, 1977), pp. 147–52. It is the God of this Protestantism which Hegel tries to overturn with his affirmation of the death of God, 'the speculative Good Friday in place of the historic Good Friday'. Hegel, *Faith & Knowledge*, p. 191.

Conclusion

become once more fully itself. When Kant stated that he needed to set thinking aside in order to make room for faith, he carried this programme forward with a radicalism that the Reformers could never have foreseen. He thus anchored faith exclusively in practical reason, denying it access to reality as a whole. The liberal theology of the nineteenth and twentieth centuries ushered in a second stage in the process of dehellenization, with Adolf von Harnack as its outstanding representative.[15]

Here, Benedict XVI is tracing a line from Luther to Harnack. What we have been arguing is that this interpretation of Luther is radicalized in Heidegger's thought. This utterly refigures the question of postmodernity from one of Protestantism's end, to its role in the formation of a post-metaphysical future. On the one hand Protestantism is bound up within a post-Heideggerian dehellenization of faith and theology, and the fideist theological liberalism this implies. But it is precisely here that we asked if Protestantism could offer any credible alternative theological ontology. Must Protestantism adopt a being-less faith devoid of reason, and be 'deprived of the truth of existence'[16] as Benedict XVI suggests? Said another way, must it remain tied to the Heideggerian divide between theology and ontology? I would suggest that the future of ecumenical relations between Roman Catholic and Protestant traditions depends upon our answers to these questions.

If treatises on postmodern theology are going to offer any substantive answer to this question, then they must pay closer attention to the complex interrelationship between postmodernism and Protestantism itself. Taking Kevin Vanhoozer's 'Introduction' to the *Cambridge Companion to Postmodern Theology*, as an example,[17]

---

15 Pope Benedict XVI, 'Faith, Reason and the University: Memories and Reflections' (paper presented at the Apostolic Journey of His Holiness Benedict XVI to München, Altötting and Regensburg (September 9–14, 2006), Regensberg, 12 September 2006).
16 Pope Benedict XVI, 'Faith, Reason and the University', n. 13.
17 Vanhoozer, *The Cambridge Companion to Postmodern Theology*. See also Graham Ward, *The Postmodern God: A Theological Reader* (Oxford: Blackwell Publishers, 1997); Graham Ward, *The Blackwell Companion to Postmodern Theology* (Oxford: Blackwell Publishers, 2001); David Ray Griffin, William A. Beardslee and Joe Holland, *Varieties of Postmodern Theology* (Albany, NY: State University of New York Press, 1989).

postmodernism is defined as 'an "exodus" from the constraints of modernity'.[18] In an attempt to delineate what is new about postmodern theology, however, they fail to interrogate Protestant metaphysics in any significant way and this leaves its relationship to modernity and postmodernity in an ambiguous state.[19] This oversight can, in part, be explained by the ecumenical veneer which coats the issue of postmodern theological thought today, an oversight which we have been arguing can equally be seen in the ecumenical generalizations applied to Heidegger's theology. The Protestant nature of postmodern theology is further confused by the role of ostensibly Roman Catholic theologians working in Heidegger's wake. For instance, Thomas Carlson's essay on 'Postmetaphysical Theology', again in the *Cambridge Companion to Postmodern Theology*, reflects upon the postmodern critique of metaphysics in the terms of the Roman Catholic theologian, Jean-Luc Marion. Here we learn that

> The highest name for God, Marion insists, is not to be found in the metaphysical predication of Being or essence but rather in the theological praise of goodness or love, for while finite creatures must first be in order to love, God loves 'before Being,' and through that love alone God's goodness gives all – including the Being of beings itself.[20]

Carlson positions Marion at the end of a particular narration of metaphysics which deeply relies upon the work of Martin Heidegger,[21] and although his explication of Marion's *God without Being* is superb, Marion's relation to Protestant theology is never addressed. On the one hand, therefore, we are contending that it is utterly inappropriate to gloss over Marion's Protestant heritage as a kind

---

18 Vanhoozer, *The Cambridge Companion to Postmodern Theology*, p. xiv.
19 The nearest address of overtly Protestant themes is Vanhoozer's own essay on 'Scripture and Tradition'. Here, he deals with the linguistic heritage of the Reformation emphasis upon Scripture, but he does so in a way that never engages the metaphysical differences between Luther and Hans-Georg Gadamer. Rather, Gadamer's *Truth and Method* is cited without ever addressing its ontological heritage and relation to Heidegger's *Being and Time*. Vanhoozer, *The Cambridge Companion to Postmodern Theology*, p. 152.
20 Thomas A. Carlson, 'Postmetaphysical Theology', in *The Cambridge Companion to Postmodern Theology*, p. 58.
21 Carlson, 'Postmetaphysical Theology', p. 58.

Conclusion

of Heideggerian Barthianism.[22] But, on the other hand, and this is the crucial qualification we are raising here, in so far as Marion inherits Heidegger's understanding of onto-theology, then of necessity he is inheriting one distinct interpretation of Protestant metaphysics. Thus, our arguments above are designed to uncover the various ways that Protestant theology is bound up within contemporary post-Heideggerian notions of onto-theology and, as such, postmodern theology more generally. Our aim in doing so was not only to explicate the idiosyncratic manner in which Heidegger appropriated Protestant theological ideas, but also, why alternative accounts of the onto-theological problem such as Barth's remain so relevant to the future of Protestant theology.

As we turned to Barth's theological ontology in Part 2 above, our aim was to demonstrate the profound differences between Barth's theological ontology and Heidegger's critique of onto-theology.[23] As we have seen, Barth's early tautology 'God is God' drew different conclusions from Luther's theology than his predecessors such as Ludwig Feuerbach and Wilhelm Herrmann. After Feuerbach, it was clear that no differentiation would be possible between theological and other forms of knowledge. The subjective projection of God as an abstraction demanded a more thoroughgoing account of the manner in which human being was not the limit of divine being. Barth responded to Feuerbach and Kant's critiques of anthropocentric theology by emphasizing the Lutheran *Deus absconditus*, the hiddenness of God on the cross. Christ is not self-evident and cannot be limited to the human subject's reasoning capacities. This is the form of the cross which Barth placed upon any attempt to apprehend true being directly. However, it is precisely in this manner that Barth most inhabits the persona of that deserving *'theologian ... who comprehends the visible and manifest things of God*

---

[22] John Milbank, *The Word Made Strange: Theology, Language, Culture* (Cambridge: Blackwell Publishers, 1997), p. 37.
[23] Cf. Graham Ward, *Barth, Derrida, and the Language of Theology* (New York: Cambridge University Press, 1995), pp. 100–1; Westphal, *Transcendence and Self-Transcendence: On God and the Soul*, p. 145. And for a reading of Barth along the lines of Derrida's post-Heideggerian différance, cf. William Stacy Johnson, *The Mystery of God: Karl Barth and the Postmodern Foundations of Theology*, 1st ed. (Louisville, KY: Westminster John Knox Press, 1997), pp. 21ff; Walter James Lowe, *Theology and Difference: The Wound of Reason* (Bloomington: Indiana University Press, 1993), p. 45.

seen through suffering and the cross',[24] in thesis 20 of Luther's *Heidelberg Disputation*. It was for these reasons that Barth was unwilling to concede a pure theologically quarantined religious subjectivity to Kant's critique of metaphysics. Rather, Barth challenged Kant on his own metaphysical grounds. For Barth, Kant's comments on theology were inevitably onto-theological in so far as they could never speak of any other existence apart from that of the thinking subject. In so far as God was justified as an idea necessary for morality, whatever Kant said of theology would inevitably be an onto-theology. This was precisely why Barth was so drawn to Anselm.[25] Barth, therefore, went well beyond Heidegger's attempt to justify his fundamental ontology based on its purity from all other ontic sciences, and the divide between theology and ontology which this implied. Rather, Barth began to work out a theologically grounded notion of ontological difference through his explication of Anselm's *Proslogion* 2–4. It was this theological ontology which offers one of the most thoroughgoing alternatives to Heidegger's thought. Barth's theology does in fact develop these ontological nuances at this point in his book on Anselm and explains why he would consistently cite its importance to his mature theology in the *Church Dogmatics*. It is this insight which we must bring to Barth's understanding of the being of the Church, Jesus Christ.

For much of the commentary which followed after Barth, the emphasis was upon analogy and dialectic. This can be noted in particular with Balthasar's *The Theology of Karl Barth*,[26] but so too, in the comparative account of Henri Chavannes in his *The Analogy between God and the World in Saint Thomas Aquinas*

---

24 Luther, *Works*, vol. 31, p. 52.

25 Again I must emphasize at this point that Barth's misattribution of the term ontological must be read as a critique of Kantian univocity, not of the unique being of God which Barth confirms in his explication of Anselm's *Proslogion* 2–4. See Chapter 4 above.

26 The chief examples of this infatuation can be found firstly in Hans Urs von Balthasar, *The Theology of Karl Barth: Exposition and Interpretation*, trans. Edward T. Oakes (San Francisco: Communio Books, Ignatius Press, 1992), pp. 116–17, 124. And the cottage industry which followed from this text, best summarized and critiqued in Bruce L. McCormack, *Karl Barth's Critically Realistic Dialectical Theology: Its Genesis and Development, 1909–1936* (New York: Oxford University Press, 1995), p. 3. For a summary of the discrepancy between them, see Timothy Stanley, 'Before Analogy: Recovering Barth's Ontological Development', *New Blackfriars* 90, no. 1029 (2009).

Conclusion

and Karl Barth. Here, Chavannes rightly points out that it was Erich Przywara's account of *analogia entis* that Barth inherits and not Thomas's.[27] He goes on to note Barth's positive appraisal of Gottlieb Söhngen's Roman Catholic understanding of *analogia fidei*,[28] and again rightly comments upon the possibilities which Barth's account of Söhngen's notion of analogy opens up for ecumenical dialogue.[29] As such, Chavannes pursues a renewed analysis of the relationship between Barth's account of analogy and Saint Thomas's. To this end, Chavannes will ultimately draw his readers' attention to Barth's later account of creation in *Church Dogmatics* III.3, where Barth explicates the ambiguous 'twofold character and aspect of creaturely existence'.[30] As we have explained in the previous chapters, however, the emphasis in Barth's work is not upon analogy, but upon the ontological difference inherent to his understanding of the doctrine of the Trinity. For instance, the negative references to analogy in his Anselm book all refer to the unqualified relation between the ontic object and the divine object, or the ontological univocity assumed by the *insipiens*. However, the positive references to analogy begin precisely where Anselm recognized the true possibility of God's existence, in so far as it cannot fail to be.[31] Hence, the aim of our initial chapters on Barth was to set out the proper context of his arrival at the ontological difference he develops in his book on Anselm and the *Church Dogmatics*. Chavannes is right therefore to emphasize Barth's discussion of creation at this point in his *Dogmatics*, but it is our contention that he was wrong to presume that 'this wish of Barth to withstand the slander on creation is a new note in his theology emphasising without destroying what the earlier volumes gave us to understand'.[32] Furthermore, Chavannes' belief that Barth refuses to admit philosophical knowledge is at work in his thinking[33] misunderstands just how important philosophical reflection actually was for Barth's theology. As Barth

---

27 Henry Chavannes, *The Analogy between God and the World in Saint Thomas Aquinas and Karl Barth* (New York: Vantage Press, 1992), p. 4.
28 Karl Barth, *Church Dogmatics*, ed. G. W. Bromiley and T. F. Torrance, trans. G. W. Bromiley, vol. II.1 (Edinburgh: T. & T. Clark, 1962), p. 81.
29 Chavannes, *The Analogy between God and the World*, pp. 6–7.
30 Barth, *Church Dogmatics*, III.3, p. 295/KD III.3, 335.
31 Barth, *Anselm*, p. 167/G170.
32 Chavannes, *The Analogy between God and the World*, p. 209.
33 Chavannes, *The Analogy between God and the World*, pp. 215–16.

himself says, 'A free theologian does not deny, nor is he ashamed of, his indebtedness to a particular *philosophy* or ontology, to ways of thought and speech'.[34] Barth is not concerned to completely extricate philosophical language and terminology from his theology. Rather, his concern is that the knowing capacity of the human being is inadequate for apprehending divine being. For Barth, no human ontology can claim full existence apart from God, and no account of divine ontology can claim truth status apart from an act of God. Our contention is that the reason Barth did not develop a more nuanced account of analogy is not because of a rejection of philosophical categories, but because he did not see it as necessary given the structure of the Trinitarian ontology he *did* develop. This occurred early on in the first volume of his *Church Dogmatics*, and it was maintained throughout as a governing theological ontology.

From the first volume to the last, Barth retained the title *Church Dogmatics*, and it has been our aim to demonstrate the ontological difference this title always implied concerning the being of Jesus Christ as a mode of being in relation to the Father and the Holy Spirit. For Barth, as for Luther, God had come to save us, and we participate in this divine ontology in so far as we are returned to our true ontological humanity which was given in creation and finds its paragon in Christ. This cross simultaneously prohibits and obscures any direct apprehension of being (*absconditus*), and yet, nonetheless, reveals true being in so far as it arrives for us there (*revelatus*). It is here that Barth's theological ontology does indeed present us with the possibility of an ecclesial existence which has *real* ethical teeth. Barth's theology has sometimes been depicted as little more than otherworldly ecclesiocentrism that showed his nonchalance towards political engagement in the real world.[35]

---

34 Karl Barth, *The Humanity of God* (London: Collins, 1967), p. 92.

35 Charles C. West, *Communism and the Theologians: Study of an Encounter* (London: SCM Press, 1958), p. 313. See also the criticisms in Jürgen Habermas, 'Transcendence from Within, Transcendence in This World', in *Habermas, Modernity, and Public Theology*, ed. Francis Schussler Fiorenza and Don S. Browning (New York: The Crossroad Publishing Company, 1992), p. 231; Reinhold Niebuhr, *Essays in Applied Christianity* (New York: Meridian Books, 1959); Richard H. Roberts, *A Theology on Its Way?: Essays on Karl Barth* (Edinburgh: T&T Clark, 1991); Helmut Thielicke, *Theological Ethics*, 3 vols., vol. 1 (Grand Rapids, MI: William B. Eerdmans, 1979); Helmut Thielicke, *Modern Faith and Thought* (Grand Rapids, MI.: William B. Eerdmans, 1990).

Conclusion

Barth was often seen as a Protestant separatist who made a choice between the natural world of historical experience and faith. In choosing faith he neglected the political concerns most important to those like the reporters who interviewed Heidegger as we noted above. This interpretation, however, needs to be challenged. In addition to Barth's own statements,[36] the works of Friedrich-Wilhelm Marquardt and Helmut Gollwitzer[37] have drawn out the relationship between Barth's theology and the socialism he participated in as a pastor in Safenwil. Building on this foundation has been the continuing work of Nigel Biggar and John Webster who both have shown the inherent connection between Barth's theology and his ethics and politics.[38] Though Biggar believes Barth's position on political leadership became more nuanced in his later work,[39] he nonetheless draws upon the ongoing and consummate interest Barth had in politics and ethics. The question is never whether or not Barth's theology was oriented around political and ethical action, but how and to what degree. In like manner Webster points out the way Barth saw his theology as the foreground for an ongoing political subtext.[40] What is increasingly acknowledged is that Barth was deeply invested in the political nature of theology. This compounded with the historical weight of Barth's involvement with the Confessing Church in Germany during World War Two

---

36 '"Don't forget to say that I have always been interested in politics"', remarked Karl Barth toward the end of his career, "and consider that it belongs to the life of a theologian. My whole cellar is full of political literature. I read it all the time. I am also an ardent reader of the newspaper".' George Hunsinger, *Karl Barth and Radical Politics* (Philadelphia, PA: Westminster Press, 1976), p. 181, citing John Deschner, 'Karl Barth as Political Activist', *Union Seminary Quarterly Review* 28 (1972), p. 55.

37 Friedrich-Wilhelm Marquardt, 'Socialism in the Theology of Karl Barth', in *Karl Barth and Radical Politics*, ed. George Hunsinger (Philadelphia, PA: Westminster Press, 1976), pp. 47–8. In this essay you can find a summary of Marquardt's larger thesis, *Theology and Socialism: The Example of Karl Barth*. See also Helmut Gollwitzer, 'Kingdom of God and Socialism in the Theology of Karl Barth', in *Karl Barth and Radical Politics*, ed. George Hunsinger (Philadelphia, PA: Westminster Press, 1976).

38 See for instance J. B. Webster, *Barth's Moral Theology: Human Action in Barth's Thought* (Grand Rapids, MI: William B. Eerdmans, 1998), and Nigel Biggar, *The Hastening That Waits: Karl Barth's Ethics* (New York: Oxford University Press, 1993).

39 Biggar, *The Hastening That Waits*, p. 61.

40 Webster, *Barth's Moral Theology*, pp. 4–5, citing Karl Barth, *Letters 1961–1968* (Edinburgh: T & T Clark, 1981), p. 251.

gives ample evidence that Barth was by no means politically, nor ethically complacent.[41] Although we do not have the space here to spell out the full implications of the theological ontology we have explicated above, it should be clear that it is precisely because Jesus Christ was and is that being who can not fail to be, that true human being arrives as a real possibility for us. That Barth retained the title *Church Dogmatics* for this theological ontology, however, is not to suggest that a sufficient Protestant ecclesiology was worked out in its necessary detail for us today.[42] Rather, Barth developed one of the most profound alternatives to a Heideggerian framing of the onto-theological problem. It is hoped that in this sense, Barth's theology may indeed inspire the future of Protestant theology.[43]

---

41 See, for instance, the Barmen Declaration, which opens with, 'In view of the errors of the "German Christians" and of the present Reich Church Administration, which are ravaging the church and at the same time also shattering the unity of the German Evangelical Church, we confess the following evangelical truths'. Karl Barth, *The Barmen Declaration* (United Church of Christ, 1934; available from http://www.ucc.org/faith/barmen.htm.

42 I began writing this book as a dissertation on Protestant ecclesiology. However, I found myself in the opposite situation to Dietrich Bonhoeffer. Rather than writing an ecclesiology (*Communion of Saints*) which would clear the way for his metaphysics (*Act and Being*), the crisis of contemporary postmodern critique forced me to write a metaphysics which could clear the way for an ecclesiology. This ecclesiology remains as my primary aim.

43 As William Stacy Johnson suggests, 'With a new generation of theologians re-evaluating the theology of Karl Barth, some are suggesting that this pivotal figure of the 20th century may enjoy his greatest influence in the 21st'. William Stacy Johnson, 'Barth and Beyond', *The Christian Century*, May 2, 2001, p. 16.

Bibliography

Anselm, *The Major Works*, edited by Brian Davies and G. R. Evans. Oxford: Oxford University Press, 1998.
Aristotle, *The Metaphysics: Books I–IX*, translated by Hugh Tredennick. Cambridge, MA: Harvard University Press, 1980.
Aristotle, *Aristotle's Metaphysics*, Vol. 1, translated by W. D. Ross. Oxford: The Clarendon Press, 1924.
Baillie, Donald Macpherson, *God Was in Christ: An Essay on Incarnation and Atonement*. London: Faber and Faber, 1948.
Baillie, John, 'Introduction' in *Natural Theology: Comprising 'Nature and Grace' by Professor Dr. Emil Brunner and the Reply 'No!' by Dr. Karl Barth*, edited by Peter Fraenkel. London: Geoffrey Bles, 1946, pp. 5–13.
Balthasar, Hans Urs von, *The Theology of Karl Barth: Exposition and Interpretation*, translated by Edward T. Oakes. San Francisco: Communio Books, Ignatius Press, 1992.
Barth, Karl, *Die christliche Dogmatik im Entwurf*, edited by Gerhard Sauter. Zürich: Theologischer Verlag, 1927.
Barth, Karl, *The Word of God and the Word of Man*, translated by Douglas Horton. London: Hodder and Stoughton, 1928.
Barth, Karl, *The Epistle to the Romans*, translated by Edwyn Clement Hoskyns. 2nd ed. London: Oxford University Press, 1933.
Barth, Karl, 'The Barmen Declaration' United Church of Christ. Available online at http://www.ucc.org/faith/barmen.htm. Originally published 1934.
Barth, Karl, 'No! Answer to Emil Brunner', in *Natural Theology: Comprising 'Nature and Grace' by Professor Dr. Emil Brunner and the Reply 'No!' by Dr. Karl Barth*, edited by Peter Fraenkel. London: Geoffrey Bles, 1946.
Barth, Karl, *Die protestantische Theologie im 19. Jahrhundert: Ihre Vorgeschichte und ihre Geschichte*. Zürich: Evangelischer Verlag, 1947.
Barth, Karl, 'Introductory Essay', in Ludwig Feuerbach, *The Essence of Christianity*. New York: Harper and Row, 1957, pp. x–xxxii.
Barth, Karl, *Anselm: Fides Quaerens Intellectum*. London: SCM Press, 1960.

Barth, Karl, *Church Dogmatics*, translated by G. W. Bromiley, edited by G. W. Bromiley and T. F. Torrance. Vol. I.1. Edinburgh: T. & T. Clark, 1962.
Barth, Karl, *Church Dogmatics*, translated by G. W. Bromiley, edited by G. W. Bromiley and T. F. Torrance. Vol. I.2. Edinburgh: T. & T. Clark, 1962.
Barth, Karl, *Church Dogmatics*, translated by G. W. Bromiley, edited by G. W. Bromiley and T. F. Torrance. Vol. II.1. Edinburgh: T. & T. Clark, 1962.
Barth, Karl, *Church Dogmatics*, translated by G. W. Bromiley, edited by G. W. Bromiley and T. F. Torrance. Vol. II.2. Edinburgh: T. & T. Clark, 1962.
Barth, Karl, *Church Dogmatics*, translated by G. W. Bromiley, edited by G. W. Bromiley and T. F. Torrance. Vol. III.2. Edinburgh: T. & T. Clark, 1962.
Barth, Karl, *Church Dogmatics*, translated by G. W. Bromiley, edited by G. W. Bromiley and T. F. Torrance. Vol. III.3. Edinburgh: T. & T. Clark, 1962.
Barth, Karl, *Church Dogmatics*, translated by G. W. Bromiley, edited by G. W. Bromiley and T. F. Torrance. Vol. III.4. Edinburgh: T. & T. Clark, 1962.
Barth, Karl, *Church Dogmatics*, translated by G. W. Bromiley, edited by G. W. Bromiley and T. F. Torrance. Vol. IV.1. Edinburgh: T. & T. Clark, 1962.
Barth, Karl, *Church Dogmatics*, translated by G. W. Bromiley, edited by G. W. Bromiley and T. F. Torrance. Vol. IV.2. Edinburgh: T. & T. Clark, 1962.
Barth, Karl, *Theology and Church: Shorter Writings, 1920–1928*. New York: Harper & Row, 1962.
Barth, Karl, 'Ludwig Feuerbach (1920)', in *Theology and Church: Shorter Writings, 1920–1928*. New York: Harper & Row, 1962, pp. 217–37.
Barth, Karl, 'Martin Luther's Doctrine of the Eucharist (1923)', in *Theology and Church: Shorter Writings, 1920–1928*. New York: Harper & Row, 1962.
Barth, Karl, 'The Principles of Dogmatics According to Wilhelm Herrmann (1925)', in *Theology and Church: Shorter Writings, 1920–1928*. New York: Harper & Row, 1962, pp. 238–71.
Barth, Karl, *Die Kirchliche Dogmatik*. Vol. I.1. Zürich: Evangelischer Verlag, 1964.
Barth, Karl, *Die Kirchliche Dogmatik*. Vol. III.3. Zürich: Evangelischer Verlag, 1964.
Barth, Karl, *How I Changed My Mind*. Richmond, VA: John Knox Press, 1966.
Barth, Karl, *The Humanity of God*. London: Collins, 1967.

Bibliography

Barth, Karl, 'An Answer to Professor von Harnack's Open Letter', in *The Beginnings of Dialectical Theology*, edited by James M. Robinson. Richmond, VA: John Knox Press, 1968, pp. 175-85.

Barth, Karl, *Fides Quaerens Intellectum*, Gesamtausgabe Vol. 13. Zürich: Theologischer Verlag, 1981.

Barth, Karl, *The Christian Life: Church Dogmatics IV, 4: Lecture Fragments*, translated by G. W. Bromiley. Grand Rapids, MI: William B. Eerdmans, 1981.

Barth, Karl, *Letters 1961-1968*. Edinburgh: T. & T. Clark, 1981.

Barth, Karl, *The Theology of Schleiermacher: Lectures at Göttingen, Winter Semester of 1923-24*, translated by Dietrich Ritschl. Grand Rapids, MI: William B. Eerdmans, 1982.

Barth, Karl, *The Way of Theology in Karl Barth: Essays and Comments*, edited by Martin Rumscheidt. Allison Park, PA: Pickwick Publications, 1986.

Barth, Karl, 'Fate and Idea', in *The Way of Theology in Karl Barth: Essays and Comments*. Allison Park, PA: Pickwick Publications, 1986, pp. 25-61.

Barth, Karl, 'The First Commandment as an Axiom of Theology', in *The Way of Theology in Karl Barth: Essays and Comments*. Allison Park, PA: Pickwick Publications, 1986, pp. 63-78.

Barth, Karl, 'Philosophy and Theology', in *The Way of Theology in Karl Barth: Essays and Comments*. Allison Park, PA: Pickwick Publications, 1986, pp. 79-95.

Barth, Karl, *The Göttingen Dogmatics: Instruction in the Christian Religion*, edited by Hannelotte Reiffen. Vol. 1. Grand Rapids, MI: W. B. Eerdmans, 1991.

Barth, Karl, *Gespräche 1964-1968*. Zürich: Theologische Verlag Zürich, 1997.

Barth, Karl, *Protestant Theology in the Nineteenth Century: Its Background & History*, translated by G. W. Bromiley. New ed. London: SCM Press, 2001.

Barth, Karl, 'Feuerbach', in *Protestant Theology in the Nineteenth Century: Its Background & History*. London: SCM Press, 2001, pp. 520-26.

Barth, Karl, *The Theology of the Reformed Confessions, 1923*, translated by Darrell L. Guder and Judith J. Guder. Louisville, KY: Westminster John Knox Press, 2002.

Barth, Karl and Eduard Thurneysen, *Revolutionary Theology in the Making: Barth-Thurneysen Correspondence, 1914-1925*. Richmond, VA: John Knox Press, 1964.

Bartsch, Hans Werner, *Kerygma und Mythos: ein theologisches Gespräch*. London: SPCK, 1964.

Bauman, Zygmunt, 'The Re-Enchantment of the World, or How Can One Narrate Postmodernity? (1992)', in *The Bauman Reader*, edited by Peter Beilharz. Oxford: Blackwell Publishers, 2001, pp. 188-99.

Beck, Lewis White, 'Neo-Kantianism' in *Encyclopedia of Philosophy*, edited by Paul Edwards. New York: The Macmillan Company & The Free Press, 1967.

Beintker, Michael, 'Unterricht in der christlichen Religion', in *Verküdigung und Forschung: Beihefte zur 'Evangelische Theologie'*, edited by Gerhard Sauter. Munich: Kaiser Verlag, 1985, pp. 58–65.

Beintker, Michael, *Die Dialektik in der 'dialektischen Theologie' Karl Barths: Studien zur Entwicklung der Barthschen Theologie und zur Vorgeschichte der 'Kirchlichen Dogmatik'*, Beiträge zur evangelischen Theologie; Bd. 101. München: C. Kaiser, 1987.

Beiser, Frederick C., *The Cambridge Companion to Hegel*. Cambridge: Cambridge University Press, 1993.

Benedict XVI, Pope, 'Faith, Reason and the University: Memories and Reflections', Paper presented at the Apostolic Journey of His Holiness Benedict XVI to München, Altötting and Regensburg (9–14 September 2006), Regensburg, 12 September 2006. Available online at http://www.vatican.va/holy_father/benedict_xvi/speeches/2006/september/documents/hf_ben-xvi_spe_20060912_university-regensburg_en.html.

Bettenson, Henry and Chris Maunder, 'The Definition of Chalcedon, 451', in *Documents of the Christian Church*. Oxford: Oxford University Press, 1999, pp. 56–7.

Bielfedlt, Dennis, 'The Ontology of Deification', in *Caritas Dei: Beiträge zum Verständnis Luthers und der gegenwärtigen Ökumene*, edited by Oswald Bayer, Robert W. Jenson and Simo Knuuttila. Helsinki: Luther-Agricola-Gesellschaft, 1997, pp. 90–113.

Biggar, Nigel, *The Hastening That Waits: Karl Barth's Ethics*. New York: Oxford University Press, 1993.

Bouillard, Henri, *The Knowledge of God*. London: Burns & Oates, 1969.

Bouyer, Louis, *The Spirit and Forms of Protestantism*. Westminster, MD: Newman Press, 1956.

Braaten, Carl E. and Robert W. Jenson, *Union with Christ: The New Finnish Interpretation of Luther*. Grand Rapids, MI: William B. Eerdmans Publishing Company, 1998.

Brunner, Emil, 'Nature and Grace', in *Natural Theology: Comprising 'Nature and Grace' by Professor Dr. Emil Brunner and the Reply 'No!' by Dr. Karl Barth*, edited by Peter Fraenkel. London: Geoffrey Bles, 1946, pp. 15–64.

Busch, Eberhard, *Karl Barth: His Life from Letters and Autobiographical Texts*. London: SCM Press, 1976.

Busch, Eberhard, 'God is God: The Meaning of a Controversial Formula and the Fundamental Problem of Speaking about God', *The Princeton Seminary Bulletin* 7, no. 2 (1986), pp. 101–13.

Busch, Eberhard, *Karl Barth & the Pietists: The Young Karl Barth's Critique of Pietism and Its Response*. Downers Grove, IL: InterVarsity Press, 2004.

Bibliography

Butchvarov, Panayot, 'Metaphysics', in *The Cambridge Dictionary of Philosophy*, edited by Robert Audi. New York: Cambridge University Press, 1999.

Calvin, John, *The Institutes of the Christian Religion*. Grand Rapids, MI: William B. Eerdmans Publishing Company, 2001.

Caputo, John D., 'Phenomenology, Mysticism and the *Grammatica Speculativa*: A Study in Heidegger's *Habilitationsschrift*', *The Journal of the British Society for Phenomenology* 5, no. 2 (1974), pp. 101–17.

Caputo, John D., *Heidegger and Aquinas: An Essay on Overcoming Metaphysics*. New York: Fordham University Press, 1982.

Caputo, John D., *Radical Hermeneutics: Repetition, Deconstruction, and the Hermeneutic Project*. Bloomington, IN: Indiana University Press, 1987.

Caputo, John D., 'Heidegger and Theology', in *The Cambridge Companion to Heidegger*, edited by Charles B. Guignon. Cambridge: Cambridge University Press, 1993, pp. 270–88.

Caputo, John D., 'Introduction: Who Comes after the God of Metaphysics?', in *The Religious*, edited by John D. Caputo. Malden, MA: Blackwell, 2002, pp. 1–22.

Caputo, John D., *The Weakness of God: A Theology of the Event*. Bloomington, IN: Indiana University Press, 2006.

Carlson, Thomas A., 'Postmetaphysical Theology', in *The Cambridge Companion to Postmodern Theology*, edited by Kevin J. Vanhoozer. Cambridge: Cambridge University Press, 2003, pp. 58–75.

Caygill, Howard, 'Existence', in *A Kant Dictionary*. Oxford: Blackwell Publishing, 1995.

Chavannes, Henry, *The Analogy between God and the World in Saint Thomas Aquinas and Karl Barth*. New York: Vantage Press, 1992.

Cohen, Hermann, *Logik der reinen Erkenntnis*. Berlin: B. Cassirer, 1902.

Cohen, Hermann, *Reason and Hope: Selections from the Jewish Writings of Hermann Cohen*, edited by Eva Jospe. Cincinnati, OH: Hebrew Union College Press, 1993.

Cunningham, Conor, *A Genealogy of Nihilism: Philosophies of Nothing and the Difference of Theology*. London and New York: Routledge, 2002.

Dalferth, Ingolf U., 'Karl Barth's Eschatological Realism', in *Karl Barth: Centenary Essays*, edited by Stephen Sykes. Cambridge: Cambridge University Press, 1989, pp. 14–45.

Deegan, Daniel L., 'The Theology of Wilhelm Herrmann: A Reassessment', *The Journal of Religion* 45, no. 2 (1965), pp. 87–99.

Denifle, Heinrich and Albert Maria Weiss, *Luther und Luthertum*, 2nd ed. Vol. I. Mainz: F. Kirchheim, 1906.

Derrida, Jacques, 'How to Avoid Speaking: Denials', in *Derrida and Negative Theology*, edited by Harold G. Coward, Toby Foshay and Jacques

Derrida. Albany, NY: State University of New York Press, 1992, pp. 73–142.
Derrida, Jacques, *On the Name*, edited by Thomas Dutoit. Stanford, CA: Stanford University Press, 1995.
Deschner, John, 'Karl Barth as Political Activist', *Union Seminary Quarterly Review* 28, (1972), pp. 55–66.
Dillenberger, John and Claude Welch, *Protestant Christianity Interpreted Through its Development*. New York: Scribner & Sons, 1954.
Drescher, Hans-Georg, *Ernst Troeltsch: His Life and Work*. 1st Fortress Press ed. Minneapolis, MN: Fortress Press, 1993.
Dreyfus, Hubert L., 'Heidegger on the Connection between Nihilism, Art, Technology, and Politics', in *The Cambridge Companion to Heidegger*, edited by Charles B. Guignon. Cambridge: Cambridge University Press, 1993, pp. 289–316.
Dulles, Avery, *The Assurance of Things Hoped for: A Theology of Christian Faith*. New York: Oxford University Press, 1994.
Durkheim, Emile, *The Elementary Forms of Religious Life*. New York: Alan and Unwin, 1976.
Ebeling, Gerhard, *Luther: An Introduction to His Thought*, translated by R. A. Wilson. London: Collins, 1970.
Ebeling, Gerhard, *Lutherstudien*, translated by R. A. Wilson. Vol. 3. Tübingen: J. C. B Mohr, 1985.
Engels, Frederick. 'Origin of the Family, Private Property, and the State', http://www.marxists.org/archive/marx/works/1884/origin-family/cho2d.htm.
Ferreira, Jamie M., 'Faith and the Kierkegaardian Leap', in *The Cambridge Companion to Kierkegaard*, edited by Alastair Hannay and Gordon Daniel Marino. Cambridge: Cambridge University Press, 1998, pp. 207–34.
Feuerbach, Ludwig, *The Essence of Christianity*, translated by George Eliot. New York: Prometheus, 1989.
Fisher, Simon, *Revelatory Positivism?: Barth's Earliest Theology and the Marburg School*. Oxford: Oxford University Press, 1988.
Frei, Hans W., 'The Doctrine of Revelation in the Thought of Karl Barth 1909–1922', Doctoral Dissertation, Yale, 1956.
Gadamer, Hans-Georg, 'Wilhelm Dilthey nach 150 Jahren', in *Dilthey und die Philosophie der Gegenwart*, edited by E. W. Orth. Freiburg: Alber, 1985, pp. 157–82.
Gerrish, B. A., *Grace and Reason: A Study in the Theology of Luther*. Oxford: Clarendon Press, 1962.
Gerrish, B. A., *The Old Protestantism and the New: Essays on the Reformation Heritage*. Chicago: University of Chicago Press, 1982.
Gilson, Etienne, *Being and Some Philosophers*. Toronto: Pontifical Institute of Mediaeval Studies, 1949.

Bibliography

Gockel, Matthias, 'A Dubious Christological Formula? Leontius of Byzantium and the *Anhypostasis-Enhypostasis* Theory', *Journal of Theological Studies* 51, no. 2 (2000), pp. 515–32.

Gogarten, Friedrich, 'Historicism', in *The Beginnings of Dialectic Theology*, edited by James McConkey Robinson and Jürgen Moltmann. Richmond, VA: John Knox Press, 1968, pp. 341–58.

Gollwitzer, Helmut, 'Kingdom of God and Socialism in the Theology of Karl Barth', in *Karl Barth and Radical Politics*, edited by George Hunsinger. Philadelphia, PA: Westminster Press, 1976, pp. 77–120.

Gordon, Peter Eli, *Rosenzweig and Heidegger: Between Judaism and German Philosophy*. Berkeley: University of California Press, 2003.

Griffin, David Ray, William A. Beardslee and Joe Holland, *Varieties of Postmodern Theology*. Albany, NY: State University of New York Press, 1989.

Gunton, Colin E., *Becoming and Being: The Doctrine of God in Charles Hartshorne and Karl Barth*. Oxford: Oxford University Press, 1978.

Guyer, Paul, 'Thought and Being: Hegel's Critique of Kant's Theoretical Philosophy', in *The Cambridge Companion to Hegel*, edited by Frederick C. Beiser. Cambridge: Cambridge University Press, 1993, pp. 171–210.

Habermas, Jürgen, 'Transcendence from Within, Transcendence in This World', in *Habermas, Modernity, and Public Theology*, edited by Francis Schüssler Fiorenza and Don S. Browning. New York: The Crossroad Publishing Company, 1992, pp. 226–50.

Harnack, Adolf von, *Das Wesen des Christentums*, 1st ed. Gütersloh: Gütersloher Verlagshaus Mohn, 1977.

Harnack, Adolf von, *What is Christianity?* Philadelphia, PA: Fortress Press, 1986.

Hauerwas, Stanley, *With the Grain of the Universe: The Church's Witness and Natural Theology: Being the Gifford Lectures Delivered at the University of St. Andrews in 2001*. Grand Rapids, MI: Brazos Press, 2001.

Hector, Kevin, 'God's Triunity and Self-Determination: A Conversation with Karl Barth, Bruce McCormack and Paul Molnar', *International Journal of Systematic Theology* 7, no. 3 (2005), pp. 246–61.

Hegel, Georg Wilhelm Friedrich, 'Dialectic and the *Science of Logic*', in *Hegel: The Essential Writings*, edited by Frederick G. Weiss. New York: Harper & Row, 1974, pp. 86–123.

Hegel, Georg Wilhelm Friedrich, *Faith & Knowledge*, translated by Walter Cerf and H. S. Harris. Albany, NY: State University of New York Press, 1977.

Hegel, Georg Wilhelm Friedrich, *Phenomenology of Spirit*, translated by A. V. Miller. Oxford: Clarendon Press, 1977.

Heidegger, Martin, *Sein und Zeit*. 7th ed. Tübingen: Neomarius Verlag, 1953.

Heidegger, Martin, *The Question of Being*. New York: Twayne Publishers, 1958.
Heidegger, Martin, *Being and Time*, translated by John Macquarrie and Edward Robinson. New York: Harper Collins Publishers, 1962.
Heidegger, Martin, *On Time and Being*, translated by Joan Stambaugh. New York: Harper & Row, 1972.
Heidegger, Martin, 'The End of Philosophy and the Task of Thinking', in *On Time and Being*, edited by Joan Stambaugh. New York: Harper & Row, 1972, pp. 55–73.
Heidegger, Martin, *Zur Bestimmung der Philosophie*, Gesamtausgabe, Vol. 56/57. Frankfurt am Main: Klostermann, 1976.
Heidegger, Martin, *The Piety of Thinking*, edited by James G. Hart and John C. Maraldo. Bloomington, IN: Indiana University Press, 1976.
Heidegger, Martin, 'Phenomenology and Theology', in *The Piety of Thinking*, edited by James G. Hart and John C. Maraldo. Bloomington, IN: Indiana University Press, 1976, pp. 5–21.
Heidegger, Martin, 'The Theological Discussion of 'The Problem of A Non-Objectifying Speaking and Thinking in Today's Theology' – Some Pointers to Its Major Aspects', in *The Piety of Thinking*, edited by James G. Hart and John C. Maraldo. Bloomington, IN: Indiana University Press, 1976, pp. 22–31.
Heidegger, Martin, *Zur Sache des Denkens*, Gesamtausgabe, Vol. 14. Frankfurt am Main: Vittorio Klostermann, 1976.
Heidegger, Martin, *Wegmarken*, Gesamtausgabe, Vol. 9. Frankfurt am Main: Vittorio Klostermann, 1976.
Heidegger, Martin, 'The Question Concerning Technology', in *The Question Concerning Technology and Other Essays*. New York: Harper & Row, 1977, pp. 3–35.
Heidegger, Martin, '"Only a God Can Save Us": The *Spiegel* Interview (1966)', in *Heidegger: The Man and the Thinker*, edited by Thomas Sheehan. Chicago: Precedent, 1981, pp. 45–67.
Heidegger, Martin, *The Basic Problems of Phenomenology*, translated by Albert Hofstadter. Bloomington, IN: Indiana University Press, 1982.
Heidegger, Martin, *Phänomenololgische Interpretationen zu Aristotles*, Gesamtausgabe Vol. 61. Frankfurt am Main: Klostermann, 1985.
Heidegger, Martin, *Ontologie (Hermeneutik der Faktizität)*, Gesamtausgabe Vol. 63. Frankfurt am Main: Klostermann, 1988.
Heidegger, Martin, 'The Way Back into the Ground of Metaphysics', in *Existentialism: From Dostoevsky to Sartre*, edited by Walter Kaufmann. New York: Penguin Books, 1989, pp. 265–79.
Heidegger, Martin, 'The Reply to the Third Question at the Seminar in Zürich, 1951', in *God without Being: Hors-texte*, edited by Jean-Luc Marion. Chicago: University of Chicago Press, 1991, pp. 61–62.
Heidegger, Martin, 'What is Metaphysics?' in *Basic Writings: From Being*

Bibliography

and Time (1927) to The Task of Thinking (1964), edited by David Farrell Krell. San Francisco: HarperSanFrancisco, 1993, pp. 92–110.

Heidegger, Martin, 'Letter on Humanism', in *Basic Writings: From Being and Time (1927) to The task of Thinking (1964)*, edited by David Farrell Krell. San Francisco: HarperSanFrancisco, 1993, pp. 213–66.

Heidegger, Martin, *Phänomenologie des Religiösen Lebens*, Gesamtausgabe Vol. 60. Frankfurt am Main: Klostermann, 1995.

Heidegger, Martin, *Ontology: The Hermeneutics of Facticity*. Bloomington, IN: Indiana University Press, 1999.

Heidegger, Martin, *Contributions to Philosophy (From Enowning)*, translated by Parvis Emad and Kenneth Maly. Bloomington, IN: Indiana University Press, 1999.

Heidegger, Martin, *Towards the Definition of Philosophy: With a Transcript of the Lecture Course 'On the Nature of the University and Academic Study'*, translated by Ted Sadler. New Brunswick, NJ: Athlone Press, 2000.

Heidegger, Martin, 'The Idea of Philosophy and the Problem of Worldview: War Emergency Semester 1919', in *Towards the Definition of Philosophy: With a Transcript of the Lecture Course 'On the Nature of the University and Academic Study'*. New Brunswick, NJ: Athlone Press, 2000, pp. 3–102.

Heidegger, Martin, *Phenomenological Interpretations of Aristotle: Initiation into Phenomenological Research*. Bloomington, IN: Indiana University Press, 2001.

Heidegger, Martin, *Identity and Difference*, translated by Joan Stambaugh. Chicago: The University of Chicago Press, 2002.

Heidegger, Martin, *Supplements: From the Earliest Essays to Being and Time and Beyond*, edited by John Van Buren. Albany, NY: State University of New York Press, 2002.

Heidegger, Martin, 'Vorwort', in *Heidegger. Through Phenomenology to Thought*, edited by William J. Richardson. New York: Fordham University Press, 2003, pp. ix–xxiii.

Heidegger, Martin, *The Phenomenology of Religious Life*. Bloomington, IN: Indiana University Press, 2004.

Hemming, Laurence Paul, *Heidegger's Atheism: The Refusal of a Theological Voice*. Notre Dame, IN: University of Notre Dame Press, 2002.

Heppe, H., *Dogmatics*. London: Allen & Unwin, 1950.

Herrmann, Wilhelm, *The Communion of the Christian with God: A Discussion in Agreement with the View of Luther*, translated by J. Sandys Stanyon. London: Williams & Norgate, 1895.

Herrmann, Wilhelm, *Systematic Theology*, translated by Nathaniel Micklem and Kenneth A. Saunders. London: George Allen & Unwin Ltd, 1927.

Hoyle, Richard Birch. *The Teaching of Karl Barth: An Exposition*. London: Student Christian Movement Press, 1930.

Hunsinger, George, *Karl Barth and Radical Politics*. Philadelphia, PA: Westminster Press, 1976.
Hunsinger, George, *How to Read Karl Barth: The Shape of His Theology*. Oxford: Oxford University Press, 1991.
Hunsinger, George, 'Karl Barth's Christology: Its Basic Chalcedonian Character', in *Disruptive Grace: Studies in the Theology of Karl Barth*. Grand Rapids, MI: William B. Eerdmans, 2000, pp. 131–47.
Hunsinger, George, 'What Karl Barth Learned from Martin Luther', in *Disruptive Grace: Studies in the Theology of Karl Barth*. Grand Rapids, MI: William B. Eerdmans, 2000, pp. 279–304.
Hunsinger, George, 'Election and the Trinity: Twenty-Five Theses on the Theology of Karl Barth', *Modern Theology* 24, no. 2 (2008), pp. 179–98.
Inwood, M. J., *A Hegel Dictionary*. Oxford: Blackwell, 1992.
James, William, *Varieties of Religious Experience: A Study in Human Nature*. Centenary ed. London: Routledge, 2002.
Jaspers, Karl, *Philosophy*, translated by E. B. Ashton. Chicago: University of Chicago Press, 1969.
Jaspers, Karl, 'On Heidegger', *Graduate Faculty Philosophy Journal* 7 (1978), pp. 107–28.
Jenson, Robert W., *Alpha and Omega: A Study in the Theology of Karl Barth*. New York: Nelson, 1963.
John Duns Scotus, *Philosophical Writings: A Selection*, edited and translated by Allan Wolter. Edinburgh: Nelson, 1962.
Johnson, William Stacy, *The Mystery of God: Karl Barth and the Postmodern Foundations of Theology*. 1st ed. Louisville, KY: Westminster John Knox Press, 1997.
Johnson, William Stacy, 'Barth and Beyond', *The Christian Century*, 2 May 2001, pp. 16–17.
Jonas, Hans, *The Phenomenon of Life: Toward a Philosophical Biology*. Chicago: University of Chicago Press, 1982.
Jüngel, Eberhard, 'Der Schritt zurück: Eine Auseinandersetzung mit der Heidegger-Deutung Heinrich Otts', *Zeitschrift für Theologie und Kirche* LVIII (1961), pp. 104–22.
Jüngel, Eberhard, *Karl Barth: A Theological Legacy*. Philadelphia, PA: Westminster Press, 1986.
Jüngel, Eberhard, *God's Being Is in Becoming: The Trinitarian Being of God in the Theology of Karl Barth*. Grand Rapids, MI: W.B. Eerdmans, 2001.
Kant, Immanuel, *Religion within the Limits of Reason Alone*. London: Open Court Pub. Co., 1960.
Kant, Immanuel, *Grundlegung der Metaphysik der Sitten*. Berlin: Bruyter, 1968.
Kant, Immanuel, *Lectures on Philosophical Theology*, translated by Allen W. Wood and Gertrude M. Clark. Ithaca, NY: Cornell University Press, 1978.

Bibliography

Kant, Immanuel, *Religion and Rational Theology*, translated by Allen W. Wood and George Di Giovanni. Cambridge: Cambridge University Press, 1996.

Kant, Immanuel, *Critique of Practical Reason*, edited by Mary J. Gregor. Cambridge: Cambridge University Press, 1997.

Kant, Immanuel, *Prolegomena to Any Future Metaphysics That Will Be Able to Come Forward as Science: With Selections from the Critique of Pure Reason*, translated by Gary C. Hatfield. Cambridge: Cambridge University Press, 1997.

Kant, Immanuel, *Critique of Pure Reason*, edited by Paul Guyer and Allen W. Wood. Cambridge: Cambridge University Press, 1998.

Kant, Immanuel, 'Kritik der reinen Vernunft (1787)', edited by Gerd Bouillon. Project Gutenberg, 2004. Available online at http://www.gutenberg.org/dirs/etext04/8ikc210.txt.

Kärkkäinen, Veli-Matti, 'Salvation as Justification and Theosis: The Contribution of the New Finnish Luther Interpretation to Our Ecumenical Future', *Dialog* 45, no. 1 (2006), pp. 74–82.

Kelsey, David H., *The Fabric of Paul Tillich's Theology*. New Haven, CT: Yale University Press, 1967.

Kerr, Fergus, 'Karl Barth's Christological Metaphysics', in *Immortal Longings: Versions of Transcending Humanity*. Notre Dame, IN: University of Notre Dame Press, 1997, pp. 23–45.

Kerr, Fergus, *After Aquinas: Versions of Thomism*. Malden, MA: Blackwell Publishers, 2002.

Kierkegaard, Søren, *Concluding Unscientific Postscript to Philosophical Fragments*, translated by David F. Swenson and Walter Lowrie. Princeton, NJ: Princeton University Press, 1968.

Kierkegaard, Søren, *Journals and Papers*, translated by Howard Vincent Hong, Edna Hatlestad Hong and Gregor Malantschuk. Vol. III. Bloomington, IN: Indiana University Press, 1975.

Kisiel, Theodore J., 'The Missing Link in the Early Heidegger', In *Hermeneutic Phenomenology: Lectures and Essays*, edited by Joseph J. Kockelmans. Washington DC: University Press of America, 1988, pp. 1–40.

Kisiel, Theodore J., *The Genesis of Heidegger's Being and Time*. Berkeley: University of California Press, 1993.

Kisiel, Theodore J., 'Heidegger on Becoming a Christian', in *Reading Heidegger from the Start: Essays in His Earliest Thought*, edited by Theodore J. Kisiel and John Van Buren. Albany, NY: State University of New York Press, 1994, pp. 175–94.

Kluback, William, *The Idea of Humanity: Hermann Cohen's Legacy to Philosophy and Theology*, Studies in Judaism. Lanham, MD: University Press of America, 1987.

Kluback, William, 'Friendship without Communication: Wilhelm Herrmann and Hermann Cohen', in *The Idea of Humanity: Hermann Cohen's*

Legacy to Philosophy and Theology. Lanham, MD: University Press of America, 1987, pp. 163–86.

Krell, David Farrell, 'Introduction to "What is Metaphysics?"', in *Basic Writings: From Being and Time (1927) to The Task of Thinking (1964)*. San Francisco: HarperSanFrancisco, 1993, pp. 90–91.

Lamm, Julia A., *The Living God: Schleiermacher's Theological Appropriation of Spinoza*. University Park, PA: Pennsylvania State University Press, 1996.

Lang, U. M., 'Anhypostatos-Enhypostatos: Church Fathers, Protestant Orthodoxy and Karl Barth', *Journal of Theological Studies* 49, no. 2 (1998), pp. 630–57.

Lessing, Gotthold Ephraim, 'On the Proof of the Spirit and of Power (1777)', in *Philosophical and Theological Writings*, edited by Hugh Barr Nisbet. Cambridge: Cambridge University Press, 2005, pp. 51–6.

Liddell, Henry George and Robert Scott, *An Intermediate Greek-English Lexicon, Founded Upon the Seventh Edition of Liddell and Scott's Greek-English Lexicon*. New York: Harper & Brothers, 1889.

Loewenich, Walther von, *Luther's Theology of the Cross*. Minneapolis, MN: Augsburg Pub. House, 1976.

Lohmann, Johann Friedrich, *Karl Barth und der Neukantianismus: die Rezeption des Neukantianismus im 'Römerbrief' und ihre Bedeutung für die weitere Ausarbeitung der Theologie Karl Barths*. Berlin and New York: de Gruyter, 1995.

Lohse, Bernhard, *Martin Luther's Theology: Its Historical and Systematic Development*. Fortress Press ed. Minneapolis, MN: Fortress Press, 1999.

Loisy, Alfred Firmin, *The Gospel and the Church*. Buffalo, NY: Prometheus Books, 1988.

Lowe, E. J., *A Survey of Metaphysics*. Oxford: Oxford University Press, 2002.

Lowe, Walter James, *Theology and Difference: The Wound of Reason*. Bloomington, IN: Indiana University Press, 1993.

Löwith, Karl, *My Life in Germany Before and After 1933: A Report*. London: Athlone, 1994.

Löwith, Karl, *Martin Heidegger and European Nihilism*, edited by Richard Wolin. New York: Columbia University Press, 1995.

Luther, Martin, *Luther's Works*, edited by Jaroslav Jan Pelikan, Hilton C. Oswald and Helmut T. Lehmann. American ed. 55 vols. Vols 14, 26, 27, 29, 31, 34, 38, 41, 51. Philadelphia, PA: Fortress Press, 1999.

Lyotard, Jean-François, *The Postmodern Condition*, translated by Geoff Bennington and Brian Massumi. Minneapolis, MN: The University of Minnesota Press, 1984.

McCormack, Bruce L., *Karl Barth's Critically Realistic Dialectical Theology: Its Genesis and Development, 1909–1936*. New York: Oxford University Press, 1995.

Bibliography

McCormack, Bruce L., 'Grace and Being: The Role of God's Gracious Election in Karl Barth's Theological Ontology', in *The Cambridge Companion to Karl Barth*, edited by J. B. Webster. New York: Cambridge University Press, 2000, pp. 92–110.

McCormack, Bruce L., 'Seek God Where He May Be Found: A Response to Edwin Chr. van Driel', *Scottish Journal of Theology* 60, no. 1 (2007), pp. 62–79.

McCormack, Bruce L., 'Karl Barth's Historicized Christology: Just How 'Chalcedonian' Is It?', in *Orthodox and Modern: Studies in the Theology of Karl Barth*. Grand Rapids, MI: Baker Academic, 2008, pp. 201–34.

McCormack, Bruce L., 'Participation in God, Yes; Deification, No: Two Modern Protestant Responses to an Ancient Question', in *Orthodox and Modern: Studies in the Theology of Karl Barth*. Grand Rapids, MI: Baker Academic, 2008, pp. 235–60.

McGrath, Alister E., *Luther's Theology of the Cross: Martin Luther's Theological Breakthrough*. Oxford: Blackwell, 1985.

McGrath, Alister E., *The Making of Modern German Christology, 1750–1990*. 2nd ed. Grand Rapids, MI: Zondervan, 1994.

McGrath, Alister E., *Reformation Thought: An Introduction*. 3rd ed. Oxford: Blackwell Publishers, 1999.

McGrath, Alister E., and Darren C. Marks, *The Blackwell Companion to Protestantism*. Oxford: Blackwell, 2004.

MacCulloch, Diarmaid, *The Reformation*. New York: Viking, 2004.

Macleod, Alistair M., *Paul Tillich: An Essay on the Role of Ontology in His Philosophical Theology*. London: Allen & Unwin, 1973.

Macquarrie, John, *An Existentialist Theology: A Comparison of Heidegger and Bultmann*. Westport, CT: Greenwood Press, 1979.

Macquarrie, John, *Heidegger and Christianity: The Hensley Henson Lectures, 1993–94*. New York: Continuum, 1994.

Macquarrie, John, *Jesus Christ in Modern Thought*. London: SCM Press, 2003.

Mann, William E., 'Duns Scotus on Natural and Supernatural Knowledge of God', in *The Cambridge Companion to Duns Scotus*, edited by Thomas Williams. Cambridge: Cambridge University Press, 2003, pp. 238–62.

Marion, Jean-Luc, *God without Being: Hors-texte*. Chicago: University of Chicago Press, 1991.

Marion, Jean-Luc, 'In the Name', in *God, the Gift, and Postmodernism*, edited by John D. Caputo and Michael J. Scanlon. Bloomington, IN: Indiana University Press, 1999, pp. 20–41.

Marion, Jean-Luc, 'Is the Ontological Argument Ontological? The Argument according to Anselm and Its Metaphysical Interpretation according to Kant', in *Flight of the Gods: Philosophical Perspectives on Negative Theology*, edited by Ilse Nina Bulhof and Laurens ten Kate. New York: Fordham University Press, 2000, pp. 78–99.

Marion, Jean-Luc, *The Idol and Distance: Five Studies*. New York: Fordham University Press, 2001.
Marquardt, Friedrich-Wilhelm, 'Socialism in the Theology of Karl Barth', in *Karl Barth and Radical Politics*, edited by George Hunsinger. Philadelphia, PA: Westminster Press, 1976, pp. 47–76.
Marty, Martin E., *Protestantism*, History of Religion. London: Weidenfeld and Nicolson, 1972.
Marx, Karl, 'Introduction to A Contribution to the Critique of Hegel's Philosophy of Right', http://www.marxists.org/archive/marx/works/1843/critique-hpr/intro.htm.
Milbank, John, *The Word Made Strange: Theology, Language, Culture*. Oxford: Blackwell Publishers, 1997.
Milbank, John, 'The Programme of Radical Orthodoxy', in *Radical Orthodoxy?: A Catholic Enquiry*, edited by Laurence Paul Hemming. Aldershot: Ashgate, 2000, pp. 33–45.
Milbank, John, *Theology and Social Theory: Beyond Secular Reason*. 2nd ed. Malden, MA: Blackwell Publishers, 2006.
Milbank, John and Catherine Pickstock, *Truth in Aquinas*, Radical Orthodoxy series. London: Routledge, 2001.
Milbank, John, Catherine Pickstock and Graham Ward, *Radical Orthodoxy: Suspending the Material*. New York: Routledge, 1999.
Miller, Allen O. and M. Eugene Osterhaven (eds), *The Heidelberg Catechism*. Cleveland, OH: United Church Press, 1962.
Monsma, Peter Halman, *Karl Barth's Idea of Revelation*. Somerville, NJ: Somerset Press Inc., 1937.
Muller, Richard, 'Scholasticism in Calvin: A Question of Relation and Disjunction', in *The Unaccomodated Calvin: Studies in the Foundation of a Theological Tradition*. Oxford: Oxford University Press, 2000, pp. 39–61.
Niebuhr, Reinhold, *Essays in Applied Christianity*. New York: Meridian Books, 1959.
Nielsen Jr, Niels C., 'Przywara's Philosophy of the Analogia Entis', *Review of Metaphysics* 5, (1952), pp. 599–620.
Oberman, Heiko Augustinus, *The Harvest of Medieval Theology: Gabriel Biel and Late Medieval Nominalism*. Durham, NC: Labyrinth Press, 1983.
Oberman, Heiko Augustinus, *Luther: Man Between God and the Devil*. New Haven, CT: Yale University Press, 1989.
Oberman, Heiko Augustinus, *The Dawn of the Reformation: Essays in Late Medieval and Early Reformation Thought*. Grand Rapids, MI: W. B. Eerdmans, 1992.
Oberman, Heiko Augustinus, 'The 'Extra' Dimension in the Theology of Calvin', in *The Dawn of the Reformation: Essays in Late Medieval and Early Reformation Thought*. Grand Rapids, MI: W.B. Eerdmans, 1992, pp. 234–58.

Bibliography

Oberman, Heiko Augustinus, *The Reformation: Roots and Ramifications*. Grand Rapids, MI: William B. Eerdman's Publishing Company, 1994.

O'Meara, Thomas F., 'Tillich and Heidegger: A Structural Relationship', *Harvard Theological Review* 61, no. 2 (1968), pp. 249–61.

O'Meara, Thomas F., *Erich Przywara, S.J.: His Theology and His World*. Notre Dame, IN: University of Notre Dame Press, 2002.

Ormerod, Neil, 'Milbank and Barth: A Catholic Perspective', in *Karl Barth – A Future for Postmodern Theology?*, edited by Christiaan Mostert and Geoff Thompson. Adelaide: Australian Theological Forum, 2000, pp. 276–89.

Ott, Heinrich, *Denken und Sein: Der Weg Martin Heideggers und der Weg der Theologie*. Zürich: EVZ Verlag, 1959.

Ott, Hugo, *Martin Heidegger: A Political Life*, translated by Allan Blunden. London: HarperCollins Publishers, 1993.

Parsons, Charles, 'The Transcendental Aesthetic', in *The Cambridge Companion to Kant*, edited by Paul Guyer. Cambridge: Cambridge University Press, 1992, pp. 62–100.

Pauck, Wilhelm and Marion Pauck, *Paul Tillich, His Life & Thought*. San Francisco: Harper & Row, 1989.

Pickstock, Catherine, *After Writing: On the Liturgical Consummation of Philosophy*. Oxford: Blackwell Publishers, 1998.

Pickstock, Catherine, 'Duns Scotus: His Historical and Contemporary Significance', *Modern Theology* 21, no. 4 (2005), pp. 543–74.

Pöggeler, Otto, *Martin Heidegger's Path of Thinking*, translated by Daniel Magurshak and Sigmund Barber. New York: Humanity Books, 1987.

Pöggeler, Otto, *The Paths of Heidegger's Life and Thought*, translated by John Bailiff. Amherst, MA: Humanity Books, 1998.

Poma, Andrea, *The Critical Philosophy of Hermann Cohen*. Albany, NY: State University of New York Press, 1997.

Poma, Andrea, *Yearning for Form and Other Essays on Hermann Cohen's Thought*. Dordrecht: Springer, 2006.

Prudhomme, Jeff Owen, *God and Being: Heidegger's Relation to Theology*. Atlantic Highlands, NJ: Humanities Press, 1997.

Przywara, Erich, 'Drei Richtungen der Phänomenologie', *Stimmen der Zeit* 115 (1928), pp. 252–64.

Przywara, Erich, 'Gott in uns oder Gott über uns? (Immanenz und Transzendenz im heutigen Geistesleben)', *Stimmen der Zeit* 105 (1923), pp. 343–62.

Przywara, Erich, *Polarity: A German Catholic's Interpretation of Religion*, translated by Alan Coates Bouquet. London: Oxford University Press, 1935.

Przywara, Erich, 'Religionsphilosophie katholischer Theologie (1927)', in *Religions-Philosophische Schriften*. London: Johannes-Verlag, 1962, pp. 376–512.

Pugh, Jeffrey C., *The Anselmic Shift: Christology and Method in Karl Barth's Theology*. New York: P. Lang, 1990.

Richardson, William J., *Heidegger. Through Phenomenology to Thought*. New York: Fordham University Press, 2003.

Rickert, Heinrich, *The Limits of Concept Formation in Natural Science: A Logical Introduction to the Historical Sciences*. Abridged ed. Cambridge: Cambridge University Press, 1986.

Ritschl, Albrecht, 'Theology and Metaphysics', in *Three Essays*. Philadelphia, PA: Fortress Press, 1972, pp. 149–218.

Robbins, Jeffrey W., *Between Faith and Thought: An Essay on the Ontotheological Condition*. Charlottesville, VA: University of Virginia Press, 2003.

Roberts, Richard H., 'Barth's Doctrine of Time: Its Nature and Implications', in *Karl Barth: Studies of His Theological Method*, edited by Stephen Sykes. New York: Oxford University Press, 1979, pp. 88–146.

Roberts, Richard H., *A Theology on Its Way?: Essays on Karl Barth*. Edinburgh: T. & T. Clark, 1991.

Robinson, James McConkey and John B. Cobb, *The Later Heidegger and Theology*. New York: Harper & Row, 1963.

Rogers, Eugene F., *Thomas Aquinas and Karl Barth: Sacred Doctrine and the Natural Knowledge of God*, Revisions. Notre Dame, IN: University of Notre Dame Press, 1995.

Rosato, Philip J., *The Spirit as Lord: The Pneumatology of Karl Barth*. Edinburgh: T. & T. Clark, 1981.

Rosen, Stephen, 'Is Metaphysics Possible?', *The Review of Metaphysics* 45 (1991), pp. 235–7.

Rowland, Tracey, *Culture and the Thomist Tradition: After Vatican II*. London: Routledge, 2003.

Saarinen, Risto, *Faith and Holiness: Lutheran–Orthodox Dialogue 1959–1994*. 1st Fortress Press ed. Göttingen: Vandenhoeck & Ruprecht, 1997.

Saarinen, Risto, *God and the Gift: An Ecumenical Theology of Giving*, Unitas Books. Collegeville, PA: Liturgical Press, 2005.

Safranski, Rüdiger, *Martin Heidegger: Between Good and Evil*. Cambridge, MA: Harvard University Press, 1998.

Saltzman, Judy Deane, *Paul Natorp's Philosophy of Religion within the Marburg Neo-Kantian Tradition*. New York: Olms, 1981.

Schleiermacher, Friedrich Daniel Ernst, *On Religion: Speeches to Its Cultured Despisers*, translated by John Oman. Louisville, KY: Westminster John Knox Press, 1994.

Schüssler Fiorenza, Francis, 'Being, Subjectivity, Otherness: The Idols of God', in *Questioning God*, edited by John D. Caputo, Mark Dooley and Michael J. Scanlon. Bloomington, IN: Indiana University Press, 2001, pp. 341–70.

Schwartz, Regina M., *Transcendence: Philosophy, Literature, and Theology Approach the Beyond*. New York: Routledge, 2004.

Bibliography

Schweitzer, Albert, *The Quest of the Historical Jesus: A Critical Study of Its Progress from Reimarus to Wrede*, translated by W. Montgomery. New York: Dover Publications, 2005.

Scott, William A., *Historical Protestantism: An Historical Introduction to Protestant Theology*. Englewood Cliffs, NJ: Prentice-Hall, 1970.

Sheehan, Thomas, 'Heidegger's Early Years: Fragments for a Philosophical Biography', in *Heidegger: The Man and the Thinker*, edited by Thomas Sheehan. Chicago: Precedent, 1981, pp. 3-20.

Shults, F. LeRon, 'A Dubious Christological Formula: From Leontius of Byzantium to Karl Barth', *Theological Studies* 57, no. 3 (1996), pp. 431-47.

Spieckermann, Ingrid, *Gotteserkenntnis: ein Beitrag zur Grundfrage der neuen Theologie Karl Barths*. München: Chr. Kaiser, 1985.

Stanley, Timothy, 'Heidegger on Luther on Paul', *Dialog: A Journal of Theology* 46, no. 1 (2007), pp. 41-5.

Stanley, Timothy, 'Returning Barth to Anselm', *Modern Theology* 24, no. 3 (2008), pp. 413-37.

Stanley, Timothy, 'Before Analogy: Recovering Barth's Ontological Development', *New Blackfriars* 90, no. 1029 (2009), pp. 577-601.

Steiner, George, *Heidegger*. 2nd ed. London: Fontana, 1992.

Sykes, Stephen, *The Identity of Christianity: Theologians and the Essence of Christianity from Schleiermacher to Barth*. Philadelphia, PA: Fortress Press, 1984.

Taylor, Charles, *Sources of the Self: The Making of the Modern Identity*. Cambridge, MA: Harvard University Press, 1989.

Thielicke, Helmut, *Theological Ethics*. 3 vols. Vol. 1. Grand Rapids, MI: Wiliam B. Eerdmans, 1979.

Thielicke, Helmut, *Modern Faith and Thought*. Grand Rapids, MI: William B. Eerdmans, 1990.

Thiselton, Anthony C., *The Two Horizons: New Testament Hermeneutics and Philosophical Description with Special Reference to Heidegger, Bultmann, Gadamer, and Wittgenstein*. Grand Rapids, MI: W. B. Eerdmans, 1980.

Tillich, Paul, *Systematic Theology*. 3 vols. Vol. 1. London: SCM Press, 1978.

Tillich, Paul, *The Courage to Be*. 2nd ed. New Haven, CT: Yale University Press, 2000.

Torrance, Thomas Forsyth, *Karl Barth: An Introduction to His Early Theology, 1910-1931*. London: SCM Press, 1962.

Toulmin, Stephen Edelston, *Cosmopolis: The Hidden Agenda of Modernity*. Chicago: The University of Chicago Press, 1992.

Troeltsch, Ernst, *Psychologie und Erkenntnistheorie in der Religionswissenschaft*. Tübingen: J. C. B. Mohr, 1905.

Troeltsch, Ernst, 'Historische und dogmatische Methode in der Theologie', in *Gesammelte Schriften: Zur religiösen Lage, Religionsphilosophie und Ethik*. Aalen: Scientia Verlag, 1962, pp. 729–53.

Troeltsch, Ernst, 'Rückblick auf ein halbes Jahrhundert der theologischen Wissenschaft', in *Gesammelte Schriften: Zur religiösen Lage, Religionsphilosophie und Ethik*. Aalen: Scientia Verlag, 1962, pp. 193–226.

Troeltsch, Ernst, 'Was heißt "Wesen des Christentums"?', in *Gesammelte Schriften: Zur religiösen Lage, Religionsphilosophie und Ethik*. Aalen: Scientia Verlag, 1962, pp. 386–451.

Troeltsch, Ernst, 'Wesen der Religion und der Religionswissenschaft', in *Gesammelte Schriften: Zur religiösen Lage, Religionsphilosophie und Ethik*. Aalen: Scientia Verlag, 1962, pp. 452–99.

Troeltsch, Ernst, 'Half a Century of Theology: A Review', in *Writings on Theology and Religion*, edited by Robert Morgan and Michael Pye. London: Duckworth, 1977, pp. 53–81.

Troeltsch, Ernst, 'Religion and the Science of Religion', in *Writings on Theology and Religion*, edited by Robert Morgan and Michael Pye. London: Duckworth, 1977, pp. 82–123.

Troeltsch, Ernst, 'What Does 'Essence of Christianity' Mean?', in *Writings on Theology and Religion*, edited by Robert Morgan and Michael Pye. London: Duckworth, 1977, pp. 124–79.

Troeltsch, Ernst, *Protestantism and Progress: A Historical Study of the Relation of Protestantism to the Modern World*, translated by W. Montgomery. Eugene, OR: Wipf and Stock, 1986.

Troeltsch, Ernst, 'Historical and Dogmatic Method in Theology (1898)', in *Religion in History*. Minneapolis, MN: Fortress Press, 1991, pp. 11–32.

Van Buren, John, 'Martin Heidegger, Martin Luther', in *Reading Heidegger from the Start: Essays in His Earliest Thought*, edited by Theodore J. Kisiel and John Van Buren. Albany, NY: State University of New York Press, 1994, pp. 159–74.

Van Buren, John, *The Young Heidegger: Rumor of the Hidden King*. Bloomington, IN: Indiana University Press, 1994.

Vanhoozer, Kevin J., *The Cambridge Companion to Postmodern Theology*. Cambridge: Cambridge University Press, 2003.

Vattimo, Gianni, *The End of Modernity: Nihilism and Hermeneutics in Post-modern Culture*. Cambridge: Polity Press, 1988.

Vattimo, Gianni, 'The Trace of the Trace', in *Religion*, edited by Jacques Derrida and Gianni Vattimo. Cambridge: Polity Press, 1998, pp. 79–94.

Vattimo, Gianni, *Belief*. Cambridge: Polity Press, 1999.

Waldrop, Charles T. *Karl Barth's Christology: Its Basic Alexandrian Character*. New York: Mouton Publishers, 1984.

Ward, Graham, *Barth, Derrida, and the Language of Theology*. New York: Cambridge University Press, 1995.

Bibliography

Ward, Graham, *The Postmodern God: A Theological Reader*. Oxford: Blackwell Publishers, 1997.

Ward, Graham, 'The Theological Project of Jean-Luc Marion', in *Postsecular Philosophy: Between Philosophy and Theology*, edited by Phillip Blond. New York: Routledge, 1998, pp. 229-39.

Ward, Graham, 'Barth, Modernity, and Postmodernity', in *The Cambridge Companion to Karl Barth*, edited by John Webster. Cambridge: Cambridge University Press, 2000, pp. 274-95.

Ward, Graham, *The Blackwell Companion to Postmodern Theology*. Oxford: Blackwell Publishers, 2001.

Ward, Graham, 'Barth, Hegel and the Possibility for Christian Apologetics', in *Conversing with Barth*, edited by Mike Higton and John C. McDowell. Burlington, VT: Ashgate, 2004, pp. 53-67.

Ward, Graham, *Cultural Transformation and Religious Practice*. New York: Cambridge University Press, 2004.

Ward, Graham, 'The Future of Protestantism: Postmodernity', in *The Blackwell Companion to Protestantism*, edited by Alister E. McGrath and Darren C. Marks. Malden, MA: Blackwell, 2004, pp. 453-67.

Ward, Graham, *Christ and Culture*. Malden, MA: Blackwell Publishing, 2005.

Weber, Joseph C., 'Feuerbach, Barth and Theological Methodology', *The Journal of Religion* 46, no. 1 (1966), pp. 24-36.

Webster, John B., *Barth's Moral Theology: Human Action in Barth's Thought*. Grand Rapids, MI: William B. Eerdmans, 1998.

Webster, John B., 'Barth, Modernity and Postmodernity', in *Karl Barth - A Future for Postmodern Theology?*, edited by Christiaan Mostert and Geoff Thompson. Adelaide: Australian Theological Forum, 2000, pp. 1-28.

Webster, John B., *The Cambridge Companion to Karl Barth*, New York: Cambridge University Press, 2000.

Webster, John B., 'Balthasar and Karl Barth', in *The Cambridge Companion to Hans Urs von Balthasar*, edited by Edward T. Oakes and David Moss. Cambridge: Cambridge University Press, 2004, pp. 241-55.

Webster, John B., *Barth's Earlier Theology*. New York: T. & T. Clark International, 2005.

Welch, Claude, *Protestant Thought in the Nineteenth Century*. Vol. II. New Haven, CT: Yale University Press, 1972.

West, Charles C., *Communism and the Theologians: Study of an Encounter*. London: SCM Press, 1958.

Westphal, Merold, *Postmodern Philosophy and Christian Thought*. Bloomington, IN: Indiana University Press, 1999.

Westphal, Merold, *Overcoming Onto-theology: Toward a Postmodern Christian Faith*. New York: Fordham University Press, 2001.

Westphal, Merold, *Transcendence and Self-Transcendence: On God and the Soul*. Bloomington, IN: Indiana University Press, 2004.

White, Graham, 'Barth's Theological Realism', *Neue Zeitschrift für systematische Theologie und Religionsphilosophie* 26 (1984), pp. 54–70.

Wigley, Stephen, 'The von Balthasar Thesis: A Re-Examination of von Balthasar's Study of Barth in the Light of Bruce McCormack', *Scottish Journal of Theology* 56, no. 3 (2003), pp. 345–59.

Willey, Thomas E., *Back to Kant: The Revival of Kantianism in German Social and Historical Thought, 1860–1914*. Detroit, MI: Wayne State University Press, 1978.

William of Occam, *Philosophical Writings: A Selection*, edited by Philotheus Boehner and Stephen F. Brown. Indianapolis: Hackett Publishing Company, 1990.

Williams, Thomas, 'The Doctrine of Univocity is True and Salutary', *Modern Theology* 21, no. 4 (2005), pp. 575–85.

Wippel, John F.,'Essence and Existence', in *The Cambridge History of Later Medieval Philosophy: From the Rediscovery of Aristotle to the Disintegration of Scholasticism, 1100–1600*, edited by Norman Kretzmann, Anthony John Patrick Kenny and Jan Pinborg. Cambridge: Cambridge University Press, 1982, pp. 385–410.

Wolfe, Tom, 'Pleasure Principles', *New York Times*, 12 June 2005.

Wood, Allen W., 'Rational Theology, Moral Faith, and Religion', in *The Cambridge Companion to Kant*, edited by Paul Guyer. Cambridge: Cambridge University Press, 1992, pp. 394–416.

Wrathall, Mark A., *Religion after Metaphysics*. Cambridge: Cambridge University Press, 2003.

Wyman, Walter E., *The Concept of Glaubenslehre: Ernst Troeltsch and the Theological Heritage of Schleiermacher*. Chico, CA: Scholars Press, 1983.

Yasukata, Toshimasa, 'Lessing's 'Ugly Broad Ditch'', in *Lessing's Philosophy of Religion and the German Enlightenment*. Oxford: Oxford University Press, 2002, pp. 56–71.

Index

analogy, 96, 97, 105, 127, 128, 142, 145, 147, 149–52, 154, 161, 166, 191, 193–94, 217, 244–46, *analogia entis*, 170, 190, 191–193, 224–25, 245, *analogia fidei*, 193, 224–25, 245
Anselm of Canterbury, xvii, 96, 125, 126ff, 161–64, 166–67, 174–75, 177, 185, 190, 198, 204–05, 217, 229, 244–45
anthropomorphism, 111, 114
Antiochene vs. Alexandrian Christology, 209
Aquinas, Thomas, 16, 65–66, 127, 141–42, 191, 244–45
ascension, 224
atheism, 198, 98–9, 137
Augustine of Hippo, 29, 65–66, 71–72, 80, 188, 193, 207, and Augustinianism, 15
Averroes, 17, 19
Avicenna, 17, 19

Balthasar, Hans Urs von, 96–97, 102, 105, 127–28, 149–52, 216–217, 244
Barmen Theological Declaration, 248

being and becoming, 174, 198, 210, 223–26
Bonhoeffer, Dietrich, 248
Bouillard, Henri, 127, 150, 193–94, 224–25
Braaten, Carl, 16, 69, 239
Brunner, Emil, 123, 125, 153–54, 165–66, 192
Buber, Martin, 123
Bultmann, Rudolf, 60, 63, 66, 74, 79–83, 89–92, 123, 125, 154, 167–68, 239
Busch, Eberhard, 91, 95–103, 110–11, 115, 126, 131, 160, 221

Caputo, John, xviii, 55, 61, 65–66, 89, 237–38
Chalcedonianism, 102, 109, 162, 209, 222–23
Church, xx, 4, 8, 13–14, 33, 37, 56, 69, 90, 108–09, 119, 162, 164–65, 168–87, 195, 205–07, 212, 222, 232–33, 244, 247, and confessing church, 247–48, ecclesiology, 248
Cohen, Hermann, 105–07, 114, 191
covenant, 220

creation, 71, 103–04, 161, 187, 191, 204–05, 208, 212, 214, 218, 223, 226, 228–34, 245–46, *ex nihilo*, 187

Dalferth, Ingolf U., 148, 233–34
daseiend, 129–30, 135, 140, 142, 147, 151–53, 205
Dasein, xxi, 40, 49–50, 63, 82, 84, 86, 91, 129–30, 134–53, 158, 165, 167–70, 174, 204–05, 219, 225–27, 232, 234
Derrida, Jacques, 34–38, 53–55, 59–61, 242
Descartes, Rene, 51, 70, 141–42, 165
deus absconditus/revelatus (see revelation)
dialectic, 40, 96, 105, 122, 127, 147, 149, 154, 255, 161, 176–77, 184–86, 188, 197, 205, 207, 209–10, 212, 217, 226–27, 231, 244
die Kehre (the Turn), 84–88
dogma, 109–10, 196, 207, 210–11

Ebeling, Gerhardt, 67–68, 100
election, 214–21, 231
Enlightenment, 9, 58–59, 164–65
epistemology, 3, 10, 13, 16, 65, 77, 152, 194, 219, (see revelation)
Ereignis, 60, 88, 151, 178, 200, 227, and event, 38, 44, 50, 52–56, 59–60, 91, 108, 151, 159, 168, 171, 174, 178–80,

185–86, 195, 201–02, 211–12, 218, 226–28, 232–34
eschatology, 148, 158, 176, 233
esse, 132, 135, 138–41
eternity (see time)
eternity, 15, 25, 63, 71, 118, 121, 215, 217
ethics, 6, 10, 74, 106, 117, 172, 246–48

facticity, 62, 64–65
faith, 7, 13, 27, 33, 37–38, 46–51, 54, 60, 64–65, 69, 72, 74, 76, 90, 103, 106, 110, 121, 130–32, 137, 143, 148, 151–52, 157, 160, 164–65, 168–71, 174, 177, 182, 185, 189–94, 204, 210, 224–25, 228, 240–41, 247
Fall, 23, 68, 193, 212, 230
Father, 5–7, 120, 122, 200, 203–04, 207, 212, 218, 220, 222, 231–32, 246
Feuerbach, Ludwig, 102, 110–18, 243
Fisher, Simon, 105, 114
foundationalism, 36, 52, 58–59, 78, 168, 171, 219
Frei, Hans, 96, 105, 161,–163
Freiburg, 39, 45, 65, 67, 73–74, 86, 123
Freud, Sigmund, 2

Gadamer, Hans–Georg, 88, 242
Gogarten, Friedrich, 95, 154, 177, 183
Göttingen, 99, 118, 149, 160–61

Index

grace, v, 23–25, 120, 165, 171, 179, 184, 192–94, 214, 225, 232
Greek, xxi, 5, 7, 18, 68, 71–73, 77 107, 163
guilt, 189

Habermas, Jürgen, 246
Harnack, Adolf von, 4–9, 13–14, 77, 103, 241
Hauerwas, Stanley, 158
Hegel, FGW, 11–12, 39–41, 49, 56, 81, 129–30, 184, 216–17, 238, 240
Heidelberg Disputation, 15, 23, 26, 68, 72–73, 101, 117, 124, 181, 211, 237, 244
Hemming, Laurence Paul, 62–63, 85, 87, 89
hermeneutics, 59, 65, 69, 74, 82, 86 (see also language)
Herrmann, Wilhelm, 99–100, 102, 104–11, 114, 117, 124–25, 172, 191, 216, 243
history/historicity, xix, 2, 4–15, 18, 42, 57, 59, 62, 65–66, 69–71, 77, 86, 95, 167–68, 174, 176, 201–203, 247, and metaphysics, 42, 70, 86–88, and Protestantism, 4–15, 18, 116, and Jesus, 107–108, 110, 159, 162, 176, 180, 201–203, 217, 228, 232, 234, 240
Holy Spirit, 25, 174, 185, 201, 203–04, 207, 218, 220, 231, 246
humanity, 23, 97–98, 101, 110–19, 154, 166, 184, 191–92, 200, 209, 211–13, 217, 219–20, 230, 232–33, 246, and *humanitas Christi*, 182, 200–201, *imago dei*, 166–67, 192–93
Hunsinger, George, 99–101, 174, 209, 214–15, 218–23, 231, 247
Husserl, Edmund, 45, 65–66, 191
hypostatic union (*anhypostasis-enhypostasis*), 221–22, 225–27, 231–32

I and thou, 194, 204
idealism, 8–9, 73, 81, 106, 113–15, 117, 122–23
impossibility, 27, 117, 135, 137, 140–41, 151, 175–76, 178, 182, 198 (see also possibility)
incarnation, 6, 53–55, 59–61, 112, 120, 181–82, 214–15, 220, 222, 225, 231, 234, 237
infinite, 7, 10, 25, 76, 78, 118–19, 157, 172, 191, 229, 231 (see also eternal)

Jacobi, Friedrich Heinrich, 240
Jaspers, Karl, 67, 129
Jenson, Robert, 16, 159, 239
Judaism, 123, 181
Jüngel, Eberhard, 173–74, 211–12
justification, 24–26, 101

Kant, Immaneul, 6, 11–12, 36, 40–41, 47–48, 105–07, 113–14, 123, 125, 127, 129,

144–46, 157–58, 161, 172–73, 241, 243–44, and Neo-Kantianism, 12, 76, 82, 105–07, 114, 191
kenosis, 109
Kerr, Fergus, 142, 158–59
Kierkegaard, Søren, 65, 80, 103, 167, 184, 216–17
Kingdom of God, v, 7, 122, 247
Kisiel, Theodore, 63–65, 88

language, 35, 51, 84, 129, 134–35, 145, 151, 174, 185, 204–05, 207, 227, 232, 246
Lessing, Gotthold Ephraim, 82, 107
Logos, 7, 221–23, *asarkos*, 214–15, 221–22, *ensarkos*, 221–22, 231, *incarnandus*, 214, 221, 215, *incarnatus*, 221, 215, *extra Calvinisticum*, 222
Lord's Supper/Eucharist, 27, 101, 120–21
Luther, Martin, xx, 2, 4, 7–8, 13–29, 33–34, 38, 63, 65–77, 79, 90, 92, 97–104, 107–12, 115, 117, 118, 120–25, 181–82, 193–94, 211, 237, 239–42, 244, 246
Lutheran theology, xx, 37, 61, 64, 73, 98, and Finnish School 16, 69, 239
Lyotard, Jean-Francois, 2

Macquarrie, John, 6, 64, 80
Marburg, 27, 45, 60, 66, 73–74, 81–82, 85, 96, 99, 104–06, 123

Marcion, 103, 230
Marion, Jean-Luc, xviii, 33–34, 36–38, 50, 53–55, 59, 80, 157–58, 169, 242–43
Marx, Karl, 2, 56, 240
McCormack, Bruce, 95–97, 128, 131, 147–55, 157, 161–62, 172, 184, 214–19, 226–27, 231–32, 244
mediation, 108, 197–98
Melanchthon, Philip, 6, 73
Milbank, John, 1, 57–58, 179
modernity, 1–4, 16, 39, 57–58, 164, 167–70, 174, 191, 206–07, 226, 240–42, and *via moderna*, 16–17, 20–29, 120 (see also nominalism)
mystery, 112, 179–185, 189–90, 199–200

Natorp, Paul, 66, 105–07
natural theology, 10, 12, 23, 25, 27–28, 166, 176, 247
Nestorianism, 209
Nietzsche, Friedrich, 2, 58
nihilism, 45, 53, 59, 167, 178, (see also Creation)
nominalism, 1, 15–17, 22–23, 29, 101, 120–21

objectivity, 9, 20–21, 35, 37, 41, 45, 47–49, 52–53, 64, 73, 78, 82, 106–107, 112, 129–135, 137–40, 142–44, 147–52, 155, 168, 186, 188, 190, 192, 196, 198, 201, 204, 214, 220–21, 224, 245
onto-theology, xvii, xix, xxi, 35–39, 42, 50, 53, 84, 89–

Index

90, 92, 123, 125, 128, 147, 153, 156–57, 164–65, 168–70, 181, 211–12, 237–39, 243–44, 248
Origen, 205–06
Otto, Rudolf, 76
Ott, Heinrich, xviii, 83

paradox, 22, 36, 103, 119, 184, 216
Paul, 14, 60, 65, 68, 71–72, 74, 82, 180
Pelagianism, 188
phenomenology, 8–14, 45–50, 54, 60, 65–67, 71, 75–76, 78–79, 114, 155, 161, 177, 182, 191, 228, 237–38
Plato, 15, 66, 71
Pögeller, Otto, 75, 88
political, 2, 86, 95, 120, 123, 153, 246–48
possibility, 12, 20, 23, 26–27, 46, 48, 54–55, 59, 112–114, 123, 143, 146, 155, 164, 168–69, 171, 173–74, 178, 182, 184–87, 190, 193–96, 198, 201, 203, 212, 215, 224, 229, 232–33, 236–38, 245–48 (see also impossibility)
postmodernism, xix–xx, 1–4, 14, 16, 29, 57, 92, 239–43, 248
predestination, 57
presence, 10, 108, 119–122, 203
primordiality, 79, 107, 240, and Christianity (*Urchristentum*), 70–72, 75, and phenomena (*Urphänomen*), 10, and science, 69, 75, priority, 117, 150, 152–54, 205, 215, 220
prolegomena, 162, 164–65, 167–69
Przywara, Erich, 102, 150, 183, 190–92, 197, 245

realism, 5, 16, 18, 26, 121–23, 144, 148, 159, 161
reality, 57, 78, 95, 106, 108, 116, 131, 133, 140, 144–45, 148, 150, 152, 172–73, 175, 182, 188, 194, 197–98, 210–11, 217, 222, 225–28, 234, 241
reconciliation, 27, 174, 184, 208, 212, 232
redemption, 193, 195, 212, 224, 232
Reformed theology, xx, 29, 99, 101–04, 109–10, 118–22, 160–61, 222
revelation, 27, 46, 48, 98, 103, 108–10, 113, 117, 122, 130, 151, 160, 166, 170, 174, 176, 179, 182–83, 185, 189, 194–211, 224–25, 228–29, 233–34, and *deus absconditus/revelatus*, 98–99, 102–03, 113, 117, 122, 200, 243, and *deus dixit*, 160–61, 196–97, and knowledge of God, 21, 106, 132, 144–45, 154, 161, 163, 166, 181–87, 190, 193, 195, 198, 203–04, 209, 211, and hiddeness of

273

God, 27–28, 48, 98–99, 108–09, 115, 117, 121, 132, 180–82, 199, 211, 221, 243, and 'in a mirror dimly' (1 Cor 13.12), 180, and unconcealment, 42 (see also truth)
Richardson, William J., 85–87
Ritschl, Albrecht, 6, 8, 106–07, 124
Roberts, Richard, 233–34
Roman Catholicism, xviii, 1, 5, 7, 11, 13, 37, 63–66, 70, 74, 150, 170, 174, 190–91, 240–42, 245
Römerbrief, 95–96, 98–99, 105, 111, 113, 156, 216–17, 221, 229
Rosenzweig, Franz, 123

Saarinen, Risto, 16, 239
salvation, 23, 25, 212, 236, and Heidegger's 'only a god can save us,' 183, 236
Sartre, Jean-Paul, 91–92
Schelling, F. W. J von, 80
Schleiermacher, Friedrich, 9, 75–79, 100–01, 107, 113, 167–69, 177, 179, 187, 206, 240
scholasticism, xvii, xx, 1, 5, 6, 13–16, 22–23, 29, 65, 68–74, 77, 101, 120–21, 125, 163, 174, 191, 207, 222, 240
science, 12, 17–21, 27, 39–41, 45–57, 69–70, 75, 77, 79, 106, 155–57, 167–69, 173, 244
Scotus, John Duns, 1, 17, 19–20, 29, 65

Scripture, 13, 23, 112, 160, 180, 204, 228, 242, *sola scriptura*, 240, Bible, 67, 82, 108, 160, 165, 179, 196, 200, 202, Proverbs, 67, New Testament, 65, 82, 202, 229, Old Testament, 199, 228, Genesis, 68, 95, 178, 221, Romans, 14, 22, 68, 71–73, 90, 162, 217, 221, 1 Corinthians, 53, 180–81
secularity, 56, 62, 179–85, 189, 234, 240
Sein, xxi, 34, 36, 39, 46, 83, 129, 134, 146, 151, 155, 162, 164, 168–71, 174, 187, 197, 201, 208, 216, 218, 223
Seinsweise (mode of being), 197, 203–05, 207–08, 220–22, 226–27, 231, 246
sin, 23, 25, 28, 74–75, 166, 194
socialism, 95, 247
Son of God, 200–01, 203–04, 207, 210, 212, 215, 218, 220–23, 231–32, 235
Suarez, Franciscus, 65
subjectivity, 1, 9–10, 19–21, 23, 28, 36, 41, 64, 84–85, 106, 113–114, 142–43, 148, 158, 166, 194, 196, 204, 214, 225, 243–44
sublation (see also Hegel), 40, 49–50
substance, xix, 10, 12, 19–20, 196, 206–07
suffering, 26–27, 101, 112, 117, 124, 211, 244

technology, 3, 48, 57–58

Index

Thurneysen, Eduard, 105
Tillich, Paul, 63, 80–81, 89–90
time, xix, 7, 44–46, 52, 57, 84, 87, 199, 202, 215, 218, 222, 228–35, and temporality, 192, 214–15, 219, 230 (see also eternity)
Torrance, Thomas F., 96, 152,
Toulmin, Stephen, 2
transcendence, 35, 44, 52–54, 59–60, 83, 110, 112, 183, 191, 229
Trinity, 174, 176, 182–83, 185, 195–99, 203–10, 214–22, 226, 245–46, and *perichoresis* (*circumincessio*), 210, and modalism, 206, 208, 212, 218 (see also separate entries on Father, Son and Holy Spirit)
Troeltsch, Ernst, 5–14, 71, 75, 77–78, 107, 202
Truth, 5–6, 27, 40, 45, 51, 84–86, 111, 113, 129–36, 142, 144, 148–53, 160, 162, 164, 175, 178, 286, 198, 202, 205, 211, 228, 235, 241, 246, 248, (see also revelation)

universality, 18–19, 21, 82, 234

Van Buren, John, xx, 67, 75
Vattimo, Gianni, 56–61, 237

Ward, Graham, xv, xvii, 1–3, 14, 21–22, 37, 91, 95, 155–58, 176, 205, 212, 226, 240, 243
Webster, John, xix, 102, 247
Westphal, Merold, xviii, 72, 155–57, 238–39, 243
'wholly other', 98, 102–03
Word of God, 7, 14, 160–61, 174–81, 183, 185–94, 198, 220, 225
World War I, 2, 117, 123, 167
World War II, 11, 86, 247
worldview, 46, 50, 56, 69

www.ingramcontent.com/pod-product-compliance
Lightning Source LLC
Chambersburg PA
CBHW021655230426
43668CB00008B/629